C000205647

FreeSWITCH 1.2

Second Edition

Build robust, high-performance telephony systems using FreeSWITCH

Anthony Minessale

Michael S Collins

Darren Schreiber

Raymond Chandler

BIRMINGHAM - MUMBAI

FreeSWITCH 1.2
Second Edition

Copyright © 2013 Packt Publishing

All rights reserved. No part of this book may be reproduced, stored in a retrieval system, or transmitted in any form or by any means, without the prior written permission of the publisher, except in the case of brief quotations embedded in critical articles or reviews.

Every effort has been made in the preparation of this book to ensure the accuracy of the information presented. However, the information contained in this book is sold without warranty, either express or implied. Neither the authors, nor Packt Publishing, and its dealers and distributors will be held liable for any damages caused or alleged to be caused directly or indirectly by this book.

Packt Publishing has endeavored to provide trademark information about all of the companies and products mentioned in this book by the appropriate use of capitals. However, Packt Publishing cannot guarantee the accuracy of this information.

First edition: July 2010

Second edition: May 2013

Production Reference: 1170513

Published by Packt Publishing Ltd.
Livery Place
35 Livery Street
Birmingham B3 2PB, UK.

ISBN 978-1-78216-100-4

www.packtpub.com

Cover Image by Suresh Mogre (suresh.mogre.99@gmail.com)

Credits

Authors
Anthony Minessale
Michael S Collins
Darren Schreiber
Raymond Chandler

Reviewers
Norm Brandinger
Kristian Kielhofner
Jeff Leung
Brian Wiese

Acquisition Editor
Usha Iyer

Lead Technical Editor
Ankita Shashi

Technical Editors
Chirag Jani
Soumya Kanti
Ankita Meshram
Dheera Meril Paul
Zafeer Rais

Project Coordinator
Arshad Sopariwala

Proofreader
Paul Hindle

Indexer
Monica Ajmera Mehta

Graphics
Abhinash Sahu

Production Coordinator
Pooja Chipulunkar

Cover Work
Pooja Chipulunkar

About the Authors

Anthony Minessale has been working with computers for nearly 30 years. He is the primary author of FreeSWITCH and Director of Engineering for CudaTEL at Barracuda Networks.

He created and continues to run the ClueCon Telephony Developers Conference, held every August in Chicago.

He has extensive experience in the Internet industry and VoIP. Before creating FreeSWITCH, he contributed heavily to the Asterisk open source project, producing many features that are still in use today. At Barracuda Networks, Anthony oversees the production and development of the CudaTEL PBX appliance that uses FreeSWITCH as its core telephony engine.

I would like to thank my awesome family: my wife, Jill, son, Eric, and daughter, Abbi, for putting up with the long hours and supporting me on my cause to revolutionize the telephony industry. Thanks to my dogs, Chewie and Gypsy, for staying up with me at 2 a.m. on long nights. I would also like to thank the open source community at large, especially those involved in the FreeSWITCH project, and I hope to see you all every summer at ClueCon!

Michael S Collins is a telephony and open source software enthusiast. He is a PBX veteran, having worked as a PBX technician for five years and as the head of IT for a call center for more than nine years. He is an active member of the FreeSWITCH community and has co-authored *FreeSWITCH Cookbook, Packt Publishing*. He resides in Central California with his wife and two children and currently works for Barracuda Networks, Inc.

I would like to thank first and foremost my wife, Lisa, my daughter, Katherine, and my son, Sean, who keep me going each day. Without them I could not contribute to open source projects like FreeSWITCH, much less co-author a book.

I would also like to thank the many FreeSWITCH experts around the world who are so willing to answer technical questions: Anthony Minessale, Michael Jerris, Moises Silva, Raymond Chandler, Ken Rice, Travis Cross, and many more. I would especially like to thank Brian K. West for patiently educating me in the ways of VoIP.

I am also grateful to the many people who devote themselves to answering questions on the FreeSWITCH mailing list and IRC channel: Steven Ayre, Avi Marcus, Steve Underwood, and all the rest. The FreeSWITCH worldwide community is a great example of what an open source community should be. Well done!

Darren Schreiber is the CEO and Co-founder of 2600 Hz. He began working heavily in open source voice with the FreeSWITCH project, where he engaged with Brian, Mike, and Anthony. His projects have since evolved into two enterprise VoIP platforms that allow a multitude of development of voice, SMS, and video applications to be delivered to customers.

He has 15 years of voice and IT experience including developing multiple enterprise SaaS infrastructures for hosting and remotely managing IT, voice, and e-commerce services. He is a guest lecturer at major universities on VoIP technology and leads paid international VoIP trainings. As a serious telephony enthusiast since a young age, he has worked extensively with VoIP technologies. He graduated from Rensselaer Polytechnic Institute with a degree in Computer Science and Business Management.

He is also a co-author of *FreeSWITCH Cookbook, Packt Publishing*.

I'd like to thank, first and foremost, the FreeSWITCH team. Without them, I wouldn't have been challenged with some of the most intriguing technology and people I've ever worked with. It has been a gift working with them.

I'd also like to thank my family and friends who have put up with my crazy work schedule and constant tardiness, and have helped provide funds and moral support for our work. Thanks for everything.

Finally, I'd like to thank the open source community. Their tireless patience and countless selfless contributions are a constant reminder that the world is not an evil place, and that people are generally out for the greater good of society.

Raymond Chandler(@intralanman) has been working with, and contributing to, open source projects for over a decade. Raymond's VoIP experience started with a small CLEC/ITSP using SER for call routing, and Asterisk for voicemail and advanced services. After encountering limits in Asterisk and looking for features not easily found in SER, he moved to using OpenSER and CallWeaver (then known as OpenPBX.org). While that combination was better, he still had not found his perfect solution.

In 2006, he was introduced to FreeSWITCH. Since then, he's been using FreeSWITCH and regularly contributing to the community. He is the author of mod_lcr and several utility PHP/Perl scripts. He now works with Anthony Minessale as a CudaTel Software Engineer at Barracuda Networks (@CudaTel and @Barracuda). In the spring of 2011, he was among the founding members of the Open Source Telephony Advancement Group (@OSTAG), whose mission is to advance open source telephony to new heights by funding open source projects through funds received by generous contributions and grants from those who share the OSTAG vision.

I'd like to thank my loving wife, Samantha, our daughters Makenzie, Trinity, Alecsys, and Kristian, and our sons Kaiden and Casper for their support while they get less time with me than any of us would like. I'd also like to thank the countless volunteers who step up to help out in the FreeSWITCH and other open source project communities. It would be impossible to keep any project running without them.

About the Reviewers

Norm Brandinger has worked in the computer industry focusing in the areas of systems programming and communications for many years. He graduated with an Engineering Degree in Computer Science from the University of Florida just before the industry began experiencing the exponential growth that continues today. He has worked on the communication challenges that Fortune 100, mid-sized, and small companies all face as an owner, employee, and consultant. Today he balances his high-tech career with a love of the outdoors. Hiking in the woods, climbing mountains, and biking are just some of the ways he finds some balance.

He would not be where he is today without the support, love, guidance, and good genes from his parents. His mom is a retired Special Education professor from Trenton State College. Most recently, his dad was the Executive Director of the New Jersey Commission on Science and Technology. His brother Paul also inherited some good genes as he now works for NASA's Goddard Space Flight Center.

> I would like to acknowledge and thank my partner, Donna. She works full time as a nurse, yet manages to find the time to take care of much of the home and social responsibilities. Her tireless efforts are the reason I have had the time to work on this project.

Kristian Kielhofner is the Co-founder and Chief Technology Officer of Star2Star Communications, The World's Most Reliable Business Grade Communications Solution. He is the inventor and architect of Star2Star's patent-pending StarPath and Constellation technologies. Prior to joining Star2Star, he was most well known as the creator and maintainer of AstLinux, the first Linux distribution to target embedded devices for open source telephony applications.

Jeff Leung is a Small Business Networking Consultant and a Telecommunications Technician. He has seven years of experience in various networking protocols and network architectures including Microsoft Active Directory Networks, Legacy Nortel PBX systems, and FreeSWITCH IP-PBX systems.

He started learning networking protocols at the age of 14 when he stumbled across a book about Active Directory networks at his local library, and the experiences and self-teaching of networking protocols started to snowball from there, eventually turning a hobby into a career that he is very passionate about.

I extend my thanks to the Richmond Public Library located in Richmond, British Columbia for jumpstarting my career with the selection of printed material, and my family for the support they have given me during my tenure at British Columbia Institute of Technology for further training in the Telecommunications and Networking career.

Brian Wiese maintains IT systems for school districts in Central Wisconsin, USA. For more than 12 years he has brought cost-effective and sustainable solutions to education, including recommending open source software such as FreeSWITCH. Brian has also authored many programs and scripts to increase productivity and streamline daily operations for both education and the business sector. In his spare time he enjoys experimenting with new technology, tinkering with his home network, and giving back to his community.

First, I want to thank Anthony for creating FreeSWITCH and giving it to the world, as well as the community for being so willing to help others. I want to express my sincere gratitude to my parents for always pushing me to achieve success. Finally, I want to thank everyone who gave me unprecedented opportunities and inspiration to pursue my passion for technology.

www.PacktPub.com

Support files, eBooks, discount offers, and more

You might want to visit www.PacktPub.com for support files and downloads related to your book.

Did you know that Packt Publishing offers eBook versions of every book published, with PDF and ePub files available? You can upgrade to the eBook version at www.PacktPub.com and as a print book customer, you are entitled to a discount on the eBook copy. Get in touch with us at service@packtpub.com for more details.

At www.PacktPub.com, you can also read a collection of free technical articles, sign up for a range of free newsletters, and receive exclusive discounts and offers on Packt Publishing books and eBooks.

 PACKTLiB®

http://PacktLib.PacktPub.com

Do you need instant solutions to your IT questions? PacktLib is Packt Publishing's online digital book library. Here, you can access, read, and search across Packt Publishing's entire library of books.

Why Subscribe?

- Fully searchable across every book published by Packt Publishing
- Copy and paste, print, and bookmark content
- On demand and accessible via web browser

Free Access for Packt Publishing account holders

If you have an account with Packt at www.PacktPub.com, you can use this to access PacktLib today and view nine entirely free books. Simply use your login credentials for immediate access.

Table of Contents

Preface

A lot has happened in the three years since the original *FreeSWITCH 1.0.6* book was released. At the time, FreeSWITCH 1.0 was only about two years old. A number of early adopters became staunch believers in this relative newcomer. Many others became introduced to FreeSWITCH with the help of a shiny new FreeSWITCH book from Packt Publishing. A few short years later the *FreeSWITCH Cookbook* was also released. Things were happening quickly.

In the meantime the FreeSWITCH team remained active in their development efforts. New features have been added and existing features have been optimized and enhanced. Even prior to the release of *FreeSWITCH 1.2.0* we knew that we would eventually want to revise what we affectionately called the bridge book.

When writing of this edition began, FreeSWITCH 1.2.1 had just come out. In the ensuing months a number of subsequent versions were released. At the time of this writing, the FreeSWITCH project had just moved Version 1.2.8 to stable status, meaning no more features will be added, only bug fixes. The new development branch will eventually result in FreeSWITCH Version 1.4. Will we see a FreeSWITCH 1.4 book released in 2016? Only time will tell, but we wouldn't bet against it.

Like we did with the previous edition of this book, we want to answer a few important questions.

Is FreeSWITCH right for me? The correct answer is always the same, it depends. The FreeSWITCH development team and long-time users are often asked which telephony platform to use. The answer is always the same: use what works for you and your scenario. While we may favor FreeSWITCH we also recognize that every situation is different. If Asterisk or Yate is a better fit for what you want to accomplish then by all means use them. We are very bullish on open source software.

What is FreeSWITCH? FreeSWITCH is a scalable softswitch. In practical terms, this means that it can do anything a traditional PBX can do and much more. It can (and does) act as the core switching software for commercial carriers. It can scale up to handle thousands of simultaneous calls. It can also scale down to act as a simple softphone for your laptop or personal computer. It can also work in a cluster of servers. FreeSWITCH is the telephony engine that powers the CudaTel Communication Server from Barracuda Networks.

FreeSWITCH is not a proxy server. If you need proxy server functionality, then consider OpenSIPS, Kamailio, Repro, or other similar software. FreeSWITCH is a **back-to-back user agent** or **B2BUA**. In this regard, it is similar to Asterisk and other IP PBX software.

Which open source license does FreeSWITCH use? FreeSWITCH is released under the **Mozilla Public License** (**MPL**) Version 1.1. Since FreeSWITCH is a library that can be implemented in other software applications and projects, the developers felt it important to strike a balance between the extremely liberal BSD license and the so-called viral GPL. The MPL fits this paradigm well and allows businesses to create commercial products based on FreeSWITCH without licensing concerns.

However, what about using FreeSWITCH with GPL-based software? It should suffice if we said that the developers wanted to make sure that anyone, including proprietary and GPL-based software users, could use FreeSWITCH. The powerful event socket gives us this functionality, a simple TCP socket-based interface that allows an external program to control FreeSWITCH. Regardless of the license you may be using for your own software, you can still connect to a FreeSWITCH server without any licensing issues.

What this book covers

Chapter 1, Architecture of FreeSWITCH, gives a brief, but thorough introduction to the underlying architecture of FreeSWITCH.

Chapter 2, Building and Installation, shows how to download and install FreeSWITCH on Windows and Unix-like operating systems.

Chapter 3, Test Driving the Example Configuration, provides a hands-on look at the powerful and feature-rich example FreeSWITCH configuration.

Chapter 4, SIP and the User Directory, offers an introduction to the concept of users and the directory as well as a brief look at SIP user agents.

Chapter 5, Understanding the XML Dialplan, explains the basics of creating and editing Dialplan extensions to add advanced functionality to a FreeSWITCH install.

Chapter 6, Using XML IVRs and Phrase Macros, discusses how to create menus and sound phrases for interacting with callers as well as the useful Phrase Macro system.

Chapter 7, Dialplan Scripting with Lua, introduces the concept of advanced call handling using the lightweight scripting language Lua.

Chapter 8, Advanced Dialplan Concepts, builds upon the foundation laid in *Chapter 5, Understanding the XML Dialplan*, and shows how to handle more challenging routing scenarios.

Chapter 9, Moving Beyond the Static XML Configuration, explains concepts necessary for configuring and controlling FreeSWITCH dynamically, such as with a database system.

Chapter 10, Controlling FreeSWITCH Externally, introduces the incredibly powerful Event Socket and the Event Socket library that can be used to access and control a FreeSWITCH server.

Chapter 11, Web-based Call Control with mod_httapi, shows the reader how to use the new `mod_httapi` module to create telephony applications controlled via HTTP.

Chapter 12, Handling NAT, provides much needed insight into understanding how NAT causes issues with VoIP and how to work around them.

Chapter 13, VoIP Security, offers suggestions on how to secure VoIP communications from prying eyes as well as securing a FreeSWITCH server against various attacks.

Chapter 14, Advanced Features and Further Reading, highlights some of the more powerful FreeSWITCH features such as conferencing and offers some ideas on where to learn more about FreeSWITCH.

Appendix A, The FreeSWITCH Online Community, gives a brief introduction to the worldwide online community and the tools used to stay in contact.

Appendix B, Migrating from Asterisk to FreeSWITCH, helps those familiar with Asterisk to get up and running quickly with FreeSWITCH.

Appendix C, The History of FreeSWITCH, is a description of how FreeSWITCH came to be, written by FreeSWITCH master architect and lead developer Anthony Minessale.

What you need for this book

At the very least you will need a computer on which you can run FreeSWITCH. Typically this is a server although that isn't an absolute requirement. You will also need at least one SIP device, be it a softphone, desk phone, or analog telephone adapter (ATA) device. Without such a phone you will not be able to make any phone calls into your FreeSWITCH system.

Although not a requirement, having an account with a SIP provider will enable you to make calls to the Public Switched Telephone Network or PSTN.

Who this book is for

This book is for prospective FreeSWITCH administrators as well as enthusiasts who wish to learn more about how to set up, configure, and extend a FreeSWITCH installation. If you are already using FreeSWITCH, you will find that the information in this book compliments what you have already learned from your personal experience.

A solid understanding of basic networking concepts is very important. Previous experience with VoIP is not required, but will certainly make the learning process go faster.

Conventions

In this book, you will find a number of styles of text that distinguish between different kinds of information. Here are some examples of these styles and an explanation of their meaning.

Code words in text are shown as follows: "We can see FreeSWITCH status information by issuing the stuts command at the FreeSWITCH console."

A block of code is set as follows:

```
<extension name="get voicemail">
  <condition field="destination_number" expression="^\*98$">
    <action application="answer"/>
    <action application="voicemail"
    data="check auth default ${domain_name}"/>
  </condition>
</extension>
```

When we wish to draw your attention to a particular part of a code block, the relevant lines or items are set in bold:

```
<extension name="get voicemail">
  <condition field="destination_number" expression="^\*98$">
    <action application="answer"/>
  <action application="voicemail"
  data="check auth default ${domain_name}"/>

  </condition>
</extension>
```

Any command-line input or output is written as follows:

```
# /usr/local/freeswitch/bin/fs_cli -x version
```

New terms and **important words** are shown in bold. Words that you see on the screen, in menus or dialog boxes for example, appear in the text like this: "Numerous messages will appear in the **Output** window."

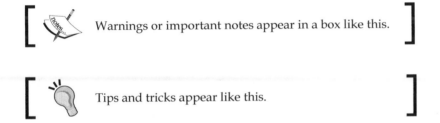

Warnings or important notes appear in a box like this.

Tips and tricks appear like this.

Reader feedback

Feedback from our readers is always welcome. Let us know what you think about this book—what you liked or may have disliked. Reader feedback is important for us to develop titles that you really get the most out of.

To send us general feedback, simply send an e-mail to feedback@packtpub.com, and mention the book title via the subject of your message.

If there is a topic that you have expertise in and you are interested in either writing or contributing to a book, see our author guide on www.packtpub.com/authors.

Customer support

Now that you are the proud owner of a Packt book, we have a number of things to help you to get the most from your purchase.

Downloading the example code

You can download the example code files for all Packt books you have purchased from your account at `http://www.packtpub.com`. If you purchased this book elsewhere, you can visit `http://www.packtpub.com/support` and register to have the files e-mailed directly to you.

Errata

Although we have taken every care to ensure the accuracy of our content, mistakes do happen. If you find a mistake in one of our books—maybe a mistake in the text or the code—we would be grateful if you would report this to us. By doing so, you can save other readers from frustration and help us improve subsequent versions of this book. If you find any errata, please report them by visiting `http://www.packtpub.com/submit-errata`, selecting your book, clicking on the **errata submission form** link, and entering the details of your errata. Once your errata are verified, your submission will be accepted and the errata will be uploaded on our website, or added to any list of existing errata, under the Errata section of that title. Any existing errata can be viewed by selecting your title from `http://www.packtpub.com/support`.

Piracy

Piracy of copyrighted material on the Internet is an ongoing problem across all media. At Packt, we take the protection of our copyright and licenses very seriously. If you come across any illegal copies of our works, in any form, on the Internet, please provide us with the location address or website name immediately so that we can pursue a remedy.

Please contact us at `copyright@packtpub.com` with a link to the suspected pirated material.

We appreciate your help in protecting our authors and our ability to bring you valuable content.

Questions

You can contact us at `questions@packtpub.com` if you are having a problem with any aspect of the book, and we will do our best to address it.

Architecture of FreeSWITCH

Welcome to FreeSWITCH! If you are reading this, then undoubtedly you are interested in things like telecommunications and **Voice over Internet Protocol (VoIP)**. FreeSWITCH is revolutionary software created during a telephony revolution. Before looking at the architecture of this powerful software, let's take a look at the colorful world of telecommunications. This will help to put FreeSWITCH into perspective.

In this chapter we will cover:

- A telephony revolution
- Advantages of FreeSWITCH
- Endpoint and Dialplan modules
- How FreeSWITCH simplifies complex applications like voicemail

A revolution has begun and secrets have been revealed

How and why the telephone works is a mystery to most people. It has been kept secret for years. We just plugged our phones into the wall and they worked, and most people do just that and expect it to work. The **telephony revolution** has begun, and we have begun to pry its secrets from the clutches of the legacy of the telephony industry. Now, everyday individuals like you and me are able to build phone systems that outperform traditional phone services and offer advanced features for relatively low cost. Some people even use FreeSWITCH to provide telephone services for making a profit. FreeSWITCH has been designed to make all of this easier, so we will go over the architecture to get a better understanding of how it works.

Do not be concerned if some of the concepts we introduce seem unnaturally abstract. Learning telephony takes time, especially VoIP. In fact, we recommend that you read this chapter more than once. Absorb as much as you can on the first pass, then come back after you complete *Chapter 5, Understanding the XML Dialplan*. You will be surprised at how much your understanding of VoIP and FreeSWITCH has improved. Then come back and skim it a third time after you have completed *Chapter 10, Controlling FreeSWITCH Externally*; at this point, you will have a firm grasp of VoIP and FreeSWITCH concepts. Give yourself plenty of time to digest all of these strange new concepts, and soon you will find that you are a skilled FreeSWITCH administrator. If you keep at it, you will be rewarded with a meaningful understanding of this strange and wonderful world we call telephony.

Telephones and **telephony systems** (such as telephone switches and PBXs) are very complicated and have evolved over the years into several varieties. The most popular type of phone in the U.K. and the U.S. is the traditional analog phone, which we affectionately refer to as **POTS lines** or **Plain Old Telephone Service**. From the traditional Ma Bell phone up to the long-range cordless phones that most of us have today, one thing has remained the same—the underlying technology. In the last 10-15 years, there has been a convergence of technology between computers and telephones that has produced a pair of affordable alternatives to POTS lines—Mobile phones and VoIP phones (also called Internet Phones).

FreeSWITCH fits into this big tangled mess of various telephone technologies by bridging them together, so that they can communicate despite being otherwise completely incompatible. FreeSWITCH also bridges telephone calls with computer programs that you can write yourself, and controls what happens in ways like never before. FreeSWITCH is software that runs on Windows and several UNIX varieties such as Mac OS X, Linux, Solaris, and BSD. This means you can install FreeSWITCH on your home PC or even a high-end server and use it to process phone calls. Installing FreeSWITCH is discussed in detail in *Chapter 2, Building and Installation*. We will be doing this as soon as we review the basic architecture.

The FreeSWITCH design – modular, scalable, and stable

The design goal of FreeSWITCH is to provide a modular, scalable system around a stable switching core, and to provide a robust interface for developers to add to and control the system. Various elements in FreeSWITCH are independent of each other and do not have much knowledge about how the other parts are working, other than what is provided in what are called **exposed functions**. The functionality of FreeSWITCH can also be extended with loadable modules, which tie a particular external technology into the core.

FreeSWITCH has many different module types that revolve around the central core, much like satellites orbiting a planet. The list includes:

Module type:	Purpose:
Endpoint	Telephone protocols like SIP/H.323 and POTS lines
Application	Performs a task such as playing audio or setting data
Application Programming Interface (API)	Exports a function that takes text input and returns text output, which could be used across modules or from an external connection
Automated Speech Recognition (ASR)	Interfaces with speech recognition systems
Chat	Bridges and exchanges various chat protocols
Codec	Translates between audio formats
Dialplan	Parses the call details and decides where to route the call
Directory	Connects directory information services, such as LDAP, to a common core lookup API
Event handlers	Allows external programs to control FreeSWITCH
File	Provides an interface to extract and play sound from various audio file formats
Formats	Plays audio files in various formats
Languages	Programming language interfaces used for call control
Loggers	Controls logging to the console, system log, or log files
Say	Strings together audio files in various languages to provide feedback to say things like phone numbers, time of day, spell words, and so on
Text-To-Speech (TTS)	Interfaces with text-to-speech engines
Timers	POSIX or Linux kernel timing in applications
XML Interfaces	Uses XML for **Call Detail Records (CDRs)**, RADIUS, CURL, LDAP, RPC, and/or SCGI

The following image shows what the FreeSWITCH architecture looks like and how the modules orbit the core of FreeSWITCH:

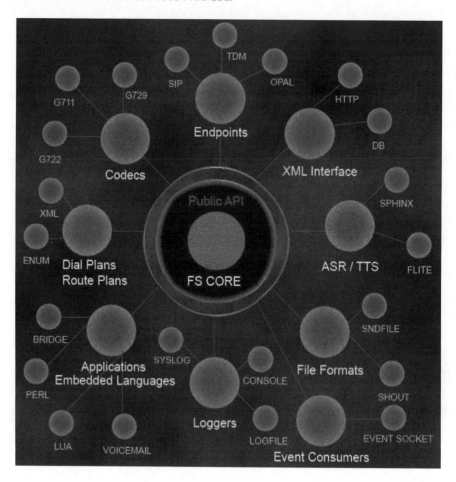

By combining the functionality of the various module interfaces, FreeSWITCH can be configured to connect IP phones, POTS lines, and IP-based telephone services. It can also translate audio formats and interfaces with a custom menu system, which you can create by yourself. You can even control a running FreeSWITCH server from another machine. Let's start by taking a closer look at a pair of important module types.

Important modules – Endpoint and Dialplan

Endpoint modules are critically important and add some of the key features that make FreeSWITCH the powerful platform it is today. The primary role of these modules is to take certain common communication technologies and normalize them into a common abstract entity which we refer to as a **session**. A session represents a connection between FreeSWITCH and a particular protocol. There are several Endpoint modules that come with FreeSWITCH, which implement several protocols such as SIP, H.323, Jingle (Google Talk), and some others. We will spend some time examining one of the more popular modules named mod_sofia.

Sofia-SIP (http://sofia-sip.sourceforge.net) is an open source project sponsored by Nokia, which provides a programming interface for the **Session Initiation Protocol** (**SIP**). We use this library in FreeSWITCH in a module we call mod_sofia. This module registers to all the hooks in FreeSWITCH necessary to make an Endpoint module, and translates the native FreeSWITCH constructs into SIP constructs and back again. Configuration information is taken from the central FreeSWITCH configuration files, which allows mod_sofia to load user-defined preferences and connection details. This allows FreeSWITCH to accept registration from SIP phones and devices, register to other SIP Endpoints such as service providers, send notifications, and provide services to the phones such as voicemail.

> The SIP protocol is defined by a number of **RFC (request for comment)** documents. The primary RFC can be found at http://www.ietf.org/rfc/rfc3261.txt.

When a SIP call is established between FreeSWITCH and another SIP device, it will show up in FreeSWITCH as an active session. If the call is inbound, it can be transferred or bridged to **interactive voice response** (**IVR**) menus, hold music, or one or more extensions, though numerous other options are available. Let's examine a typical scenario where an SIP phone registered as extension 2000 dials extension 2001 with the hope of establishing a call.

First, the SIP phone sends a call setup message to mod_sofia over the network (mod_sofia is *listening* for such messages). After receiving the message, mod_sofia in turn parses the relevant details and passes the call into the **core state machine** in FreeSWITCH. The state machine (in the FreeSWITCH core) then sends the call into the ROUTING state.

The next step is to locate the Dialplan module based on the configuration data for the calling Endpoint. The default and most widely used Dialplan module is the XML Dialplan module. This module is designed to look up a list of instructions from the central XML registry within FreeSWITCH. The XML Dialplan module will parse a series of XML extension objects using **regular expression pattern-matching**.

As we are trying to call 2001, we hope to find an XML extension testing the `destination_number` field for something that matches 2001 and routes accordingly. The Dialplan is not limited to matching only a single extension. In fact, in *Chapter 5, Understanding the XML Dialplan*, you will get an expanded definition of the term **extension**. The XML Dialplan module builds a sort of task list for the call. Each extension that matches it will have its actions added to the call's task list.

Assuming FreeSWITCH finds at least one extension, the XML Dialplan will insert instructions into the session object with the information it needs to try and connect the call to 2001. Once these instructions are in place, the state of the calling session changes from ROUTING to EXECUTE, where the next handler drills down the list and executes the instructions obtained during the ROUTING state. This is where the application interface comes into the picture.

Each instruction is added to the session in the form of an application name and a data argument that will be passed to that application. The one we will use in this example is the `bridge` application. The purpose of this application is to create another session with an outbound connection, then connect the two sessions for direct audio exchange. The argument we will supply to `bridge` will be `user/2001`, which is the easiest way to generate a call to extension 2001. A Dialplan entry for 2001 might look like this:

```
<extension name="example">
  <condition field="destination_number"
             expression="^2001$">
    <action application="bridge" data="user/2001"/>
  </condition>
</extension>
```

The extension is named `example`, and it has a single condition to match. If the condition is matched, it has a single application to execute. In plain language, the mentioned extension could be expressed like this: If the caller dialed 2001, this establishes a connection between the calling party and the endpoint (that is, telephone) at 2001. Consider how this happens.

Once we have inserted the instructions into the session, the session's state will change to `EXECUTE`, and the FreeSWITCH core will use the data collected to perform the desired action. First, the default execute state handler will parse the command to execute `bridge` on `user/2001`, then it will look up the `bridge` application and pass the `user/2001` data in. This will cause the FreeSWITCH core to create a new outbound session of the desired type. User 2001 is also a SIP phone, so `user/2001` will resolve into a SIP dial string, which will be passed to `mod_sofia` to ask it to create a new outbound session.

If the setup for that new session is successful, there will now be two sessions in the FreeSWITCH core. The `bridge` application will take the new session and the original session (the caller's phone) and call the **bridge function** on it. This allows the audio to flow in both directions once the person at extension 2001 actually answers the phone. If that user was unable to answer or was busy, a **timeout** (that is, a failure) would occur and send the corresponding message back to the caller's phone. If a call is unanswered or an extension is busy, many routing options are possible, including call forwarding or voicemail.

All of this happens from the simple action of picking up the phone handset and dialing 2 0 0 1. FreeSWITCH takes all of the complexity of SIP and reduces it to a common denominator. From there, it reduces the complexity further by allowing us to configure a single instruction in the Dialplan to connect the phone at 2000 to the phone at 2001. If we want to allow the phone at 2001 to be able to call the phone at 2000, we can add another entry in the Dialplan going the other way:

```
<extension name="example 2">
  <condition field="destination_number" expression="^2000$">
    <action application="bridge" data="user/2000"/>
  </condition>
</extension>
```

In this scenario, the Endpoint module turned SIP into a FreeSWITCH session and the Dialplan module turned XML into an extension. The `bridge` application turned the complex code of creating an outbound call and connecting the audio into a simple application/data pair. Both the Dialplan module and the application module interface are designed around regular FreeSWITCH sessions. Therefore, not only does the abstraction make life easier for us at the user level, it also simplifies the design of the application and the Dialplan because they can be made agnostic of the actual endpoint technology involved in the call. It is because of this abstraction, when we make up a new Endpoint module tomorrow for something like Skype (there is actually such a thing present, by the way), that we can reuse all the same application and Dialplan modules. The same principle applies to the **Say**, **Automatic Speech Recognition (ASR)**, **Text-to-Speech (TTS)**, and other such modules.

It is possible that you may want to work with some specific data provided by the Endpoint's native protocol. In SIP, for instance, there are several arbitrary headers as well as several other bits of interesting data from the SIP packets. We solve this problem by adding variables to the channel. Using channel variables, `mod_sofia` can set these arbitrary values as they are encountered in the SIP data where you can retrieve them by name from the channel in your Dialplan or application. This way, we share our knowledge of these special variables with the SIP Endpoint. However, the FreeSWITCH core just sees them as arbitrary channel variables that the core can ignore. There are also several special reserved channel variables that can influence the behavior of FreeSWITCH in many interesting ways. If you have ever used a scripting language or configuration engine that uses variables (sometimes called **attribute-value pairs** or **AVPs**), you are at an advantage because channel variables are pretty much the same concept. There is simply a variable name and a value that is passed to the channel and the data is set.

There is even an application interface for this, the `set` application, which lets you set your own variables from the Dialplan:

```
<extension name="example 3">
  <condition field="destination_number" expression="^2000$">
    <action application="set" data="foo=bar"/>
    <action application="bridge" data="user/2000"/>
  </condition>
</extension>
```

This example is almost identical to the previous example, but instead of just placing the call, we first set the variable `foo` equal to the value `bar`. This variable will remain set throughout the call and can even be referenced at the end of the call in the detail logs.

The more we build things in small pieces, the more the same underlying resources can be reused, making the system simpler to use. For example, the codec interface knows nothing else about the core, other than its own isolated world of encoding and decoding audio packets. Once a proper codec module has been written, it becomes usable by any Endpoint interface capable of carrying that codec in its audio stream. This means that if we get a Text-To-Speech module working, we can generate synthesized speech on any and all Endpoints that FreeSWITCH supports. It does not matter which one comes first as they have nothing to do with each other. However, the addition of either one instantly adds functionality to the other. The TTS module becomes more useful because it can use more codecs; the codecs have become more useful because we added a new function that can take advantage of them. The same idea applies to applications. If we write a new application module, the existing endpoints will immediately be able to run and use that application.

Complex applications made simple

FreeSWITCH removes much of the complexity of the more advanced applications. Let's look at two examples of a more complex application.

Voicemail

The first application we will discuss is the `voicemail` application. The general purpose of this application is probably pretty easy to deduce. It provides voicemail service. This application is useful to add right after the `bridge` application as a second option, in case the call was not completed. We can do this with a careful combination of application choices and one of those fancy special variables that we were discussing earlier. Let's look at a new version of our last extension that also allows us to leave a voicemail:

```
<extension name="example 4">
  <condition field="destination_number" expression="^2000$">
    <action application="set"
           data="hangup_after_bridge=true"/>
    <action application="bridge" data="user/2000"/>
    <action application="voicemail"
           data="default ${domain} 2000"/>
  </condition>
</extension>
```

Here we see two uses of channel variables. First we set `hangup_after_bridge=true` telling the system to just hang up once we have had at least one successfully bridged call to another phone and to disregard the rest of the instructions. We are also using the `domain` variable as seen in brackets prefixed with a dollar sign, `${domain}`. This is a special variable that defaults to the auto-configured domain name, which all the phones are using from the configuration.

In this example, we check if someone is dialing 2000. We then try to bridge the call to the phone registered to extension 2000. If the call fails or if there is no answer, we will continue to the next instruction, which is to execute the `voicemail` application. We provide the information the application needs to know and which extension the voicemail is for, so it knows how to handle the situation. Next, the `voicemail` application plays the pre-recorded greeting or generates one for you using the Say module's interface we briefly discussed earlier. It strings together sound files to make a voice say something like, "The person at extension 2 0 0 0 is not available, please leave a message." Next, `mod_voicemail` prompts you to record a message, and now is your chance to leave your mark in that person's inbox by leaving a voice message. As an additional feature, if you are not satisfied with your recording, you can repeat it as many times as you wish. Once you finally commit, a FreeSWITCH MESSAGE_WAITING event is fired into the core event system, which is picked up by mod_sofia by way of an event consumer, where the event information is translated into SIP — in this case a SIP NOTIFY message that lets the SIP phone know that there is a message waiting. If everything goes as planned, the phone registered on extension 2000 will illuminate its message-waiting indicator light!

Again in this example, not only have we seen how to play a greeting, record a message, and send it to a user, we have also uncovered another unsung hero of the FreeSWITCH core — the **event system**. The FreeSWITCH event system is not a module interface like the other examples, it is a core engine that you can use to bind to named events and react accordingly when an event is received. In other words, throughout the FreeSWITCH core, there are events that are sent and received. Modules can bind to (that is listen for) various events. They can also fire events into the event engine; other modules can listen for those events. As we discussed, the Sofia SIP module binds or subscribes to the event designated for MESSAGE_WAITING information. This allows our `mod_voicemail` module to interact with `mod_sofia` without either system having any knowledge about the other's existence. The event is fired by `mod_voicemail`, received by `mod_sofia`, and translated into the proper SIP message — all seemingly magical, courtesy of the event system.

There are several challenges with such a complex interactive system when considering all of the possible languages it may need to support, as well as what files to play for the automated messages and how they are strung together. The Say module supplies a nice way to string files together, but it is limited to something specific like spelling a word, counting something, or saying a certain date. The way we overcome this is by defining a more complex layer on top of the Say module called **Phrase Macros**. Phrase Macros are a collection of XML expressions that pull out a list of arguments by matching a regular expression and executing a string of commands. This is very similar to how the XML Dialplan works, only custom-tailored for **interactive voice response (IVR)** scenarios. For example, when mod_voicemail asks you to record your message, rather than coding in the string of files to make it say what you want, the code just calls a Phrase Macro called voicemail_record_message. This arbitrary string is shared between mod_voicemail and the Phrase Macro section in the configuration allowing us, the users, to edit the file without doing any fancy programming.

```
<macro name="voicemail_record_message">
  <input pattern="^(.*)$">
    <match>
      <action function= "play-file"
         data="voicemail/vm-record_message.wav"/>
    </match>
  </input>
</macro>
```

When mod_voicemail executes the voicemail_record_message macro, it first matches the pattern, which, in this case, is just to match everything, as this particular macro has no input. If the macro did have input, the pattern matching could be used to perform different actions based on different input. Once a match is found, the match tag is parsed in the XML for action tags just like in our Dialplan example. This macro just plays the file vm-record_message.wav, but more complicated macros, like the ones for verifying your recording or telling you how many messages you have in your inbox, may use combinations of various Say modules and play various audio files. Phrase Macros are discussed in detail in *Chapter 6, Using XML IVRs and Phrase Macros* and used extensively in *Chapter 7, Dialplan Scripting with Lua*.

Once again, we have cooperation among the phrase system, the audio file, and the Say modules loaded by the core being joined together to enable powerful functionality. The Say modules are written specifically for a particular language or voice within a language. We can programmatically request to say a particular time and have it translated into the proper Say module based on input variables. The Phrase Macro system is a great way to put bigger variable concepts into your code, which can be easily tweaked later by everyday users. For example, if we wanted to make a small IVR that asks us to dial a four-digit number and then just read it back and hang up, we could make one macro called `myapp_ask_for_digits` and the other called `myapp_read_digits`. In our code, we would execute these macros by name—the former when it is time to ask for the digits and the later to read back the digits by passing in the value we entered. Once this is in place, a less-experienced individual could implement the XML files to play the proper sounds. He or she can use the Say modules to read back the number, and it should all be working in multiple languages with no further coding necessary. Voicemail is just one example of FreeSWITCH in use as an application server. There are endless possibilities when we use FreeSWITCH to connect phone calls with computers.

Multi-party conferencing

Another popular feature of FreeSWITCH is delivered by the `mod_conference` conferencing module. The `mod_conference` module provides dynamic conference rooms that can bridge together the audio from several audio channels. This can be used to hold meetings where there are several callers who want to interact on the same call. Each new session that connects to the same conference room will join the others, and instantly be able to talk to all of the other participants at the same time. By using a Dialplan example, similar to the one we used for bridging to another phone, we can make an extension to join a conference room:

```xml
<extension name="example 4">
  <condition field="destination_number"  expression="^3000$">
    <action application="conference" data="3000@default"/>
  </condition>
</extension>
```

This is just as simple as bridging a call, but what is special about this extension is that many callers can call extension 3000 and join the same conference. If three people joined this conference and one of them decides to leave, the other two would still be able to continue their conversation.

The conference module also has other special features, such as the ability to play sound files or Text-To-Speech to the whole conference or even just to a single member of the conference. As you may have guessed, we are able to do this by using the TTS and sound file interfaces provided by their respective modules. Once again, the smaller pieces come together to extend the functionality without needing explicit knowledge of the other components in the system.

The conference module also uses the event system in a special way, employing what are called **custom events**. When it first loads, a module such as `mod_conference` can reserve a special event namespace called a **subclass**. When something interesting happens, such as when a caller joins or leaves a conference, it fires those events on the CUSTOM event channel in the core. When we are interested in receiving such events, all we have to do is subscribe to the CUSTOM event supplying an extra subclass string, which specifies the specific CUSTOM events we are interested in. In this case, it is `conference::maintenance`. This makes it possible to look out for important things such as when someone joins or leaves the conference, or even when they start and stop talking. Conferencing is discussed in detail in *Chapter 14*, *Advanced Features and Further Reading*.

The FreeSWITCH API (FSAPI)

Another very powerful module interface in FreeSWITCH is the **FSAPI** module. The principle of this type of interface is very simple—it takes a single string of text as input, which may or may not be parsed, and performs a particular action. The return value is also a string that can be of any size, from a single character up to several pages of text, depending on the function that was called. One major benefit of FSAPI functions is that a module can use them to call routines in another module without directly linking into the actual code. The command-line interface of FreeSWITCH or CLI uses FSAPI functions to pass FreeSWITCH API commands from an operating system's command prompt.

Here is a small example of how we can execute the `status` FSAPI command from the FreeSWITCH CLI:

```
freeswitch@internal> status
UP 0 years, 3 days, 2 hours, 25 minutes, 5 seconds, 49 milliseconds, 603 microseconds
FreeSWITCH (Version 1.3.13b git 1a3a11f 2013-02-15 11:16:49Z) is ready
0 session(s) since startup
0 session(s) - 0 out of max 30 per sec
1000 session(s) max
min idle cpu 0.00/98.00
Current Stack Size/Max 240K/8192K
```

What's really happening here is that when we type status and press the *Enter* key, the word "status" is used to look up the status FSAPI function from the module in which it is implemented. The underlying function is then called, and the core is queried for its status message. Once the status data is obtained, the output is written to a stream that comes back and prints as the result of the command.

We have already learned that a module can create and export FSAPI functions that can be executed from anywhere such as the CLI. But wait, there's more! Modules can also be written to push commands into the FSAPI interface and send the result over a specific protocol. There are two modules included in FreeSWITCH that do just that—mod_xml_rpc and mod_event_socket (discussed respectively in *Chapter 9, Moving Beyond the Static XML Configuration* and *Chapter 10, Controlling FreeSWITCH Externally*). Consider the example of mod_xml_rpc. This module implements the standardized XML-RPC protocol as a FreeSWITCH module. Clients using an XML-RPC interface can connect to FreeSWITCH and execute any FSAPI command they choose. So a remote client could execute an RPC call to status, and get a similar status message to the one we saw in the previous example. This same module also provides FreeSWITCH with a general web server, which allows FSAPI commands to be accessed with a direct URL link. For example, one could point a browser to http://example.freeswitch.box:8080/api/status to access the status command directly over the World Wide Web. By using this technique, it's possible to create FSAPI commands that work similar to a CGI, providing a dynamic web application that has direct access to FreeSWITCH internals.

As we have shown, the FSAPI interface is very versatile. Now we know it can be used to provide a CLI interface, a way for modules to call functions from each other, and a way to export WWW or XML-RPC functions. There is still one more use for FSAPI functions that we have not covered. We touched briefly on the concept of channel variables earlier, noting that we can use the expression ${myvariable} to get the value of a certain variable. FSAPI functions can also be accessed this way in the format ${myfunction()}. This notation indicates that the FSAPI command myfunction should be called, and that the expression should be replaced with the output of that function call. Therefore, we can use ${status()} anywhere when variables are expanded to gain access to the status command. For example:

```
<action application="set" data="my_status=${status()}"/>
```

The value placed in the my_status variable will be the output from the status command.

The drawback to all the versatility provided by a single module interface is that, in order to achieve all of this, we have to loosely type the functionality. This means that there are several cases where a single FSAPI command could easily be accessed using all of the ways we have discussed. In addition, there are also some other specific functions that are specifically designed for a particular access method. For instance, if we made an FSAPI command that produced HTML intended to be accessed with a web browser, we would not want to access it from the CLI or by referencing it as a variable. Similarly, if we made an FSAPI function that computed some kind of value based on call details, which was designed to be used from the Dialplan, it would not be very useful at the CLI or from the Web. So, with great power comes great responsibility, and this is one case where we need to use common sense to decide when and where to use the proper FSAPI functions to get the most out of them.

The XML registry

We have now discussed many of the fundamental components of the FreeSWITCH core and how they interact with each other. We have seen how the event system can carry information across the core, and how the XML Dialplan can query the XML registry for data. This would be a good time to explain the XML registry a bit more. The **XML registry** is a centrally managed XML document that holds all of the critical data that FreeSWITCH needs to operate properly. The initial document is loaded from your hard drive and passed into a special **pre-processor**. This pre-processor can include other XML documents and other special operations, such as setting global variables, which can be resolved by the pre-processor further down in the document.

Once the entire document and all of the included files are parsed, replaced, and generated into a static XML document, this document is loaded into memory. The XML registry is divided into several sections— *configuration, odbc, dialplan, directory, locations, chatplan, languages,* and *phrases*. The core and the modules draw their configuration from the **configuration** section. The XML Dialplan module draws its Dialplan data from the **dialplan** section. The SIP authentication, user lookup, and the voicemail module read their account information from the **directory** section. The Phrase Macros pull their configuration from the **phrases** section. If we make a change to any of the documents on the disk, we can reload the changes into memory by issuing the `reloadxml` command from the CLI. (This is an example of using the FSAPI interface to communicate with the FreeSWITCH core.)

Language modules

One distinct type of module that does not have a direct interface to FreeSWITCH-like files and Endpoints, but still offers an immensely powerful connection to existing technology, is the **Language** module. Language modules embed a programming language like Lua, JavaScript, Perl, and even C# (using mod_managed) into FreeSWITCH, and transfer functionality between the core and the language's runtime. This allows things like IVR applications to be written in the embedded language, with a simple interface back to FreeSWITCH for all the heavy lifting. Language modules usually register into the core with the application interface and the FSAPI interface and are executed from the Dialplan. Language modules offer lots of opportunities and are very powerful. Using language modules, you can build powerful voice applications in a standard programming language. In some respects, you can actually control a telephone with a programming language.

The demonstration configuration

Understanding all of these concepts right off the bat is far from easy, and as the maintainers of the software, we do not expect most people to have everything *just click*. This is the main reason that every new layer we put on top of the core makes things simpler and easier to learn. The demonstration configuration of FreeSWITCH is the last line of defense between new users of the software and all of the crazy, complicated, and sometimes downright evil stuff better known as telephony. We try very hard to save the users from such things.

The main purpose of the demonstration configuration in FreeSWITCH is to showcase all of the hundreds of parameters there are to work with. We present them to you in a working configuration that you could actually leave untouched and play with a bit before venturing into the unknown and trying your own hand at changing some of the options. Think of FreeSWITCH as a Lego set. FreeSWITCH and all of its little parts are like a brand new bucket Lego bricks, with plenty of parts to build anything we can imagine. The demonstration configuration is like the sample spaceship that you find in the instruction booklet. It contains step-by-step instructions on exactly how to build something you know will work. After you pick up some experience, you might start modifying your Lego ship to have extra features, or maybe even rebuild the parts into a car or some other creation. The good news about FreeSWITCH is that it comes out of the box already assembled. Therefore, unlike the bucket of Lego bricks, if you get frustrated and smash it to bits, you can just re-install the defaults and you won't have to build it again from scratch. The demonstration configuration is discussed in *Chapter 3, Test Driving the Example Configuration*.

Once FreeSWITCH has been successfully built on your system, you simply have to launch the program without changing one line in the configuration file. You will be able to point a SIP telephone or software-based SIP **softphone** to the address of your computer and make a test call. If you are brave and have the ambition of connecting a traditional analog phone, you may want to get the SIP thing under your belt first. This is because it involves a little more work (including purchasing a hardware card for your computer or a magic device called an **ATA—analog telephone adapter**).

If you have more than one phone, you should be able to configure them to each having an individual extension in the range 1000-1019, which is the default extension number range that is pre-defined in the demonstration configuration. Once you get both phones registered, you will be able to make calls across them or have them to meet in a conference room in the 3000-3399 range. If you call an extension that is not registered or let the phone ring at another extension for too long, the voicemail application will use the phrase system to indicate that the party is not available, and ask you to record a message. If you dial 5000, you can see an example of the IVR system at work, presenting several menu choices demonstrating various other neat things FreeSWITCH can do out of the box. There are a lot of small changes and additions that can be made to the demonstration configuration while still leaving it intact.

For example, using the pre-processor directives we went over earlier, the demonstration configuration loads a list of files into the XML registry from certain places, meaning that every file in a particular folder will be combined into the final XML configuration document. The two most important points where this takes place are where the user accounts and the extensions in the Dialplan are kept. Each of the 20 extensions that are preconfigured with the defaults are stored into their own file. We could easily create a new file with a single user definition and drop it into place to add another user, and simply issue the `reloadxml` command at the FreeSWITCH CLI. The same idea applies to the example Dialplan. We can put a single extension into its own file and load it into place whenever we want.

Summary

FreeSWITCH is a complex system of moving parts that are intertwined to produce a solid, stable core with flexible and easy-to-extend add-ons. The core extends its interfaces to modules. These modules simplify the functionality further and extend it up to the user. The modules also can bring outside functionality into FreeSWITCH by translating various communication protocols into a common, well-known format. We looked at the various module types, and demonstrated how they revolve around the core and interact with each other to turn simple abstract concepts into higher-level functionalities. We touched base on a few of the more popular applications in FreeSWITCH—the conferencing and voicemail modules and how they, in turn, make use of other modules in the system without ever knowing it. This agnosticism is accomplished by means of the event system. We also saw how the demonstration configuration provides several working examples to help take the edge off of an otherwise frightening feat of staring down the business end of a full-featured soft-switch.

Now that we have a general idea of what makes FreeSWITCH tick, we will take a closer look at some of these concepts with some real-world examples for you to try. First we obtain a copy of the source code from the Internet, so we can build the software package and install it. From there, we will test out the configuration, so be sure to get yourself a SIP phone or at least a softphone. Once we try a few things, we will dive a litter deeper into how things work and create a few things of our own, like an extension or two and an IVR menu. So take a deep breath and get ready to dive into the world of telephony with FreeSWITCH!

In the following chapter we will take our first steps in getting a FreeSWITCH system up and running.

2
Building and Installation

FreeSWITCH is open source software. Basically, this means that anyone can obtain, read, compile, mangle, fix, or do anything that comes to mind, the raw source code of the application. Many users, especially beginners, will find that dealing with source code is somewhat a daunting task, but rest assured, we are doing our best to make this experience as painless as possible. In the future, we will be adding binary packages into various popular Linux distributions, but for the time being, we will explain how to manually obtain and install FreeSWITCH for Unix and Windows. (For the purpose of this chapter, the terms **Unix-like** and **Linux/Unix** refer not only to Unix and Linux, but also to FreeBSD and Mac OS X.) Try not to fret if it seems overwhelming. With a little patience and luck, the whole process will go smoothly. It's not entirely unlike a root canal. It's been said that many root canals are pulled off without a hitch and when they go wrong, they go horribly wrong; and that is where the horror stories, which we all hear, come from.

In this chapter, we will discuss how to download and install FreeSWITCH from the source code for Unix-like environments as well as for Windows. We will cover the necessary prerequisites for each operating system. Finally, we will explain how to launch FreeSWITCH and how to run it in the background.

In this chapter, we will cover the following topics:

- Setting up the FreeSWITCH environment
- Laying the ground work for our FreeSWITCH installation
- Downloading and installing FreeSWITCH
- Launching FreeSWITCH and running it in the background

Setting up the FreeSWITCH environment

FreeSWITCH, like many other software applications, requires a suitable environment. Primarily that means choosing an appropriate operating system for your hardware and having the proper LAN/WAN connectivity and physical environment.

Operating system

The first question to consider here is: which operating system should be used? Generally speaking, it is good to use an operating system with which you are comfortable and familiar. One caveat to consider is 32-bit versus 64-bit. Some users have reported problems when running a 32-bit OS on a 64-bit hardware platform. We strongly recommend that you use a 64-bit OS if you have 64-bit hardware.

Those who prefer a Windows environment can use XP, Vista, Windows 7, Server 2003, Server 2008 R2, or Server 2012. Several users have reported good success with production systems running on modern hardware and using Windows Server 2008.

On the other hand, there is a wide variety of Unix-like operating systems available, many of which are freely downloadable. Most of us have an operating system (Linux, BSD, Solaris, and so on) and distribution (CentOS, Debian, Ubuntu, and so on) that we prefer to use. The FreeSWITCH developers do not advocate any particular operating system or distribution.

Some have asked which platform is the best for FreeSWITCH. There are many factors to consider when choosing a platform on which to run a telephony application. FreeSWITCH is cross-platform, and therefore, it compiles and runs on numerous systems. However, through hard-earned experience, we know which operating systems and distributions lend themselves to real-time telephony applications. The bottom line is that you want your system to be stable and reliable. The FreeSWITCH community has overwhelmingly endorsed CentOS 5 and Debian 6 as production-ready Linux distributions.

 As of the time of writing, there were concerns with the performance of FreeSWITCH under CentOS 6. Many members of the FreeSWITCH community report that these issues do not occur in CentOS 6.3. If you experience unusual symptoms in prior versions of CentOS Version 6 then try using CentOS 6.3.

Keep in mind that bleeding edge distributions generally are not appropriate for real-time telephony systems. Boring and predictable are preferable to latest and greatest.

Operating system prerequisites

Each operating system has its own set of prerequisites. Make sure that you have met the prerequisites for your platform. In the following sections we discuss Linux/Unix, Mac OS X, and Windows.

Linux/Unix

The following items are usually already installed on your system. Note that a Git client is not required:

- **Git**: A Git client also gives you access to the current code repository (recommended especially for developers and those who want the latest code)
- **GNUMAKE**: The GNU version of Make
- **AUTOCONF**: Version 2.60 or higher
- **AUTOMAKE**: Version 1.9 or higher
- **LIBTOOL**: Version 1.5.14 or higher
- **GCC**: Version 3.3 or higher
- **WGET**: Any recent version
- **LIBNCURSES**: Any recent version
- **BZIP2**: Any recent version

Mac OS X

It is strongly recommended that Mac users have, at the very least, OS X Version 10.4. Compiling FreeSWITCH on OS X requires the installation of the Apple XCode Developer Tools. You may download them from `http://connect.apple.com`. Free registration is required.

 Apple has been making some changes in the tools supported on OS X. The FreeSWITCH community does their best to keep people informed of the latest information with respect to building and running FreeSWITCH on OS X. Stay informed by visiting `http://wiki.freeswitch.org/wiki/Installation_and_Setup_on_OS_X`.

Windows

FreeSWITCH in a Windows environment has two primary requirements. They are as follows:

1. Microsoft Visual C++ 2008 or 2010 (or 2008 or 2010 Express Edition).
2. A file decompression utility.

FreeSWITCH in Windows is compiled and built using **Microsoft Visual C++ (MSVC)** or **Visual C++ Express Edition (MSVCEE)**. The Express Edition is free to download, though registration is required. It can be obtained at `http://www.microsoft.com/Express/VC`. The other requirement for Windows is a file decompression utility like WinZip (`www.winzip.com`), or WinRAR (`www.rarlab.com`). A free alternative is 7-Zip (`www.7-zip.org`). Each of these utilities will add a right-click (context) menu option to Windows Explorer.

> The Express Editions of Visual C++ do not support 64-bit targets by default. If you are intending to build 64-bit versions of FreeSWITCH for Windows, it is recommended that you have the Professional Editions of Visual Studio instead of Visual C++ Express.

Text editors and XML

Working with FreeSWITCH requires you to have a text editor with which you are comfortable. Regardless of your editor choice, we strongly recommend that you use a text editor that supports XML syntax highlighting. You will find that editing XML configuration files is much easier on the eyes with highlighting turned on.

If you do not already have a preferred editor, we suggest trying one or two for your platform. Be aware that if you are in a Linux/Unix environment that does not have a **Graphical User Interface (GUI)**, your choices will be fewer. However, there are several excellent text-only editors available:

- **Emacs**: A text-only editor available for just about any Unix-like environment, including Mac OS X. It can highlight source code, XML, HTML, and more. This is the editor of choice for the FreeSWITCH development team. (A GUI version of Emacs is also available.)
- **Vi/Vim**: A text-only editor available for just about any Unix-like environment. Like Emacs, it can highlight source code and markup languages. (A GUI version of Vim is also available.)
- **Notepad++**: A graphical text editor for a Windows environment. It supports highlighting of many programming and markup languages. It is a very useful and free text editor for Windows.

- **Microsoft Visual Studio/Visual C++ Express**: This **Integrated Development Environment (IDE)** has a graphical editor that plays out very well with XML files. It supports highlighting and auto-completion of the XML tags and will display a red underline for any improperly closed or edited XML tags and/or elements.

Downloading the source

Most open source projects have their source code divided into two general categories: **stable** and **latest**. The FreeSWITCH project recently formed these two branches. Version 1.2.x is the stable branch and Version 1.3.x is the latest branch. Future releases will follow the even/odd numbering plan, where 1.4.x is stable and 1.5.x is the **unstable** or **development** branch. You can update to the latest branch at any time if you are using Git (see the *Building from the latest code* section in this chapter) One other point to keep in mind: binary distributions of FreeSWITCH might be available for your platform. While they are certainly convenient, in our experience it is easier to troubleshoot, update, and customize your FreeSWITCH installation when compiling from the source.

Be sure that your system has the Internet access because the build process will occasionally need to download additional files.

The source code can be obtained from the following FreeSWITCH download site:

http://files.freeswitch.org

Locate a file named `freeswitch-1.2.x.tar.gz` (where x is the latest build number), and download it into a local directory on your computer, then decompress it. A typical session in Linux might look like the following:

```
#>cd /usr/src
#>wget http://files.freeswitch.org/freeswitch-1.2.1.tar.bz2
#>tar jxvf freeswitch-1.2.1.tar.bz2
```

This will create a new directory that contains the FreeSWITCH source code ready for you to compile on your system. (From now on, this will be referred to as the FreeSWITCH source directory.)

Windows users should create a new directory and download the source file. See the *Compiling FreeSWITCH For Windows* section later in this chapter.

Building from the latest code

If you prefer to be on the latest version of FreeSWITCH, you will need a Git client. Use yum, apt, or whichever package manager your distribution has to install Git. In Windows, a popular (and free) client is TortoiseGit (`code.google.com/p/tortoisegit`).

In Linux/Unix environments a typical Git checkout and compile session would look like this:

```
#>cd /usr/src
#>git clone git://git.freeswitch.org/freeswitch.git
#>cd freeswitch
#>./bootstrap.sh
#>./configure -C
#>make install
#>make cd-sounds-install
#>make cd-moh-install
```

The preceding commands will take some time to complete. You can automate the process a bit by chaining the commands together with the `&&` operator. These commands are discussed in more detail in the following sections.

Compiling FreeSWITCH for Linux/Unix/Mac OS X

The install procedure is essentially the same for Linux, Unix, or Mac OS X. However, make sure that your system has met the prerequisites listed in the previous section.

Compiling FreeSWITCH

Compiling FreeSWITCH requires just a few steps, although it will take some time depending upon the speed of your system. The basic procedure for compiling FreeSWITCH is as follows:

1. Run the `bootstrap.sh` script.
2. Edit the `modules.conf` file to customize which modules are compiled by default.
3. Run the `configure` script.
4. Run the `make` and `make install` utilities to compile and install.
5. Edit `modules.conf.xml` to customize which modules are loaded by default.
6. Install the sound and music files.

Following are detailed step-by-step instructions for compiling FreeSWITCH.

Step 1 – edit modules.conf

The `modules.conf` file contains a list of the various FreeSWITCH modules that will be configured and compiled. The default `modules.conf` file has a sensible set of modules pre-selected to be compiled. However, there is one optional module that we will enable now. You should have a new subdirectory named `freeswitch-1.2.x`, where `1.2.x` is the version number. For example, if the latest stable version is 1.2.1 then your source directory will be `/usr/src/freeswitch-1.2.1`. Perform the following steps:

1. Change the directory into the new FreeSWITCH source directory:

    `#>cd /usr/src/freeswitch-1.2.x`

2. Open `modules.conf` in a text editor. Scroll down to the following line:

    `#asr_tts/mod_flite`

3. Remove the # character from the beginning of the line, then save and exit. The `mod_flite` module enables FreeSWITCH to use the open source **Festival Lite text-to-speech** (TTS) engine. (The Flite TTS engine does not produce a particularly high quality speech synthesis. However, it is very handy for doing TTS testing.)

> More information about Festival Lite can be found at `http://www.speech.cs.cmu.edu/flite/`.

After editing `modules.conf`, we are ready to start the build process.

> Removing the # character at the beginning of a line in `modules.conf` will cause the module on that line to automatically be built when issuing the `make` command. Likewise, adding a # at the beginning of the line will prevent the corresponding module from being built automatically.

Step 2 – run the configure script

Like many open source projects, FreeSWITCH in UNIX-like environments makes use of the now famous `configure` script. From within the FreeSWITCH source directory, launch the configure script, as follows:

`#>./configure -C`

The `configure` script performs many tasks, including making sure that the prerequisites have been met. If a prerequisite has not been met then the `configure` script will exit and tell you which dependency has not been met. If this occurs then you must resolve the issue and rerun the `configure` script. You will need to make sure that all of the prerequisites have been met before the `configure` script will run to completion. The `-c` argument tells the `configure` module to create a `config.cache` file that will be used by subsequent `configure` scripts with the various libraries included in the source tree.

> The `configure` script is a common tool in building open source software in the Linux/Unix environment. It has many options to modify the behavior. Launch `configure` with the `--help` argument to see a complete list.

During the configuration process, you will see the `configure` script run multiple times. FreeSWITCH makes use of many libraries like **Apache Portable Runtime (APR)** and **Perl Compatible Regular Expressions (PCRE)**. Each of these elements has its own specific `configure` script that is customized to its own needs.

After some time, the `configure` script finishes and returns you to the system prompt. You will undoubtedly see a lot of output on the screen from the configuration process, but if you do not see any errors then you may proceed to the compilation process.

Step 3 – run the make and make install utilities

The configuration process in the previous step actually creates what is called a **Makefile** for FreeSWITCH, its libraries, and its various modules. The compilation and installation of FreeSWITCH are both handled by the make utility. First run `make`, and then run `make install`. Many users will run them both with one command line, which is as follows:

```
#>make && make install
```

Like the `configure` script, the `make` process takes a while, and it will stop if there are any errors. Usually things go well, and at the end of the compilation and installation, you are greeted with the following message:

```
+-------- FreeSWITCH install Complete ----------+
+ FreeSWITCH has been successfully installed.   +
+                                               +
+       Install sounds:                         +
+       (uhd-sounds includes hd-sounds, sounds) +
+       (hd-sounds includes sounds)             +
```

```
+       -----------------------------------       +
+               make cd-sounds-install            +
+               make cd-moh-install               +
+                                                 +
+               make uhd-sounds-install           +
+               make uhd-moh-install              +
+                                                 +
+               make hd-sounds-install            +
+               make hd-moh-install               +
+                                                 +
+               make sounds-install               +
+               make moh-install                  +
+                                                 +
+       Install non english sounds:               +
+       replace XX with language                  +
+       (ru : Russian)                            +
+       -----------------------------------       +
+               make cd-sounds-XX-install         +
+               make uhd-sounds-XX-install        +
+               make hd-sounds-XX-install         +
+               make sounds-XX-install            +
+                                                 +
+       Upgrade to latest:                        +
+       -------------------------------           +
+               make current                      +
+                                                 +
+       Rebuild all:                              +
+       -------------------------------           +
+               make sure                         +
+                                                 +
+       Install/Re-install default config:        +
+       -------------------------------           +
+               make samples                      +
+                                                 +
+                                                 +
+       Additional resources:                     +
```

```
+       ----------------------------------      +
+       http://www.freeswitch.org               +
+       http://wiki.freeswitch.org              +
+       http://jira.freeswitch.org              +
+       http://lists.freeswitch.org             +
+                                               +
+       irc.freenode.net / #freeswitch          +
+                                               +
+-----------------------------------------------+
```

If you see a message like the last one then you have successfully compiled FreeSWITCH, and can proceed to the next step. If an error occurs then the compilation process will stop and report it. You will need to correct the problem before you can continue. If the error message is unfamiliar to you then you should contact the FreeSWITCH community using the resources listed in *Appendix A, The FreeSWITCH Online Community*.

Step 4 – edit modules.conf.xml

The modules.conf.xml file contains a list of modules that FreeSWITCH will load when it is launched. The default modules.conf.xml file corresponds with the default modules.conf file. The modules that are built by default in modules.conf are also enabled by default in modules.conf.xml. As we enabled mod_flite to be built in modules.conf, we need to enable mod_flite in modules.conf.xml so that it will be loaded automatically when FreeSWITCH starts. As a rule of thumb, any module that you wish to load automatically when FreeSWITCH starts must be enabled in modules.conf.xml.

The modules.conf.xml file is located in the conf/autoload_configs subdirectory. The default location is /usr/local/freeswitch/conf/autoload_configs/modules.conf.xml. Open the file in a text editor and locate the following line near the end of the file:

```
<!-- <load module="mod_flite"/> -->
```

Remove the <!-- and --> tags so that it looks like the following:

```
<load module="mod_flite"/>
```

Save the file and exit. You are almost ready to start the FreeSWITCH application.

What's the difference between `modules.conf` and `modules.conf.xml` files? The `modules.conf` file is found in the source directory, and is used to control FreeSWITCH modules that are compiled when running `make`. It is a simple text file that uses a leading # character to denote a comment. The `modules.conf.xml` file is part of the example XML configuration, and is found in the FreeSWITCH `autoload_configs` subdirectory. It uses standard XML `<!--` and `-->` pairs to denote a comment. It controls which modules are loaded when FreeSWITCH is launched.

Step 5 – install sound and music files

Sound and music files are not absolutely required. However, they are highly recommended. Without them, you will not have music on hold, and features like voicemail and the sample IVR will not be functional. FreeSWITCH has sample sound and music files available in four different sampling rates. We recommend installing all of them so that you can take advantage of high quality audio connections wherever possible.

To install the sound files, just issue the following command in the FreeSWITCH source directory:

```
#>make cd-sounds-install
```

To install the music files, issue the following command:

```
#>make cd-moh-install
```

These commands will download and install the sound and music files in 8 kHz, 16 kHz, 32 kHz, and 48 kHz sampling rates. FreeSWITCH will use the appropriate sampling rate when playing a sound or music file to a caller.

You are now ready to start FreeSWITCH. The next section covers compiling FreeSWITCH in the Windows environment, so skip down to the *Starting FreeSWITCH* section.

Compiling FreeSWITCH for Windows

As mentioned in the *Operating system prerequisites* section, FreeSWITCH is built with MSVC or MSVCEE. The steps presented here are specifically for MSVCEE 2010; however, the steps for the various editions of MSVC are essentially the same.

Important considerations for Windows users

Unless you are a developer, you may find that using the FreeSWITCH binary installer is more than adequate for your needs. Simply download the x86 or x64 `freeswitch.msi` from `http://files.freeswitch.org/windows/installer/` and run the installer. It is extremely simple to do. More information about the binaries can be found online at `http://wiki.freeswitch.org/wiki/Installation_for_Windows#Precompiled_Binaries`.

With the new features present in Microsoft's Visual Studio 2010, it is now highly advisable that users should use this development environment instead of Visual Studio 2008. Please do note that the recommendation also applies to the Express Editions. Some of the exciting new modules added in FreeSWITCH since 1.0.6 may not be present in the Visual Studio 2008 project files, as the contributors of the project mainly focused on developing applications with Visual Studio 2010.

At the time of writing, please do not attempt to import the Visual Studio 2010 solution file in a Visual Studio 2012 build environment, as FreeSWITCH currently does not build correctly with it.

Building the solution with MSVC/MSVCEE

There are several small steps to take prior to building with MSVCEE. They are as follows:

1. Create a new folder and copy the `bz2` file into it. In our example, we'll use the following:

    ```
    C:\FreeSWITCH\freeswitch-1.2.1.tar.bz2
    ```

2. Right-click on `freeswitch-1.2.1.tar.bz2` and extract the files with your decompression utility. You will now have a new file named `freeswitch-1.2.1.tar`.

3. Right-click on `freeswitch-1.2.1.tar` and extract the files. This process will take a few moments. For 7-zip, you will then see a window similar to the following screenshot:

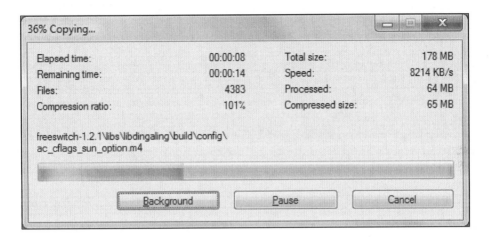

 WinRAR decompresses both the `.gz` and `.tar` files in a single step.

4. After extraction, you will have a new sub-folder named after the latest version of FreeSWITCH. In our example, we now have a sub-folder named `freeswitch-1.2.1`. Double-click on the folder to see the complete FreeSWITCH source tree. It will be similar to the screen in the following screenshot:

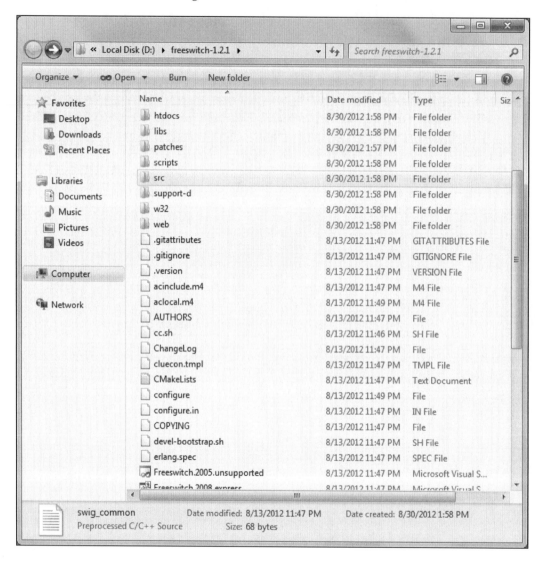

5. While there are many files, the only ones we care about right now are the two solution files. For MSVC, the file is named `Freeswitch.2010.sln`, and for MSVCEE, it is named `Freeswitch.2010.express.sln`. Double-click on the appropriate solution file for your edition of MSVC. The screenshots in this example will show MS Visual C++ Express Edition. However, the Professional and Ultimate editions will be very similar.

6. After the solution file loads, click on the drop-down box (located on the toolbar) and change from `Debug` to `Release`, then go to **Build | Build Solution** or press *F7*. If you are using the Visual Studio 2010 IDE, then go to **Build | Build Solution** or enter the *Ctrl + Shift + B* key sequences. The solution will start building. Numerous messages will appear in the **Output** window. When the solution has finished building, you will see a message at the bottom of the **Output** window as shown in the following screenshot:

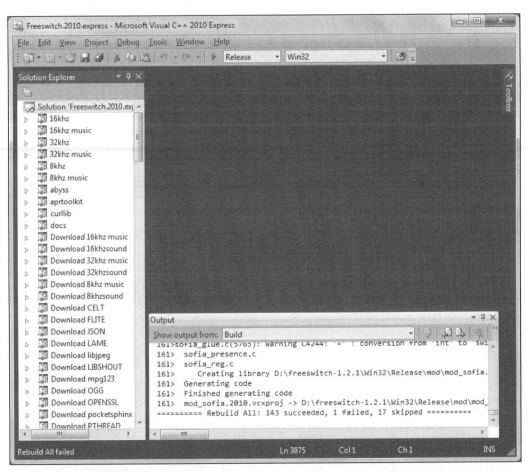

The MSVC/MSVCEE solution files will automatically perform several steps that are usually done manually in a Linux/Unix installation. These include downloading all the sound and music files and building optional modules like Flite (text-to-speech) and PocketSphinx (speech recognition). However, these optional modules still need to be enabled in `modules.conf.xml` if you wish to have them automatically loaded when FreeSWITCH starts. More information about PocketSphinx can be found at `http://cmusphinx.sourceforge.net/wiki/start`. Go back to the Windows Explorer. You will see that the build process has created a new folder named `Release`. This is the FreeSWITCH installation directory. The last step before launching FreeSWITCH is to edit the `modules.conf.xml` file in order to enable `mod_flite` to be loaded by default when FreeSWITCH is started. We will be using the `mod_flite` text-to-speech (TTS) engine in several examples throughout this book.

7. Double-click on the `conf` folder, then double-click on the `autoload_configs` folder. Open `modules.conf.xml` in an editor. In our example, we'll use MSVCEE to edit the file as seen in the following screenshot:

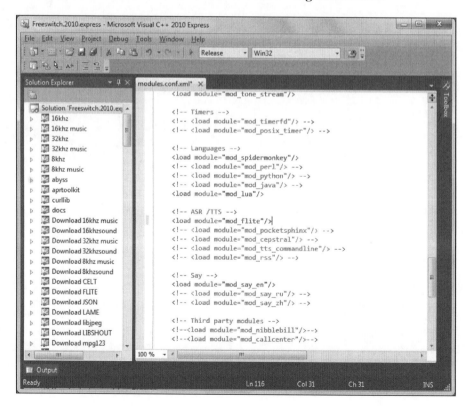

8. Locate the following line near the end of the file:

```
<!-- <load module="mod_flite"/> -->
```

Remove the `<!--` and `-->` tags so that it looks like the following:

```
<load module="mod_flite"/>
```

9. Save the file and exit the editor. You are now ready to launch FreeSWITCH for the first time.

Starting FreeSWITCH

Once you have compiled and installed FreeSWITCH, it is time to launch the application:

- **Linux/Unix/OS X**: run `/usr/local/freeswitch/bin/freeswitch`
- **Windows**: run `freeswitchconsole.exe` from the `Release` directory

The system will start loading, and numerous messages will display on the screen. Console messages are color-coded for readability. Do not worry about all of the messages right now, just make sure that your system starts up and you get to the FreeSWITCH console, which we call the **command-line interface (CLI)**. The CLI prompt looks like the following:

```
freeswitch@localhost>
```

Let's issue a few commands to verify that the system is operational. First, issue the `version` command to verify the version of FreeSWITCH that we have installed. You'll see something similar to this:

```
FreeSWITCH Version 1.2.1
```

Next, issue the `status` command, which displays a few statistics about your system. You'll see output similar to this:

```
freeswitch@localhost> status
UP 0 years, 0 days, 0 hours, 0 minutes, 16 seconds, 808 milliseconds, 260
microseconds
FreeSWITCH is ready
0 session(s) since startup
0 session(s) 0/30
1000 session(s) max
min idle cpu 0.00/100.00
Current Stack Size/Max 240K/8192K
```

These are just a few of the many commands you will learn about in FreeSWITCH. For a complete list of commands, simply type `help` and press *Enter*. Lastly, shut down FreeSWITCH with this command: `fsctl shutdown`. The system will display numerous messages as it shuts down, and will return you to the system command prompt. (If you launched `freeswitchconsole.exe` from the Windows Explorer then the FreeSWITCH window will simply close.)

Running FreeSWITCH in the background

In most cases, you will want FreeSWITCH to run in the background. In a Unix/Linux environment this is frequently called running as a **daemon**. In Windows this is called running as a **service**.

To launch FreeSWITCH as a daemon in Unix/Linux, execute the following command:

```
#>/usr/local/freeswitch/bin/freeswitch -nc
```

The various Linux and Unix distributions take different approaches to automatically running a daemon at system start up. Several initialization or `init` script examples are available on the FreeSWITCH wiki: `wiki.freeswitch.org/wiki/Freeswitch_init`. Consult the system administration documentation for your specific distribution for instructions on how to configure the `init` script to launch FreeSWITCH at system start up.

Windows requires just a few steps to have FreeSWITCH run as a service. They are as follows:

1. Open a Windows command-line session (click on **Start** | **Run**, type `cmd`, and then click on the **OK** button).

2. Change the directory into your FreeSWITCH installation directory, as follows:

   ```
   cd FreeSWITCH\freeswitch-1.2.1\Release
   ```

3. Run `freeswitchconsole.exe` with the `-install` argument, as follows:

   ```
   freeswitchconsole -install FreeSWITCH
   ```

4. The last step is to configure the service itself.

   If you are using Windows XP or Server 2003, open the services tool and click on **Start** | **Control Panel** | **Administrative Tools** | **Services**.

   Otherwise, if you are using later versions of Windows, simply type in `Services` in the **Start** menu's search textbox. Select the **Services** icon in the results bar.

   Alternatively, you can also bring up the Services MMC Console by entering

Windows Key + *R* and typing in `services.msc`, and then click on **OK**. FreeSWITCH should now appear in the list of services:

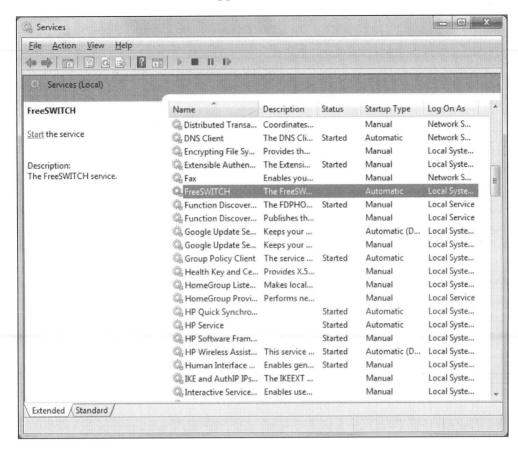

5. Right-click on **FreeSWITCH** and click on **Start**. The service will take a moment to start up.

6. Confirm that the service is running by using the `fs_cli.exe` utility found in the `Release` folder.

7. You will see a welcome screen and a command prompt. Issue the `status` command to confirm that the system is running.

8. Type `/exit` to close the `fs_cli.exe` program.

You now have FreeSWITCH running as a service in Windows.

The `fs_cli` utility is discussed in greater detail in *Chapter 10, Controlling FreeSWITCH Externally*.

Summary

In this chapter, we accomplished a number of objectives. They are as follows:

- Downloaded and installed FreeSWITCH

- Customized the installation by modifying the `modules.conf` file to compile the `mod_flite` TTS module (Linux/Unix/Mac OS X only)

- Customized the FreeSWITCH configuration by modifying `modules.conf.xml` to automatically load `mod_flite` when FreeSWITCH is launched

- Launched FreeSWITCH and issued several commands to confirm its operational status

- Launched FreeSWITCH as a daemon (Linux/Unix) or as a service (Windows)

In the following chapter, we will put our new installation into action as we explore the demonstration configuration of FreeSWITCH.

3
Test Driving the Example Configuration

Now that you have FreeSWITCH installed, it is time to explore the **example configuration** (or example config). The **example config** is preconfigured with users, a Dialplan, security settings, and more. The example config is designed to make your first experience with FreeSWITCH as simple as possible by showing you what FreeSWITCH can do.

In this chapter we will cover the following topics:

- Important VoIP and FreeSWITCH concepts
- Using the FreeSWITCH command-line interface (`fs_cli`)
- Configuring a phone to work with FreeSWITCH
- Calling various extensions in the system

Important concepts to understand

FreeSWITCH is a very versatile piece of software. One of the biggest reasons that it's so versatile is because the world of telephony is very dynamic. As the developers of the software, we often faced difficult choices when making decisions about how FreeSWITCH should behave in various situations. Quite often, we faced conundrums where a large number of potential users required the software to work in a specific way, and the others expected the exact opposite behavior. We easily support devices that behave properly, but at the same time we must adapt to tolerate many devices that blatantly violate specifications. FreeSWITCH was designed to scale, so we also had to design things so you can start out with a self-contained static configuration and be able to scale into using live dynamic configurations without missing a beat. This is a lot to swallow for a new user but don't fret. When you installed FreeSWITCH in the previous chapter, you also installed a fully functional example configuration that will get you through most of this book, with only a few minor modifications.

As we discussed in *Chapter 1, Architecture of FreeSWITCH*, FreeSWITCH is based on a central core fuelled by a central XML registry and orbited by several modules that communicate with each other via the core. We are going to use the example settings in the XML registry to register some phones and make a few test calls. When you make a call, the SIP module will push a request to the XML Dialplan, where the digits you dialed are matched against a series of patterns called **regular expressions**. Once a match has been found, the data from the XML extension that matched is copied into the channel locally, so it has a list of instructions that it will execute in the next stage of the call. It's possible to match more than one extension on the same pass of the Dialplan depending on the choice of configuration keywords. For these first few tests, just a single extension will be put to use, and you will have a chance to see all of the call data that is available whenever a channel is in the ROUTING state. (For details on channel states, see the *Putting it all together* section in *Chapter 8, Advanced Dialplan Concepts*.)

In telephony jargon, we call a connection between two devices a **call leg**. The term **A leg** is used to describe the communication path between the calling party (or caller) and FreeSWITCH. The term **B leg** is used to describe the communication path between the receiving party (or callee) and FreeSWITCH. Consider the following illustration:

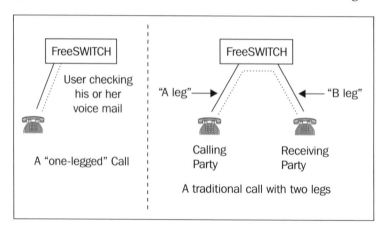

If you are using a phone to call and listen to a demo extension then there is one call leg in use, that is, the connection between your phone and FreeSWITCH. If you dial digits that end up calling another phone currently registered to FreeSWITCH or push the call to a service provider to call your cellular phone, you then have two call legs — the first one, *A leg*, we explained, and another one, *B leg*, that connects FreeSWITCH and the other phone or service provider. Each leg of the call has its own unique properties, and a special relationship with the opposite leg in that particular call. When one or more legs of a call are exchanging media with each other, we call that a **bridge**. In a bridged, call, either leg of the call can perform certain operations on the other leg in the same bridge such as putting it on hold, transferring it to another extension, or joining it with a third party to form a **three-way call**.

Some calls only have one leg—there is a connection between one phone and FreeSWITCH, and FreeSWITCH interacts with the caller directly. Frequently, this type of interface is referred to as an **IVR** or **Interactive Voice Response** menu. Other examples of one-legged calls include a user connected to voicemail, as well as a caller connected to a conference room. IVRs are very powerful and you certainly have used them before if you have ever called a system that provides a list of choices and asks you to dial a digit indicating the choice you want to make. If you have ever used a calling card, this is also a form of IVR that asks you to dial your account number, PIN, and destination digits before completing your call. Some IVRs can even detect speech and react purely on special words that you may say at the appropriate time. With FreeSWITCH, it is simple to make an IVR, and we will learn a few ways to do this in *Chapter 6, Using XML IVRs and Phrase Macros* and *Chapter 7, Dialplan Scripting with Lua*.

The XML Dialplan separates the extensions into special groups called **contexts**. A context is an XML tag containing several extension elements. An **extension** is a collection of patterns to match against the dialed digits and a relative set of instructions to execute based on a positive or negative match against the patterns. Consider the following figure:

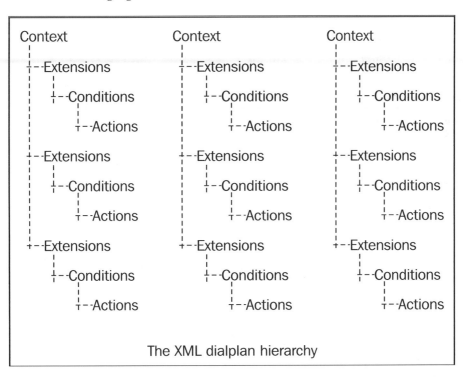

The XML dialplan hierarchy

Every new call that enters the FreeSWITCH core must have a pre-ordained set of context, Dialplan, and extension digits to indicate where the call should be routed. In our examples, we will be using the XML Dialplan and the `default` Dialplan context. The extension digits will depend on what you dialed when you placed the call. Once you dial an extension, the SIP Endpoint module will insert all of the call data it has decoded from your SIP phone, set the Dialplan to XML, the context to default, and push the call's state to ROUTING. The default ROUTING logic in the core will look up the XML Dialplan module and push the call into its call hunt handler routine. This routine connects to the XML registry and searches the list of contexts for the default context. Once the context has been located, it parses each extension in the context, testing the patterns held in the `condition` tag until it finds one that matches. Each `action` tag within that `condition` tag contains an **application** and an optional data argument. These applications provided by the application modules that we discussed in *Chapter 1, Architecture of FreeSWITCH*, will be executed in order until the last one is reached or the call ends.

The arguments to the applications can contain **channel variables**, a special group of name/value pairs that are designed to influence the channel behavior, and provide a way to store important call data. They look similar to the special pre-processor variables we recently discussed, but only a single dollar sign is used rather than two. `${destination_number}`, for instance, tells you what digits the caller dialed, and is the primary value used to route calls. The condition tags use the `field` attribute to denote which value to run the pattern match against. If this value is one of the special variables held in the caller profile, you can omit the `${}` for simplicity's sake.

The special **caller profile** variables are as follows. Some may seem unusual at first, but as you use FreeSWITCH more, you will see where these all come into play:

- `username`
- `dialplan`
- `caller_id_name`
- `caller_id_number`
- `callee_id_name`
- `callee_id_number`
- `network_addr`
- `ani`
- `aniii`
- `rdnis`
- `destination_number`
- `source`
- `uuid`
- `context`

The caller profile is just a collection of special information that every call has in common, which is passed along from one leg to another. This information can be accessed the same way as other variables, and should be considered read-only, as the data is provided by the initial call setup. Following is a real example from the default configuration, which uses the tone generator in the core to play a rendition of the popular song from the 1980's video game, Tetris:

```
<extension name="tone_stream">
  <condition field="destination_number"
    expression="^9198$">
    <action application="answer"/>
    <action application="playback"
      data="tone_stream://path=${base_dir}
      /conf/tetris.ttml;loops=10"/>
  </condition>
</extension>
```

As you can see, it uses `field="destination_number"` to check if you dialed *9198*, and if you did, it answers the call and plays the **tone stream**. It uses `${base_dir}` to denote the location where the configuration is stored so it can deduce the path to the correct file containing the tone data. (Don't worry if this seems like a lot to digest. We will be explaining this information in more detail.) You have had a chance to see FreeSWITCH in action by making a few test calls to the various example extensions that are found in the example config. Channel variables can be very useful when integrating outside information about a call, which you may want to set and retrieve later in your own applications. These variables might contain information such as the caller's account number, which is useful if someone calls in to manage their account. There is an interface to set variables in the application interface provided by the `set` application. Consider the following example:

```
<action application="set" data="customer_id=1234"/>
```

From this point on, the channel variable `customer_id` will contain the value `1234`. If the value is not changed prior to the call ending then this value will also be available in the **Call Detail Record (CDR)** data.

As the XML registry can be rather large and scary, we have designed it to be loaded from several smaller files spread out into the configuration directory in logical order. This means that rather than digging into one giant file, you can locate smaller, simpler files, each of which can be used to configure a specific type of functionality in FreeSWITCH.

The FreeSWITCH wiki contains a large diagram showing how the example config is laid out: `http://wiki.freeswitch.org/wiki/Default_config#Overview_Diagram_of_the_Demo_Configuration`.

Once FreeSWITCH loads the **main registry** (a file called `freeswitch.xml`), the file is run through a special pre-processor that scans the file for special directives, which are replaced in the file with the contents of other files. In some cases, the pre-processor also sets **global variables**. This means that you can set important variables once in the top-level configuration file and reference them later in the deeper sections of the registry. Take an IP address or domain name for instance. Pretend that you have some significant IP address, say, `74.112.132.98`. If you use this value multiple times in your configuration, you can put the following line somewhere at the top of the first file that is loaded:

```
<X-PRE-PROCESS cmd="set" data="my_ip=74.112.132.98"/>
```

Now you can place `$${my_ip}` in your configuration where you want your IP address to appear. This expansion is done by the pre-processor, so in the final XML generated and loaded by FreeSWITCH, the IP will appear as if it was hardcoded into the file everywhere `$${my_ip}` appeared.

Another great feature of the XML pre-processor is the ability to include other files with a single line. Following is an example line used in the example config to load all the files from a particular directory in place inside the default Dialplan context:

```
<X-PRE-PROCESS cmd="include" data="default/*.xml"/>
```

This means that every single file in the default folder that ends with `.xml` will be included in place of the preceding line. This makes it possible to create new extensions in their own dedicated files and include them into your Dialplan without disturbing the `default.xml` file (the file containing the default Dialplan context).

Putting FreeSWITCH to work

Now that we have covered the basics, it is time to roll up our sleeves and really put FreeSWITCH to work. We will first learn a bit more about the main tool for controlling FreeSWITCH, the **Command Line Interface** (or **CLI**), after which we will configure one or two telephones and make some test calls.

Controlling FreeSWITCH with the CLI

In *Chapter 2, Building and Installation*, we briefly discussed a utility called `fs_cli`. As we generally will run FreeSWITCH as a daemon (Linux/Unix) or a service (Windows), it is important to become familiar with using `fs_cli`. For convenience, you can add `fs_cli.exe` to your path in Windows. In Linux/Unix you can create a symbolic link, as follows:

```
#>ln -s /usr/local/freeswitch/bin/fs_cli /usr/local/bin/fs_cli
```

Some Linux users prefer to add `/usr/local/freeswitch/bin` to the Linux path.

Now, if you simply type `fs_cli` at the system command prompt, it will launch the `fs_cli` program for you.

 Generally speaking, Windows executable files will have `.exe` at the end of the filename. On Windows systems, the `fs_cli` program is named `fs_cli.exe`. Windows users can type `fs_cli.exe` or just `fs_cli`, whereas Linux/Unix users should type `fs_cli` to launch the FreeSWITCH command-line utility.

Launch the command-line utility:

```
#>fs_cli
```

You will be greeted with the following FS CLI welcome message as shown in the following screenshot:

```
fs:/usr/src/freeswitch#
fs:/usr/src/freeswitch# fs_cli




                        F S   C L I




  Anthony Minessale II, Ken Rice,
  Michael Jerris, Travis Cross
  FreeSWITCH (http://www.freeswitch.org)
  Paypal Donations Appreciated: paypal@freeswitch.org
  Brought to you by ClueCon http://www.cluecon.com/
```

Once connected, everything you type will be sent to the FreeSWITCH server, except for commands that begin with a / (slash) character. These **slash commands** control the behavior of the `fs_cli` program itself. Issue the `/help` command to see the list of available `fs_cli` slash commands as shown in the following screenshot:

```
freeswitch@internal> /help
Command                                Description
-----------------------------------    ------------------------
/help                                  Help
/exit, /quit, /bye, ...                Exit the program.
/event, /noevents, /nixevent           Event commands.
/log, /nolog                           Log commands.
/uuid                                  Filter logs for a single call uuid
/filter                                Filter commands.
/debug [0-7]                           Set debug level.
```

Note that there are several different slash commands for exiting the system: /exit, /quit, and /bye. Also, there is the ellipsis (…) shortcut for exiting out of the fs_cli program. All four of these commands will exit the fs_cli utility and return you to the system prompt. They are all equivalent, so use whichever suits you. Keep in mind that when running FreeSWITCH from the console, that is, not as a daemon or service, the ellipsis shortcut will perform a FreeSWITCH system shutdown!

The other slash command to keep in mind is /log. By default, fs_cli starts up with full debug logging enabled. (The welcome screen mentions this fact with **+OK log level [7]** displayed at start up.) The /log command will let you control what level of debug logging will be displayed during your fs_cli session. You can change the log level at any point during your session. When you exit and restart fs_cli, the log level will reset to 7. (This behavior can be controlled with the -d or --debug command-line parameters.) Unless you wish to see a lot of debug information, it is best to set the log level to 6, as follows:

```
freeswitch@internal>/log 6
+OK log level 6 [6]
```

Each number from 0 to 7 represents a different debug level as noted in the following table:

Debug level:	Name:	Text display color:
0	Console	White
1	Alert	Red
2	Critical (Crit)	Red
3	Error (Err)	Red
4	Warning	Violet
5	Notify	Light Blue
6	Information (Info)	Green
7	Debug	Yellow

You may use the name (case-insensitive) as well as the number when specifying the log level:

```
freeswitch@internal>/log info
+OK log level info [6]
```

All the other commands you type will be sent to the FreeSWITCH server. There are a few basic commands to become familiar with. They are as follows:

- `help`: Displays a list of available CLI commands; these commands are called FSAPI commands or just APIs for short
- `version`: Displays the FreeSWITCH version you are running
- `status`: Displays some statistics about the currently running instance of FreeSWITCH
- `show channels`: Displays a list of individual channels that are active
- `show calls`: Displays a list of bridged calls

A channel is a single call leg. An example of a one-legged call is a user checking his or her voicemail. On the other hand, a call is two individual call legs bridged (that is, connected) together. Be sure to understand the difference between `show channels` and `show calls`.

In the next section, we will learn a few more commands that will help us configure phones to work with FreeSWITCH.

Configuring a SIP phone to work with FreeSWITCH

Most of the devices that we connect to FreeSWITCH will be SIP-based. **SIP** or **Session Initiation Protocol** is a very common signaling protocol for telephone calls. (SIP is not limited to voice; it can handle chat, video, and other session types.) SIP phones come in two varieties: hard phones and soft phones. A **hard phone** is a standalone device with a headset, keypad, and usually a digital display. A **soft phone** is a software application that runs on a computer and utilizes the computer's speaker and microphone or an external headset. We will examine the setup process for a free soft phone called X-Lite, as well as the basic SIP configuration options for hard phones from Aastra, Polycom, and Snom.

SIP settings

All SIP devices have a minimum set of configuration parameters that must be set. Like all complex protocols, SIP has its share of obscure and sometimes arcane configuration options. However, they are well beyond the scope of this book. We will be limiting our discussion to the basics that are necessary to make a SIP device connect to FreeSWITCH and perform standard PBX functions: make and receive calls, transfer calls, put calls on hold, and so on.

In our SIP configuration, we will have our SIP devices register with our FreeSWITCH server. When a SIP device is registered with an **SIP registrar**, then that registrar knows how to route calls to the SIP device. FreeSWITCH acts as a SIP registrar. SIP allows for **digest authentication** for SIP endpoints that wish to register. It is possible to allow unauthorized SIP endpoints to register, but it is not recommended. (A good analogy might be that of an open relay SMTP server. If you just let anyone into your system to send an e-mail or make phone calls, bad things are bound to happen. Please do not do it!)

SIP users bear other semblances to e-mail. A SIP URI contains user@domain just like an e-mail address. There is also a real name or display name in addition to the username, as well as a domain. There is also an authorization username and password. The authorization username does not need to be the same as the username but in many cases it is.

FreeSWITCH comes preconfigured with 20 SIP user accounts. (In *Chapter 4, SIP and the User Directory*, we will discuss these in more detail, including how to configure additional users.) The user names are 1000 through 1019. You can use any of these users for testing.

The following are the SIP settings for user 1000:

- **Username**: 1000
- **Authorization Username**: 1000
- **Password**: 1234
- **Domain**: [IP address of your FreeSWITCH server]

Keep these settings handy for setting up your SIP device. Let's look at the configuration process for several different SIP phones. Even if your device is not specifically mentioned here, you can still use the basic principles of configuring the SIP device and you should be able to get your phone connected without much hassle. In each of the following examples, we will connect a different telephone to a FreeSWITCH server running on a local LAN.

X-Lite soft phone

X-Lite (http://www.counterpath.com) is a free soft phone. (X-Lite is, however, not open source.) Download and install X-Lite on a computer that is on the same LAN as your FreeSWITCH server.

While it is technically possible to run a soft phone on the same machine as your FreeSWITCH server, this is neither recommended nor supported.

Launch the X-Lite application. You will see a phone as shown in the following screenshot:

Click on **Softphone**, and then click on **SIP Account Settings...** to open the SIP account menu. X-Lite supports just a single SIP account. Click on **Add** to open up the **SIP Account** screen. Fill in the form fields.

Setting up extension 1005 would look like the following screenshot:

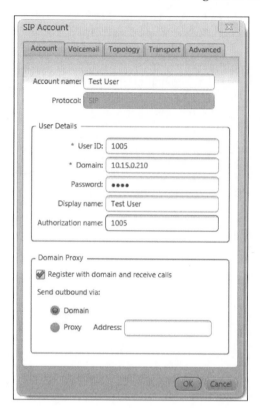

Click on **OK** to accept these settings. The phone will attempt to register with FreeSWITCH. A successful registration looks like the following screenshot:

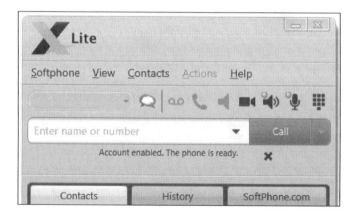

This phone is now registered. If you receive a different message in the display, there was most likely a configuration error. Several common errors are 403, 404, and 408:

- **403 – Forbidden**: This means that the authorization username or password is incorrect.

- **404 – Not Found**: This means that the username specified was not found by the FreeSWITCH server.

- **408 – Timeout**: Usually, this means that the domain is not correct or there is a network problem. Be sure to check firewall settings to make sure that port 5060 traffic is not being blocked.

Now that your phone is registered, you can begin making test calls. Skip to the *Testing the example Dialplan* section.

Hard phones

We will take a brief look at setting up a few different kinds of hard phones. After reviewing the sample setup for Aastra, Polycom, and Snom phones, you will know the basic principles and should be able to set up any SIP-compliant telephone.

Before you start, be sure that you have at least the following basic information for your phone:

- **IP address**: You will need to know the IP address of the phone if you wish to use the web interface. Most phones also have a small menu system for configuring the phone itself.

- **Admin name**: Most phones will have an admin user.

- **Admin password**: Most phones also require an admin password.

If you are unsure of the telephone's default username and password, consult the manufacturer's website for more information.

 Most hard phones are field upgradable, that is, the manufacturer supplies updated firmware that can be downloaded and installed on each phone. Visit the manufacturer's website to find out if there is an updated firmware available for your phone as well as what features it includes.

Aastra phones

Aastra phones have a standard web-based interface. Point a browser to the phone's IP address and then log in. Click on the **Global SIP** link on the navigation pane. The interface for the Aastra 9112i will look as shown in the following screenshot:

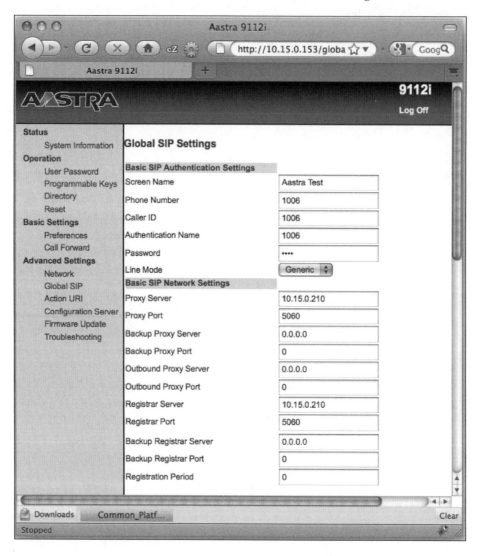

Fill in all the fields under **Basic SIP Authentication Settings**. Under **Basic SIP Network Settings**, fill in the **Proxy Server**, **Proxy Port**, **Registrar Server**, and **Registrar Port** fields. Scroll down and click on **Save Settings**, then restart the phone by clicking on the **Reset** link on the navigation pane. The phone will restart and connect to FreeSWITCH.

If the registration is successful then the display name (**Aastra Test**), and the phone number (**1006**) will show in the telephone display. Now that your phone is registered, you can begin making test calls. Skip to the *Testing the example Dialplan* section.

Polycom phones

Polycom phones have a web interface as well as a menu on the phone. You can use either; however, it is easier to use the web interface. Point a browser at the phone's IP address and log in. Click on the **Lines** link. Like many SIP phones, the SoundPoint IP 330 can register to more than one server. In this example, we'll use **Line 1** to connect to FreeSWITCH. The web interface for a Polycom SoundPoint IP 330 looks like the following screenshot:

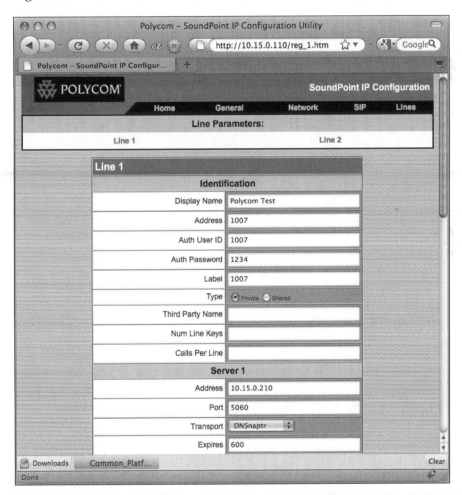

For **Line 1**, fill in the following fields: **Display Name**, **Address**, **Auth User ID**, **Auth Password**, and **Label**. Under **Server 1**, fill in the **Address** and **Port** fields. Scroll down and click on the **Submit** button. The phone will reboot and then connect to FreeSWITCH.

Now that your phone is registered, you can begin making test calls. Skip to the *Testing the example Dialplan* section.

Snom phones

Snom phones have a full-featured web interface for configuration. Point a browser at your phone's IP address to open up the web interface. Notice that Snom phones have the concept of **identities**, which allow you to connect to more than one server. Click on the **Identity 1** link on the navigation pane and fill in the SIP configuration fields. The web interface for a Snom 300 looks like the following screenshot:

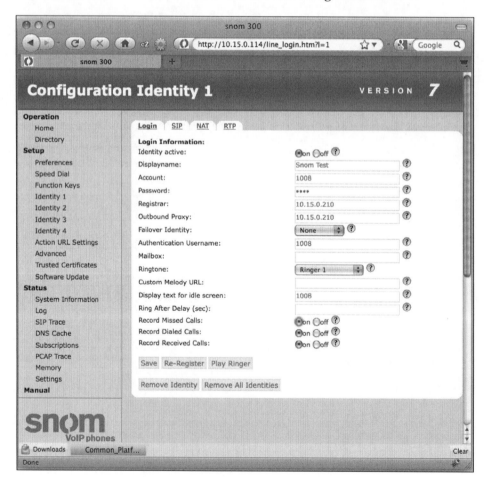

Configure **Identity 1** by filling in the fields under **Login Information**: **Displayname, Account, Password, Registrar, Outbound Proxy, Authentication Username**, and **Display test for idle screen**. Click on **Save** then click on **Re-Register**. The phone will immediately connect to FreeSWITCH.

Now that your phone is registered, you can begin making test calls. Skip to the *Testing the example Dialplan* section.

> FreeSWITCH supports the use of the local sound card or an external headset that is connected to the FreeSWITCH server. The optional PortAudio module (`mod_portaudio`) can be compiled and enabled in the same manner as the `mod_flite` example discussed in *Chapter 2, Building and Installation*. See `http://wiki.freeswitch.org/wiki/Mod_portaudio` for details on how to configure and use the PortAudio module with FreeSWITCH.

Testing the example Dialplan

Now that you have a phone configured, you can perform several kinds of test calls. If you can get two different phones configured, you can make a few additional types of test calls. Before you begin dialing, be sure that you have installed the default sounds and music files. (Windows users will have them installed by default. Linux/ Unix users should refer to the *Step 5 – install sound and music files* section in *Chapter 2, Building and Installation*, for more information.)

Test calls for a single phone

The following tests are simple ways to confirm that FreeSWITCH is operating properly, as well as learning more about what it can do. In each case, you simply need to dial the four-digit number and click on your phone's **Send** button.

The Tetris extension

Dial *9198*. You will hear what hopefully sounds like the Tetris theme song. The sound is generated solely using tone generation. (See `http://wiki.freeswitch.org/wiki/TGML` for more information on **TGML**, the **tone generation markup language** used in FreeSWITCH.)

Echo test

Dial *9196*. Speak into the phone and the audio will be echoed back to you. This test confirms that audio is flowing in both directions. (Keep in mind that if your phone and the FreeSWITCH server are on the same LAN then the echoed audio will return very quickly. Try dialing *9195*, which will do an echo test with a 5-second delay.)

Music on hold

Dial *9664*. The system will play the default music on hold. If you hear the music, your `music on hold` files are properly installed, and FreeSWITCH is correctly playing those sound files.

Demonstration IVR

Dial *5000*. The demonstration IVR menu will play. You will be given the options that are described as follows:

- Call FreeSWITCH public conference
- Echo test
- Music on hold
- Register for ClueCon
- Screaming Monkeys (yes, really)
- Sample IVR sub-menu

The **FreeSWITCH public conference** is quite literally a public conference room, which anyone may call into. Note that your FreeSWITCH system will need to have the Internet access, and that your firewall and NAT must be configured to allow SIP and RTP traffic.

The **echo test** and **music on hold** options are identical to dialing *9196* and *9664*, respectively.

ClueCon is an annual telephony developer conference. Dialing 4 will transfer you to an operator who will be glad to get you registered for the conference.

The **sample sub-menu** is very simple— press * to return to the main menu.

The **demonstration IVR menu** is found at `conf/ivr_menus/demo_ivr.xml`.

The information application

Dial *9192*. This extension is very simple. Before dialing, be sure to open up the `fs_cli` utility. The `info` application will dump a lot of debug data about the current phone call. Change the debug level to 6 (INFO) before you dial. You can find the sample output of this in the `Chapter 3` folder of the code bundle.

Don't worry about what all of that means right now. Just remember that FreeSWITCH stores a lot of information for each call leg that is active. The `info` Dialplan application is useful for debugging your custom Dialplan entries.

Test calls for two or more phones

The true power of FreeSWITCH is seen in how it can handle calls from multiple endpoints. The following tests will give you an idea of some of the features that FreeSWITCH supplies. The tests in this section require at least two different telephones to be configured.

Calling another telephone

Dial *1000, 1001*, and so on. Simply dial the other phone's extension number and it should ring. Most SIP phones are like regular telephones, so just pick up the handset to answer. If a telephone isn't configured for a particular extension, you will be connected to the voicemail application and prompted to leave a message in the mailbox for the extension you called.

Parking a call

Call another telephone and wait for an answer. Click on the **Transfer** button and dial *6001*. Hang up. The other party is now **parked** and will hear music on hold. Retrieve the call in one of the following ways:

1. Dial *6001*. The parked call is automatically unparked.
2. Dial *6000* and wait for the system to answer. The system will prompt you for the extension number.

   Dial *6001*. The parked call is automatically unparked.

Calling a conference

Dial *3000* from several different phones. All parties will be able to hear each other.

Example Dialplan quick reference

Consult the following table for a list of extension numbers and their functions:

Extension	Function
1000 - 1019	Local extensions
** + extension number	Intercepts a ringing phone (that is, call pickup)
2000	Samples call group: Sales
2001	Samples call group: Support
2002	Samples call group: Billing
3000 - 3399	Samples conference rooms
4000 or *98	Retrieves voicemail
5000	Demo IVR
5900	FIFO queue park
5901	FIFO queue retrieve
6000	Valet park/retrieval, manual
6001-6099	Valet park/retrieval, automatic
7243	RTP multicast page
0911	Group intercom example #1
0912	Group intercom example #2
0913	Emergency outbound conference example
9178	Example fax receive
9179	Example fax transmit
9180	Ring test, far end generates ring tone
9181	Ring test, send U.K. ring tone
9182	Ring test, send music as ring tone
9183	Answer, then send U.K. ring tone
9184	Answer, then send music as ring tone
9191	ClueCon registration
9192	Information dump
9195	Delayed echo test
9196	Echo test
9197	Milliwatt tone (test signal quality)
9198	Tetris
9664	Music on hold

The bulk of the example Dialplan is defined in `conf/dialplan/default.xml`.

Summary

In this chapter, we were introduced to the default configuration of FreeSWITCH. Among the topics we discussed were the following:

- The important concepts behind how and why FreeSWITCH behaves when you make calls
- Basic use of fs_cli, the FreeSWITCH command-line interface utility
- How to configure SIP devices to connect to FreeSWITCH using the predefined user accounts
- Testing the default Dialplan by dialing a number of different extensions

We now turn our attention to another important aspect of FreeSWITCH: the user directory.

In the next chapter, we will take a closer look at the FreeSWITCH user directory.

4

SIP and the User Directory

In the previous chapter, we briefly introduced SIP, the **Session Initiation Protocol**, where we discussed how to register a telephone with FreeSWITCH. In this chapter, we will build upon that foundation and learn more about how we use SIP to connect users, both locally and around the world. SIP is a ubiquitous protocol in the VoIP landscape. In this chapter, we will cover the following topics:

- Learning the principles behind the FreeSWITCH user directory
- Exploring and configuring the FreeSWITCH user directory for the first time
- Learning how to connect FreeSWITCH to service providers
- Making modifications to the Dialplan and directory XML configuration
- Briefly discussing SIP profiles and user agents

Understanding the FreeSWITCH user directory

The FreeSWITCH user directory is based on a centralized XML document, comprising of one or more <domain> elements. Each <domain> can contain either <users> elements or <groups> elements. A <groups> element contains one or more <group> elements, each of which contains one or more <users> elements. In turn, a <users> element contains one or more <user> elements. A small, simple example would look like the following:

```
<section name="directory">
  <domain name="example.com">
    <groups>
      <group name= "default">
        <users>
          <user id="1001">
```

```
              <params>
                <param name="password" value="1234"/>
              </params>
              </users>
            </user>
          </group>
        </groups>
      </domain>
    </section>
```

Downloading the example code

You can download the example code files for all Packt books you have purchased from your account at http://www.packtpub.com. If you purchased this book elsewhere, you can visit http://www.packtpub.com/support and register to have the files e-mailed directly to you.

Some more basic configurations may not have a need to organize the users in groups so it is possible to omit the <groups> element completely, and just insert several <user> elements into the top <domain> element.

The important thing is that each user@domain derived from this directory is available to all components in the system—it's a single centralized directory for storing all FreeSWITCH user information. If you register as a user with a SIP phone or if you try to leave a voicemail message for a user, FreeSWITCH looks in the same place for user data. This is important because it limits duplication of data, and makes it more efficient than it would be if each component kept track of its users separately.

This system should work well for a small system with a few users in it, but what about a large system with thousands of users? What if a user wants to connect his or her existing database to FreeSWITCH to provide the user directory? Well, using mod_xml_curl that we discussed in *Chapter 1, Architecture of FreeSWITCH*, we can create a web service that gets the request for the entries in the user directory, in much the same way a web page sends the results of an HTML form submission. In turn, that web service can query an existing database of users regardless of the format, and construct the XML records in the format that the FreeSWITCH registry expects. mod_xml_curl returns the data to the module requesting the lookup. This means that instant, seamless integration with your existing setup is possible; your data is still kept in its original, central location.

The user directory can be accessed by any subsystem within FreeSWITCH. This includes modules, scripts, and the FSAPI interface among others. In this chapter, we are going to learn how the **Sofia** SIP module employs the user directory to authenticate your soft phone or hardware SIP phone. If you are a developer, you may appreciate some nifty things you can do with your user directory, such as adding a <variables> element to either the <domain>, the <group>, or the <user> element. In this element you can set many <variable> elements, allowing you to set channel variables that will apply to every call made by a particular authenticated user. This can come in very handy in the Dialplan because it allows you to make user-specific routing decisions. It is also possible to define IP address ranges using CIDR notation, which can be used to authenticate particular users based on what remote network address they connect from. This removes the need for a login and password, if your user always logs in from the same remote IP address.

Authentication is the process of identifying a user. **Authorization** is the process of determining the level of access of a user. Authentication answers the question, "Is this person really who he says he is?" Authorization answers the question, "What is this person allowed to do here?" When you see expressions such as IP Auth and Digest Auth, remember that they are referring to the two primary ways of identifying (that is, authenticating) a user. **IP authorization** is based upon the user's IP address. **Digest authentication** is based upon the user supplying a username and password. SIP (and FreeSWITCH) can use either method. Visit http://en.wikipedia.org/wiki/Digest_access_authentication for a discussion of how digest authentication works.

The directory is implemented in pure XML. This is advantageous for several reasons, not least of which is the X in XML: **Extensible**. Since XML is, by definition, extensible, the directory structure is also extensible. If we need to add a new element to the directory, we can do so simply by adding to the existing XML structure.

Working with the FreeSWITCH user directory

The example configuration has one domain with a directory of 20 users. Users can be added or removed very easily. There is no set limit to how many users can be defined on the system. The list of users is collectively referred to as the **directory**. Users can belong to one or more groups. Finally, all the users belong to a single domain. By default, the **domain** is the IP address of the FreeSWITCH server.

 FreeSWITCH also supports multiple domains. You can find more information at http://wiki.freeswitch.org/wiki/Multi-tenant.

In the following sections we will discuss these topics:

- User features
- Adding a user
- Testing voicemail
- Groups of users

User features

Let's begin by looking at the XML file that defines a user. Locate the file conf/directory/default/1000.xml and open it in an editor. You should see a file like the following:

```
<include>
  <user id="1000">
    <params>
      <param name="password" value="$${default_password}"/>
      <param name="vm-password" value="1000"/>
    </params>
    <variables>
      <variable name="toll_allow"
        value="domestic,international,local"/>
      <variable name="accountcode" value="1000"/>
      <variable name="user_context" value="default"/>
      <variable name="effective_caller_id_name"
      value="Extension 1000"/>
      <variable name="effective_caller_id_number"
      value="1000"/>
```

```
        <variable name="outbound_caller_id_name"
        value="$${outbound_caller_name}"/>
        <variable name="outbound_caller_id_number"
        value="$${outbound_caller_id}"/>
        <variable name="callgroup" value="techsupport"/>
    </variables>
  </user>
</include>
```

The XML structure of a user is simple. Within the `<include>` tags the user has the following:

- The `user` element with the `id` attribute
- The `params` element, wherein parameters are specified
- The `variables` element, wherein channel variables are defined

Even before we know what many of the specifics mean, we can glean from this file that the user ID is 1000 and that there is both a password and a vm-password. In this case, the `password` parameter refers to the SIP authorization password. (We discussed this in the *Configuring a SIP phone to work with FreeSWITCH* section in *Chapter 3, Test Driving the Example Configuration*.) The expression `$${default_password}` refers to the value contained in the global variable `default_password`, which is defined in the `conf/vars.xml` file. If you surmised that vm-password means voicemail password then you are correct. This value refers to the digits that the user needs to dial when logging in to check his or her voicemail messages. The value of `id` is used both as the authorization username and the SIP username.

Additionally, there are a number of channel variables that are defined for this user. Most of these are directly related to the default Dialplan. The following table lists each variable and what it is used for:

Variable	Purpose
`toll_allow`	Specifies which types of calls the user can make
`accountcode`	Arbitrary value that shows up in CDR data
`user_context`	The Dialplan context that is used when this person makes a call
`effective_caller_id_name`	Caller ID name displayed on called party's phone when calling another registered user
`effective_caller_id_number`	Caller ID number displayed on called party's phone when calling another registered user

Variable	Purpose
outbound_caller_id_name	Caller ID name sent to provider on outbound calls
outbound_caller_id_number	Caller ID number sent to provider on outbound calls
callgroup	Arbitrary value that can be used in Dialplan or CDR

In summary, a user in the default configuration has the following:

- A username for SIP and for authorization
- A voicemail password
- A means of allowing/restricting dialing
- A means of handling caller ID being sent out
- Several arbitrary variables that can be used or ignored as needed

Let's now add a new user to our directory.

Adding a user

Adding one or more users is a simple two-step process, which is as follows:

1. Create a new XML file for the user, usually by copying an existing file.
2. Modify the Local_Extension Dialplan entry.

In this example, we will create a new user for a person named Gwen and a username of 1100. Perform the following steps:

1. Open a terminal window, and change the directory to conf/directory/default.
2. Make a copy of 1000.xml and name it 1100.xml. A Linux/Unix session looks as follows:
   ```
   #>cd /usr/local/freeswitch/conf/directory/default
   #>cp 1000.xml 1100.xml
   ```
3. Open 1100.xml in an editor and make the following changes:
   - Replace all occurrences of 1000 with 1100
   - Change the value of effective_caller_id_name to Gwen

4. The new file should look as follows:

```
<include>
  <user id="1100">
    <params>
      <param name="password" value="$${default_password}"/>
      <param name="vm-password" value="1100"/>
    </params>
    <variables>
      <variable name="toll_allow"
        value="domestic,international,local"/>
      <variable name="accountcode" value="1100"/>
      <variable name="user_context" value="default"/>
      <variable name="effective_caller_id_name" value="Gwen"/>
      <variable name="effective_caller_id_number"
        value="1100"/>
      <variable name="outbound_caller_id_name"
        value="$${outbound_caller_name}"/>
      <variable name="outbound_caller_id_number"
        value="$${outbound_caller_id}"/>
      <variable name="callgroup" value="techsupport"/>
    </variables>
  </user>
</include>
```

5. Save the file. Next, we need to edit the Dialplan entry for
   Local_Extension. Open conf/dialplan/default.xml in an editor
   and locate the following lines:

```
<extension name="Local_Extension">
  <condition field="destination_number"
    expression="^(10[01][0-9])$">
```

This Dialplan extension, as its name implies, routes calls to local extensions. In our
case, a local extension is a phone registered to a user in our directory. Recall that
FreeSWITCH comes with 20 directory users predefined, numbered 1000 through 1019.
This extension corresponds to those 20 users. By default, any call made to 1000, 1001,
…, 1019 will be handled by the Local_Extension Dialplan entry. We need to add 1100
to the regular expression. Edit the expression value so that it looks as follows:

```
^(10[01][0-9]|1100)$
```

Save the file. (Regular expressions are discussed in greater detail in *Chapter 5,*
Understanding the XML Dialplan, in the *Regular expressions* section.)

The last thing we need to do is reload the XML configuration. Launch `fs_cli` and issue the `reloadxml` command as follows:

```
freeswitch@internal> reloadxml

+OK [Success]

2012-09-14 14:27:32.942464 [INFO] mod_enum.c:871 ENUM Reloaded

2012-09-14 14:27:32.942464 [INFO] switch_time.c:1163 Timezone reloaded
530 definitions
```

> Linux/Unix users can save time by opening two terminal windows. Run `fs_cli` in one window and your editor in the other. For advanced handling of multiple windows check out the GNU Screen utility. More information can be found at `http://www.gnu.org/software/screen`.

Our new extension has been defined, and we should now be able to register a SIP phone to user 1100. Using the methods described in *Chapter 3, Test Driving the Example Configuration*, register a SIP phone to user 1100. An X-Lite configuration looks like the following screenshot:

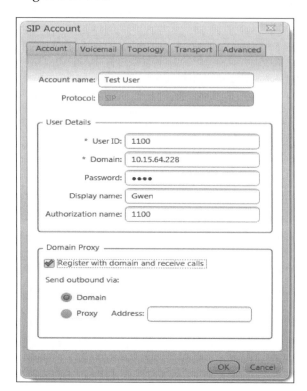

The registered phone can now make outbound calls, and can receive inbound calls from those who dial *1100*.

 To see which SIP phones are registered, issue this command at the FreeSWITCH command line: `sofia status profile internal reg`.

Now that we have successfully added a user, let's test a common feature: voicemail.

Testing voicemail

Each user in the directory has a voice mailbox, where others can leave voice messages. In the example Dialplan configuration, unanswered calls to a user will go to the user's voicemail after 30 seconds. Make a test call to confirm that everything is working. Dial the destination extension and let it ring. After about 30 seconds, the voicemail system will answer; record a message of at least three seconds (the minimum message length), and then hang up. (If you have only one phone for testing, try dialing your own extension.)

The user's phone will now have a message-waiting indicator. An X-Lite soft phone with a message waiting looks like the following screenshot:

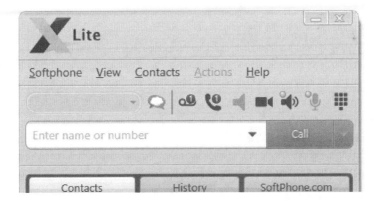

Notice the recording icon and the telephone handset icon. Each has a red circle indicating the number of voicemail messages and missed calls, respectively.

 Save time when leaving a voice message by pressing #, to skip past the user's outbound greeting.

Retrieving the message is also simple; dial *98* or *4000*. The voicemail system will guide you through logging in and listening to new or saved messages. A typical session would sound like the following:

4000

"Welcome to your voicemail. Please enter your ID, followed by pound."

1100#

"Please enter your password, followed by pound"

1100#

"You have one new message."

When a user has a new message, the system will automatically play it along with the date and time that the message was left. The default voicemail menus are configured as follows:

Main menu:

1—Listen to new messages

2—Listen to saved messages

5—Options menu (recorded name, greeting, and so on)

#—Exit voicemail

While listening to a message:

1—Replay message from the beginning

2—Save message

4—Rewind

6—Fast-forward

After listening to a message:

1—Replay message from the beginning

2—Save message

4—Send to e-mail (requires configuration)

7—Delete message

Feel free to try out some of these options. Log in to your voicemail and record an outbound greeting. By default, you can record up to 10 different greetings; however, most users only record a single greeting. Typically, we will use greeting number one.

 All of the voicemail options are customizable. Look in the file `conf/autoload_configs/voicemail.conf.xml`. You can edit the `default` voicemail profile or even create your own custom voicemail profiles.

Now that we have voicemail working, we can concentrate on one other useful feature: groups of users.

Groups of users

Larger installations frequently need the ability to dial multiple telephones. For example, a department in a company might have several users, all of whom are responsible for answering calls to that department. At the same time, they each have their own extension number, so they can individually receive calls. FreeSWITCH has a directory feature that allows users to be grouped together. A user can belong to multiple groups.

 Some PBX systems employ an advanced form of inbound call routing called **ACD** or **Automatic Call Distribution**. Call groups are not used for this kind of application. Although it is beyond the scope of this publication, FreeSWITCH users wanting advanced functionality are encouraged to investigate FIFO queues. See `http://wiki.freeswitch.org/wiki/Mod_fifo` for more information.

Groups are defined in the file `conf/directory/default.xml`. Open the file and locate the `groups` node. Notice that there are four groups already defined. They are as follows:

- Default — All users in the directory
- Sales — 1000 to 1004
- Billing — 1005 to 1009
- Support — 1010 to 1014

The latter three groups are merely arbitrarily defined groups that can be modified or removed as needed. The default group, though, is a bit more interesting. It contains every user in the directory. (Use with caution!) Let's add a new group and then examine how groups work. Perform the following steps:

1. Open `conf/directory/default.xml`. Add the following lines inside the `groups` node:

```
<group name="custom">
  <users>
    <user id="1000" type="pointer"/>
    <user id="1100" type="pointer"/>
  </users>
</group>
```

2. If you have two or more telephones registered then use their extension numbers instead of 1000 and 1100. Save the file.

3. Launch `fs_cli` and press *F6* or issue the `reloadxml` command.

   Confirm that the new custom group has been added by using the `group_call` command. Your output should be similar to the following:

```
freeswitch@internal> group_call custom

[sip_invite_domain=10.15.64.229,presence_
id=1000@10.15.64.229]error/user_not_registered,[sip_invite_
domain=10.15.64.229,presence_id=1100@10.15.64.229]sofia/internal/
sip:1100@10.15.129.38:5060;rinstance=8eecf059256b51f1;fs_
nat=yes;fs_path=sip%3A1100%4010.15.129.38%3A5060%3Brinstance%3D8ee
cf059256b51f1
```

What significance does this chunk of apparently random gibberish hold? The `group_call` command is used to create a SIP dialstring for calling multiple telephones. In our example, user 1000 is not registered and therefore would not receive a call. (Hence the error of `user_not_registered`.) However, user 1100 is indeed registered. If a user in a group is not registered, when the group is called, that user is effectively ignored. Before we can call our new group we need to add it to the Dialplan as follows:

1. Open `conf/dialplan/default.xml` and locate the `group_dial_billing` extension:

```
<extension name="group_dial_billing">
  <condition field="destination_number" expression="^2002$">
    <action application="bridge"
      data="group/billing@${domain_name}"/>
  </condition>
</extension>
```

2. Insert the following new lines after the `</extension>` tag of the `group_dial_billing` extension:

```
<extension name="group_dial_custom">
  <condition field="destination_number" expression="^2003$">
    <action application="bridge"
      data="group/custom@${domain_name}"/>
  </condition>
</extension>
```

3. Save the file.

4. Launch `fs_cli` and issue the `reloadxml` command.

5. Test your group by dialing *2003*. All the extensions in your group should ring.

When all of the phones in a group are ringing, the first one to answer will win and receive the call. All the other phones will stop ringing.

We have seen how we can connect telephones to FreeSWITCH, as well as the many features they have. Now let's discuss how to make phone calls outside the local FreeSWITCH server.

Connecting to the world with gateways

The counterpart to having a user register to your FreeSWITCH server is to have your server register as a user on a remote server. This is accomplished using **gateways**. A gateway is quite simply a way to authenticate with another SIP server. This includes authentication challenges to SIP REGISTER attempts as well as INVITE messages. Telephone service providers use very large servers (including some running FreeSWITCH!) to provide SIP trunks to their subscribers. In FreeSWITCH, we can use a gateway to connect to a SIP provider. We can also use a gateway to connect to another SIP server, such as another FreeSWITCH server or any SIP-compliant IP-PBX.

Setting up a new gateway

A gateway simply connects to a SIP server just like a SIP phone connects to FreeSWITCH. As such, a gateway configuration bears some resemblance to a SIP phone configuration. Like a SIP phone registering to FreeSWITCH, a gateway has some minimum requirements. They are as follows:

- Username and password
- Server address or IP, and port

These values are supplied by the service provider. Occasionally there are other parameters, like a proxy server and port. If you already have an account with a SIP provider then you can use it for your gateway. In this example, we will use an account from `iptel.org`.

> Visit `http://www.iptel.org/service` to sign up for a free SIP account.

To add a new gateway, perform the following steps:

1. Create a new XML file in `conf/sip_profiles/external`. This example will use `iptel.org.xml`. Add the following lines, inserting the proper values for your provider:

```
<include>
 <gateway name="iptel">
  <param name="username" value="MY_USER_NAME"/>
  <param name="password" value="MY_PASSWORD"/>
  <param name="realm" value="iptel.org"/>
  <!-- iptel.org requires a 'proxy' parameter -->
  <param name="proxy" value="sip.iptel.org"/>
 </gateway></include>
```

2. Save the file and then launch `fs_cli`.

3. Issue the command `/log 6` to decrease the verbosity of debug messages.

4. Simply reloading the XML configuration will not add the new gateway. Issue the following command: `sofia profile external restart reloadxml`.

   The output will look as follows:

```
freeswitch@internal> sofia profile external restart reloadxml

Reload XML [Success]

restarting: external

freeswitch@internal> 2012-09-14 16:29:23.509986 [INFO] mod_
enum.c:808 ENUM Reloaded

2012-09-14 16:29:23.511578 [INFO] switch_time.c:661 Timezone
reloaded 530 definitions

2012-09-14 16:29:24.118566 [NOTICE] sofia_reg.c:85 UN-Registering
iptel

2012-09-14 16:29:24.713768 [NOTICE] sofia.c:1218 Waiting for
worker thread

2012-09-14 16:29:24.713768 [NOTICE] sofia_glue.c:3690 deleted
gateway example.com
```

```
2012-09-14 16:29:24.713768 [NOTICE] sofia_reg.c:2237 Added gateway
'iptel' to profile 'external'

2012-09-14 16:29:24.713768 [NOTICE] sofia_reg.c:2237 Added gateway
'example.com' to profile 'external'

2012-09-14 16:29:24.713768 [NOTICE] sofia.c:3149 Started Profile
external [sofia_reg_external]

2012-09-14 16:29:25.736445 [NOTICE] sofia_reg.c:333 Registering
iptel
```

5. Confirm that the gateway is registered properly. Issue the command `sofia status`. The output should look similar to the following:

```
freeswitch@internal> sofia status
                        Name            Type
Data        State
========================================================================
=============================
                external         profile        sip:mod_
sofia@10.15.0.91:5080     RUNNING    (0)
                example.com      gateway             sip:joeuser@
example.com    NOREG
                    iptel        gateway        sip:MY_USER@sip.
iptel.org      REGED
                internal         profile        sip:mod_
sofia@10.15.0.91:5060     RUNNING    (0)
            internal-ipv6        profile        sip:mod_sofia@
[::1]:5060        RUNNING    (0)
                10.15.0.91       alias
internal        ALIASED
========================================================================
=============================
3 profiles 1 alias
```

The gateway's state should be REGED, which means that the registration was successful. If it says something else, like FAIL_WAIT, most likely there is a configuration problem. Confirm your settings and try again.

 Warning: Restarting a profile will disconnect all active calls that are currently routed through that profile. An alternate command to add a newly created gateway without restarting the entire profile is: `sofia profile <profile name> rescan reloadxml`.

Now that our gateway is added, we need to modify the Dialplan so that we can make and receive calls.

Making calls

We will make a simple Dialplan entry that sends calls out to our new gateway. Our new extension will accept the digit 9 and then the digit 1, followed by exactly 10 more digits representing the telephone number to be dialed. (In a production environment there are many other possible strings, which can even be alphanumeric. Some of these will be considered in *Chapter 5, Understanding the XML Dialplan*.)

To get started with making outbound calls, add your new extension to the Dialplan, by performing the following steps:

1. Create a new file in `conf/dialplan/default` named `01_custom.xml`.

2. Add the following text to the file:

```xml
<include>
  <extension name=" iptel-outbound">
    <condition field="destination_number"
      expression="^9(1\d{10})$">
      <action application="bridge"
        data="sofia/gateway/iptel/$1"/>
    </condition>
  </extension>
</include>
```

3. Save the file. Launch `fs_cli` and press *F6* or issue the `reloadxml` command.

The new extension is now ready to be tested. From a phone that is registered to FreeSWITCH, dial 9 plus a 10-digit phone number. For example, dial 9, 1-800-555-1212. It may take a moment for the call to be established. Confirm that audio is flowing in both directions and that each party can hear the other. If audio is flowing in only one direction, most likely there is a problem with the NAT device on your local network. NAT traversal is discussed in more detail in *Chapter 14, Handling NAT*.

Receiving calls

Generally, when you register your gateway with a SIP provider, the provider allows you to receive calls. (Telephones that register with FreeSWITCH are an example of this.) In the example configuration, FreeSWITCH treats incoming calls as inherently untrusted, even if they come from the corresponding end of a registered gateway. These calls come into the `public` Dialplan context. From there they can be discarded or routed as needed. Let's set up a simple Dialplan entry for handling inbound calls to our `iptel.org` account. This works for any SIP trunk or gateway connection you have created.

1. Create a new file in `conf/dialplan/public` named `01_iptel.xml`.

2. Add these lines to the file, using your account name as follows:

```
<include>
  <extension name="iptel-inbound">
    <condition field="destination_number"
      expression="^(MY_IPTEL_USERNAME)$">)$">
      <action application="set"
        data="domain_name=${domain}"/>
      <action application="bridge" data="1000 XML default"/>
    </condition>
  </extension>
</include>
```

3. Save the file. Launch `fs_cli` and press *F6* or issue the `reloadxml` command.

Be sure to use your actual iptel username. Inbound calls will now be routed to extension 1000. You can route calls to any valid extension, including all the extensions we tested in *Chapter 3, Test Driving the Example Configuration*.

Making calls without a gateway

Sometimes it is not necessary to use a gateway. For example, not all services require digest authorization. An example of this is the FreeSWITCH public conference server. In fact, the default Dialplan contains an extension for dialing the conference: **9888**. (Actually, there are several different conference rooms on the public FreeSWITCH conference server.) Let's look at this extension. Open `conf/dialplan/default.xml` in an editor and locate the `freeswitch_public_conf_via_sip` extension. Note the bridge line:

```
<action application="bridge"
  data="sofia/${use_profile}/$1@conference.freeswitch.org"/>
```

In the example configuration, the value in `${use_profile}` is set to internal (as defined in `conf/vars.xml`). When a user dials *9888* the dialstring that is sent out is actually as follows:

```
sofia/internal/888@conference.freeswitch.org
```

Notice that there is no mention of a gateway. Instead, FreeSWITCH simply sends the call out to the internal SIP profile. In other words, the local FreeSWITCH server sends a call to `conference.freeswitch.org` without actually authorizing it. This is possible because the server at `conference.freeswitch.org` does not require authorization for incoming calls. (This is where the gateway comes in—if the target server issues a challenge then the gateway will respond to that challenge with authorization credentials, namely the username and password.)

Not all SIP providers explicitly require digest authorization of calls; some perform IP authorization instead. In those cases you do not need to create a gateway. Instead, simply send the call out to a SIP profile. Usually, the `internal` SIP profile is sufficient for these kinds of calls.

SIP profiles and user agents

Before we finish our discussion of SIP and the user directory, it would be good to touch upon a subject that some users initially find a bit daunting: **SIP profiles**. In the strictest sense of the word, a SIP profile in FreeSWITCH is a **user agent**. In practical terms, this means that each SIP profile *listens* on a particular IP address and port number. In the example configuration, the `internal` profile listens on port 5060, and the `external` profile listens on port 5080. Not only does the profile listen, but it can respond as well. For example, when a phone sends a SIP `REGISTER` packet to FreeSWITCH (at port 5060), the `internal` profile *hears* the registration request and acts accordingly. The files in `conf/sip_profiles/` are ones which determine how the profiles behave. Many of the parameters in these profiles are used to customize how FreeSWITCH handles various SIP traffic scenarios. In most cases the defaults are reasonable and should work. In other cases, though, you may find that because of the peculiarities in various VoIP phones, vendors, or your local environment, you will need to make adjustments.

Lastly, do not let the profile names, `internal` and `external`, be a source of confusion. Each profile is simply a user agent that is streamlined for a specific purpose. The **internal** profile is optimized to handle telephone registrations and calls between registered phones, even phones that are not on the local LAN. The **external** profile is optimized for outbound gateway connections and several NAT traversal scenarios.

For a deeper discussion of user agents and the concept of a **back-to-back user agent (B2BUA)** see `http://en.wikipedia.org/wiki/Back-to-back_user_agent`.

Summary

In this chapter, we discussed the following:

- How FreeSWITCH collects users into a directory
- How FreeSWITCH uses a VoIP protocol, SIP, to connect users to each other, and to the world
- SIP is similar to e-mail in that it has users and domains
- Employing various user features such as voicemail
- Adding a new user and modifying the Dialplan accordingly
- Connecting to the outside world with gateways
- SIP profiles and user agents

In this chapter, we made some minor modifications to the `default` XML Dialplan, and we learned how to set up users and domains within the XML user directory. Now that we have a general understanding of how these modifications work, we will continue to build upon this foundation. In the next chapter, we will now begin to form a much more detailed understanding of FreeSWITCH as we further explore the XML Dialplan module, the default and most commonly used call routing engine available in FreeSWITCH.

5
Understanding the XML Dialplan

The Dialplan is a crucial part of any FreeSWITCH installation. Indeed, any PBX must have a Dialplan, sometimes called a numbering plan, in order to handle the routing of calls. In simple terms, a Dialplan is a list of instructions on where to route a call. For example, when a user picks up a phone and dials 1000, how does the system know what to do with that call? The example Dialplan knows to connect the calling party to the telephone registered as user ID 1000. However, the Dialplan can do much more than merely connect the calling and called parties. The Dialplan contains instructions on what the call should do and how it should behave.

In the previous chapter we made small modifications to the Dialplan. In this chapter, we will build upon that foundation and introduce the basics of routing and controlling calls as we discuss the following topics:

- Overview of the XML Dialplan
- Contexts, extensions, and actions
- Conditions, patterns, and regular expressions
- Channel variables
- Creating and testing a new extension
- Important Dialplan applications
- Writing Dialstrings

FreeSWITCH XML Dialplan elements

The example FreeSWITCH XML Dialplan is a good place to start learning about XML Dialplan concepts. The configuration is contained in three main files and two directories, located at `conf/dialplan/`:

- `default.xml`: This contains the primary FreeSWITCH Dialplan configuration
- `public.xml`: This contains configurations for handling calls coming in to FreeSWITCH from another location
- `features.xml`: This contains a special context for handling specific dialing features
- `default/`: Files in this directory get included in the `default` context
- `public/`: Files in this directory get included in the `public` context

The example XML configuration has many instructions for routing calls, all of which make use of the basic building blocks of a Dialplan: contexts, extensions, conditions, and actions. A context is a logical grouping of one or more extensions. An extension contains one or more conditions that must be met. Conditions contain actions that will be performed on the call, depending on whether the condition is met or not. Before further discussing these building blocks, let's revisit some of the concepts we first considered in *Chapter 3, Test Driving the Example Configuration*.

Contexts

Contexts are logical groups of extensions. Think of contexts as sections of the Dialplan. Each section has a specific purpose and contains only extensions that are related to the purpose. One such purpose is to isolate extensions from one another. A typical example of this is "multi-tenancy". A FreeSWITCH server can service more than one business entity (tenant), and providing each tenant with its own context prevents numbering conflicts. Each tenant could, for example, have a "dial zero for the operator" extension. Users in one tenant can dial 0 to reach their front-desk extension, while users in another tenant can also dial 0 to reach a completely different extension. Another consideration for contexts is security. Phone calls that are being routed through a context have access only to the resources specifically allotted, perhaps long-distance or international dialing, or use other resources such as multi-party audio conference rooms.

There is no limit to the number of extensions that may be defined. The example XML Dialplan defines three different contexts, which we'll look at next.

Default

The default context contains all of the extension definitions that are available to registered users of the system. When we added extension 1100 to conf/dialplan/default.xml, we were actually modifying an extension in the default context. Most of the features of the example XML Dialplan are defined in this file.

Public

The public context is a good example of using contexts for the sake of security. All unauthorized calls coming in to the FreeSWITCH server will be handled by the public context. The name "public" means "inherently untrusted". By default, FreeSWITCH is paranoid about what unauthorized callers can do in the system. Generally speaking, the public context is used to route incoming **DID (Direct Inward Dial)** phone numbers to a specific internal extension (see conf/dialplan/public/00_inbound_did.xml for an example). You can use the public context to let in only the calls that you deem appropriate for your system.

Features

The features context is a good example of grouping together extensions by function. These extensions could just as easily be added to the default context; however, putting them in their own context helps keep things organized. The extensions defined in the features context mostly are not Endpoints in themselves but rather helper extensions, which perform a function and then transfer the caller elsewhere. An example of this is the please_hold extension that sets the music on hold for the caller, tells the caller, "Please hold while I connect your call", and then transfers the caller to the destination extension.

Extensions

The term extension can sometimes be misleading. In the traditional PBX environment, an extension is simply a phone connected to the phone system, typically with a three-digit or four-digit extension number. In FreeSWITCH an extension is actually a set of instructions that define what to do with a call. It can be as simple as dialing a three-digit or four-digit number, and having someone's desk phone ring. In fact, this is precisely what we did in *Chapter 4, SIP and The User Directory*, in the *Adding a user* section, when we added a new user and a corresponding extension to allow her phone to be dialed.

An extension definition begins with an `<extension>` tag and ends with a closing `</extension>` tag. All the conditions, actions, and anti-actions in between are part of the extension definition. Extensions have two optional attributes: `name` and `continue`. The `name` attribute is used primarily to keep your Dialplan readable. You can imagine how difficult it would be to look at a Dialplan file with dozens of `<extension>` tags without any names. The `continue` attribute determines the Dialplan parser's behavior when it finds a matching extension. An extension is said to match if all of the conditions for that extension evaluate to true. By default, extensions do not continue after the first Dialplan match. Setting `continue="true"` will cause the parser to keep looking for more extensions to match (see the *How Dialplan Processing works* section later in this chapter).

Conditions

Conditions decide the requirements to take the actions listed inside an extension. For example, you might have a condition that says "When 999 is dialed" and then runs the actions within the extension block. Keep in mind that conditions are not limited just to which phone number was dialed. Conditions can also be based on date and time, caller ID, the IP address of the sending server, and even channel variables. Looking through the example Dialplan files, you will mostly see conditions like the following:

```
<condition field="destination_number" expression="^(1234)$">
```

The `destination_number` field is by far the most common field tested, as most of the time we need to route a call based upon the digits dialed by a user.

Many extensions have just a single condition:

```
<extension name="Simple example">
  <condition field="destination_number" expression="^(1234)$">
    <!-- actions performed here -->
  </condition>
</extension>
```

However, you can also stack conditions to create a logical AND, as shown in the following example:

```
<extension name="Two condition tags example">
  <condition field="ani" expression="^(1111)$"></condition>
  <condition field="destination_number" expression="^(1234)$">
    <!-- actions performed here but only if both of the above
       conditions are true -->
  </condition>
</extension>
```

In the preceding example, both conditions must be true for the actions inside the second `<condition>` tag to be executed. The `ani` field (which is the calling party's phone number) must be `"1111"`, and the `dialed_number` field must be `"1234"` for the actions to be executed. The plain-language description of this extension would be, "If the caller is 1111 and the destination is 1234 then execute these actions". Putting multiple `<condition>` tags inside a single extension is sometimes called stacking the conditions. Note that the first condition is still a valid XML node and requires a closing tag. XML allows a syntactic shortcut for this, which is as follows:

```
<condition field="ani" expression="^(1111)$"/>
```

The trailing / (forward slash) character closes the `<condition>` tag.

An additional feature of the `<condition>` tags is the `break` attribute. (Sometimes you will hear this being referred to as the break flag or break parameter.) When stacking multiple conditions, the `break` attribute can control how the parser behaves after each condition is evaluated. The `break` attribute can have the following four values:

- `on-true`: Stop searching further conditions in this extension if the current condition is true
- `on-false`: Stop searching further conditions in this extension if the current condition is false (this is the default)
- `never`: Keep searching further conditions regardless of whether the current condition is true or false
- `always`: Stop searching further conditions regardless of whether the current condition is true or false (very rarely used)

The default behavior is to break out of searching for more conditions as soon as the first failed match occurs. Let's try the same extension with a `break` attribute:

```
<extension name="Two condition tags example">
  <condition field="ani" expression="^(1111)$" break="never">
    <!-- actions performed here if caller is 1111 -->
  </condition>
  <condition field="destination_number" expression="^(1234)$">
    <!-- actions performed here if caller dialed 1234 even if caller
      was not 1111 -->
  </condition>
</extension>
```

We added `break="never"` to the first condition. The parser will now behave differently when it gets to this condition. Regardless of whether or not the first condition fails, the parser moves on to the next condition within the same extension. Without the `break="never"` attribute, the parser would have stopped all further parsing of this extension, and moved on in the Dialplan. But what happens if this condition is true? The actions inside the first condition will be added to the task list, and then the parser moves on to the next condition in this extension. The net result is that we get a set of actions performed if the caller dialed *1234*, but we have other actions that get performed if the caller happens to be *1111*.

 More advanced conditions are considered in *Chapter 8, Advanced Dialplan Concepts.*

Call legs and channel variables

Phone calls to and from FreeSWITCH consist of one or more call legs. A one-legged connection might be something like a user dialing into his or her voicemail. A traditional call between two parties is a connection with two call legs. Recall the following diagram from *Chapter 3, Test Driving the Example Configuration*:

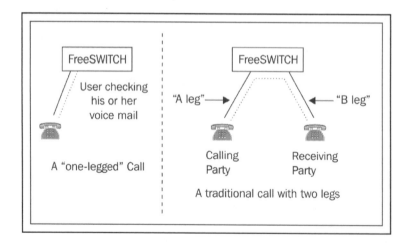

A call between two different telephones consists of an **A leg** (calling or originating party) and a **B leg** (receiving party). Each call leg is also known as a **channel**, as in an audio channel. Each channel has a set of logical attributes that you might call a list of facts about that particular call leg. Each of these attributes is stored in a corresponding channel variable. In the previous chapter, we learned that a registered user has several channel variables defined, and these variables are included in call legs involving that user. To get an idea of just how much information is available for a call, you can call the information extension at *9192* by following these steps:

1. Launch `fs_cli` and issue the command `/log 6`.
2. From a registered phone dial *9192*.

You will see dozens of lines of information. The following is an excerpt from an info dump:

```
2012-09-28 12:26:27.862464 [INFO] mod_dptools.c:1504 CHANNEL_DATA:
Channel-State: [CS_EXECUTE]
Channel-Call-State: [ACTIVE]
Channel-State-Number: [4]
Channel-Name: [sofia/internal/1010@10.15.64.229]
Unique-ID: [660e8db4-09a2-11e2-98a1-a759c95c7090]
Call-Direction: [inbound]
Presence-Call-Direction: [inbound]
Channel-HIT-Dialplan: [true]
Channel-Presence-ID: [1010@10.15.64.229]
Channel-Call-UUID: [660e8db4-09a2-11e2-98a1-a759c95c7090]
Answer-State: [answered]
Channel-Read-Codec-Name: [PCMU]
Channel-Read-Codec-Rate: [8000]
Channel-Read-Codec-Bit-Rate: [64000]
Channel-Write-Codec-Name: [PCMU]
Channel-Write-Codec-Rate: [8000]
Channel-Write-Codec-Bit-Rate: [64000]
Caller-Direction: [inbound]
Caller-Username: [1010]
Caller-Dialplan: [XML]
Caller-Caller-ID-Name: [1010]
Caller-Caller-ID-Number: [1010]
Caller-Network-Addr: [10.15.64.123]
Caller-ANI: [1010]
Caller-Destination-Number: [9192]
...
```

```
variable_sip_from_user: [1010]
variable_sip_from_uri: [1010@10.15.64.229]
variable_sip_from_host: [10.15.64.229]
variable_channel_name: [sofia/internal/1010@10.15.64.229]
variable_sip_call_id: [3c27e62339dd-652d94imggcb]
variable_sip_local_network_addr: [10.15.64.229]
variable_sip_network_ip: [10.15.64.123]
variable_sip_network_port: [2048]
variable_sip_received_ip: [10.15.64.123]
variable_sip_received_port: [2048]
variable_sip_via_protocol: [udp]
variable_sip_authorized: [true]
variable_sip_number_alias: [1010]
variable_sip_auth_username: [1010]
variable_sip_auth_realm: [10.15.64.229]
...
variable_toll_allow: [domestic,international,local]
variable_accountcode: [1010]
variable_user_context: [default]
variable_effective_caller_id_name: [Extension 1010]
variable_effective_caller_id_number: [1010]
variable_outbound_caller_id_name: [FreeSWITCH]
variable_outbound_caller_id_number: [0000000000]
...
```

The lines beginning with `variable_` show the values in the respective channel variables. For example, the line `variable_sip_authorized: [true]` is showing that the value of the `sip_authorized` channel variable is `true`. You will also notice that there are numerous other data elements such as `Unique-ID` and `Call-Direction`. These are `info` application variables. Most (but not all) of these are available as read-only values, which can be accessed just like channel variables.

Accessing channel variables

Within the Dialplan, variables are accessed with a special notation: `${variable_name}`. Consider the following example:

```
<action application="log" data="INFO The value in sip_authorized
  is '${sip_authorized}'"/>
```

This action would print a log message to the FreeSWITCH command line as follows:

```
2009-12-09 14:32:48.904383 [INFO] mod_dptools.c:897 The value in sip_
authorized is 'true'
```

Accessing the read-only values is much the same. Each of these values has a corresponding channel variable name. For example:

```
<action application="log" data="INFO The value of Unique-ID is
    '${uuid}'"/>
```

This will print a log line on the FreeSWITCH command line as follows:

```
2009-12-09 14:46:31.695458 [INFO] mod_dptools.c:897 The value of Unique-
ID is '169ae42e-29f5-4e1c-9505-8ee6ef643081'
```

A complete list of info application variables and their corresponding channel variable names can be found at the following address: http://wiki.freeswitch.org/wiki/Channel_Variables#Info_ Application_Variable_Names_.28variable_xxxx.29

Channel variables are discussed further in *Chapter 8, Advanced Dialplan Concepts*.

Regular expressions

The FreeSWITCH XML Dialplan makes extensive use of **Perl-compatible regular expressions (PCRE)**. A regular expression is a means of executing a true/false test on a string of characters. This is commonly called pattern matching. When a regular expression is applied to a string of characters, we answer a simple question: does it match the pattern? If the answer is yes, then usually it means that a particular condition is met, and therefore, the extension in question can be executed. In some cases, we want to do something if a pattern is not met (see the *Actions and anti-actions* section of this chapter.)

Perl-compatible regular expressions follow a very specific syntax. It can be overwhelming at first. However, once you learn the basics you will appreciate just how powerful they are. The following are some sample regular expressions and their meanings:

Pattern	Meaning
123	Match any string containing the sequence "123"
^123	Match any string beginning with the sequence "123"
123$	Match any string ending with the sequence "123"
^123$	Match any string that is exactly the sequence "123"
\d	Match any single digit (0-9)
\d\d	Match two consecutive digits
^\d\d\d$	Match any string that is exactly three digits long
^\d{7}$	Match any string that is exactly seven digits long
^(\d{7})$	Match any string that is exactly seven digits long, and store the matched value in a special variable named $1
^1?(\d{10})$	Matching any string that optionally begins with the digit "1" and contains an additional ten digits; store the ten digits in $1
^(3\d\d\d)$	Match any four-digit string that begins with the digit "3", and store the matched value in $1

You can no doubt see that regular expressions can be used to match virtually any conceivable pattern of dialed digits. They also can match letters and punctuation marks. Look through `conf/dialplan/default.xml` and you will see many different regular expressions used.

If you would like to know if a particular string matches a specific pattern, then use the `regex` command at the FreeSWITCH command line. (The term `regex` is short for regular expression and is generally pronounced "REJ-ex".) The `regex` command needs at least two arguments: the data to test and the pattern to match against. The arguments are separated by a | (pipe) character. The `regex` command will return `true` if the data and the pattern match, otherwise it will return `false`. You can try the following examples at `fs_cli`:

```
freeswitch@internal> regex 1234|\d
true
freeswitch@internal> regex 1234|\d\d\d\d
true
freeswitch@internal> regex 1234|\d{4}
true
freeswitch@internal> regex 1234|\d{5}
```

```
false
freeswitch@internal> regex 1234|^1234$
true
freeswitch@internal> regex 1234|234
true
freeswitch@internal> regex 1234|^234
false
```

The `regex` command also has a capture syntax that will store and return the values that matched instead of a `true` or `false` value. The expression `%0` contains the entire matched value whereas `%1` contains the first captured value, `%2` contains the second, and so forth. Try the following commands:

```
freeswitch@internal> regex 18005551212|1?(\d\d\d)(\d\d\d)(\d\d\d\d)
true
freeswitch@internal> regex 18005551212|1?(\d\d\d)(\d\d\d)(\d\d\d\d)|%0
18005551212
freeswitch@internal> regex 18005551212|1?(\d\d\d)(\d\d\d)(\d\d\d\d)|%1
800
freeswitch@internal> regex 18005551212|1?(\d\d\d)(\d\d\d)(\d\d\d\d)|%2
555
freeswitch@internal> regex 18005551212|1?(\d\d\d)(\d\d\d)(\d\d\d\d)|%3
1212
freeswitch@internal> regex 18005551212|1?(\d\d\d)(\d\d\d)(\d\d\
d\d)|%1%2%3
8005551212
freeswitch@internal> regex 18005551212|1?(\d\d\d)(\d\d\d)(\d\d\
d\d)|%1-%2-%3
800-555-1212
freeswitch@internal> regex 18005551212|^7|%0
18005551212
```

Use the `regex` command to quickly test data strings and patterns.

 Regular expressions are useful in numerous other computer-related endeavors. You may find it handy to know more than just the basic pattern matching syntax. The FreeSWITCH wiki contains links to many online resources for learning more:

http://wiki.freeswitch.org/wiki/Regular_Expression

Actions and anti-actions

Actions represent the actual steps to take when a Dialplan match has been found. The actions are always present inside an `extension` and `condition` block.

Actions and anti-actions both tell FreeSWITCH to act upon a call. The difference between the two is simple: actions are executed if the condition is met and anti-actions are executed if the condition is not met. Consider the following example:

```
<extension name="Action vs. anti-action example">
  <condition field="destination_number" expression="^(9101)$">
    <action application="log" data="INFO You dialed 9101"/>
    <anti-action application="log"
      data="INFO You did NOT dial 9101"/>
  </condition>
</extension>
```

In the preceding example, `<extension>` will log some information to the FreeSWITCH command line depending upon what the user dialed. If the user dials 9101, the action is executed and the log displays, "You dialed 9101". If the user dials anything other than 9101, then the anti-action is executed and the log displays, "You did NOT dial 9101".

Most extensions you create (and indeed those in the example Dialplan) will have many actions but few anti-actions. In most cases, actions execute Dialplan applications, which in turn may accept arguments. In the preceding example, the `log` application is executed and the `data` attribute contains the argument passed to it.

How Dialplan processing works

Understanding the Dialplan is easier if you can visualize what happens when a call comes in. Often, we hear expressions like "the call traverses the Dialplan" or "the call hits the Dialplan". What exactly does that mean? Let's walk through the processing of a call, so that we can really understand what the XML Dialplan is doing.

The Dialplan has two phases: **parsing** and **executing**. The Dialplan parser looks for extensions to execute. When it finds a matching extension, it then adds the actions (or anti-actions) to a list of tasks to be executed. When the parser finishes looking for extensions, the execution phase begins, and the actions in the task list are performed.

A good way to see all of this in action is to watch the FreeSWITCH console in debug mode while making a test phone call. Launch `fs_cli`, make a test call to 9196 (echo test), and then hang up the phone. Scroll back in your terminal and look for a line that looks like the following example:

```
2012-09-28 20:10:21.930188 [INFO] mod_dialplan_xml.c:485 Processing Test
User <1010>->9196 in context default
```

This is the start of the Dialplan processing. A telephone whose user is named Test User has dialed 9196. (Your console will display the name of the user associated with the phone from which you dialed.) The lines that follow begin with `Dialplan:` and are debug messages, showing which extensions matched and which ones did not. The first extension parsed is called **unloop**. It is an important extension, but is not very interesting for our Dialplan discussion. Look at the next extension that gets parsed. In our example, the debug output is as follows:

```
Dialplan: sofia/internal/1010@10.15.64.229 parsing [default->unloop]
continue=false

Dialplan: sofia/internal/1010@10.15.64.229 Regex (PASS) [unloop]
${unroll_loops}(true) =~ /^true$/ break=on-false

Dialplan: sofia/internal/1010@10.15.64.229 Regex (FAIL) [unloop] ${sip_
looped_call}() =~ /^true$/ break=on-false

Dialplan: sofia/internal/1010@10.15.64.229 parsing [default->tod_example]
continue=true

Dialplan: sofia/internal/1010@10.15.64.229 Date/TimeMatch (FAIL) [tod_
example] break=on-false

Dialplan: sofia/internal/1010@10.15.64.229 parsing [default->holiday_
example] continue=true

Dialplan: sofia/internal/1010@10.15.64.229 Date/TimeMatch (FAIL)
[holiday_example] break=on-false
```

The extension `tod_example` (time of day example) shown is being parsed. These debug lines correspond to the `tod_example` extension found in `conf/dialplan/default.xml`:

```xml
<extension name="tod_example" continue="true">
  <condition wday="2-6" hour="9-18">
    <action application="set" data="open=true"/>
  </condition>
</extension>
```

This extension simply checks the time of the day and the day of the week. If the call is made on a weekday (Monday through Friday) during business hours (9:00 AM to 6:59 PM) then it sets the channel variable open to `true`. This call was made on a Friday at 10:10 PM. Therefore, it passed the `wday` (day of week) test but not the `hour` (hour of day) test. Had the call been made between 9 AM and 6 PM then both conditions would have been met, and the `set` application would have been added to the task list. Notice that the `tod_example` extension has `continue="true"`. This means that the Dialplan will continue parsing extensions even if `tod_example` matches.

The parser continues trying to match extensions, most of which fail:

```
Dialplan: sofia/internal/1010@10.15.64.229 Regex (FAIL) [Check IVR-based
CF] ${cf_target}() =~ /^\d+$/ break=on-false

Dialplan: sofia/internal/1010@10.15.64.229 parsing [default->global-
intercept] continue=false

Dialplan: sofia/internal/1010@10.15.64.229 Regex (FAIL) [global-
intercept] destination_number(9196) =~ /^886$/ break=on-false

Dialplan: sofia/internal/1010@10.15.64.229 parsing [default->group-
intercept] continue=false

Dialplan: sofia/internal/1010@10.15.64.229 Regex (FAIL) [group-intercept]
destination_number(9196) =~ /^\*8$/ break=on-false

Dialplan: sofia/internal/1010@10.15.64.229 parsing [default->intercept-
ext] continue=false

Dialplan: sofia/internal/1010@10.15.64.229 Regex (FAIL) [intercept-ext]
destination_number(9196) =~ /^\*\*(\d+)$/ break=on-false

Dialplan: sofia/internal/1010@10.15.64.229 parsing [default->redial]
continue=false

Dialplan: sofia/internal/1010@10.15.64.229 Regex (FAIL) [redial]
destination_number(9196) =~ /^(redial|870)$/ break=on-false

Dialplan: sofia/internal/1010@10.15.64.229 parsing [default->global]
continue=true

Dialplan: sofia/internal/1010@10.15.64.229 Regex (FAIL) [global] ${call_
debug}(false) =~ /^true$/ break=never

Dialplan: sofia/internal/1010@10.15.64.229 Regex (FAIL) [global] ${sip_
has_crypto}() =~ /^(AES_CM_128_HMAC_SHA1_32|AES_CM_128_HMAC_SHA1_80)$/
break=never
```

The preceding debug lines are all failed matches, which is completely normal. Next, we see some interesting output as follows:

```
Dialplan: sofia/internal/1010@10.15.64.229 Absolute Condition [global]

Dialplan: sofia/internal/1010@10.15.64.229 Action hash(insert/${domain_
name}-spymap/${caller_id_number}/${uuid})

Dialplan: sofia/internal/1010@10.15.64.229 Action hash(insert/${domain_
name}-last_dial/${caller_id_number}/${destination_number})

Dialplan: sofia/internal/1010@10.15.64.229 Action hash(insert/${domain_
name}-last_dial/global/${uuid})

Dialplan: sofia/internal/1010@10.15.64.229 Action set(RFC2822_
DATE=${strftime(%a, %d %b %Y %T %z)})
```

Notice the debug line that mentions `Absolute Condition`. An absolute condition simply means that the condition is always evaluated as `true`, and the actions within are always executed. This `condition` tag is located in the `global` extension further down in `default.xml`. It is listed as follows:

```
<extension name="global" continue="true">
  <condition field="${call_debug}"
      expression="^true$"
      break="never">
    <action application="info"/>
  </condition>
  <!--
      This is an example of how to auto detect if telephone-event
      is missing and activate inband detection
  -->
  <!--
  <condition field="${switch_r_sdp}"
      expression="a=rtpmap:(\d+)\stelephone-event/8000"
      break="never">
    <action application="set" data="rtp_payload_number=$1"/>
    <anti-action application="start_dtmf"/>
  </condition>
  -->
  <condition field="${sip_has_crypto}"
      expression="^(AES_CM_128_HMAC_SHA1_32|AES_CM_128_HMAC_SHA1_80)$"
      break="never">
    <action application="set" data="sip_secure_media=true"/>
    <!-- Offer SRTP on outbound legs if we have it on inbound. -->
    <!-- <action application="export" data="sip_secure_media=true"/>
  -->
  </condition>

  <condition>
    <action application="hash" data="insert/${domain_name}-
      spymap/${caller_id_number}/${uuid}"/>
    <action application="hash" data="insert/${domain_name}-
      last_dial/${caller_id_number}/${destination_number}"/>
    <action application="hash" data="insert/${domain_name}-
      last_dial/global/${uuid}"/>
    <action application="set" data="RFC2822_DATE=${
      strftime(%a, %d %b %Y %T %z)}"/>
  </condition>
</extension>
```

The third `<condition>` tag (highlighted) in the `global` extension has no field or expression and thus always evaluates to `true`, and therefore, the actions within are added to the task list. This does raise a good question: normally the parser stops parsing the current extension as soon as a condition fails, so why did the parser not skip past the `global` extension after its first condition failed? The answer lies in the `break` attribute. Notice that we have `break="never"` specified in the first two `<condition>` tags in this extension. This tells the parser to keep parsing the current extension for further conditions regardless of whether this condition is true or false (see the *Conditions* section earlier in this chapter).

Most of the following conditions fail to match until the parser reaches the music on hold extension:

```
Dialplan: sofia/internal/1010@10.15.64.229 Regex (PASS) [echo]
destination_number(9196) =~ /^9196$/ break=on-false
```

```
Dialplan: sofia/internal/1010@10.15.64.229 Action answer()
```

```
Dialplan: sofia/internal/1010@10.15.64.229 Action echo()
```

The parser adds the `answer` and `echo` Dialplan applications to the task list.

At this point, the parsing is done and now the execution phase begins. You will see some debug lines that begin with EXECUTE and show exactly what is being executed, as shown in the following example:

```
EXECUTE sofia/internal/1010@10.15.64.229 hash(insert/10.15.64.229-
spymap/1010/1e67fc46-09e5-11e2-8893-b106a33054f8)
```

```
EXECUTE sofia/internal/1010@10.15.64.229 hash(insert/10.15.64.229-last_
dial/1010/9196)
```

```
EXECUTE sofia/internal/1010@10.15.64.229 hash(insert/10.15.64.229-last_
dial/global/1e67fc46-09e5-11e2-8893-b106a33054f8)
```

```
EXECUTE sofia/internal/1010@10.15.64.229 set(RFC2822_DATE=Fri, 28 Sep
2012 20:24:03 -0700)
```

```
EXECUTE sofia/internal/1010@10.15.64.229 answer()
```

```
EXECUTE sofia/internal/1010@10.15.64.229 echo()
```

The previous output is a complete example of a call hitting the Dialplan and being processed. Though it took us several minutes to discuss this process, it happens very quickly on the server. This "parse first, execute second" processing strategy makes the XML Dialplan relatively efficient. As an exercise, try watching the debug output while calling 9664 (music on hold) and dialing from one registered telephone to another.

Now that you have seen the Dialplan parser in action, let's create a new extension.

Creating a new extension

Let's create a brand new extension. Start by opening the `conf/dialplan/default/01_custom.xml` file we created in *Chapter 4, SIP and the User Directory*. This file will contain the custom extensions that we will create from now on.

 Always begin your custom Dialplan filenames with a digit sequence. The reason for this is that the XML parser reads the XML files in the order represented by their ASCII filenames. The last file at `conf/dialplan/default/` that we want parsed is `99999_enum.xml`. This file contains the ENUM extension that is used as a last resort if the dialed number does not match any other extensions. See `http://wiki.freeswitch.org/wiki/Mod_enum` for more information.

A Dialplan XML file can contain one or more extension definitions. The only restriction is that the file should begin and end with the XML tags `<include>` and `</include>` respectively.

Our new extension will be simple, but it will also demonstrate the power and flexibility of the FreeSWITCH Dialplan. The extension will have the following characteristics:

- Answering the call
- Reading back the calling user's extension number in two different formats, waiting one second after each reading
- Sleeping for two seconds
- Saying goodbye to the caller
- Hanging up
- The extension will be executed when the caller dials 9101

To create the new extension follow these steps:

1. Add the following content to your `01_custom.xml` file:

```
<include>
  <extension name="simple test">
    <condition field="destination_number"
     expression="^(9101)$">
      <action application="answer"/>
      <action application="say"
       data="en number iterated ${ani}"/>
      <action application="sleep" data="1000"/>
      <action application="say"
       data="en number pronounced ${ani}"/>
```

```
            <action application="sleep" data="1000"/>
            <action application="playback"
             data="voicemail/vm-goodbye.wav"/>
            <action application="sleep" data="2000"/>
            <action application="hangup"/>
        </condition>
      </extension>
    </include>
```

2. Save the file. Launch `fs_cli` and issue the `reload_xml` command, or press *F6*.

The new extension is now added. To test your new extension, simply dial 9101. (You can also watch the FreeSWITCH command line to get a sense of what the system is doing as it processes your extension.) The system should answer, play the two sound prompts, and then hang up. Let's step through each line of the extension and discuss what it does:

```
<extension name="simple test">
```

This tag simply marks the beginning of the extension definition. The `name` attribute is actually optional. However, it helps with making the Dialplan more readable. Also, the extension name will appear in the FreeSWITCH logs, which makes troubleshooting a little easier. The extension definition ends with the `</extension>` tag.

```
<condition field="destination_number" expression="^(9101)$">
```

The `condition` tag defines the matching parameters for this extension. Here we match the value in `destination_number` against the pattern `^(9101)$`. In plain language, this condition says, "If the user dialed the exact digits 9101, then execute the actions inside this condition block." All of the actions between this tag and the closing `</condition>` tag will be executed.

```
<action application="answer"/>
```

The `answer` application does just what it says: it answers the call.

```
<action application="say" data="en number iterated ${ani}"/>
```

This executes the `say` application, which uses the pre-recorded sound prompts to voice numbers, letters, currency amounts, and so on. The first three arguments to the `say` application are: the say engine (usually a language), pronunciation type, and pronunciation method. In this example, we are telling the `say` application to use the `en` engine (that is, use the English sound files) and to pronounce a number in iterated fashion. The number 1234 will be voiced as, "One-two-three-four". The `say` application is further described in the *Important Dialplan applications* section of this chapter.

```
<action application="sleep" data="1000"/>
```

The preceding action simply sleeps, that is, pauses the execution for 1000 milliseconds (1 second).

```
<action application="say" data="en number pronounced ${ani}"/>
```

This executes the `say` application again, this time using the `pronounced` method. With the `pronounced` method, the `say` application will pronounce the number instead of merely listing the digits. The number 1234 will be voiced as, "One thousand, two hundred thirty-four".

```
<action application="sleep" data="1000"/>
```

This action pauses the execution for another 1000 milliseconds.

```
<action application="playback" data="voicemail/vm-goodbye.wav"/>
```

The preceding action executes the `playback` application. The `playback` application plays an audio file to the caller. The filename is specified as the argument. In this case, we specify a file normally used with the FreeSWITCH voicemail application. The `playback` application is further described in the *Important Dialplan applications* section of this chapter.

 FreeSWITCH contains a number of pre-recorded audio files. The English filenames and contents are listed in `docs/phrase/phrase_en.xml` under the FreeSWITCH source directory.

```
<action application="sleep" data="2000"/>
```

This pauses execution for 2000 milliseconds (2 seconds).

```
<action application="hangup"/>
```

The last action of our extension hangs up, disconnecting the caller.

That's it! You have now gone through the basic steps necessary to add custom extensions to your system. Most of the extensions that we create will go into the `default` context, because they are designed for the users of our system. In a few cases we may add extensions to another context. For example, to handle incoming DID calls you would update the `public` Dialplan context. We may also define a custom context to handle a specific need, such as when using a single FreeSWITCH server to handle multiple departments or multiple companies.

Important Dialplan applications

FreeSWITCH has more than 140 Dialplan applications. However, a few of them are particularly important because they are used very frequently. In this section we consider the most important and widely used Dialplan applications.

bridge

The `bridge` application connects two Endpoints together.

Argument syntax:

```
<target_endpoint>[,<target_endpoint>] [|<target_endpoint>]
```

Endpoints separated by commas are dialed simultaneously. Endpoints separated by pipes are dialed sequentially. The first Endpoint to answer receives the call, at which time dialing to all other Endpoint is discontinued.

Examples:

```
<action application="bridge" data="user/1000"/>
<action application="bridge"
  data="sofia/gateway/my_gateway_name/$1"/>
```

See the *Dialstring formats* section later in this chapter.

playback

The `playback` application simply plays an audio file to the caller. Files can be in many formats. The sound and music files included in FreeSWITCH are all .wav files.

Argument syntax: absolute path to a sound file or relative path to an installed sound file.

Examples:

```
<action application="playback"
  data="/absolute/path/to/sound.wav"/>
<action application="playback" data="voicemail/vm-goodbye.wav"/>
```

You can also playback from a stream location (for mp3 files, you'll need mod_shout loaded). That would look like this:

```
<action application="playback"
  data="http://sounds.com/path/to/sound.mp3"/>
```

say

The `say` application uses the built-in say engine to voice to the caller some piece of information. This is not text-to-speech. See the `speak` application.

Argument syntax:

```
<module_name> <say_type> <say_method> <text>
```

The `module_name` is usually the language, for example `en` or `es`.

The `say_type` parameter can be any of the following:

- `number`
- `items`
- `persons`
- `messages`
- `currency`
- `time_measurement`
- `current_date`
- `current_time`
- `current_date_time`
- `telephone_number`
- `telephone_extension`
- `url`
- `ip_address`
- `e-mail_address`
- `postal_address`
- `account_number`
- `name_spelled`
- `name_phonetic`
- `short_date_time`

The `say_method` parameter can be any of the following:

- `n/a` (a method is not applicable)
- `pronounced` ("one hundred, twenty-three")
- `iterated` ("one two three")
- `counted` (special case, similar to "pronounced")

Examples:

```
<action application="say" data="en number pronounced 1234"/>
<action application="say" data="en number iterated 1234"/>
<action application="say" data="en currency pronounced 1234"/>
<action application="say" data="en items pronounced 1234"/>
```

play_and_get_digits

The `play_and_get_digits` application will play a sound file to the caller, while at the same time listening for digits dialed by the caller. This allows you to create interactive Dialplans without necessarily creating an entire IVR.

Argument syntax:

```
<min> <max> <tries> <timeout> <terminators> <file> <invalid_file>
<var_name> <regex> [<digit_timeout>] ['<failure_ext> [failure_dp
[failure_context]]']
```

Arguments:

- `min`: Minimum number of digits to collect
- `max`: Maximum number of digits to collect
- `tries`: Number of attempts to play the file and collect digits
- `timeout`: Number of milliseconds to wait before assuming the caller is done entering digits
- `terminators`: Digits used to end input if less than `min` digits have been pressed (typically #)
- `file`: Sound file to play while digits are fetched
- `invalid_file`: Sound file to play when digits don't match the `regex` argument
- `var_name`: Channel variable that digits should be placed in
- `regex`: Regular expression to match digits
- `digit_timeout` (optional): Number of milliseconds to wait in between digits (defaults to timeout value)
- `failure_ext` (optional): Destination extension to which the call should be transferred if the caller does not enter a valid input value
- `failure_dp` (optional with `failure_ext`): Destination Dialplan type when using `failure_ext`
- `failure_context` (optional with `failure_dp`): Destination Dialplan context when using `failure_dp`

Example:

```
<action application="play_and_get_digits"
  data="2 5 3 8000 # /path/to/sound_file.wav
    /path/to/invalid_sound.wav my_digits \d+ "/>
<action application="log" data="User entered these digits:
  ${my_digits}"/>
```

This example executes `play_and_get_digits` with the following parameters:

- Looks for a minimum of two digits
- Looks for a maximum of five digits
- Tries three times
- Waits 8 seconds before assuming the caller is done entering digits
- Uses the # key as the terminator
- Plays the sound file `/path/to/sound_file.wav` while collecting digits
- Plays the sound file `/path/to/invalid_sound.wav` if invalid digits are dialed
- Stores the dialed digits in the channel variable `my_digits`
- Matches against the pattern `\d+`

ivr

The `ivr` application sends the caller to a predefined IVR.

Argument syntax: Name of IVR to execute.

Example:

```
<action application="ivr" data="ivr_demo"/>
```

See *Chapter 6, Using XML IVRs and Phrase Macros*, and also the `ivr_demo` extension in `conf/dialplan/default.xml`.

sleep

The `sleep` application pauses Dialplan execution for the specified number of milliseconds.

Argument syntax: Number of milliseconds to sleep.

Example:

```
<action application="sleep" data="1000"/>
```

answer

The `answer` application picks up the phone by establishing an audio path to the calling party. In SIP terms, this causes FreeSWITCH to send a "200 OK" message, establish a codec to use (if not already determined), and begin the flow of RTP packets.

Example:

```
<action application="answer"/>
```

pre_answer

The `pre_answer` application is similar to `answer`, except it establishes early media. In SIP terms, this causes FreeSWITCH to send a "183 Session Progress with SDP" message.

Example:

```
<action application="pre_answer"/>
```

hangup

The `hangup` application disconnects the audio path and ends the call.

Argument syntax: Optional hang up cause.

Examples:

```
<action application="hangup"/>
<action application="hangup" data="USER_BUSY"/>
```

set

The `set` application sets a channel variable or processes an API command from within the Dialplan. (This latter feature is demonstrated in *Chapter 8, Advanced Dialplan Concepts*.)

Argument syntax:

```
<variable_name=value>
```

Example:

```
<action application="set" data="my_chan_var=example value"/>
<action application="log"
   data="INFO my_chan_var contains ${my_chan_var}"/>
```

transfer

The `transfer` application sends the call back through the Dialplan. This causes an entirely new parse phase and execution phase to take place.

Argument syntax:

```
<destination number> [destination dialplan [destination context]]
```

Example:

```
<action application="transfer" data="9664"/>
<action application="transfer"
  data="12345 XML custom"/>
```

Dialstring formats

Before we leave our discussion of the Dialplan, it would be good to consider one more topic: Dialstrings. A **Dialstring** is exactly what it sounds like—a string of characters that defines a destination to be dialed by FreeSWITCH. All Dialstrings have a specific syntax. The syntax varies depending upon the type of Endpoint being dialed. The most important types of Dialstring in FreeSWITCH are those for Sofia, because they represent how we dial SIP Endpoints. However, as we will see, there are several different kinds of Dialstrings. They are used primarily in two places, which are as follows:

- Bridging an existing call leg in the Dialplan with the `bridge` application
- Creating a new call leg at the CLI with the `originate` command

 Dialstring syntax is the same whether using the `bridge` dialplan application or the `originate` API command.

Let's learn a bit more about Dialstrings by considering a few examples, starting with some Sofia Dialstrings. The basic Sofia Dialstring takes two different formats:

- `sofia/<profile name>/<user@domain>`
- `sofia/gateway/<gateway name>/<user>`

As we learned in *Chapter 4, SIP and the User Directory*, we can dial another SIP Endpoint, either with or without a gateway. When using Sofia to dial through a SIP profile, it is necessary to specify both the user and domain. However, when dialing through a gateway it is not necessary to include the domain because this is already defined in the gateway configuration. Therefore, the following is not allowed:

```
<!-- Wrong -->
<action application="bridge"
  data="sofia/gateway/my_gateway/user@1.2.3.4"/>
```

The correct syntax is as follows:

```
<!-- Correct -->
<action application="bridge"
  data="sofia/gateway/my_gateway/user">
```

The equivalent for dialing through the `internal` profile would look like the following:

```
<!--Also correct -->
<action application="bridge"
  data="sofia/internal/user@1.2.3.4 /">
```

Knowing these two syntaxes will cover the vast majority of your SIP dialing needs. However, there are many edge cases. For a complete discussion on dial strings see `http://wiki.freeswitch.org/wiki/Dialplan_XML#SIP-Specific_Dialstrings`.

When dialing a user who is registered on your FreeSWITCH server there is a shortcut available:

```
user/<user id>[@domain]
```

This syntax makes it very easy to dial another phone registered on your system. In fact, `Local_Extension` in `conf/dialplan/default.xml` uses this method to connect calls to registered users:

```
<action application="bridge"
  data="user/${dialed_extension}@${domain_name}"/>
```

The `@domain` parameter is optional if you have only one domain defined on your FreeSWITCH server.

The following are a few more types of Dialstrings:

- `loopback/<destination number>`: This creates a call leg and puts it in the Dialplan at `<destination_number>`
- `freetdm/<span>/<channel>/<phone number>`: This creates a call leg on a telephony interface card (see `http://wiki.freeswitch.org/wiki/FreeTDM` for more information on using traditional telephony hardware with FreeSWITCH)
- `error/<error code>`: This simulates an error condition; useful for testing
- `group/<group name>[@domain]`: This calls a group of users (see *Chapter 4, SIP and the User Directory*)

Feel free to try some of these. If you have a phone registered to your FreeSWITCH server, then use the `originate` command from `fs_cli`. The basic syntax of `originate` is as follows:

```
originate <dialstring> <destination number>
```

Try the following and see what happens. Replace `1000` with the extension number of your phone:

```
originate loopback/9664 1000
originate user/1000 9664
originate error/USER_BUSY 1000
originate loopback/9192 1000
originate loopback/4000 1000
```

As you can see, FreeSWITCH has many tools for creating calls. There is virtually no scenario that it cannot handle or emulate.

Summary

Completing this chapter is an important milestone for a beginner. Understanding the concepts presented here is a large part of being able to configure and maintain a FreeSWITCH server. A number of topics were discussed:

- The basic hierarchy of the FreeSWITCH XML Dialplan:
    - The Dialplan consists of one or more contexts
    - Contexts consist of one or more extensions
    - Extensions contain one or more conditions
    - Conditions usually have one or more actions or anti-actions

- Regular expressions and pattern matching
- An introduction to the concept of channel variables
- How Dialplan parsing and processing works
- Creating our own custom extension
- A list of some of the more common and useful Dialplan applications

Having these basic skills, you should now be able to create truly useful extensions that do more than merely connect one telephone user to another. Although the Dialplan is very powerful and flexible, it is not in and of itself an IVR engine or a programming language. FreeSWITCH has modules that work with the Dialplan to add these more advanced features to your system.

In the next chapter, we will look at two aspects of FreeSWITCH that help us interact with callers: the XML IVR subsystem and FreeSWITCH phrase macros.

6
Using XML IVRs and Phrase Macros

The built-in **IVR (Interactive Voice Response)** engine is a powerful component of the FreeSWITCH system. It allows messages to be played and interactive responses (usually touch-tones) to be processed, in order to direct calls to particular destinations. It can ultimately allow callers to hear information without needing to speak to a live person, select options that enable/disable features, or to enter data that can be used in account, billing, or other operations.

Most people are familiar with an IVR as an auto-attendant that answers a main number for your company and provides a list of options to reach people (that is, "For sales press one, for support press two"). This avoids disruptions to unintended call recipients, and reduces or removes the need for a dedicated receptionist. More advanced IVRs can also be used for collecting information from a caller, such as a caller's account number or the PIN number for a conference bridge. In this chapter, we will explore utilizing the built-in IVR engine that FreeSWITCH provides natively. You will use the skills you learned in *Chapter 5, Understanding the XML Dialplan*, to route calls to an IVR application via the Dialplan, and we will build an IVR menu using the built-in XML configuration files native to FreeSWITCH.

The following topics will be discussed:

- IVR engine overview
- IVR XML configuration file
- IVR menu definitions
- IVR menu destinations
- Routing calls to your IVR
- Nesting IVRs
- Using phrases with IVRs
- Advanced routing

IVR engine overview

Unlike many applications within FreeSWITCH which are built as modules, IVR is considered the core functionality of FreeSWITCH. It is used anytime a prompt is played and digits are collected. Even if you are not using the IVR application itself from your Dialplan, you will see IVR-related functions being utilized from various other applications. As an example, the `voicemail` application makes heavy use of IVR functionality when playing messages, while awaiting digits to control deleting, saving, and otherwise managing voicemails.

In this section, we will only be reviewing the IVR functionality that is exposed from within the `ivr` Dialplan application. This functionality is typically used to build an auto-attendant menu, although other functions are possible as well.

IVR XML configuration file

FreeSWITCH ships with a sample IVR menu, typically invoked by dialing 5000 from the sample Dialplan. When you dial 5000, you will hear a greeting welcoming you to FreeSWITCH, and will present your menu options. The menu options consist of options such as calling the FreeSWITCH conference, calling the echo extension, hearing music on hold, or going to a submenu. We will start off by reviewing the XML that powers this example.

IVR engine overview

Open `conf/ivr_menus/demo_ivr.xml`, which contains the following XML:

```
<!-- demo IVR setup -->
<!-- demo IVR, Main Menu -->
<menu name="demo_ivr"
    greet-long="phrase:demo_ivr_main_menu"
    greet-short="phrase:demo_ivr_main_menu_short"
    invalid-sound="ivr/ivr-that_was_an_invalid_entry.wav"
    exit-sound="voicemail/vm-goodbye.wav"
    confirm-macro=""
    confirm-key=""
    tts-engine="flite"
    tts-voice="rms"
    confirm-attempts="3"
    timeout="10000"
    inter-digit-timeout="2000"
    max-failures="3"
    max-timeouts="3"
```

```
    digit-len="4">

    <!-- The following are the definitions for the digits the user dials
    -->
    <!-- Digit 1 transfer caller to the public FreeSWITCH conference -->
    <entry action="menu-exec-app" digits="1" param="bridge
    sofia/$${domain}/888@conference.freeswitch.org"/>
    <entry action="menu-exec-app" digits="2" param="transfer 9196
    XML default"/> <!-- FS echo -->
    <entry action="menu-exec-app" digits="3" param="transfer 9664
    XML default"/> <!-- MOH -->
    <entry action="menu-exec-app" digits="4" param="transfer 9191
    XML default"/> <!-- ClueCon -->
    <entry action="menu-exec-app" digits="5" param="transfer
    1234*256 enum"/> <!-- Screaming monkeys -->
    <entry action="menu-sub" digits="6" param="demo_ivr_submenu"/>
    <!-- demo sub menu -->
    <!-- Using a regex in the digits tag lets you define a dial
    pattern for the caller
        You may define multiple regexes if you need a different
        pattern for some reason -->
    <entry action="menu-exec-app" digits="/^(10[01][0-9])$/"
    param="transfer $1 XML features"/>
    <entry action="menu-top" digits="9"/> <!-- Repeat this menu -->
</menu>

<!-- Demo IVR, Sub Menu -->
<menu name="demo_ivr_submenu"
    greet-long="phrase:demo_ivr_sub_menu"
    greet-short="phrase:demo_ivr_sub_menu_short"
    invalid-sound="ivr/ivr-that_was_an_invalid_entry.wav"
    exit-sound="voicemail/vm-goodbye.wav"
    timeout="15000"
    max-failures="3"
    max-timeouts="3">

    <!-- The demo IVR sub menu prompt basically just says, "press
    star to return to previous menu..." -->
    <entry action="menu-top" digits="*"/>
</menu>
```

In the preceding example, there are two IVR menus defined: demo_ivr and demo_ivr_submenu. Let's break apart the first one and examine it, starting with the IVR menu definition itself.

IVR menu definitions

The following XML defines an IVR menu named `demo_ivr`:

```
<menu name="demo_ivr"
    greet-long="phrase:demo_ivr_main_menu"
    greet-short="phrase:demo_ivr_main_menu_short"
    invalid-sound="ivr/ivr-that_was_an_invalid_entry.wav"
    exit-sound="voicemail/vm-goodbye.wav"
    confirm-macro=""
    confirm-key=""
    tts-engine="flite"
    tts-voice="rms"
    confirm-attempts="3"
    timeout="10000"
    inter-digit-timeout="2000"
    max-failures="3"
    max-timeouts="3"
    digit-len="4">
```

We'll use the previously mentioned menu's name later when we route calls to the IVR from the Dialplan. Following the name, various XML attributes specify how the IVR will behave. The following options are available when defining an IVR's behavior.

greet-long

The `greet-long` attribute specifies the initial greeting that is played when a caller reaches the IVR. This is different from the `greet-short` sound file which allows for introductions to be played, such as "Thank you for calling XYZ Company". In the demo IVR, the `greet-long` attribute is a **Phrase Macro** that plays an introductory message to the caller ("Welcome to FreeSWITCH...") followed by the menu options the caller may choose from.

Argument syntax: Sound filename (or path + name), TTS, or Phrase Macro.

Examples:

```
greet-long="my_greeting.wav"
greet-long="phrase:my_greeting_phrase"
greet-long="say:Welcome to our company. Press 1 for sales, 2 for
support."
```

greet-short

The `greet-short` attribute specifies the greeting that is replayed if the caller enters invalid information, or no information at all. This is typically the same sound file as `greet-long` without the introduction. In the sample IVR, the `greet-short` attribute is a Phrase Macro that simply plays the menu options to the caller, and does not play the lengthy introduction found in `greet-long`.

Argument syntax: Sound filename (or path + name), TTS, or Phrase Macro.

Examples:

```
greet-short="my_greeting_retry.wav"
greet-short="phrase:my_greeting_retry_phrase"
greet-short="say:Press 1 for sales, 2 for support."
```

invalid-sound

The `invalid-sound` attribute specifies the sound that is played when a caller makes an invalid entry.

Argument syntax: Sound filename (or path + name), TTS, or Phrase Macro.

Examples:

```
invalid-sound="invalid_entry.wav"
invalid-sound="phrase:my_invalid_entry_phrase"
invalid-sound="say:That was not a valid entry"
```

exit-sound

The `exit-sound` attribute specifies the sound, which is played when a caller makes too many invalid entries or too many timeouts occur. This file is played before the IVR exits. (The call will continue in the Dialplan.)

Argument syntax: Sound filename (or path + name), TTS, or Phrase Macro.

Examples:

```
exit-sound="too_many_bad_entries.wav"
exit-sound="phrase:my_too_many_bad_entries_phrase"
exit-sound="say:Hasta la vista, baby."
```

timeout

The `timeout` attribute specifies the maximum amount of time the IVR will wait for the user to start entering digits after the greeting has played. If this time limit is exceeded, the menu is repeated until the value in the `max-timeouts` attribute has been reached.

Argument syntax: Any number, in milliseconds.

Examples:

```
timeout="10000"
timeout="20000"
```

inter-digit-timeout

The `inter-digit-timeout` attribute specifies the maximum amount of time to wait in between each digit the caller presses. This is different from the overall timeout. It is useful to allow enough time to enter as many digits as necessary, without frustrating the caller by pausing too long after they are done making their entry. For example, if both 1000 and 1 are valid IVR entries, the system will continue waiting for the `inter-digit-timeout` length of time after 1 is entered, before determining that it is the final entry.

Argument syntax: Any number, in milliseconds.

Example:

```
inter-digit-timeout="2000"
```

max-failures

The `max-failures` attribute specifies how many failures due to invalid entries to tolerate before exiting the IVR. (The call will continue in the Dialplan.)

Argument syntax: Any number.

Example:

```
max-failures="3"
```

max-timeouts

The `max-timeouts` attribute specifies how many timeouts to tolerate before exiting the IVR. (The call will continue in the Dialplan.)

Argument syntax: Any number.

Example:

```
max-timeouts="3"
```

digit-len

The `digit-len` attribute specifies the maximum number of digits that the user can enter before determining the entry is complete.

Argument syntax: Any number greater than or equal to one.

Example:

```
digit-len="4"
```

tts-voice

The `tts-voice` attribute specifies the specific Text-To-Speech voice that should be used.

Argument syntax: Any valid Text-To-Speech voice.

Example:

```
tts-voice="Mary"
```

tts-engine

The `tts-engine` attribute specifies the specific Text-To-Speech engine that should be used.

Argument syntax: Any valid Text-To-Speech engine.

Example:

```
tts-engine="flite"
```

confirm-key

The `confirm-key` attribute specifies the key which the user can press to verify the entry of a target extension number. It is used with the `confirm-macro` attribute.

Argument syntax: Any valid DTMF digit.

Example:

```
confirm-key="#"
```

confirm-macro

The `confirm-macro` attribute specifies which Phrase Macro to play while waiting for the `confirm-key` to be pressed. When set, the macro is played after the caller enters a destination extension number at the IVR.

Argument syntax: Any valid Phrase Macro.

Example:

```
confirm-macro="my_confirm_macro"
```

These attributes dictate the general behavior of the IVR.

IVR menu destinations

After defining the global attributes of the IVR, you need to specify what specific destinations (or options) are available for the caller to press. You do this with `<entry>` XML elements. Let's review the first six XML options used by this IVR:

```
<entry action="menu-exec-app" digits="1" param="bridge
sofia/$${domain}/888@conference.freeswitch.org"/>
<entry action="menu-exec-app" digits="2" param="transfer 9196 XML
default"/> <!-- FS echo -->
<entry action="menu-exec-app" digits="3" param="transfer 9664 XML
default"/> <!-- MOH -->
<entry action="menu-exec-app" digits="4" param="transfer 9191 XML
default"/> <!-- ClueCon -->
<entry action="menu-exec-app" digits="5" param="transfer 1234*256
enum"/> <!-- Screaming monkeys -->
<entry action="menu-sub" digits="6" param="demo_ivr_submenu"/>
<entry action="menu-exec-app" digits="/^(10[01][0-9])$/"
param="transfer $1 XML features"/>
```

Each entry defines an individual action that a caller can take from within the menu. There are three parameters for each entry—an `action` to be taken, the `digits` the caller must press to activate that action, and the parameters (the `param` attribute) that are passed to the action. In most cases you will probably use the `menu-exec-app` action, which transfers control of the call to a Dialplan application along with Dialplan parameters, just as you would from the regular Dialplan (`bridge`, `transfer`, `hangup`, and so on.).

In the previous examples, the available options are pretty simple—they define a single digit (`digits="3"` for example) which, when pressed either bridges a call directly to an endpoint (digit 1) or transfers the call to an extension in the Dialplan (digits 2, 3, 4, and 5). Lastly, the destinations for digits 6 and 9 are related to IVR submenus (described in the following section).

There is one entry that is a bit different from the rest, which is the second to last IVR entry. It deserves a closer look.

```
<entry action="menu-exec-app" digits="/^(10[01][0-9])$/"
param="transfer $1 XML features"/>
```

This entry definition specifies a regular expression for the digits field. This regular expression field is identical to the expressions you would use in the Dialplan. In this example, the IVR is looking for any four-digit extension number from 1000 through 1019 (which is the default extension number range for the predefined users in the directory). Notice that the regular expression here has parentheses that capture the value that is matched. This captured value is stored in the special variable $1 and is used in the argument of the `transfer` application. This effectively allows the IVR to accept 1000-1019 as entries, and transfer the caller directly to those extensions when they are entered into the IVR.

The remaining IVR entry actions are a bit different. They introduce `menu-sub` as an action, which transfers the caller to an IVR submenu, and `menu-top`, which restarts the current IVR and replays the menu.

```
<entry action="menu-sub" digits="6"
 param="demo_ivr_submenu"/>
<entry action="menu-top" digits="9"/>
```

These two entries transfer control of the running IVR to a new IVR. Note that by transferring to a `sub-menu` in this manner you build a history of IVRs. So, a **go back** button is available to the caller, which sends them to the previous IVR.

Several other actions exist that can be used within an IVR. The complete list of actions you can use from within the IVR is covered in the following sections.

menu-exec-app

The `menu-exec-app` action, combined with a `param` field, executes the specified application and passes the parameters listed to that application. This is equivalent to using `<action application="app" data="data">` in your Dialplan. The most common use of `menu-exec-app` is to transfer a caller to another extension in the Dialplan.

Argument syntax: `application <params>`

Example:

```
<entry digits="1" action="menu-exec-app"
param="application param1 param2 param3 ..."/>
<entry digits="2" action="menu-exec-app"
param="transfer 9664 XML default"/>
```

menu-play-sound

The `menu-play-sound` action, combined with a `param` field, plays a specified sound file.

Argument syntax: valid sound file.

Example:

```
<entry digits="1" action="menu-play-sound" param="screaming_monkeys.
wav"/>
```

menu-back

The `menu-back` action returns to the previous IVR menu, if any.

Argument syntax: None.

Example:

```
<entry digits="1" action="menu-back"/>
```

menu-top

The `menu-top` action restarts this IVR's menu.

Argument syntax: None.

Example:

```
<entry digits="1" action="menu-top"/>
```

Routing calls to your IVR

Now that you've built an IVR, you need some way to get calls to reach the IVR.

Routing calls to your IVR is simple and can be done from within the Dialplan. Add the following XML application to your Dialplan extension where you want to invoke an IVR:

```
<action application="ivr" data="demo_ivr"/>
```

This will cause FreeSWITCH to look for an IVR named demo_ivr and invoke it.

The XML Dialplan entry for invoking the demo_ivr, which is included with the sample FreeSWITCH configuration files, is as follows:

```
<!-- a sample IVR  -->
<extension name="ivr_demo">
  <condition field="destination_number" expression="^5000$">
    <action application="answer"/>
    <action application="sleep" data="2000"/>
    <action application="ivr" data="demo_ivr"/>
  </condition>
</extension>
```

> Note that in the preceding example, a sleep application appears before the IVR is executed. This is important as it allows media to start flowing between your caller and your FreeSWITCH instance, before the IVR's greeting begins to play. If the Dialplan does not do this, you may get complaints from some callers saying that the beginning of the greeting in being clipped.

Nesting IVRs

There are two ways to nest or otherwise combine IVRs. The first way is to use the submenu system list, as previously mentioned. Simply create two or more IVR menus as if they were independent menus, with each one having a unique name. Then, from the main IVR, create an entry option with action of menu-sub, and a param field containing the name of the child IVR. For example:

```
<entry digits="1" action="menu-sub" param="child_ivr"/>
```

The advantage of creating your menus this way is that you gain the ability to use the menu-back action to allow callers to get to the previous IVR menu. It is useful if you have multiple parents calling the same child menu.

The other way to use submenus is to assign each IVR a unique extension number and simply transfer the caller from one extension to another, in order to get to and from the parent and child menus. In this way, you can always guarantee that you can get from one specific IVR to another and back again, regardless of how an IVR was invoked. This also makes your Dialplan more consistent and allows for testing individual IVRs (by dialing their extension directly) at any time without having to navigate the entire tree.

Using phrases with IVRs

You may have noticed that the `greet-long` and `greet-short` options in the examples use `phrase:demo_ivr_main_menu` as opposed to a specific sound filename and path. IVRs allow you to specify sound files using the phrase and Text-To-Speech macros. This is useful for several reasons; most notably the ability to chain together multiple sounds into one phrase and the ability to have different languages presented to the caller, based on the caller's information.

Calling Phrase Macros

Phrase Macros can be called from the Dialplan, from an IVR, or from a Dialplan script (such as Lua script, which is discussed in the next chapter). The latter will be covered in the next chapter. Phrase Macros can be used virtually in all places where a sound filename can be used. Phrase Macros are used only for playback purposes, so they cannot be used when specifying a filename for a recording operation. We have already seen examples of using phrases in our XML IVR configuration files. The following are a few examples of using Phrase Macros from the Dialplan:

```
<action application="playback"
data="phrase:myphrase:arg1:arg2:arg3"/>
<action application="play_and_get_digits"
data="2 5 3 7000 # phrase:myphrase:arg1 /invalid.wav my_var
\d+"/>
```

Note that there is no requirement to have an argument. The following code is valid as well:

```
<action application="playback" data="phrase:myphrase"/>
```

Now let's look at some phrases to see what they can accomplish for you.

Phrase Macro examples – voicemail

Remember that the FreeSWITCH voicemail system is a heavy user of IVRs. It is also exemplary in its use of Phrase Macros to simplify the task of combining prerecorded sound prompts in a reusable way. By looking at the Phrase Macros used in the FreeSWITCH voicemail implementation, we can learn virtually all there is to know about using these powerful tools.

Open `conf/lang/en/vm/sounds.xml` in a text editor and scan through the file. You will notice the familiar opening `<include>` tag and the subsequent `<macro>` tags. Just by looking at the definitions of these macros, you can get an idea of what some of them do.

The basic syntax of a Phrase Macro looks as follows:

```
<macro name="<macro name>">
  <input pattern="<pattern>">
    <match>
      <action/>
    </match>
    <nomatch>
      <action/>
    </nomatch>
  </input>
  <input pattern="<pattern>">
    <match>
      <action/>
    </match>
    <nomatch>
      <action/>
    </nomatch>
  </input>
</macro>
```

The macro is defined by the contents within the `<macro>` and `</macro>` tags. The `input pattern` expression is a regular expression (pattern) that is matched against any arguments that are passed to the Phrase Macro. The actions inside of the `<match>` and `</match>` tags are executed if there is a positive match, otherwise the actions inside the `<nomatch>` and `</nomatch>` are executed. If a match is found, then the special regular expression capture variables (`$1`, `$2`, and so on) are available inside the `<match>` node. Note that you may have multiple input patterns. This functions in a way that is very similar to the XML Dialplan functions. See the following code for an example of using multiple `input pattern` nodes.

Let's review a few simple macros. Locate the `voicemail_goodbye` macro as follows:

```
<macro name="voicemail_goodbye">
  <input pattern="(.*)">
    <match>
      <action function="play-file"
      data="voicemail/vm-goodbye.wav"/>
    </match>
  </input>
</macro>
```

This macro is called by the voicemail system when the caller logs out. In this case the input pattern is (.*), which will always match, even if the phrase was called without an argument. This pattern is very common in Phrase Macros. At first glance, it may not seem advantageous to have seven lines of code just to play a single sound file. However, using this Phrase Macro allows us to customize what happens when a caller logs out of voicemail, and we can do so without editing any source code. There are, though, other advantages.

Locate the `voicemail_enter_pass` macro:

```
<macro name="voicemail_enter_pass">
    <input pattern="(.*)">
      <match>
        <action function="play-file" data="voicemail/vm-
          enter_pass.wav"/>
        <action function="say" data="$1" method="pronounced"
        type="name_spelled"/>
      </match>
    </input>
  </macro>
```

Note that this macro captures the arguments and places them in the special variable $1. In the example configuration, the voicemail module sends # as the argument. This macro is what controls the dialog when the caller is logging into voicemail. Specifically, it plays the sound file that says, "Please enter your password, followed by…" and then uses the `say` application to say the word "pound". The net effect then, is that the caller hears "Please enter your password, followed by… pound". This macro lets us customize what the caller hears when he or she is prompted to enter a password.

 Watch the `fs_cli` program while logging into voicemail and checking messages. You can observe the phrases being parsed and executed.

At this point, we can already see that Phrase Macros are good for customization, and they stitch together various sound prompts to create meaningful sentences to play to the caller. A classic example of this is the IVR menu. The voicemail main menu really is just an IVR menu for a specific purpose. It is a dialog that says to the caller, "To listen to new messages, press one. To listen to saved messages, press two. For advanced options, press five. To exit, press pound". Let's look at the following macro.

Locate the macro `voicemail_menu`, listed as follows:

```
<macro name="voicemail_menu">
  <input pattern="^([0-9#*]):([0-9#*]):([0-9#*]):([0-9#*])$">
    <match>
      <!-- To listen to new messages -->
      <action function="play-file"
      data="voicemail/vm-
      listen_new.wav"/>
      <action function="play-file"
      data="voicemail/vm-press.wav"/>
      <action function="say"
      data="$1" method="pronounced"
        type="name_spelled"/>
      <action function="execute" data="sleep(100)"/>
      <!-- To listen to saved messages -->
      <action function="play-file"
      data="voicemail/vm-listen_saved.wav"/>
      <action function="play-file"
      data="voicemail/vm-press.wav"/>
      <action function="say" data="$2" method="pronounced"
      type="name_spelled"/>
      <action function="execute" data="sleep(100)"/>
      <!-- For advanced options -->
      <action function="play-file"
      data="voicemail/vm-advanced.wav"/>
      <action function="play-file"
      data="voicemail/vm-press.wav"/>
      <action function="say" data="$3" method="pronounced"
      type="name_spelled"/>
      <action function="execute" data="sleep(100)"/>
      <!-- To exit -->
      <action function="play-file"
      data="voicemail/vm-to_exit.wav"/>
      <action function="play-file"
      data="voicemail/vm-press.wav"/>
      <action function="say" data="$4" method="pronounced"
      type="name_phonetic"/>
    </match>
  </input>
</macro>
```

Most of this phrase is self-explanatory. The key piece of information is actually found in the pattern (highlighted). The voicemail module calls this macro with an argument list that looks like this: 1:2:5:#. The input pattern is simply a regular expression that parses out those values, so that $1 contains 1, $2 contains 2, $3 contains 5, and $4 contains #.

> You may be wondering where the key presses are defined, that is, where you can tell the FreeSWITCH voicemail module that the caller should press one for new messages, press two for saved messages, and so on. The answer is in the file conf/autoload_configs/voicemail. conf.xml. Look in the <profiles> node for the default voicemail profile. Notice that many of the parameters have names ending with -key. These are all customizable. The parameter play-new-messages-key defines which key the user presses to listen to new messages. The parameter config-menu-key is what the user presses to access the advanced options menu. Feel free to experiment with your own customizations. The FreeSWITCH developers recommend that you make a copy of the default voicemail profile, and then define your own custom profile if you wish to make changes to a production system.

Let's look at one more example of using Phrase Macros to solve what may otherwise be complicated IVR scenarios. The voicemail_message_count macro solves two distinct problems. First, we have two different types of voicemail messages, namely, new and saved. Second, we have the challenge of when to use messages (plural) or message (singular), when telling the caller how many messages are present. Notice how our voicemail_message_count macro elegantly solves both problems as follows:

```
<macro name="voicemail_message_count">
  <input pattern="^(1):(.*)$" break_on_match="true">
    <match>
      <action function="play-file"
      data="voicemail/vm-you_have.wav"/>
      <action function="say" data="$1" method="pronounced"
      type="items"/>
      <action function="play-file"
      data="voicemail/vm-$2.wav"/>
      <action function="play-file"
      data="voicemail/vm-message.wav"/>
    </match>
  </input>
  <input pattern="^(\d+):(.*)$">
    <match>
      <action function="play-file"
      data="voicemail/vm-you_have.wav"/>
```

```
        <action function="say" data="$1" method="pronounced"
        type="items"/>
        <action function="play-file"
        data="voicemail/vm-$2.wav"/>
        <action function="play-file"
        data="voicemail/vm-messages.wav"/>
    </match>
  </input>
</macro>
```

Again, much of this is self-explanatory, and like the previous example, the key to understanding this macro is in the input patterns (highlighted). The voicemail module calls this macro with an argument of x:new or x:saved, representing the number of new or saved messages, respectively. The number of messages is captured in $1, and then type of messages (either new or saved) will be stored in $2. The macro uses $2 to determine whether to play voicemail/vm-new.wav or voicemail/vm-saved.wav, so that problem is easily solved. However, what about saying messages versus message?

Notice that the first input has an extra attribute, namely, break_on_match. By setting this attribute to true, we tell the macro to stop looking at the rest of the input patterns in the macro. If the user has a single new message, then the voicemail module will call this phrase with an argument of 1:new. (Likewise, it would call the argument with 1:saved for a single saved message.) The first pattern will match, and no more searching for matches will be performed. Then, the actions within the first <match> will be executed. In this case the Phrase Macro stitches together a phrase that says, "You have ... one ... new ... message". However, if there is more than one message (or zero messages), then the argument would be something like 2:new. In this case, the first input pattern match would fail, and then it would continue on to the second pattern, where it would match. The actions inside this <match> node would yield a phrase that says, "You have ... two ... new ... messages". By using a more specific input pattern first, along with setting break_on_match to true, and by using the more general input pattern second, we have a simple and elegant way of handling the plural problem that is common among many languages.

Keep these principles in mind as we will put them to good use in *Chapter 7, Dialplan Scripting with Lua*.

Advanced routing

IVRs are not just limited to menus. While you most likely want to program complex IVRs using a programming language, it's possible to use the built-in XML IVRs in other ways, too.

For example, let's say you wanted to require callers to enter a PIN number in order to reach a special answering service. You might create an IVR that contains the PIN number as the only available entry, and replace the sound files with a greeting, requesting the PIN number and the invalid entry sound with an invalid password message. The menu would be simple enough, as follows:

```
<menu name="enter_pin"
greet-long="phrase:enter_your_pin"
invalid-sound="phrase:invalid_pin"
exit-sound="phrase:invalid_pin"
timeout="15000"
max-failures="3"
max-timeouts="3">
   <entry digits="1828" action="menu-exec-app"
   param="transfer after_hours XML default"/>
</menu>
```

This would effectively create a prompt, requesting a password of 1828 as previously stated, and disconnect the caller after three failed attempts.

As another option, you might create an IVR that collects some data that is later used in your Dialplan. Let's say you wanted the caller to enter the caller ID that they want to appear on their next outgoing call. You could create an IVR to collect 10 digits, pass the result to another extension which sets the digits to the current caller ID, and then go to the final destination. Your IVR menu might look like the following:

```
<menu name="set_callerid"
greet-long="phrase:enter_your_callerid"
invalid-sound="phrase:invalid_callerid"
exit-sound="phrase:invalid_callerid"
timeout="15000"
digit_len="10"
max-failures="99"
max-timeouts="99">
  <entry digits="/^(\d{10})$/" action="menu-exec-app"
  param="transfer $1 XML set_callerid"/>
</menu>
```

You would then create a special context in your Dialplan, which might look like this:

```
<context name="set_callerid">
  <extension name="SetIt">
    <condition field="destination_number"
    expression="^(\d{10})$">
      <action application="set"
      data="effective_caller_id_number=$1"/>
      <action application="bridge"
      data="sofia/external/18005551212"/>
    </condition>
  </extension>
</context>
```

The combination of the preceding IVR and helper context would allow callers to enter their Caller ID, and have it set prior to the bridge application being called.

Summary

The IVR system within FreeSWITCH is a powerful, flexible tool to use when creating anything that gathers input from a caller. When combined with the various other applications in FreeSWITCH, the possibilities for routing callers using dynamic and creative call flows are endless.

Now that we have considered the XML IVR system and the Phrase Macro system, let's turn our attention to an alternative means of controlling complex interaction with the caller, that is, Dialplan scripting with the Lua programming language.

7
Dialplan Scripting with Lua

In the previous chapter, we discussed the basics of building **Interactive Voice Response (IVR)** applications using the built-in XML IVR engine. The XML IVR engine is useful for building simple IVR applications that are relatively static in nature. FreeSWITCH has other ways of building IVR applications that are more flexible and powerful than the built-in XML IVR engine. One way is by utilizing the various scripting languages that have been integrated into FreeSWITCH. FreeSWITCH supports the following scripting languages for building voice applications:

- JavaScript
- Lua
- Perl

Any of the preceding languages can be used for building IVR applications. In this chapter we will focus on using Lua (www.lua.org), a lightweight scripting language that is designed to be embedded within other projects. A famous example of which is *World of Warcraft*.

 Each of the scripting languages has its own advantages and drawbacks. Lua is a good choice because it is fast, scalable, and easy to learn. All things being equal, Lua is a good choice for almost any Dialplan script you would want to write.

This chapter will cover the following topics:

- Getting started with Lua
- Building voice applications
- Advanced IVR
- Scripting tips

As part of our building voice applications with Lua, we will make extensive use of custom phrase macros in our examples.

Getting started with Lua

Lua is built and loaded by default when using the example configuration. To confirm that you have Lua installed and running, open up `fs_cli` and issue the `lua` command. You should see something like this:

```
freeswitch@internal> lua
-ERR no reply
```

If you see an error that says **command not found** then you'll need to build and load mod_lua for your system. Use the same technique we employed for building and loading mod_flite. See the *Compiling FreeSWITCH for Linux/Unix/Mac OS X* section in *Chapter 2, Building and Installation* for details.

Running Lua scripts from the Dialplan

The `lua` Dialplan application is called from within the `<action>` tags using the familiar syntax:

```
<action application="lua"
  data="my_script.lua arg1 arg2 arg3"/>
```

Arguments passed to the script are separated by spaces. To include an argument that contains a space, use single quote characters to delimit the argument:

```
<action application="lua"
  data="my_script.lua 'arg 1' 'arg 2' 'arg 3'"/>
```

If you put your script in the `scripts` subdirectory under the main `FreeSWITCH` installation directory, then it is not necessary to specify the full path to your script file. If needed, you can use an absolute path. For example, in Linux/Unix environments, do the following:

```
<action application="lua" data="/full/path/to/my_script.lua"/>
```

In Windows:

```
<action application="lua"
  data="C:\full\path\to\my_script.lua"/>
```

Before we start writing scripts, let's take a brief look at the syntax of the Lua language.

Basic Lua syntax

Lua has a simple syntax that is easy both to learn and to read. The following is a simple script:

```lua
-- This is a sample Lua script
-- Single line comments begin with two dashes
--[[
  This is a multi-line comment.
  Everything between the double square brackets
    is part of the comment block.
]]
-- Lua is loosely typed
var = 1          -- This is a comment
var ="alpha"     -- Another comment
var ="A1"        -- You get the idea...
--[[
  When the Lua script is called from the dialplan
  you have a few magic objects. A handy one is
  the 'freeswitch' object which lets you do things
  like this:
  freeswitch.consoleLog("INFO","This is a log line\n")

  Another important one is the 'session' object which
  Lets you manipulate the call:
  session:answer()
  session:hangup()
]]
-- Lua makes extensive use of tables
-- Tables are a hybrid of arrays and associative arrays
val1 = 1
val2 = 2
my_table = {
    key1 = val1,
    key2 = val2,
  "index 1",
  "index 2"
}
```

```
freeswitch.consoleLog("INFO","my_table key1 is '" .. my_table["key1"]
.."'\n")
freeswitch.consoleLog("INFO","my_table index 1 is '" .. my_table[1]
.."'\n")
-- Access arguments passed in
arg1 = argv[1]      -- First argument
arg2 = argv[2]      -- Second argument
-- Simple if/then
if ( var =="A1" ) then
   freeswitch.consoleLog("INFO","var is 'A1'\n")
end
--   Simple if/then/else
if ( var =="A1" ) then
   freeswitch.consoleLog("INFO","var is 'A1'\n")
else
   freeswitch.consoleLog("INFO","var is not 'A1'!\n")
end
-- String concatenation uses ..
var ="This" .." and " .. "that"
freeswitch.consoleLog("INFO","var contains '" .. var .."'\n")
-- The end
```

Every Lua script that is executed from the Dialplan receives the `session` object, which represents the call leg that is being processed. The `session` object is the primary means of manipulating the call, and is used extensively in Lua scripting.

Building voice applications

Now that we have covered the basic Lua syntax, let's create a simple Lua script and the corresponding entry in the Dialplan. First, create a new Dialplan extension that will execute the Lua script when a user dials `9910`:

1. Open the `01_custom.xml` file that we created in *Chapter 5, Understanding the XML Dialplan*, and add the following new extension:

   ```
   <extension name="Simple Lua Test">
     <condition field="destination_number" expression="^(9910)$">
       <action application="lua" data="test1.lua"/>
     </condition>
   </extension>
   ```

2. Save the file, launch `fs_cli`, and issue `reloadxml`, or press the *F6* key:

Our Dialplan is now ready to call the Lua script named `test1.lua`. Create this new script as follows.

3. Using your text editor, create the `test1.lua` script in the `freeswitch/scripts/` directory, and add the following code lines:

```
-- test1.lua
-- Answer call, play a prompt, hang up
-- Set the path separator
pathsep = '/'
-- Windows users do this instead:
-- pathsep = '\'
-- Answer the call
session:answer()
-- Create a string with path and filename of a sound file
prompt ="ivr" .. pathsep .."ivr-welcome_to_freeswitch.wav"
-- Print a log message
freeswitch.consoleLog("INFO","Prompt file is '" .. prompt .."'\n")
-- Play the prompt
session:streamFile(prompt)
-- Hangup
session:hangup()
```

4. Save the file.

The preceding script is now ready for us to test. Using a phone that is registered on your FreeSWITCH server, dial `9910`. You will hear the sound prompt being played, and then the system will disconnect the call.

After editing and saving a Lua script, there is no need to execute `reloadxml`. As soon as the script file is saved, the `lua` application called from the Dialplan will use the updated script file.

Let's look at a few lines in this script and review their functions.

```
pathsep = '/'
```

This preceding code line creates a variable named `pathsep`, whose value is a single forward slash (/) character. This is used as the path separator for Linux/Unix based systems. Windows users will, of course, need to use the backslash (\) character as the path separator.

Using a path separator variable will make scripts more portable between operating systems.

```
session:answer()
```

The preceding code line answers the call. Most scripts will answer the call as their first action.

```
prompt ="ivr" .. pathsep .. "ivr-welcome_to_freeswitch.wav"
```

The preceding line creates a variable named `prompt` that contains the relative path to one of the included sound files.

```
freeswitch.consoleLog("INFO","Prompt file is '" .. prompt .. "'\n")
```

The preceding command will print a line of information to the FreeSWITCH console. It is very handy for troubleshooting and debugging. If you watch the FreeSWITCH console while calling 9910, you should see a line like the following in the output:

```
2012-10-11 16:46:50.770343 [INFO] switch_cpp.cpp:1227 Prompt file is
'ivr/ivr-welcome_to_freeswitch.wav'
```

Be sure to include a trailing newline sequence (\n) when using `freeswitch.consoleLog`.

```
session:streamFile(prompt)
```

The preceding code line uses the `session` object's `streamFile` method to play the audio file to the caller. Keep in mind that when specifying a relative path name, FreeSWITCH will actually find the file that matches the sample rate of the call. In many cases, this will be 8000, because the sampling rate of 8000 Hz (8 kHz) is typical for a phone call. In this example, the actual Linux path to the sound file is the following: `/usr/local/freeswitch/sounds/en/us/callie/ivr/8000/ivr-welcome_to_freeswitch.wav`.

A complete list of English sound files and their contents can be found in `docs/phrase/phrase_en.xml`, under the FreeSWITCH source directory.

The last code line simply hangs up the call, disconnecting the calling party:

```
session:hangup()
```

Building simple scripts with Lua is not at all difficult. Now let's write a script that does some basic interactions with the caller.

A simple IVR – interacting with the caller

Most IVR applications require some sort of input from the caller. For example, it is quite common for an IVR application to prompt the caller to enter a PIN or an account number, and then act accordingly. Let's write a small script that demonstrates how to collect some dialed digits from the caller, and read them back, using two different pronunciation methods:

1. Open the `01_custom.xml` file and add the following new extension:

    ```
    <extension name="Read Back Entered Digits">
      <condition field="destination_number" expression="^(9911)$">
        <action application="lua" data="read_back_digits.lua"/>
      </condition>
    </extension>
    ```

2. Save the file, launch `fs_cli`, and issue `reloadxml`, or press the *F6* key.

Our Dialplan is now ready to call the Lua script named `read_back_digits.lua`. Create this new script as follows:

1. Using your text editor create `read_back_digits.lua` in the `freeswitch/scripts/` directory and add the following code lines:

```
-- read_back_digits.lua
--Answer the call
session:answer()
-- Set the path separator
pathsep = '/'
-- Windows users do this instead:
-- pathsep = '\'
-- Set a variable that contains the sound prompt to play
prompt ="ivr" .. pathsep ..
"ivr-please_enter_extension_followed_by_pound.wav"
-- Set a variable that contains the invalid message to play
invalid ="ivr" .. pathsep ..
"ivr-that_was_an_invalid_entry.wav"
-- Play file and collect digits
-- Variable 'digits' will contain the digits collected
-- Valid input is 3 digits min, 5 digits max
-- Caller presses # (pound or hash) to finish
digits = session:playAndGetDigits(3, 5, 3, 7000,"#", prompt, invalid,
"\\d+")
-- Read back digits iterated, then pause
-- "one two three four five"
session:execute("say","en number iterated " .. digits)
session:sleep(1000)
```

```
-- Read back digits pronounced, then pause
-- "twelve thousand, three hundred forty-five"
session:execute("say","en number pronounced " .. digits)
session:sleep(1000)
-- Politely hang up
thankyou = "ivr" .. pathsep .. "ivr-Thank_you.wav"
goodbye  = "voicemail" .. pathsep .. "vm-goodbye.wav"
session:streamFile(thankyou)
session:sleep(250)
session:streamFile(goodbye)
-- Hangup
session:hangup()
```

2. Save the file.

This script is now ready for us to test. Dial 9911 and listen for the prompt, which will tell you to enter an extension. Key-in several digits and then press the # key. The system will read back the digits in iterated format (one-two-three-four), then in pronounced format (one thousand, two hundred thirty-four), and will finally say, "Thank you, goodbye," before hanging up. The playAndGetDigits method will also handle invalid input for you. Try entering only two digits or a star to hear the invalid entry dialog. If the caller makes three invalid entries then playAndGetDigits will disconnect.

Conditions and looping

The previous examples demonstrate a basic dialog with the caller. Let's now examine a script that will use conditionals and looping. We will also apply what we learned in *Chapter 6, Using XML IVRs and Phase Macros*, to create a new Phrase Macro to assemble several individual sound files into a larger sound prompt.

Let's create the Phrase Macro first. We need a Phrase Macro that will stitch together individual sounds files into a prompt that says, "To continue, press one; to exit, press two". We create a new file called custom-phrases.xml and add a new macro.

1. Open the file conf/lang/en/demo/custom-phrases.xml. Add the following code lines:

```
<macro name="read_digits2_phrase" pause="100">
  <input pattern="(.*)">
    <match>
      <action function="play-file" data="voicemail/vm-continue.wav"/>
      <action function="play-file" data="voicemail/vm-press.wav"/>
      <action function="play-file" data="digits/1.wav"/>
```

```
    <action function="execute" data="sleep(250)"/>
    <action function="play-file" data="voicemail/vm-to_exit.
    wav"/>
    <action function="play-file" data="voicemail/vm-press.wav"/>
    <action function="play-file" data="digits/2.wav"/>
    <action function="execute" data="sleep(250)"/>
  </match>
 </input>
</macro>
```

2. Save the file, launch `fs_cli`, and issue `reloadxml`, or press the *F6* key.

The Phrase Macro `read_digits2_phrase` is now ready to be used.

Remember that any time you edit an XML configuration file you need to issue the `reloadxml` command, or press *F6* at the FreeSWITCH command line. It is good to get into the habit of reloading your XML configuration whenever you make a change because this will make it easier to locate the source of any errors or typos.

3. Open the `01_custom.xml` file and add the following new extension:

```
<extension name="Read Back Entered Digits #2">
  <condition field="destination_number" expression="^(9912)$">
    <action application="lua" data="read_back_digits2.lua"/>
  </condition>
</extension>
```

4. Save the file, launch `fs_cli`, and issue `reloadxml`, or press *F6*.

Our Dialplan is now ready to call the Lua script named `read_back_digits2.lua`.

Create the following new script:

1. Using your text editor create `read_back_digits2.lua` in the `freeswitch/ scripts/` directory and add the following lines:

```
-- read_back_digits2.lua
-- Demonstrates while loop and session:ready()
--Answer the call
session:answer()
-- Set the path separator
pathsep = '/'
-- Windows users do this instead:
-- pathsep = '\'
-- Set a variable that contains the sound prompt to play
prompt = "ivr" .. pathsep ..
```

```
"ivr-please_enter_extension_followed_by_pound.wav"
-- Set a variable that contains the invalid message to play
invalid = "ivr" .. pathsep ..
"ivr-that_was_an_invalid_entry.wav"
-- Set a flag for continuing or exiting
continue = true
-- Initiate while loop
-- Loop continues until caller hangs up or chooses to exit
while(session:ready() == true and continue == true) do
    -- Play file and collect digits
    -- Variable 'digits' will contain the digits collected
    -- Valid input is 3 digits min, 5 digits max
    -- Caller presses # (pound or hash) to finish
    digits = session:playAndGetDigits(3, 5, 3, 7000, "#", prompt,
invalid, "\\d+")
    -- Read back digits iterated, then pause
    -- "one two three four five"
    session:execute("say","en number iterated " .. digits)
    session:sleep(1000)
    -- Read back digits pronounced, then pause
    -- "twelve thousand, three hundred forty-five"
    session:execute("say","en number pronounced " .. digits)
    session:sleep(1000)
    -- Ask caller to continue or exit
    digits = session:playAndGetDigits(1, 1, 2, 4000, "#",
"phrase:read_digits2_phrase", invalid, "\\d{1}")
    freeswitch.consoleLog("INFO","digits is '" .. digits .. "'\n")
 if (digits == "2") then
        continue = false
        freeswitch.consoleLog("INFO","Preparing to exit...\n")
    end
end
-- Politely hang up
thankyou = "ivr" .. pathsep .. "ivr-Thank_you.wav"
goodbye = "voicemail" .. pathsep .. "vm-goodbye.wav"
session:sleep(250)
session:streamFile(thankyou)
session:sleep(250)
session:streamFile(goodbye)
-- Hangup
session:hangup()
```

2. Save the file.

We are now ready to test. At the FreeSWITCH command line issue the command `/log 6` so that the debug messages are not displayed. Watch the console while you call the new extension. Dial `9912` and enter the value to be read back. After the value is read back, there will be a second prompt that will ask you to press *1* to continue, or to press *2* to exit. (Technically, any key other than *2* will continue the script.) Try both options and watch the console. You will see the console log messages from the script that print the digit you pressed.

Let's review the two highlighted lines from our script:

```
while(session:ready() == true and continue == true) do
```

This code line initiates the `while` loop. Notice that there are two conditions that must be true or the while loop will exit; namely, `session:ready()` must be `true` and the variable `continue` must also be `true`. The `session:ready()` method is a simple way to know whether or not the caller has hung up. When the caller hangs up, the `session:ready()` method will be a non-true value. The other condition is a test on the variable `continue`, which is a simple flag that we created and set to `true`. It stays `true` until the caller presses 2 when prompted to continue or exit, and at that time `continue` is set to `false`.

```
if (digits == "2") then
```

The preceding line simply checks if the caller pressed 2 in order to exit. If digits contain 2 then the script sets the value of `continue` to false, which causes the `while` loop to exit.

 Note that the information received from `play_and_get_digits` is a string value, not an integer. The digits dialed by the caller can include the * and # key.

This example demonstrates some simple ways to use conditionals to your advantage. The `session:ready()` method is an important tool to use when you need to break out of your script's main control loop if the caller hangs up.

Even more conditions and looping

Let's look back into what we have learned so far and create a simple utility script that lets the caller make recordings. The script will prompt the user for a series of digits, which it will use for the filename, allow the caller to record a prompt, give the caller a choice to accept or re-record, and finally, let the caller choose to record another prompt or exit the script. It will also introduce the concept of functions and using setInputCallback to handle certain key presses. Finally, we will create two new Phrase Macros and reuse an existing Phrase Macro. The basic call flow looks like the following diagram:

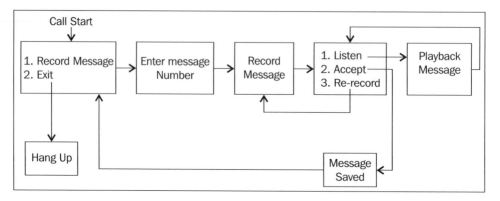

Start by adding the extension to the Dialplan as follows:

3. Open the 01_custom.xml file and add the following new extension:

```
<extension name="Record Sound Files Utility">
  <condition field="destination_number" expression="^(9913)$">
    <action application="lua" data="record_sound_files.lua"/>
  </condition>
</extension>
```

4. Save the file. Launch fs_cli and issue reloadxml, or press *F6*.

Our Dialplan is now ready to call the Lua script named record_sound_files. lua. Next, let's create some Phrase Macros. The first Phrase Macro tells the caller, "To record a greeting, press one; to exit, press two". Note that this Phrase Macro is almost identical to the read_digits2_phrase macro that we created in the previous example. The other Phrase Macro will tell the user to enter the message number (that is, the filename) and press pound (#). Add the two new Phrase Macros as shown in the following code snippet:

5. Open the file `conf/lang/en/demo/custom-phrases.xml` and add these code lines:

```xml
<macro name="record_greeting_or_exit" pause="100">
  <input pattern="(.*)">
    <match>
      <action function="play-file"
        data="voicemail/vm-to_record_greeting.wav"/>
      <action function="play-file"
        data="voicemail/vm-press.wav"/>
      <action function="play-file" data="digits/1.wav"/>
      <action function="execute" data="sleep(250)"/>
      <action function="play-file"
        data="voicemail/vm-to_exit.wav"/>
      <action function="play-file"
        data="voicemail/vm-press.wav"/>
      <action function="play-file" data="digits/2.wav"/>
      <action function="execute" data="sleep(250)"/>
    </match>
  </input>
</macro>
<macro name="enter_message_number" pause="100">
  <input pattern="(.*)">
    <match>
      <action function="play-file"
        data="ivr/ivr-please_enter_the.wav"/>
      <action function="play-file" data="ivr/ivr-file.wav"/>
      <action function="play-file" data="ivr/ivr-number.wav"/>
      <action function="execute" data="sleep(250)"/>
      <action function="play-file" data="currency/and.wav"/>
      <action function="play-file"
        data="voicemail/vm-press.wav"/>
      <action function="play-file" data="digits/pound.wav"/>
      <action function="execute" data="sleep(250)"/>
    </match>
  </input>
</macro>
```

6. Save the file, launch `fs_cli`, and issue `reloadxml`, or press *F6*.

The Phrase Macro `record_greeting_or_exit` and `enter_message_number` are now ready to be used. Finally, create the new script as follows:

1. Using your text editor, create `record_sound_files.lua` in the `freeswitch/scripts/` directory and add the following lines:

```lua
-- record_sound_files.lua
-- Lets user record one or more sound files
-- Sounds are stored in ${sounds_dir}
-- Input Callback to handle digits dialed during the recording
function onInput (s, type, obj)
  if ( type == 'dtmf' ) then
      return "break"  -- This ends the recording
  end
end
-- Answer the call
session:answer()
session:sleep(500)
-- Set the path separator
pathsep = '/'
-- Windows users do this instead:
-- pathsep = '\'
-- Set a variable that contains the sound prompt to play
prompt = "ivr" .. pathsep ..
"ivr-please_enter_extension_followed_by_pound.wav"
-- Set a variable that contains the invalid message to play
invalid ="ivr" .. pathsep ..
"ivr-that_was_an_invalid_entry.wav"
-- Set a flag for continuing or exiting
continue = true
-- Specify action when digits are dialed during the recording
session:setInputCallback("onInput","")
-- Initiate while loop
-- Loop continues until caller hangs up or chooses to exit
while(session:ready() and continue) do
  -- First menu:
  -- 1 = Record
  -- 2 = Exit
  digits = session:playAndGetDigits(1, 1, 3, 7000, "#",
"phrase:record_greeting_or_exit", invalid, "\\d{1}")
  if (digits == "2") then
    continue = false
    freeswitch.consoleLog("INFO","Preparing to exit...\n")
  else
      -- Collect message number from caller
```

```
-- Variable 'digits' will contain the digits collected
-- Valid input is 3 digits min, 5 digits max
-- Caller presses # (pound or hash) to finish
msgnum = session:playAndGetDigits(3, 5, 3, 7000, "#",
"phrase:enter_message_number", invalid, "\\d+")
-- Read back the message number
session:execute("say","en number iterated " .. msgnum)
session:sleep(1000)
-- New loop: accepted or not
accepted = false
while (session:ready() and not accepted) do
  -- Record ile
  session:streamFile("phrase:voicemail_record_message")
  -- Play a "bong" tone prior to recording
  session:streamFile("tone_stream://v=-
7;%(100,0,941.0,1477.0);v=-7;>=2;+=.1;%(1000, 0, 640)")
  filename = session:getVariable('sounds_dir') .. pathsep ..
msgnum .. ".wav"
  session:recordFile(filename,300,100,10)
  -- New loop: Ask caller to listen, accept, or re-record
  listen = true
  while ( session:ready() and listen ) do
    session:streamFile(filename)
    -- Use handy record_file_check macro courtesy of the
voicemail module
    local digits = session:playAndGetDigits(1, 1, 2, 4000,
"#", "phrase:voicemail_record_file_check:1:2:3", invalid,
"\\d{1}")
    if (digits == "1") then
      listen = true
      accepted = false
      session:execute("sleep","500")
    elseif (digits == "2") then
      listen = false
      accepted = true
      -- Let the caller know that the message is saved
      -- NOTE: you could put these into a Phrase Macro as well
      session:streamFile("voicemail/vm-message.wav")
      session:execute("sleep","100")
      session:execute("say","en number iterated " .. msgnum)
      session:execute("sleep","100")
      session:streamFile("voicemail/vm-saved.wav")
      session:execute("sleep","1500")
    elseif ( digits =="3" ) then
      listen = false
```

```
            accepted = false
            session:execute("sleep","500")
          end -- if ( digits == "1" )
        end -- while ( listen )
      end -- while ( not accepted )
    end -- if ( digits == "2" )
  end -- while ( session:ready() )
  -- Let's be polite
  thankyou = "ivr" .. pathsep .. "ivr-Thank_you.wav"
  goodbye  = "voicemail" .. pathsep .. "vm-goodbye.wav"
  session:sleep(250)
  session:streamFile(thankyou)
  session:sleep(250)
  session:streamFile(goodbye)
  -- Hangup
  session:hangup()
```

2. Save the file.

Test the script by dialing 9913. The first menu simply says, "To record a greeting, press one; to exit, press two". Press 1. The system will then ask for a message number followed by the pound (#) sign. Key-in 1234#. Next, you will be prompted to record a message. Record a message and then press any digit or stop talking to finish. The recording will be played back and then you will be in the last menu with the following options: listen, accept, or re-record. Try each one to see how the script operates. You may record as many files as you need.

 The recordings are located in the sounds directory. To see the sounds directory, go to fs_cli and issue the following command: eval ${sounds_dir}. Also, note that the recordFile method will overwrite any existing files without warning, so be careful!

Let's review a few key parts of this script in the following way, starting with the onInput function:

```
function onInput (s, type, obj)
    if ( type == 'dtmf' ) then
        return "break"  -- This ends the recording
    end
end
```

This function simply tests the type of input and returns a value of `"break"` if the user dialed a DTMF digit. When, though, is this function executed? It is closely related to this line of code, which is found later in the script:

```
session:setInputCallback("onInput", "")
```

The `setInputCallback` method specifies what to do when the caller dials a digit. Whenever a digit is dialed, the function specified here is called. (Note that this does not apply when executing `session:playAndGetDigits`, which handles digits on its own.) In our script, the function `onInput` is called whenever the caller dials a digit.

The function simply returns `"break"`, which stops both the recording and playback. So, not only can you stop recording by pressing a digit, you can also skip past the playback of various prompts. Dial 9913 again and when you get to the voice prompt that says, "Record your message at the tone", press a digit to skip past it.

Notice that we nested a pair of `while` loops inside of the main `while` loop. The main `while` loop continues to execute until the caller hangs up or presses 2 to exit. The middle `while` loop continues until the variable `accepted` is `true`. The inner `while` loop continues until the variable `listen` is `false`. The inner `while` loop allows the caller to listen to his or her recording as often as desired before accepting it, and the middle `while` loop allows the caller to re-record the file as many times as desired. The outer `while` loop lets callers record as many different sound files as they wish.

You probably noticed that we have a `session:ready()` check in each `while` loop. This is necessary to handle the case where the caller hangs up in the middle of processing a `while` loop. As a rule of thumb, any time you have a `while` loop in a Dialplan script you should check the status of `session:ready()`. Failure to do so could lead to zombie Lua scripts waiting for input from a session that has long since disconnected!

The script records all sound files as `.wav` files. You can change the file type by choosing a different file extension, such as `.ul` or `.gsm`. However, the FreeSWITCH developers recommend using `.wav` files, unless there is an extremely compelling reason not to do so.

There is one other curious line of code, which is as follows:

```
session:streamFile("tone_stream://v=-
7;%(100,0,941.0,1477.0);v=-7;>=2;+=.1;%(1000, 0, 640)")
```

The preceding line uses the built-in **Tone Generation Markup Language (TGML)** to create the "bong" tone played to the caller just prior to recording. FreeSWITCH allows you to create and playback a wide array of tones. See `http://wiki.freeswitch.org/wiki/TGML` for more information.

Using a combination of playing sound files, accepting caller input via touch-tones, as well as recording the caller's voice, you can easily build custom voice applications.

 More information about Lua and the session object can be found online at `http://wiki.freeswitch.org/wiki/Mod_lua`.

Up to this point, what we have accomplished with Lua is similar to what we did with the XML IVR engine. Let's now consider some advanced concepts that explicitly show the advantages of using a scripting language.

Advanced IVR concepts

In addition to important programming constructs such as conditionals and looping, there are other things that are possible by utilizing a scripting language. One of the advanced functions of a really useful IVR is the ability to interact with a third-party database. In some cases, this is a simple web lookup function. In other cases, it involves asking the caller for an account or ID number and a PIN code, and then polling a database. Let's consider simple examples of each method.

Connecting to a database with LuaSQL

The LuaSQL interface implements a simple interface between Lua and a DBMS. (The LuaSQL interface is provided by the Kepler project. More information is available at `http://www.keplerproject.org/luasql/`.)

 The examples in this section require some working knowledge of databases and the ability to compile LuaSQL, for the target database type to which you will be connecting. It is beyond the scope of this book to describe all the possible installation scenarios. The examples presented here were done on a 32-bit Debian 6 installation using PostgreSQL 9.1.5.

Set up your database to use the examples presented as follows:

1. Create a database user named `fsuser` with a password `fspass`.
2. Create a database named `fsbook`.

3. Create a table named `users`:

```
CREATE TABLE users (
    name character varying(20),
    pin integer,
    acct integer,
    balance numeric(9,2),
    PRIMARY KEY(acct)
);
```

4. Add some data as follows:

```
INSERT INTO users(name, pin, acct, balance) VALUES('Anthony',
7654,9898, 123.45);
INSERT INTO users(name, pin, acct, balance) VALUES('Michael',
9642,1771, 0.00);
INSERT INTO users(name, pin, acct, balance) VALUES('Darren',
3756,2316, 15.75);
```

Test to make sure that you can log in to your database with your username; otherwise, the Lua script will not be able to communicate with your database.

Add a new extension in the following way.

5. Open the `01_custom.xml` file and add the following new extension:

```
<extension name="Simple db connection">
  <condition field="destination_number" expression="^(9914)$">
    <action application="lua" data="db_connect.lua"/>
  </condition>
</extension>
```

6. Save the file, launch `fs_cli`, and issue `reload_xml`, or press *F6*.

Our Dialplan is now ready to call the Lua script named `db_connect.lua`. Our script will demonstrate the basic concepts of connecting to the database and performing an SQL query. We will accept an account number and PIN from the caller, query the database, check the PIN, and if it is correct, the script will read the customer's balance. Let's create our script in the following way.

7. Using your text editor create `db_connect.lua` in the `freeswitch/scripts/` directory and add the following lines:

```
-- db_connect.lua
-- Connects to a database, checks PIN, reads balance

-- Load the LuaSQL
```

```
require "luasql.postgres"

-- A hangup function makes the code a bit cleaner
function hangup_call ()
  session:streamFile("ivr/ivr-Thank_you.wav")
  session:sleep(250)
  session:streamFile("voicemail/vm-goodbye.wav")
  session:hangup()
end

-- Clean up if necessary
function close_db_conn()
  cur:close()
  con:close()
  env:close()
end

-- Create database environment object
env = assert (luasql.postgres())

-- Create database connection object
con = assert (env:connect("fsbook","fsuser","fspass","localhost"))

-- Set invalid entry file
invalid = "ivr/ivr-that_was_an_invalid_entry.wav"

-- Greet caller
session:answer()
session:streamFile("ivr/ivr-hello.wav")

tries = 0
while (session:ready() == true and tries < 3) do
-- Collect account number
  acct = session:playAndGetDigits(3, 5, 3, 7000, "#",
"phrase:enter_message_number", invalid, ".+")

  -- Pull account from database
  cur = assert(con:execute("SELECT * FROM users WHERE acct = '" ..
acct .. "'"))

  -- Get the results, indexed alphanumerically by column names
  row = cur:fetch ({}, "a")

  -- Confirm that we received the record
  if (cur:numrows() == 1) then
    -- We have an account, now collect PIN and check
    tries = 0
    while (tries < 3) do
      pin = session:playAndGetDigits(3, 5, 3, 7000, "#", "ivr/ivr-
please_enter_pin_followed_by_pound.wav", invalid, "\\d+")
```

```
        if (pin == row.pin) then
          bal = row.balance
          user_repeat = true
          while(session:ready() == true and user_repeat == true) do
            session:streamFile("voicemail/vm-you_have.wav")
            session:execute("sleep",200)
            session:execute("say", "en currency pronounced " .. bal)
            session:execute("sleep",200)
            digits = session:playAndGetDigits(1,1,3,7000,"#","ivr/
ivr-to_repeat_these_options.wav",invalid,"\\d+") -- repeat y/n
            freeswitch.consoleLog("INFO","User entered '" .. digits
.. "'\n")
            if (digits == "1") then
              user_repeat = true
            else
              close_db_conn()
              hangup_call()
              break
            end
          end
        else
          -- Caller entered wrong PIN
          session:streamFile("ivr/ivr-that_was_an_invalid_entry.
wav")
          tries = tries + 1;
        end
      end
    if (tries > 2) then
      -- Too many failed attempts to enter PIN
      session:streamFile("voicemail/vm-abort.wav")
      close_db_conn()
      hangup_call()
      break
    end
  else
    -- We did not find this account
    session:streamFile(invalid)
    tries = tries + 1;
  end
end -- while (tries < 3)

if (tries > 2) then
  session:streamFile("voicemail/vm-abort.wav")
  close_db_conn()
  hangup_call()
end
```

8. Save the file.

Test the new extension by dialing 9914. Enter in a four-digit account number that is found in the database and press #. In our example, you could enter 1771. Enter the corresponding PIN number for the account and press #. The system will do a database lookup and then read back the account balance. Try different combinations of valid and invalid account numbers and PIN numbers, to see how the script handles errors.

Let's review the important new features presented in this script. You will first notice that we used a pair of functions. These are not required. However, they make the code more readable. The function hangup_call simply ends the call. The function close_db_conn closes the database connection that we opened. These functions are called in various places in our script so that we can exit the script smoothly.

The database connectivity occurs with several lines in particular, which are highlighted:

```
require "luasql.postgres"
```

This line simply loads the luasql.postgres module. Depending on your database environment, it could be luasql.mysql, luasql.odbc, or even luasql.oci8 for Oracle databases.

 Some users have experienced a memory leak when using the MySQL connector with LuaSQL. If you wish to use MySQL as your database then you should strongly consider using the ODBC connector.

This line creates a database environment object for us to use:

```
env = assert (luasql.postgres())
```

This line does a little more work. It actually creates a connection object which allows us to talk to our database:

```
con = assert (env:connect("fsbook","fsuser","fspass", "localhost"))
```

The arguments to use the connect action are as follows:

*   Database name
*   Username
*   Password
*   Host name or IP address

If the connection is successful, then the connection object allows us to perform SQL queries on the target database.

```
cur = assert(con:execute("SELECT * FROM users WHERE acct = '" .. acct
.. "'"))
```

This line actually performs a SQL SELECT function on the users table in the target database. It returns a cursor object. The cursor object represents the results of the SQL statement performed on the target database. Our example uses the cursor object to return a row of data as follows:

```
row = cur:fetch ({}, "a")
```

The fetch method takes two arguments, namely, a Lua table name (optional), and either "a" or "n" to represent the kind of indices the row object will have:

- "a": This means alphanumeric indices; the columns will be accessed by the name of the column

- "n" **(default)**: This means numeric indices; the columns will be accessed by the numeric index of the field positions in the row

The table is an optional argument which will populate a Lua table with the row data. In our example, we pass in empty braces ({}) to indicate that we will not be using a Lua table. The fetch method will return a row of data or nil, if no more data is found. Note that a SELECT can return zero, one, or more rows of data. The fetch method allows the programmer to cycle through the results, one row at a time. In our example, we selected a row of data based on the acct field, which is a primary key, so our result would be either contain no records or one record. We double-check our results as follows:

```
if (cur:numrows() == 1) then
```

The PostgreSQL, MySQL, and Oracle LuaSQL drivers all support the numrows() method. In our example, we want to know if we received back exactly one row of data, which corresponds to the account number that the caller entered. We make the assumption that if the query did not return exactly one row of data, then the caller entered an invalid account number. Once it is established that a valid account has been entered, we then check to see if the caller entered the correct PIN as follows:

```
if (pin == row.pin) then
```

This check makes sure that the caller entered the PIN that is read from the database. If not, the caller is prompted again to enter the PIN. Three wrong attempts will cause the script to exit.

 More information about connection and cursor objects can be found at the following website: `http://www.keplerproject.org/luasql/manual.html`

Connecting to databases is relatively straightforward using LuaSQL. Now let's consider an alternative method of connecting to an external data source.

Making a web call with curl

Sometimes it is useful to make a web call from your script. There are varied applications where this is used, such as checking a news or weather feed, or integrating a voice application with a web application. In this example, we will do a very simple web call to get the UTC time from the U.S. Navy website, which returns the data in an easily parseable manner. We will also introduce a few new concepts, including using the `freeswitch.API` object, passing arguments to a Phrase Macro, and using Lua's string manipulation functions to do pattern-matching and data extraction.

The first step is to install `mod_curl`, which we can do just like we did with `mod_flite` in *Chapter 2, Building and Installation*. Perform the following steps:

1. Open `modules.conf` in the `FreeSWITCH` source directory and locate the following line:

   ```
   #applications/mod_curl
   ```

   Remove the # and save the file.

2. Open `modules.conf.xml` in the `conf/autoload_configs` directory and locate the following line:

   ```
   <!-- <load module="mod_curl"/> -->
   ```

   Remove the `<!--` and `-->` tags and save the file.

3. Build and compile `mod_curl` from the FreeSWITCH source directory:

   ```
   make mod_curl-install
   ```

4. Wait for the installation to finish and then restart FreeSWITCH. Launch `fs_cli` and type `help`. If `mod_curl` loaded successfully, then you will see that `curl` is now available as an API command, with the syntax listed as follows:

```
curl,curl url [headers|json] [get|head|post [url_encoded_
data]],curl API,mod_curl
```

Next, add a new extension to the Dialplan as follows:

1. Open the `01_custom.xml` file and add the following new extension:

```xml
<extension name="Web Lookup">
  <condition field="destination_number" expression="^(9915)$">
    <action application="lua" data="web-lookup.lua"/>
  </condition>
</extension>
```

2. Save the file, launch `fs_cli`, and issue `reloadxml`, or press *F6*.

Our Dialplan is now ready to call the Lua script named `web-lookup.lua`. Now let's create a new Phrase Macro that will accept an `hh:mm:ss` argument and read back the time. Perform these steps:

1. Open the file `conf/lang/en/demo/custom-phrases.xml`. Add the following lines:

```xml
<macro name="simple_time" pause="50">
  <input pattern="(\d\d):(\d\d):(\d\d)">
    <match>
      <action function="execute" data="sleep(250)"/>
      <action function="say" data="$1" method="pronounced"
      type="number"/>
      <action function="execute" data="sleep(50)"/>
      <action function="say" data="$2" method="pronounced"
      type="number"/>
      <action function="execute" data="sleep(50)"/>
      <action function="play-file" data="currency/and.wav"/>
      <action function="execute" data="sleep(50)"/>
      <action function="say" data="$3" method="pronounced"
      type="number"/>
      <action function="execute" data="sleep(50)"/>
      <action function="play-file" data="time/seconds.wav"/>
      <action function="execute" data="sleep(250)"/>
    </match>
  </input>
</macro>
```

2. Save the file, launch `fs_cli`, and issue `reloadxml`, or press *F6*.

The Phrase Macro `simple_time` is now ready to be used. It accepts the time argument in `hh:mm:ss` format and applies the input pattern of `(\d\d):(\d\d):(\d\d)` to receive the variables `$1`, `$2`, and `$3` which contain the hour, minutes, and seconds, respectively. Finally, create the new Lua script as follows:

1. Using your text editor create `web-lookup.lua` in the `freeswitch/scripts/` directory and add the following lines:

```
-- web-lookup.lua
-- Makes a curl call to http://tycho.usno.navy.mil/cgi-bin/timer.
pl
-- Extracts time information and reads back to caller

-- Set a variable with the target URL
web_url = "http://tycho.usno.navy.mil/cgi-bin/timer.pl"

-- Number of times we've read time to caller
num_reads = 0

-- Get a FreeSWITCH API object
api = freeswitch.API()

session:answer()

while(session:ready() == true and num_reads < 10) do
  freeswitch.consoleLog("INFO","URL:   " .. web_url .. "\n")
  raw_data = api:execute("curl", web_url)
  freeswitch.consoleLog("INFO","Raw data:\n" .. raw_data ..
"\n\n")

  -- Look for line that matches <BR>MMM. dd, hh:mm:ss UTC
  date_time = string.match(raw_data,"<BR>.-UTC",1)
  if (date_time == nil) then
    freeswitch.consoleLog("INFO","UTC date and time not found\n")
  else
    freeswitch.consoleLog("INFO","UTC date and time is '" .. date_
time .. "'\n")

    -- Now parse out the individual elements into smaller strings
    time = string.gsub(date_time,".-(%d+:%d+:%d+).+","%1")
    freeswitch.consoleLog("INFO","Time is '" .. time .. "'\n\n")
    session:streamFile("phrase:simple_time:" .. time)
  end

  num_reads = num_reads + 1
  session:execute("sleep","1000")
end

session:hangup()
```

2. Save the file.

Dial 9915 and listen. The script will perform the web lookup using the FreeSWITCH's curl API. If the call is successful, the raw data is parsed to extract the hour, minutes, and seconds, after which those values are passed into the simple_ time Phrase Macro. The macro then reads back the time to the caller. After 10 cycles the script will exit. You may hang up at any time.

> Be sure that your FreeSWITCH server has Internet access, otherwise the web-lookup.lua script will fail.

Let's review the new concepts presented in this example. Notice the following two related lines of code:

```
api = freeswitch.API()

raw_data = api:execute("curl", web_url)
```

The first line creates a FreeSWITCH API object, which allows us to send API commands from our script. (Remember, API commands are those that are sent from the FreeSWITCH command line.) The second line actually executes the curl command and captures the result. The script prints the raw data from the curl call, which generally looks like the following:

```
<!DOCTYPE HTML PUBLIC"-//W3C//DTD HTML 3.2 Final"//EN>
<html>
  <body>
    <TITLE>What time is it"</TITLE>
    <H2> US Naval Observatory Master Clock Time</H2> <H3><PRE>
    <BR>Feb. 28, 06:39:03 UTC    Universal Time
    <BR>Feb. 28, 01:39:03 AM EST   Eastern Time
    <BR>Feb. 28, 12:39:03 AM CST   Central Time
    <BR>Feb. 27, 11:39:03 PM MST   Mountain Time
    <BR>Feb. 27, 10:39:03 PM PST   Pacific Time
    <BR>Feb. 27, 09:39:03 PM AKST   Alaska Time
    <BR>Feb. 27, 08:39:03 PM HAST   Hawaii-Aleutian Time
    </PRE></H3><P><A HREF="http://www.usno.navy.mil"> US Naval
    Observatory</A>
  </body>
</html>
```

All this data comes in a single string of text. The following line of code extracts the line of text with the UTC time:

```
date_time = string.match(raw_data,"<BR>.-UTC",1)
```

The `date_time` variable now contains `<BR>Feb. 28, 06:39:03` UTC. The `string.match` function applies a pattern-match on the `raw_data` string. The pattern we match against is `<BR>.-UTC`. There are two meta-characters in this pattern, namely, the period and the dash. The other characters are literal. In plain language this pattern reads, "match a string of text beginning with '<BR>' and any subsequent characters until UTC is found". The `.-` means, "match as few characters as possible".

Lua string manipulation functions are documented online at `http://www.lua.org/manual/5.1/manual.html#5.4`.

Now that we have a single line of text, we need to extract the hour, minute, and second of the time:

```
time = string.gsub(date_time,".-(%d+:%d+:%d+).+","%1")
```

This line uses the `string.gsub` function to perform a "match and modify" function on a particular string. The arguments to `string.gsub` are the string to match, the pattern to match against, and the "replacement" value. In our example, we want to extract the `hour:minute:second` information from the string. The `string.gsub` function works by matching a part or all of the input string and then returning a replacement value. This is somewhat different from many other languages' string handling and pattern-matching. However, it is just as effective. The pattern that we use in this case is as follows:

```
.-(%d+:%d+:%d+).+
```

This pattern matches, from the beginning of the string, as few characters as possible until it reaches the time value. It "captures" the time value (`hh:mm:ss`), and then continues matching until the end of the string. The `hh:mm:ss` value is represented by `%1`. Putting `%1` as the "replacement" argument causes `string.gsub` to return only the captured data, which is precisely what we want. Now that we have the time information, we can pass it to our Phrase Macro in the following way:

```
session:streamFile("phrase:simple_time:" .. time)
```

The time value in the format `hh:mm:ss` is passed into the Phrase Macro, where it is matched against the input pattern as follows:

```
<input pattern="(\d\d):(\d\d):(\d\d)">
```

The hour, minute, and second values get captured in $1, $2, and $3 respectively, and are read back to the caller. The script then repeats nine more times and hangs up, unless the caller hangs up first.

In some cases, it is necessary to encode and decode string data. For reference, the following are some of the functions that you can use to URL-encode and URL-decode strings as needed in your web calls:

```
function urldecode (s)
  return (string.gsub (string.gsub (s, "+",""),
         "%%(%x%x)",
         function (str)
           return string.char (tonumber (str, 16))
           end ))
end

function urlencode (s)
  return (string.gsub (s,"%W",
         function (str)
            return string.format ("%%%02X", string.byte (str))
         end))
end
```

By now it is probably apparent that retrieving external data (via a database connection or web lookup) is relatively straightforward. The real work is in handling the possible exceptions and acting upon the retrieved data.

Lua patterns versus regular expressions

Technically speaking, Lua does not natively support regular expressions. However, the Lua pattern-matching syntax has many similarities to traditional **Perl Compatible Regular Expressions (PCRE)**. The following table shows Lua patterns and the PCRE equivalents:

Lua Metacharacter	PCRE Metacharacter
.	.
+	+
-	*?
*	*
%	\

The following table shows the Lua character classes and their PCRE equivalents:

Lua Character Class	PCRE Character Class
%d	\d
%w	\w
%s	\s

Complete Lua pattern syntax documentation can be found at `http://www.lua.org/manual/5.1/manual.html#5.4.1`.

With a little practice, anyone familiar with regular expressions will be able to write effective Lua patterns.

Scripting tips

There are a few things to keep in mind when working with Lua scripts from the Dialplan:

- When a Lua script is finished, the call automatically hangs up. If you wish for the Dialplan to continue processing, be sure to execute `session:setAutoHangup(false)`. Consider the following Dialplan snippet:

```
<condition>
    <action application="lua" data="my_script.lua"/>
    <!--the following is not executed unless setAutoHangup is
        false -->
    <action application="transfer" data="$1 XML default"/>
</condition>
```

- The proper way to exit a Lua script is for the script to run out of commands. As of the previous edition of this publication, there was no explicit command to exit a script; however, you may now use the `error()` function to force the script to terminate. If `session:setAutoHangup(false)` has been set, then the Dialplan will continue to process.

- Keeping the previous point in mind, note that calling `session:bridge()` or `session:transfer()` may not work as you expect. The `bridge` or `transfer` action will not occur until the script exits. Consider the following code snippet:

```
freeswitch.consoleLog("INFO","Before transfer...\n")
session:transfer("9664 XML default")
freeswitch.consoleLog("INFO","After transfer...\n")
```

The `transfer` action will not occur until after the second `consoleLog` call and any subsequent lines of code are executed. If you wish to use the `bridge` or `transfer` action then be sure that they occur at the logical end of your script.

- Do not use Lua (or any other scripting language) as a replacement for the Dialplan. The XML Dialplan is extremely efficient at routing calls and no scripting language can compete with it. Use Lua for interacting with the caller, or, to perform functions that are not easily executed in the Dialplan. A good rule of thumb is that if you *can* do it in the Dialplan, you *should* do it in the Dialplan.

- Do not overuse scripts called from the Dialplan. If you find that you are trying to build elaborate scripts to control calls, do inline billing, third-party call control, and so on. Then it is most likely you need to use the event socket *Chapter 10, Controlling FreeSWITCH Externally*, details some of the amazing things that are possible using the event socket.

Summary

Lua is a great choice for building simple and elegant voice applications for interacting with callers. It is very lightweight and is therefore scalable. It has a simple syntax that is easy to learn and there is ample online documentation.

In this chapter, we accomplished a number of objectives:

- Became acquainted with basic Lua syntax and control structures
- Wrote several scripts that demonstrate how to interact with a caller, including answering, hanging up, playing sound files, playing Phrase Macros, and accepting input from the caller
- Learned how to use the `freeswitch` object to send log messages to the console and to execute API commands
- Installed LuaSQL and demonstrated how to connect to a PostgreSQL database from within a Lua script
- Built `mod_curl` and enabled it to be loaded by default
- Demonstrated the use of curl requests to perform web calls from within a Lua script
- Became familiar with Lua's pattern-matching syntax

Now that we have a basis for writing scripts to interact with a caller, it is time to revisit the Dialplan. The following chapter will review a few concepts introduced in *Chapter 5, Understanding the XML Dialplan*, and then take your understanding of the Dialplan to a whole new level.

8
Advanced Dialplan Concepts

In the preceding chapters you learned a bit about the power of the XML configuration files used in FreeSWITCH. Specifically, you learned about Dialplan entries and using XML to set general configuration settings. In this chapter, we will dive deep into the general structure of Dialplan, features of the XML Dialplan processing system, and how you can use what appears to be the very basic features to achieve very complex results.

Some items in this chapter may appear to be repetitive, but we want to go back over some basic Dialplan functionality talked about in the earlier chapters, and be sure we explain the hows and whys of the Dialplan system. It is quite common for people to use the XML Dialplan in FreeSWITCH without really understanding it, hampering efforts to extend the system or debug complex problems. This chapter aims to make you an expert at exactly how and why things operate the way they do within the Dialplan.

In this chapter, we will presume you have some basic understanding of how FreeSWITCH routes and processes calls, and have seen some XML configurations. Configuring and placing some phone calls on a demo FreeSWITCH installation would work for your benefit prior to reading this chapter.

In this chapter we will discuss the following topics:

- Dialplan overview
- General Dialplan concepts
- Parsing and executing
- XML Dialplan module
- XML Dialplan pre-processing
- Utilizing variables
- Testing variables with regular expressions
- Passing variables to other legs

- Macros in Dialplans
- Pitfalls to avoid
- Multiple extensions on the same pass
- Special attributes of the XML extensions
- Alternatives to XML

Dialplan overview

The Dialplan engine in FreeSWITCH is an incredibly flexible piece of software. If you have a background of using other switching systems, you are probably familiar with Dialplan concepts being tied to a somewhat flat and static set of logic statements—you pre-program a set of decisions in the switch's native language (that is, answer calls, play files, collect digits, and transfer calls) and this happens for every call. Anything that cannot be done using the pre-built commands and logic statements available in that switch, well, they just cannot be done.

In FreeSWITCH, Dialplan processing is actually done by loadable modules. The logic in these modules is utilized every time a call is handled, and you can load multiple Dialplan modules to process calls in different ways, depending on the logic you need. This is a very important distinction between FreeSWITCH and other systems, and it is often overlooked. By making Dialplan processing modular, a new form of freedom is introduced to the way in which the calls are routed. You can write your own module or use alternative modules to open up new subsets of commands for processing your Dialplan. This freedom is comparable to other switches that allow you to invoke external scripts to handle your Dialplan. FreeSWITCH gives you tighter integration by keeping everything in C and allowing you to utilize its internal APIs and/or linked libraries (if necessary), as opposed to external calls to scripting languages. This allows processing to take place with a much lower cost for resources on your system.

Why make Dialplan processing modular? It is important to first understand why we have a Dialplan.

Let's forget about programming for a while and review a philosophy on what people want to get out of their switching system. If you break down most call handling in any voice system, you'll see that almost everything phone calls do traverses a flowchart-style logic design. In fact, if you ask people how they want their phone to behave, they often begin reciting yes/no decisions or points to take action, which can almost always be turned into a basic flowchart. No matter what you are trying to do, if you charted out your entire decision-making process as a flowchart, you have just designed your Dialplan. Inherently, you have also envisioned the requirements of decisions a Dialplan module must be able to handle.

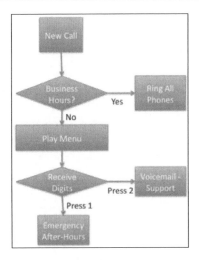

Let us take an example of a common call flow and break it apart. On close examination of the example shown here, this flowchart makes a lot of assumptions about pieces of information and logic that the Dialplan must be able to process. For example, in order to make a decision about whether or not you are currently open for business, the Dialplan processor must have access to the system's date and time, and you should be able to compare it with the time of day you are open or closed. To make the decision about whether your caller is pressing 1, the Dialplan processor must have the ability to interpret touch-tones. Based on the conditions being compared, you must then be able to do something with the call — transfer it, play a file, hang up, and so on. All these requirements make up the logic and syntactical commands that the Dialplan will utilize. In many systems, the ability to make these decisions is done by writing somewhat cryptic configuration code that can lead to certain limitations and drive you nuts. In FreeSWITCH, the logic can exist in different languages or you can write your own language.

Looking back into the history, no vision of an interpreter of Dialplan commands has been perfect. From one system to the next, the way people structure their commands for how to handle calls has changed. FreeSWITCH's forward-thinking developers knew this, so they decided to make the actual Dialplan command processing itself modular.

The technical advantages of having loadable Dialplan modules are numerous. Firstly, the switching system itself can now provide links to any existing external libraries (such as SQL libraries, YAML libraries, CURL HTTP libraries, and likewise), in order to retrieve your Dialplan configuration and turn it into the expected style of logic that FreeSWITCH needs for processing the call. Secondly, the Dialplan processing module can rely on other event-driven pieces of the system, allowing you to do things such as loading call instructions from a remote web server.

A further advantage is being able to customize logic inside a loadable module to route calls explicitly, based on the logic that you hardcode in the C programming language (native to FreeSWITCH). This allows you to make up your own Dialplan processing routines rather than rely on the ones built into FreeSWITCH. Your own routines can tie libraries together that you have linked (such as SQL) with C-based logic APIs, exposed by FreeSWITCH. For example, you could easily query a SQL database to find out if a user wants to have their call **proxied**, and then directly invoke the FreeSWITCH API to turn on proxying, all from within your Dialplan processor and with just a few lines of C code. This creates a huge advantage because you gain great flexibility without having to spawn expensive third-party processes and threads to process your Dialplan (such as invoking a shell script or a PHP script just to do a simple true/false test of a value in a SQL database). This allows FreeSWITCH to handle much higher call volumes.

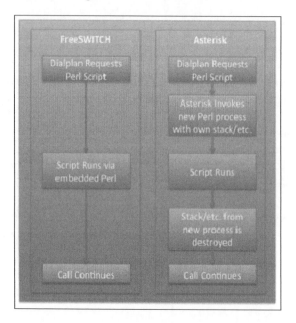

There is a common misconception that the FreeSWITCH Dialplan is based on, and requires, XML. This is simply not true. If you prefer flat files, you could use them to store your Dialplan configuration. If you prefer YAML, you could use that too. You just need to load the correct C-based Dialplan module to interpret your stored logic for the particular type of configuration file you want FreeSWITCH to utilize.

This aside, the most common (and currently, the most robust) Dialplan processing mechanism in FreeSWITCH is still the XML-based Dialplan module. Most Dialplan examples that are shipped with FreeSWITCH, or those scattered on the web, are in XML. Therefore, they will remain the focus of this chapter. Creating your own C modules is beyond the scope of this book, but it is important that you understand that this functionality exists. As you get more and more advanced in using FreeSWITCH, you may find that the built-in XML Dialplan processor will not handle your needs for all cases, and you should remember that you are not limited to using just XML! There are other avenues to achieve what you want to accomplish in terms of call routing.

Before we dig into the specifics of the XML Dialplan, let us review and expand on some basic concepts about Dialplans in general.

General Diaplan concepts

Let's briefly review some concepts that were first introduced in *Chapter 5, Understanding the XML Dialplan*. In general, a Dialplan helps generate a list of actions to take so that a caller can reach the person or people they want to talk to. A Dialplan module implements the decision-making process that powers this. While a Dialplan module is free to implement any concept it wants for organizing how calls are routed, three concepts, in particular, are generally used when processing a call. These three concepts can be broken down by asking the same three questions for every call:

- **Contexts**: Where do we look for a general list of destinations (or features) that the current caller is allowed to reach?
- **Conditions**: Whom, specifically, is the caller trying to reach?
- **Actions**: What actions need to be taken to reach that party?

These three questions are generally answered by breaking the routing decisions into three concepts—caller context, condition matching, and actions. These concepts are not necessarily unique to FreeSWITCH. We'll explore each of these concepts individually in this section.

The end result of any Dialplan's decision making is a series of actions. Every Dialplan module must return a list of actions that, when executed one after the other, results in party A reaching party B successfully.

Contexts

When we talk about **context**, we are really referring to a list of individual destinations that a caller is allowed to reach. These parties don't have to be individual people; they can be groups of people or interactive features (for example, voicemail), but ultimately, a caller wants to be connected to *someone* or *something*. A context is a collection of rules that helps determine who a caller is trying to reach, and whether they are allowed to reach that destination or not. These "rules" are called extensions.

You can think of a caller's context as the overall grouping of logic statements for a general set of destinations that can be called. In the example Dialplan the most commonly used contexts are the **"internal"** and the **"public"** contexts. The "internal" context generally refers to calls being made by users who are internal, or inside the walls of the switching system (such as people sitting inside an office building). These people can call each other with four-digit dialing, or dial *9* to call an outside number. The "public" context usually refers to people outside the system calling in. These people can usually only reach a small subset of destinations within the system, such as employee desk phones, but can't reach a destination, such as a lobby phone, directly.

Why have a group of destinations at all? Why not just have internal and public numbers? Most organizations need more flexibility than that. For example, let's look at the common scenario of phones at a hotel. If we looked at all the use cases at a hotel, we might break them into three general contexts—internal staff, internal guests, and external callers. For the purposes of this discussion, we'll nickname those use cases as "staff", "guests", and "external".

For "external" callers, the reason to group who they can call together is simple—we want external callers to be able to reach front desk staff and the hotel restaurant by calling one of two main phone numbers. However, we do not want outside callers to be able to call rooms or use the in-house hotel features (for example, our phone system's wake-up call service) directly. Therefore, we'll put together a list of externally accessible numbers in the context "external" and route all outside callers to this context for processing.

Hotel guests, on the other hand, should be able to call one another's rooms, use the wake-up call services, and call the front desk staff. Again, this group of numbers is different from those of the "external" callers—so they get their own context with those destinations.

Finally, staff have special functions, such as being able to flag a person's phone as "checked out", restricting calls from that phone while a room is empty (for safety, in order to prevent toll fraud). These functions aren't accessible to guests, and certainly not to outside callers, so staff get their own context as well.

Visually, the logic you're creating ends up looking something like this:

		Caller (context)		
		Internal Guest	**Internal Staff**	**External Caller**
Calling To	**Front Desk**	√	√	√
(Destination)	**Restaurant**	√	√	√
	Hotel Rooms	√	√	X
	Wake-up Call	√	X	X
	Set checked-out flag	X	√	X

Now we see the need for contexts. The preceding list shows that each individual type of caller has specific constraints on whom they can (and are allowed to) call.

Note carefully that the concept of a context is not for calling a specific party, but for grouping together numbers that can be dialed to reach parties. The actual decisions on who we want to reach, and what number they are assigned, is handled by conditions, which are described in the following sections.

Conditions

Once the system has determined the *general list* of who is *allowed* to be reached, it must figure out precisely who is being dialed and how to reach them. This is done using conditions.

Conditions are one or more logic statements that are used to figure out where the call should go. They typically involve comparing information about a caller (such as what number they dialed or the Caller ID of the call), with a set of rules. This information is gathered from Dialplan variables (discussed later in this chapter) and matched against regular expressions, strings, or other variables.

Conditions are most commonly used to match the dialed number with a specific destination that maps to a specific phone. For example, we might be testing to see if a person dialed a specific number; say, 415-886-7949. If they did, we would provide a list of actions that would connect to the user at the extension 7949.

Sometimes destination matching works on fields other than the dialed number. For example, you might check the calling party's Caller ID, and if it's a telemarketer, for example, you might play a busy signal. There are many combinations of field and value pairs you might check, in order to determine where to send a call. You can even check for technical or database-driven settings, such as whether someone is behind NAT or they have a call-forwarding entry saved in a database table.

It is also possible to set up the Dialplan in such a way that multiple conditions match, triggering multiple actions in the same call. Such an example might be carried out to connect a caller to someone, and when they hang up, continue the call only if they are calling from a specific area code, and play a survey for them. Multiple conditions can exist in various ways, depending on your Dialplan processor.

Using our example of a hotel discussed earlier, you might end up with three contexts that each check various conditions to determine different destinations, as follows:

"Internal Guest" Context	"Internal Staff" Context	"External" Context
Did they dial 0?	*Did they dial 0?*	
–Go to front desk	–Go to front desk	
Did they dial 2929?	*Did they dial 2929?*	*Did they dial 646-222-2929?*
–Go to restaurant	–Go to restaurant	– Go to restaurant
Did they dial 3000-3999?	*Did they dial 3000-3999?*	
–Ring room 3000-3999	–Ring room 3000-3999	
Did they dial *5?		
–Go to wake-up call		
	Did they dial *6?	
	–Set checked out flag	

By default, and in most use cases, the Dialplan is processed until a match is found. See the following *Extensions* for more information.

Actions

Actions are the steps to be taken when a condition matches. This is where the Dialplan generates a list of actions the switch will need to perform, to actually get the caller to the destination party. Actions include "answering", "bridging", "routing to voicemail", and so on.

It is very important to understand that the Dialplan module only creates a list of actions to perform—it does not actually execute those actions in real time! There are some exceptions to this rule, but the general premise of the original Dialplan structure revolves around staying modular and not requiring the module to do any of the heavy lifting, to actually connect the call and perform the actions.

To clarify this further, think of the Dialplan as generating a to-do list for what needs to happen on the call. A to-do list might consist of:

- Answer
- Play welcome file
- Transfer to user "John Doe"
- Hang up

That list would be handed back to FreeSWITCH to perform on its own.

The Dialplan is not intended to be interactive during the actual flow of the call. If you need complete interaction while a call is in progress, you should utilize a scripting language linked to FreeSWITCH. You can learn about this in *Chapter 7, Dialplan Scripting with Lua*.

Putting it all together

The time at which FreeSWITCH actually processes all the contexts, extensions, conditions, and actions you've specified is during the ROUTE phase. Every call goes through the ROUTE state. The routing state is when FreeSWITCH passes control of the call to the Dialplan module in use and the previous four concepts are used to develop a list of actions.

The process generally looks like this:

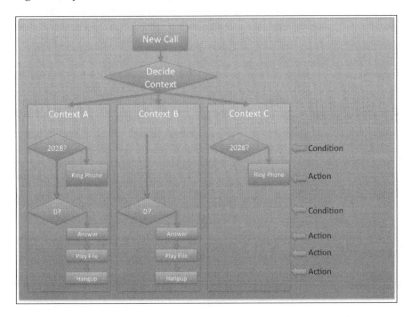

A list of resulting actions is finally returned to FreeSWITCH, such as:

- EXECUTE answer
- EXECUTE and play the `file.wav`
- EXECUTE hangup

Members of the FreeSWITCH community will often speak of the Dialplan "phases"—when they do, they are referring to this two-phase process of **ROUTE** and **EXECUTE**. Sometimes you will hear individuals referring to the ROUTE phase as the "parsing" phase. The term "parsing" loosely describes what is happening during the ROUTE phase. We also use the expression "hunting" as a synonym for the ROUTE phase. ROUTE, parsing, and hunting all refer to the same thing.

Understanding this two-phase process is crucial in mastering the operation of the XML Dialplan.

XML Dialplan module review

As we discussed in *Chapter 5, Understanding the XML Dialplan*, the XML Dialplan module is the most popular way to configure FreeSWITCH. At the time of writing this book it is also the most robust. It supports contexts, which contain lists of extensions, with each extension containing one or more conditions, and each condition containing a list of actions to be executed.

Let's review a few concepts to make sure that you are fully comfortable with them. The searching and processing of Dialplan entries is based on an expected layout that looks something like a multi-dimensional tree.

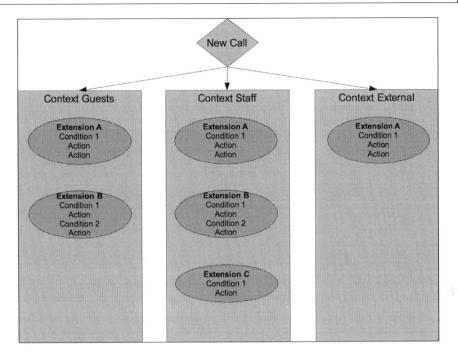

After a quick glance at the expected structure of your Dialplan and how it is used, it should be somewhat obvious why XML lends itself as a good choice for the creation of a Dialplan. The nesting attributes of XML are a perfect fit for the scenario shown. FreeSWITCH relies on a tree of configuration options in a Dialplan, and XML is naturally a limitless tree-like structure that allows for embedding values within each leaf on the tree. In addition, you can add custom tags and attributes at any time—even ones that are ignored by FreeSWITCH but are useful for your own software when reading/writing to XML. It is a great match.

At this point, you should be well versed with contexts, extensions, conditions, and actions. Let us dig a bit deeper into the XML Dialplan to see how these different Dialplan features can behave.

Extensions

Extensions are simply XML containers that group conditions and actions together. Note that the name "extensions" can be a bit misleading. Most people are used to an extension being something you attempt to reach by dialing it, such as *2900* or *3000*, but extensions in FreeSWITCH are not related to what you dial at all; they are simply named subsections of the Dialplan context. For example, to reach someone by dialing *2900*, you might actually be hitting an extension named `darren`, like this:

```
<extension name="darren">
  <condition field="destination_number" expression="^2900$">
    <action application="bridge" data="user/darren"/>
  </condition>
</extension>
```

In this example, the extension is named `darren`, but dialing *2900* is how you reach Darren, thanks to the condition.

Extensions have a variety of behaviors that can be modified. By default, when FreeSWITCH finds an extension that has matching conditions, it stops looking for additional extensions. For example, if you have an extension that modifies your Caller ID, followed by an extension that actually routes the call, FreeSWITCH will never reach the second extension by default. As an example, this will fail to reach anyone:

```
<extension name="set_callerid">
  <condition field="destination_number" expression="^2900$">
    <action application="set"
      data="effective_caller_id_number=4158867900"/>
  </condition>
</extension>
<extension name="darren">
  <condition field="destination_number" expression="^2900$">
    <action application="bridge" data="user/darren"/>
  </condition>
</extension>
```

In the preceding example, the second extension will never run. If you want to allow additional extensions to run after a successful match, you must use the `continue` flag. If we modify the previous example, the Dialplan will now operate as expected:

```
<extension name="set_callerid" continue="true">
  <condition field="destination_number" expression="^2900$">
    <action application="set"
      data="effective_caller_id_number=4158867900"/>
  </condition>
</extension>
<extension name="darren">
  <condition field="destination_number" expression="^2900$">
    <action application="bridge" data="user/darren"/>
  </condition>
</extension>
```

Note that we have added `continue="true"` only to the first extension, indicating to the Dialplan module that it should keep processing even if the extension matches. We do not add it to the second extension because we do not want to continue processing the Dialplan after the second match (where the call is actually connected).

Conditions

Conditions allow for testing regular expressions against variables. Conditions exist within extension tags. We will discuss the different types of variables available a bit later in this chapter.

Conditions can be used to test one or more expressions. By default, and at their most basic level, one or more conditions can be specified, with a group of actions executed when all conditions evaluate to `true`.

As an example, let us look at the following code snippet:

```
<extension name="test_two_things">
  <condition field="network_addr" expression="^192\.168\.1\.1$"/>
  <condition field="destination_number" expression="^2900$">
    <action application="playback" data="i-know-you.wav"/>
  </condition>
</extension>
```

In this example, there are two conditions listed. Note carefully the `/>` at the end of the first `condition` tag. While there are no actions contained within the first condition, it is still tested and, if it fails, the entire extension is skipped. However, if both the conditions pass, meaning the caller is dialing `2900` and their network IP address is `192.168.1.1`, then the action(s) will run. This effectively creates an AND logic between the two conditions—both must match before the playback action is specified.

How does this work? The secret is in the `break` attribute, also called a **break flag**. Every `condition` statement has a `break` flag associated with it that determines what should happen after the `expression` is evaluated. The default behavior for the `break` flag is `on-false`, meaning that we break out of, or stop processing, conditions and extensions as soon as we encounter a `false` or negative result during evaluation.

You can set the `break` parameter to one of four values:

- `on-false`: To stop searching after the first unsuccessful match (default behavior)
- `on-true`: To stop searching conditions after the first successful match
- `always`: To stop at this condition regardless of a match or non-match
- `never`: To continue searching regardless of a match or non-match

You can even create a pseudo `if`/`then`/`else` processing section using conditions. Let us examine the use of one of these attributes further: the `never` flag.

Let's say you want to create an extension that processes calls only from a particular IP address and checks if the user dialed *72 or *73. You can do this as two separate extensions, as follows:

```
<extension name="extension_72">
  <condition field="network_addr" expression="^192\.168\.1\.1$"/>
  <condition field="destination_number" expression="^\*72$">
    <action application="playback" data="forward-on.wav"/>
  </condition>
</extension>
<extension name="extension_73">
  <condition field="network_addr" expression="^192\.168\.1\.1$"/>
  <condition field="destination_number" expression="^\*73$">
    <action application="playback" data="forward-off.wav"/>
  </condition>
</extension>
```

You can also use the power of the break flag to consolidate this into a single extension, as follows:

```
<extension name="extension_72_or_73">
  <condition field="network_addr"
    expression="^192\.168\.1\.1$"/>
  <condition field="destination_number" expression="^\*72$"
    break="on-true">
    <action application="playback" data="forward-on.wav"/>
  </condition>
```

```
    <condition field="destination_number" expression="^\*73$">
      <action application="playback" data="forward-off.wav"/>
    </condition>
  </extension>
```

As you can see, by adding the `break="on-true"` flag to the first condition, we stop processing *only* when the condition evaluates to `true`. Otherwise, we continue processing. Think of this as an `if/then/else-if` statement; if the first condition matches, run it and stop processing, otherwise run the second condition if it matches.

As another example, consider the concept of using an `if/then` condition followed by another `if/then`. You can simulate this logic by using the `break="never"` flag. While actions inside failing conditions will not be added to the list of execution steps, the subsequent conditions will still be processed. Consider the example where we want to check two different network parameters in the same extension block:

```
  <extension name="decide_routing">
    <condition field="network_addr"
      expression="^192\.168\.1\.1$"
      break="never">
      <action application="set" data="inhouse=true"/>
    </condition>
    <condition field="source" expression="PortAudio"/>
      <action application="set" data="portaudio=true"/>
    </condition>
  </extension>
```

The preceding XML would test to see if a user is calling from `192.168.1.1` and set a variable if `true`. It would continue, in all cases, to the second condition as well and test whether the user was using `PortAudio` or not, and set a variable if `true`. This represents an effective `if/then` condition followed by another `if/then`.

A condition must exist inside every extension tag, even if you intend for the condition to be `true` always. The following code snippet is not valid:

```
  <extension name="set_callerid">
    <action application="set"
      data="effective_callerid_number=4158867900"/>
  </extension>
```

No `condition` tag exists, so this extension will be ignored and the action will never be run.

Special condition variables

While in most conditions you will encounter utilize variables and expressions, some conditions can be written to utilize special condition variables in order to make processing simpler and more flexible.

The following variables are available for use as `field` attributes in your XML `condition` tags:

- `context`: The current Dialplan context
- `rdnis`: The redirected number; that is, the directory number to which the call was last presented
- `destination_number`: The called number; that is, the number this call is trying to reach
- `dialplan`: The name of the Dialplan module in use (that is, XML or YAML)
- `caller_id_name`: The name of the caller, if available
- `caller_id_number`: The number of the party who called, if available
- `ani`: The Automatic Number Identification of the calling party
- `aniii`: The type of device placing the call, if available (for example, payphone)
- `uuid`: The unique identifier of the current call
- `source`: The name of the FreeSWITCH module that received the call (for example, `PortAudio`)
- `chan_name`: The name of the current channel (for example, `PortAudio/1234`)
- `network_addr`: The IP address of the signaling source for a call

Some simple examples are as follows:

```
<condition field="network_add" expression="^1\.2\.3\.4$">
<condition field="caller_id_number" expression="^1[01]\d\d"/>
```

The following items can be used directly as attributes inside the `condition` tag:

- `year`: Denotes the calendar year, 0-9999
- `yday`: Denotes the day of year, 1-366
- `mon`: Denotes the month, 1-12 (for example, January is equal to 1)
- `mday`: Denotes the day of month, 1-31
- `week`: Denotes the week of year, 1-53
- `mweek`: Denotes the week of month, 1-6
- `wday`: Denotes the day of week, 1-7 (for example, Sunday is equal to 1 and Monday is equal to 2)

- `hour`: Denotes the hour, 0-23
- `minute`: Denotes the minute (of the hour), 0-59
- `minute-of-day`: Denotes the minute of the day, (1-1440) (for example, midnight is equal to 1, 1 A.M. is equal to 60, and noon is equal to 720)

These `condition` attributes can be used like this:

```
<extension name="holiday_example" continue="true">
  <condition mday="1" mon="1">
    <action application="set"
      data="open=false" inline="true"/>
  </condition>
</extension>
```

This example would set a variable named `open` to `false` on New Year's Day. Note the `condition` line, which utilizes the `mday` and `mon` condition variables. A simple day/time checkout would be like this:

```
<extension name="holiday_example" continue="true">
  <condition wday="2-6" hour="8-16">
    <action application="set" data="open=true" inline="true"/>
  </condition>
</extension>
```

This would set the channel variable `open` to `"true"`, if the call came in between 8 A.M. and 5 P.M.

Inline execution

The original design of FreeSWITCH was to forbid actions from occurring during the routing/Dialplan phase. This had the intended side effect of discouraging people from evaluating and manipulating variables and call flow from within the Dialplan. Instead, it was left to the various embedded scripting languages to perform these programmatic actions. The theory was simple—rather than design a possibly obscure and limiting set of commands that can be used within the Dialplan to evaluate variables and create logic, FreeSWITCH would instead link to various scripting languages, such as Perl or Lua, which have much richer logic-processing capabilities than FreeSWITCH could ever design (and better documentation). This not only expands the possibilities of what can be performed but also avoids having to train people on the ins and outs of the XML processing system.

However, as FreeSWITCH evolved, more and more people desired the ability to handle call flow processing in the native XML Dialplan language. One of the most basic features that was noticeably absent during Dialplan routing was the ability to set, and later test (and possibly override) a variable. After numerous requests to the core developers, the `inline` flag was added to XML Dialplan processing.

The `inline` flag allows for some (but not all) commands to be executed *during* the Dialplan phase, breaking many of the previously stated rules. While its use is discouraged, it is sometimes necessary to achieve additional functionality or just make code more naturally readable.

As an example of why we need an inline execution, let us look at the following code snippet:

```
<extension name="check_for_user" continue="true">
  <condition field="${callerid}" expression="2035551212">
    <action application="set" data="user=yes"/>
  </condition>
</extension>
<extension name="route_users_only">
  <condition field="${user}" expression="yes">
    <action application="answer"/>
    <action application="playback" data="tada.wav" />
    <action application="hangup"/>
  </condition>
</extension>
```

The preceding code snippet defines two extensions that rely on each other—the first extension is supposed to set a variable named `user` to `"yes"`, if someone is calling from `203-555-1212`, and the second snippet is supposed to route all calls with the user variable set to a message playing `tada.wav`. The snippet does not work this way, though. Let us examine why not.

Recall that conditions are evaluated *before* any action is ever executed. In the previous example, `set` is an `action` application. Therefore, it will not be executed until all the conditions are evaluated. This means that `condition` that looks at the variable `${user}` will always fail, because the code that sets that variable is yet to run, hence the need for **inline** processing.

If the XML action is changed to read:

```
<action application="set" data="user=yes" inline="true"/>
```

The XML Dialplan processor will actually execute the `set` application as soon as it is encountered. Now the XML snippet works as expected.

To avoid abuse of this feature, and for various other technical reasons, the `inline` flag is only available to applications that run quickly and get or set some variable(s). Inline functions must also not access or modify the state of the current session.

The list of actions available for inline processing includes, among others, the following:

- `check_acl`: To check the access control lists
- `eval`: To execute an internal API or simply log some text to the console
- `event`: To fire arbitrary events
- `export`: To set a variable on the channel that will survive on the B legs/ transfers
- `log`: To create a log entry manually
- `presence`: To send the `PRESENCE_IN` and `PRESENCE_OUT` events
- `set`: To set a variable on the channel
- `set_global`: To set a global variable
- `set_profile_var`: To set the user's profile we want to use
- `set_user`: To set the current user and add all their channel variables to the active leg
- `sleep`: To pause the processing
- `unset`: To unset a variable
- `verbose_events`: To be verbose on events being sent
- `cidlookup`: To set the caller_id_name field via CNAM lookups
- `curl`: To make an HTTP request and receive the response
- `easyroute`: To direct to database-driven DID routing engine
- `enum`: To perform `enum` lookups or related services
- `lcr`: To take least cost routing decisions
- `nibblebill`: To bill accounts on a per-minute basis
- `odbc_query`: To perform manual ODBC queries

The details on each of these commands are documented on the FreeSWITCH wiki.

Actions and anti-actions

Another available call control mechanism is the combination of `action` and `anti-action` tags. Unlike conditions, these tags allow you to failover to an alternate set of actions if a `condition` fails. This is another version of the `if`/`then`/`else` condition, but can be easier to read and manage, especially when trying to queue multiple actions within the *same* condition.

Let us take an example to see how this works:

```
<condition field="${inhouse}"
 expression="true" break="never">
  <action application="log" data="This is an in-house call"/>
  <anti-action application="log" data="Not in-house call"/>
</condition>
```

The preceding example would output, `"This is an in-house call"` to the log if the variable `${inhouse}` is set to `true`, otherwise it would output, `"Not in-house call"` to the log. This is much easier to read than splitting the `if/then/else` logic into two separate `condition` statements.

The regex operator

Sometimes it is necessary to create more complicated logic structures. For example, it is easy to test whether the `destination_number` expression is `1000` or `1001`:

```
<condition field="destination_number" expression="^100[01]$">
```

In effect, the regular expression says, `"Match if the destination number is 1000 or is 1001"`. But what if you need to do a logical OR on two different fields? The `regex` operator can help.

The basic syntax for `regex` is:

```
<condition regex="all|any|xor">
  <regex field="some_field" expression="Some Value"/>
  <regex field="another_field"
    expression="^Another\s*Value$"/>
  <action(s) ...>
  <anti-action(s)...>
</condition>
```

You can have as many `regex` tags as need inside the `condition`. The `regex` operator can have three different values:

- `all`: It is equivalent to a logical AND operation. *All* the expressions contained in the condition *must* be true for the actions to be taken.

- `any`: It is the equivalent to a logical OR operation. *Any* of the expressions contained in the condition *may* be true for the actions to be taken.

- `xor`: It is the equivalent to a logical XOR operation. Only *one* of the expressions can be true for the actions to be taken.

To perform a more complicated logic statement, such as an OR on two different fields, try this:

```
<extension name="Regex OR example" continue="true">
  <condition regex="any">
    <!-- If either is true then perform actions-->
    <regex field="caller_id_name" expression="Some User"/>
    <regex field="caller_id_number" expression="^1001$"/>
    <action application="log"
      data="INFO At least one matched!"/>
    <!-- If *none* are true then do anti-actions -->
    <anti-action application="log"
      data="WARNING None of the conditions matched!"/>
  </condition>
</extension>
```

In the preceding example, the action tags will be executed if either the expression caller_id_name is "Some User" or the caller_id_number expression is "1001". If neither regex evaluates to true, then the anti-action tags will be executed.

You can also have more intricate regular expressions. For example, let's say that "Some User" has more than one extension. You could use this regex:

```
<regex field="caller_id_number" expression="^1001|1005$"/>
```

To perform a large AND operation, you can use an extension like this:

```
<extension name="Regex AND example" continue="true">
  <condition regex="all">
    <!-- If both are true then perform actions-->
    <regex field="caller_id_name" expression="Some User"/>
    <regex field="caller_id_number" expression="^1001$"/>
    <action application="log"
      data="INFO Both matched!"/>
    <!-- If *any* are false then then do anti-actions -->
    <anti-action application="log"
      data="WARNING At least one failed!"/>
  </condition>
</extension>
```

Again, you can stack as many <regex> tags inside the condition as you would like. All of them must evaluate to true in order to execute the apps inside the action tags. If any of the regex test fails, then any apps inside the anti-action tags will be executed.

In some rare cases, you may need to perform an XOR or exclusive OR operation; that is, where one—but only one—of the conditions can be true. If none of the tests evaluate to `true`, or if more than one test evaluates to `true`, then the whole logical operation evaluates to `false`. Here is an example:

```
<extension name="Regex XOR example" continue="true">
    <condition regex="xor">
      <!-- If only one is true then perform actions -->
      <regex field="caller_id_name" expression="Some User"/>
      <regex field="caller_id_number" expression="^1001$"/>
      <action application="log"
        data="INFO exactly one matched!"/>
      <!-- If none or 2+ are true then the XOR fails -->
      <anti-action application="log"
        data="WARNING XOR evaluated false!"/>
    </condition>
</extension>
```

Nested conditions

Starting with Version 1.2.6 of FreeSWITCH, you may now nest the `<condition>` tags to address various situations. One such condition is illustrated by this logical construct:

```
IF condition1 TRUE THEN

  IF condition2 TRUE THEN
    DO actions
  ELSE
    DO other actions
  ENDIF

  IF condition3 TRUE THEN
    DO actions
  ELSE
    DO other actions
  ENDIF

  IF condition4 TRUE THEN
    DO actions
  ELSE
    DO other actions
  ENDIF

ELSE
    DO other actions
ENDIF
```

By nesting the conditions it becomes much easier to accomplish this task. The following excerpt illustrates an example where the `destination_number` is the equivalent of `condition1` in our logical construct. We then have various other fields that are the equivalents of `condition2`, `condition3`, and `condition4`. For brevity we've left out specific `action` and `anti-action` tags:

```
<condition field="destination_number"
  expression="^1000$"
  require_nested="false">
  <action...>
  <anti-action...>
  <condition field="caller_id_number" expression="^1001$">
    <action...>
    <anti-action...>
  </condition>

  <condition field="caller_id_number" expression="1?408\d+">
    <action...>
    <anti-action...>
  </condition>

  <condition field="caller_id_number" expression="^1001$">
    <action...>
    <anti-action...>
  </condition>

  <action...>
  <anti-action...>
</condition>
```

Keep the important note in mind that all nested `conditions` get processed before the parent `condition`. This means that all `action` and `anti-action` expressions in the parent `condition` will always be executed *after* the actions/anti-actions in the nested conditions, In other words, when the Dialplan parser is looking for actions (or anti-actions) in the hunting phase, it will always add the actions/anti-actions inside the nested conditions, before it adds the actions/anti-actions of the parent condition.

In the previous example, the three nested conditions (the ones that test the `caller_id_number` field) will all be evaluated and their actions/anti-actions will be processed before the actions/anti-actions of the parent condition (the one that tests the `destination_number` field). In simple terms, the children conditions come before the parent conditions.

The following section explains more about the two phases of Dialplan processing, including a mistake that new users commonly make.

Pitfalls to avoid

There are two major places where the Dialplan design can confuse new users of FreeSWITCH—especially those with a background using Asterisk. Firstly, in understanding how variables are handled during conditional processing, and secondly, in interpreting the logs.

Keep in mind that the Dialplan is, two-phase process, the first of which is the ROUTE (also called the "hunting" or "parsing") phase. This phase completes prior to any other command being actually executed. Let us again look at the example provided, which do not work as intended. This time around, we will do what many people try to do when debugging their XML—we will add the info application to the XML, to obtain a printout of the variables that are set on a channel, on the console.

```xml
<extension name="check_for_user" continue="true">
  <condition field="${callerid}" expression="2035551212">
    <action application="set" data="user=yes"/>
    <action application="info"/>
  </condition>
</extension>
<extension name="route_users_only">
  <condition field="${user}" expression="yes">
    <action application="answer"/>
    <action application="playback" data="tada.wav"/>
    <action application="hangup"/>
  </condition>
</extension>
```

When this code snippet runs, the info application will output all variables set on the channel to the screen, and the user will see that the variable "user" is in fact set to "yes". Yet the following condition, which tests the variable user, doesn't run. Many users will think FreeSWITCH is broken, but in fact, they are misreading the output they are seeing. After careful examination, you will note in your logs that the set application executed after all the conditions were tested, and the info application ran subsequently, showing that the variable had been set, but the conditional testing had been completed long before this occurred. This can lead to many hours of frustration if you are not careful while reading the logs.

The log will show whether or not the individual Dialplan entries were matched, which can confuse people into thinking those sections of the Dialplan were actually executed. In fact, you must scroll down lower in the log to discover what actions were actually taken. Get used to looking for the EXECUTE log statements and paying more attention to those to see what is actually happening. If items are not being executed as expected, then your conditions are not set correctly.

XML Dialplan applications

While we would love to go through all the available Dialplan commands, the list far exceeds the space we have for this chapter. Therefore, we will limit our discussion of available Dialplan commands into three areas—Dialplan tools, Sofia connectivity, and general API commands. These Dialplan commands are provided by mod_ dptools, mod_sofia, and mod_commands respectively. They are also some of the most common and most popular commands in use today.

mod_dptools

The mod_dptools command is a collection of Dialplan management tools. There are many applications available from within the Dialplan. You have already learned how basic commands such as answer, hangup, bridge, and set work. Let us go over a few of the more advanced commands.

- bind_meta_app: This command binds an application to the specified call leg(s). During a bridged call, the DTMF sequence on the bound call leg will trigger the execution of the application. The call leg that is not bound will not hear the DTMF sequence being dialed. You can only bind a single digit, and the binding is usually proceeded with a * key press. As an example, let us say you want to allow *2 to begin a call recording.

  When the calling party presses *2, the recording would begin. In this case, you could utilize the following Dialplan snippet. Notice the bind_meta_app highlighted:

  ```
  <action application="bind_meta_app" data="2 a s
    record_session::recording.wav"/>
  <action application="bridge"
    data="sofia/sipprovider/+14158867900">
  ```

  This action allows the A-leg on this channel to press *2 to invoke call recording on the same leg (the third parameter s indicates the same leg).

  Note that unless otherwise specified, bind_meta_app will use * as the "meta key". Set the bind_meta_key channel variable to a different value to modify this behavior. For example, to use # instead of * you can do this:

  ```
  <action application="set" data="bind_meta_key=#"/>
  ```

  Notice the format of the bind_meta_app parameters:

  ```
  <action application="bind_meta_app"
    data="KEY LISTEN_TO RESPOND_ON
    APPLICATION[::PARAMETERS]"/>
  ```

The following list explains the previous parameters:

- KEY: This specifies the key to listen for.

- LISTEN_TO: This specifies which call leg to listen for the key. Acceptable parameters are a, b, or ab.

- RESPOND_ON: This specifies which call leg to respond when the key is dialed. For example, when playing a file as the response command, which leg will hear the playback. Acceptable parameters are s for the same leg; that is, the leg on which the key was pressed, or o for the opposite leg.

- APPLICATION: This specifies what application to run.

- PARAMETERS: This specifies the parameters to pass to the application. Note that you separate applications and parameters using double colons (APPLICATION::PARAMS).

 Once bound to a call leg, the application binding will persist for the lifetime of the call leg.

For advanced DTMF key bindings see the mechanism bind_digit_action.

- bind_digit_action: This command implements a more advanced and elegant key mapping mechanism than bind_meta_app. It allows you to capture any digit combination and does not have a requirement that it begin with a *.

The format of the bind_digit_action parameters are:

```
<action application="bind_digit_action"
   data="REALM,KEY|REGEX,COMMAND,COMMAND_ARGUMENTS,LISTEN_
TO,RESPOND_ON"/>
```

The following list explains the previous parameters:

- REALM: Specifies to Michael, the user.

- KEY|REGEX: Specifies the key to listen for, or a regex parameter containing the key(s) to listen for.

- COMMAND: Specifies the dialplan application to run. It can be either a dialplan command (prefixed with exec:) or an API command (prefixed with api:).

- COMMAND_ARGUMENTS: Specifies the arguments for the command being run.

- ○ `LISTEN_TO`: Specifies which call leg to listen for the key. Acceptable parameters are a, b, or ab.

- ○ `RESPOND_ON`: Specifies which call leg to respond. For example, when playing a file as the response command, which leg will hear `playback`. Acceptable parameters are s for the same leg; that is, the leg on which the key was pressed, or o for the opposite leg.

Here is an example. The following command will hang up all calls on the system by dialing a secret code, 9348234. It runs the API `hupall` command.

```
<action application="bind_digit_action"
  data="my_digits,9348234,api:hupall"/>
```

Be aware that `bind_digit_action` causes dialed digits to be *consumed* by `bind_digit_action` and thus will not be sent through to other applications.

- `eavesdrop`: This command allows you to listen in on other channels. As an example, the following Dialplan command would allow you eavesdrop on a UUID placed in $1.

```
<action application="eavesdrop" data="$1"/>
```

You can replace $1 with any UUID you wish, or retrieve the UUID from the database, like this:

```
<action application="eavesdrop"
  data="${db(select/spymap/${extension})}"/>
```

In this example, the variable `extension` is utilized, which can be set prior in the Dialplan, and used as a search parameter to look into the database for a UUID associated with an extension. In this scenario, if you recorded the extension number and UUID of all active calls in the database under the table `spymap`, you could later retrieve that information for eavesdropping here.

`execute_extension`: You can execute an extension from within another extension with this Dialplan application. The purpose would be to route a call temporarily to another extension, then return back to the same place we left. This is similar to the loopback function found in other switches. `execute_extension` executes an extension like a macro, and then returns. This is different from transfer, which goes to the new extension instantly and does not return. The `execute_extension` command will keep the current scope and build a one-time extension, execute it, and return right back to where it was called.

```
<action application="execute_extension"
  data="destination_number [Dialplan] [context]"/>
```

If you do not specify the Dialplan and context, it defaults to the current one.

Use `execute_extension` only when you need to execute a command and return to the Dialplan processing where you left off. When you do not need to do anything else, use the `transfer` application. If you are a programmer, then this analogy is fitting: `execute_extension` is like gosub whereas `transfer` is like goto.

- `send_display`: You can send a customized SIP INFO message to a phone, which (on some models of phones) will display the message on the phone's display.

  An example of usage:

  ```
  <action application="send_display" data="Support Call"/>
  ```

  This could be used to display a department or message on the phone that indicates who the call is for, or what department was called initially.

  There are many more commands available for review on the FreeSWITCH wiki at: `http://wiki.freeswitch.org/wiki/Mod_dptools`.

mod_sofia

The `mod_sofia` command is generally responsible for all things under SIP. This includes acting as an endpoint for sending and receiving SIP calls and managing SIP registrations and contact information. Various commands exist within `mod_sofia` that help manage not only the initiation and receiving of calls but also the management and deconstruction of endpoint information such as a device's registered IP address and whether the device is behind NAT.

While **Sofia** itself does not provide applications that you utilize from the Dialplan directly, it is used in so many command parameters that it is important to go through it more specifically here.

Sofia is generally accessed when bridging SIP calls. **Bridging** refers to connecting an A leg to a newly initiated B leg. When bridging calls, the general format is as follows:

```
<action application="bridge"
        data="sofia/profile/endpoint[@domain]"/>
```

Let us analyze the `data` portion of this command.

As the `bridge` command is a general purpose command that does not exclusively bridge SIP calls, you must specify the `sofia/` parameter first to indicate that you are working with a SIP call. Following the `sofia/` parameter, you must specify what gateway or SIP profile is to be used for connecting the call. If you specify a gateway that you have configured in your SIP configuration, the domain name of the receiving server is already known and does not need to be added at the end of the dial string (that is, you can leave off `@domain`). If you specify a profile name as the second parameter, you are telling Sofia which IP address, port, and parameters to utilize when connecting the call. In this case, you must specify a domain or IP address at the end of your Sofia `bridge` application. Finally, the endpoint parameter specifies the username to send to the remote system. This is often a DID or extension number, so that the remote end knows what party on their system to connect to.

Here are some examples of different ways in which you might bridge a call. In the following examples, let us assume we have a service provider gateway named `supersip` and a Sofia profile named `external`.

```
<action application="bridge"
  data="sofia/supersip/+14158867900"/>
```

This would bridge a caller to (415) 886-7900 using the `supersip` provider information.

```
<action application="bridge"
  data="sofia/external/+14158867900@sip.supersip.com"/>
```

This would bridge a caller to (415) 886-7900 using the `supersip` provider, except in this case, we have explicitly specified that we wish to call via the profile `external` (using whatever IP address and port are contained within that profile) and that we are routing the call via a server at `sip.supersip.com`.

```
<action application="bridge"
  data="sofia/external/someuser@otheroffice.com:5080"/>
```

This would bridge a caller to the user `someuser` located on the server `otheroffice.com` via port 5080. It is good to note that nothing is stopping you from bridging calls between FreeSWITCH, Asterisk, or other types of servers via this method—including other servers on your local network. You have complete control of the username, server, port, and routing of a call via this command when used in this way.

Now consider a more complex example. Sofia accepts parameters at the end of a dial string to specify advanced options on how a call should behave. As an example, let us say we want to send a call using TCP, instead of the default UDP transport protocol. Adding a semi-colon at the end of a dial string allows you to attach Sofia options at the end of the dial-string. In this case, we want to add the option `transport=tcp` to the end of a dial-string. It can be done like this:

```
<action application="bridge" data=
"sofia/external/+14158867900@sip.supersip.com;transport=tcp"/>
```

The purpose and importance of reviewing these examples is to expose the power that is contained within the Sofia system that is accessible via the Dialplan. Applications are not limited to basic bridging options based on defined profiles—you can connect calls to anywhere you need to via the creative use of variables, options, and Dialplan functions.

mod_commands

The `mod_commands` command provides commands on the CLI to the administrator of the system. Sometimes CLI commands may be useful within FreeSWITCH call processing too. While generally CLI commands differ from applications called from the Dialplan, you can explicitly run any CLI command you wish, by wrapping the command into an evaluation string.

As an example, the CLI command `hupall(NORMAL_CLEARING)` normally resets (hangs up on) all active calls and terminates them with the reason `NORMAL_CLEARING`. This command is normally run only from the command line. If you wanted it to be available via the Dialplan when dialing *999*, you could define an extension like this:

```
<extension name="Make API call from Dialplan">
  <condition field="destination_number" expression="^(999)$">
    <action application="set"
            data="api_result=${hupall(normal_clearing)}"/>
  </condition>
</extension>
```

Note the highlighted line. We have wrapped the CLI command `hupall` in an expression as `${hupall(normal_clearing)}` and placed it within an extension. In addition, the results of the command will be stored in the variable `api_result`, since we placed the expression in the `set` command.

While this example is not very practical, the point of the exercise is to show that any CLI command can be executed from the Dialplan and its results utilized. For a complete list of CLI commands, review the FreeSWITCH wiki at `http://wiki.freeswitch.org/wiki/Mod_commands`.

Utilizing variables

Up to this point we have considered the basic use of channel variables. FreeSWITCH has more advanced ways of using variables, including global variables. Let's round out our understanding of variables by looking at some of these.

Testing variables with regular expressions

We have already discussed the purpose and basic use of the condition XML tag. Now we will discuss the different elements you can actually test to help make decisions about call handling.

FreeSWITCH offers three general categories of variables that you can test – caller profile fields, channel variables, and global variables. In addition, you can utilize macros and API functions and utilize their output in your conditions as well. We will review each of these in detail.

Caller profile fields

Caller profile fields are variables that are retrieved when a caller is authenticated. The variables are set within the directory and can include things such as the caller's area code, codec preferences, and likewise. You can utilize caller profile fields within conditions when processing the Dialplan, like this:

```
<condition field="${caller_profile_field}">
```

The variables get set within your directory, like this:

```
<user id="bob">
  <variables>
    <variable name="caller_profile_field" value="1234"/>
  </variables>
</user>
```

In this example, when bob authenticates, it means he is set as the current caller profile. The result is that all the variables contained within his profile are accessible just like any other channel variable.

The user directory was covered in detail in *Chapter 4, SIP and the User Directory*.

Channel variables

Every channel in FreeSWITCH can have a number of variables associated with it to track state, settings, and other information about a call. Channel variables are utilized in the format:

```
${variable}
```

Channel variables may be set in the Dialplan, application, or directory. They affect progress or settings for the call. They can be used almost anywhere variable processing is invoked, such as in Dialplan conditions, application commands, and likewise.

```
<condition field="${channel_variable}">
```

Channel variables are perhaps the most utilized and most important aspect of processing a call within FreeSWITCH. There are many, many channel variables available on any single call and even more that can be set to modify the behavior of a call. You can review the complete list of channel variables available online at `http://wiki.freeswitch.org/wiki/Channel_Variables`.

Channel variables and call setup

You can utilize channel variables when setting up calls or specific call legs, such as when originating a new call or when bridging an A leg of a call to a B leg via the `bridge` command. In these instances there are two ways to set channel variables — curly brackets `{}` and square brackets `[]`. Each work differently and are useful when bridging or originating a call to multiple parties at the same time.

Curly brackets are used "globally" for the duration of a call. Take the following example, where we are bridging a call to Darren's (user) cell phone, 203-555-1212. We only want to ring the phone for 20 seconds, to avoid hitting voicemail.

```
<application action="bridge"
  data="{call_timeout=20}sofia/gateway/my_gw/2035551212"/>
```

The variable in brackets is utilized on the newly setup channel, `sofia/gateway/my_gw/2035551212`. Now, let's add in calling Darren's office phone. We want the office phone to ring for 30 seconds, but still leave the cell phone at 20 seconds. We can achieve this with square brackets before each leg of the bridge, like this:

```
<application action="bridge"
 data="[call_timeout=20]sofia/gateway/my_gw/2035551212
,[call_timeout=30]sofia/gateway/my_gw/4158867901"/>
```

By placing the variables in square brackets, they apply to each leg of the specific call.

> Curly braces are only valid at the very beginning of a dial string. Also, newlines are not valid — your `bridge` string should all be on one line with no spaces between the braces and the `sofia/` portion.

You can also "clobber" variables set with curly braces by using square brackets later. You must set a flag, named `local_var_clobber`, to make this work. We can recreate the exact same example just specified by setting the "default" timeout to 30 seconds for all legs and overriding the timeout to 20 seconds only for the cell phone, like this:

```
<application action="bridge"
data="{local_var_clobber=true,call_timeout=30}
[call_timeout=20]sofia/gateway/my_gw/2035551212
,sofia/gateway/my_gw/4158867901"/>
```

Setting multiple variables can be accomplished by comma-delimiting. For example, you can specify:

```
{call_timeout=20,sip_secure_media=true}
```

The preceding code can be used to specify two variables for all channels, or:

```
[call_timeout=20,sip_secure_media=true]
```

The preceding code can be used to specify individual channels.

There is a special notation used with an **enterprise originate**. Instead of square brackets (per-channel) or curly braces (per-originate) we use the less-than and greater-than symbols. Consider the following example:

```
<action application="bridge"
data="<ignore_early_media=true>{var1=val1}
sofia/gateway/my_gw/${dest1}:_:
{var1=val2}sofia/gateway/my_gw/${dest2}"/>
```

Note the use of `<ignore_early_media=true>` at the beginning of the dialstring. This causes the variable `ignore_early_media` to be set to `true` on both of the "originates" that get created.

An example of using enterprise originate is found later in this chapter in the section *XML Dialplan cookbook*.

Global variables

When FreeSWITCH first starts up, it loads your entire XML configuration into the memory. During this process, it looks for the following code:

```
<X-PRE-PROCESS cmd="set" data="domain=127.0.0.1"/>
```

This code defines the **global variables**.

Global variables are expanded during this initial load process when FreeSWITCH starts up. The X-PRE-PROCESS tag designates a command to be processed during the actual XML load. When you set a variable during this phase, that variable is considered global automatically and becomes accessible throughout the application as $${variable} elsewhere in the XML.

Note also that when you utilize $${variable} in your XML, it is also replaced during XML load-time with the variable that was set during the X-PRE-PROCESS tag processing.

```
<X-PRE-PROCESS cmd="set" data="domain=127.0.0.1"/>
<param name="domain" value="$${domain}"/>
```

For example, the preceding XML code would literally be compiled and seen by FreeSWITCH as one single line:

```
<param name="domain" value="127.0.0.1"/>
```

This behavior is a feature of the XML parser—not FreeSWITCH itself. The pre-processing of global variables happens prior to the XML file being utilized by any FreeSWITCH process or event.

FreeSWITCH outputs the compiled XML file to disk. You can review this file to see what happened to your pre-processor commands and global variable declarations. It is usually located in /usr/local/freeswitch/log/freeswitch.xml.fsxml.

You can utilize global variables in your conditions, your variable and parameter declarations, and pretty much anywhere, like this:

```
<condition field="$${global_variable}">
```

Dialplan functions

Dialplan functions are small pieces of functionality that run real-time when processing Dialplan conditions. They can be used to gain a little more control and flexibility when writing your condition statements.

Dialplan functions can actually be used elsewhere—not just in the Dialplan. They are not related to XML—they can be used anywhere that a FreeSWITCH string processor is invoked. Examples of other places they may appear include external scripts that execute and set variables, bridge and transfer applications, and so on.

The general format for Dialplan functions is:

```
${api_func(api_args ${var_name})}
```

Where the `api_func` function is the name of the Dialplan function, `api_args` is the name of the arguments to pass to the function, and `${var_name}` is an optional variable name to pass to the function. The format and expected parameters for `api_args` vary depending on the function being used. Each available Dialplan function is explained in more detail in the following sections.

 Virtually any API that can be executed from `fs_cli` can also be executed from within the Dialplan using the `${api(args)}` notation.

Real-time condition evaluation

You can perform conditional evaluations within a condition expression using the `cond` function.

The general format of the condition functions is:

```
${cond(<expr> ? <true val> : <false val>)}
```

An example of using the condition function:

```
${cond(5 > 3 ? true : false)}
```

This expression would return `true`. The allowed comparison operators are:

- `==` indicates equality
- `!=` indicates not equal
- `>` indicates greater than
- `>=` indicates greater than or equal to
- `<` indicates less than
- `<=` indicates less than or equal to

Note that you can compare strings with strings and numbers with numbers, but if you compare a string to a number, they will be compared as `strlen(string)` and the number.

String conditioning

You can select a portion of a variable's value, (just like a `substr` function in many programming languages) by wrapping the variable in `${var:offset:length}` tags. The arguments are:

- `var`: A string variable. It can be a literal string or a variable such as `${caller_id}`.

- `offset`: The location to start copying data. The value `0` indicates the first character.

- `length`: The number of characters to look for. It is optional and if omitted, the remainder of the string is copied.

Some examples of the arguments are as follows:

```
var = 1234567890
${var:offset:length}
${var:0:1}   // 1
${var:1}     // 234567890
${var:-4}    // 7890
${var:-4:2}  // 78
${var:4:2}   // 56
```

An example of utilizing this API call to capture the first three numbers (U.S. area code) in an outgoing caller's Caller ID, stored in a variable named `${callerid}`, via the Dialplan is as follows:

```
<application name="set" data="areacode=${callerid:0:3}"/>
```

Using anything less than or equal to `0` as the length will return from the specified position to the end of the string.

Database queries

You can arbitrarily insert, delete, select, and update values from the internal FreeSWITCH database.

The general format for database commands is:

```
${db(command/realm/key/value)}
```

Database commands can be `insert`, `select`, or `delete`, followed by the table or realm, followed by a key and a value pair.

As an example, we could program-specific hold music, based on a caller's Caller ID:

```
<action application="playback" data="${db(select/music/${caller_id_
number})}"/>
```

As another example, we could insert data into the database. In this example we insert the current caller's UUID into a table named spymap, utilizing the caller's Caller ID as the record key. Someone could later retrieve the last UUID based on a specific Caller ID.

```
<action application="db" data="insert/spymap/${caller_id_
number}/${uuid}"/>
```

When you're writing to the FreeSWITCH database, you are utilizing the sqlite or ODBC database configured for the system. This makes the data you store permanent. Sometimes this isn't desirable or practical, and you have temporary data you just wish to keep in memory. In that case, you can utilize the same application patterns as we have seen earlier but swap out db for hash.

For example, we could retrieve from the hash:

```
<action application="playback" data="${hash(select/music/${caller_id_
number})}"/>
```

Or we can store in a hash:

```
<action application="hash" data="insert/spymap/${caller_id_
number}/${uuid}"/>
```

Hash is simply an in-memory hash table that stores key/value pairs. If you restart FreeSWITCH, you will lose any data in the hash.

SIP contact parameters

You can retrieve the contact string and parameters of a registered Sofia contact (and manipulate them) using the sofia_contact command. The general format for this command is:

```
${sofia_contact(profile/foo@bar.com)}
```

This is useful for multiple reasons. At its simplest use, it can be used to retrieve the string and detect parameters such as whether NAT was detected on the registered user, or whether the user is registered at all. As a more complex example, you can use this feature to strip the contact string for pieces you wish to utilize and then manipulate them further.

The following XML snippet will look up a user named foo@domain.com and get the user's domain name or IP address and contact parameters at the time of registration from the contact string. It will strip the username from the front of the user's contact record.

```
<condition
   field="\${sofia_contact($user_id@domain.com)}"
   expression="^[^@]+@(.*)">
      <action application="set" data="to_domain=$1"/>
</condition>
```

Replace domain.com with the actual domain that you are searching. Note the regular expression pattern:

```
^[^@]+@(.*)
```

This pattern matches from the beginning of the string until it finds the @ symbol, then captures everything after the @ symbol into $1.

After you have stripped out the username, you could replace it with a new username. This is often done when routing DIDs to a customer's PBX—you could replace the recipient's username with the DID being called, like this:

```
<condition
   field="\${sofia_contact($user_id@domain.com)})}"
   expression="^[^\@]+(.*)">
      <action application="bridge"
         data="sofia/external/${DID_number}@$1"/>
</condition>
```

In this example, if a variable was set in the ${DID_number} field, it would be combined with the user's IP address and contact routing information. So if a user was registered as frank@72.44.12.28, it might be replaced in this example with 2035551212@72.44.12.28.

If you have multiple SIP profiles to which users may register their devices then you may occasionally receive an ERR/USER_NOT_REGISTERED error when using sofia_contact, even though the registration is present. Remedy this by using * as the name of the profile when calling the sofia_contact command:

```
sofia_contact(*/user@domain)
```

The * will tell Sofia to search all SIP profiles for the user.

Set, export, and legs

When performing a bridge to connect two different call legs, you may find that you have a channel variable in the originating leg (the A leg) that you wish to be available also in the B leg. Sometimes you have a value that you want only to appear in one leg or the other. The techniques presented in this section will explain how to accomplish these tasks.

Set versus export

There are two general Dialplan applications available to set and modify information about calls and the way the switch will process calls. These commands are named set and export.

The set application sets variables on a channel for the duration of the channel. These variables can then be accessed by applications (such as CDR) or by Dialplan condition testing. You have seen the set application used several times in examples throughout this book.

The export application takes the set application a step further. It sets variables on the current channel but also saves the variable for use in any future channels created that stem from the current channel or Dialplan context. In other words, export sets variables on both the A leg of a call and on any future B legs that get set up.

The difference between the two applications can be subtle until you start needing to access information on B legs (transferred calls). The export application then becomes very useful for ensuring consistency in variables that may be needed in multiple legs of calls.

Consider these examples:

```
<!--Variable "foo" is set on both legs -->
<action application="export" data="foo=bar"/>
<action application="bridge" data="/user/1001"/>
<!--Variable "foo" is set on b leg only -->
<action application="export" data="nolocal:foo=bar"/>
<action application="bridge" data="/user/1001"/>
```

In some cases you may want to have the variable foo available in both call legs. There are other times, such as when processing CDRs, when you may wish to have a particular value present in only the B leg. The highlighted line shows an example of using the nolocal: directive, which sets channel variable foo to the value of bar on the B leg, but does not set channel variable foo at all on the A leg.

Passing variables via call headers

Sometimes it is useful to add your own custom headers to outbound calls. The SIP stack is the most common place to do this.

You can add arbitrary headers to outbound SIP calls by using the same set and export commands listed, as shown, but prefixing the variable names with the string sip_h_. For example, to add the header CallerLikesTacos=1 to a call, you could add a set application prior to a bridge application, like this:

```
<action application="set" data="sip_h_X-CallerLikesTacos=1"/>
<action application="bridge"
  data="sofia/mydomain.com/1000@example.com"/>
```

If you wish to add headers to a BYE request, you will need to use the prefix sip_ bye_h_ on the channel variable.

While not required, you should prefix your headers with X- to avoid issues with interoperability with other SIP stacks. X- headers are generally seen as custom headers and are ignored in the SIP world if not recognized.

XML Dialplan cookbook

We present here a few scenarios that you may need to refer to from time-to-time because they are relatively common. The examples presented in this section are in the mold of the traditional *cookbook* full of *recipes* for the reader to try. Feel free to use and modify these recipes in your custom Dialplans.

Match by IP address and call a number

In the following example, the particular extension will be selected only if the IP address of the calling endpoint is 192.168.1.1. In the second condition, the dialed number is extracted in variable $1 and put in the data of the bridge application, in order to dial out to IP address 192.168.2.2.

```
<extension name="Test1">
  <condition field="network_addr"
    expression="^192\.168\.1\.1$"/>
  <condition field="destination_number" expression="^(\d+)$">
    <action application="bridge"
      data="sofia/profilename/$1@192.168.2.2"/>
  </condition>
</extension>
```

The first condition field is terminated by a slash. The last condition field that contains the `action` tag is terminated by a regular `</condition>` tag. Also, note that the preceding example is not the same as this example:

```
<extension name="Test1Wrong">
  <condition field="destination_number" expression="^(\d+)$"/>
  <condition field="network_addr"
    expression="^192\.168\.1\.1$">
    <action application="bridge"
      data="sofia/profilename/$1@192.168.2.2"/>
  </condition>
</extension>
```

The `Test1Wrong` example will not route the call properly because the variable `$1` will not have any value, since the destination number was matched in a different condition, field.

You can also solve the `Test1Wrong` example by setting a variable in the first condition which you then use inside the second condition's action:

```
<extension name="Test1.2">
  <condition field="destination_number" expression="^(\d+)$">
    <action application="set" data="dialed_number=$1"/>
  </condition>
  <condition field="network_addr"
    expression="^192\.168\.1\.1$">
    <action application="bridge"
      data="sofia/profile/${dialed_number}@192.168.2.2"/>
  </condition>
</extension>
```

You cannot use a variable set inside an extension for further conditions/matches as the extension is evaluated when the action is called.

If you need to do different actions based on a variable set inside an extension, you need to either use `execute_extension` to transfer the call for the variable to be set, or use inline processing. (See the section *Inline execution* earlier in this chapter.)

Match an IP address and Caller ID

In this example, we need to match a called number beginning with the prefix 1 and match the incoming IP address at the same time.

```
<extension name="Test2">
  <condition field="network_addr"
    expression="^192\.168\.1\.1$"/>
  <condition field="destination_number" expression="^1(\d+)$">
    <action application="bridge"
      data="sofia/profilename/$0@192.168.2.2"/>
  </condition>
</extension>
```

Here, although we match with the rule ^1(\d+)$, we don't use the variable $1, which would contain only the rest of the dialed number with the leading 1 stripped off. Instead, we use the variable $0 that contains the original destination number.

Match a number and strip digits

In this example we need to match a called number beginning with 00, but we also need to strip the leading digits. Assuming that FreeSWITCH receives the number 00123456789 and we need to strip the leading 00 digits, then we can use the following extension:

```
<extension name="Test3.1">
  <condition field="destination_number"
    expression="^00(\d+)$">
    <action application="bridge"
      data="sofia/profilename/$1@192.168.2.2"/>
  </condition>
</extension>
```

On the other hand, if you anticipate receiving non-digits, or you want to match on more than just digits, use .+ instead of \d+, because \d+ matches numeric digits only, whereas a .+ will match all characters from the current position to the end of the string:

```
<extension name="Test3.2">
  <condition field="destination_number" expression="^00(.+)$">
    <action application="bridge"
      data="sofia/profilename/$1@192.168.2.2"/>
  </condition>
</extension>
```

Technically, we are not "stripping off" the digits we do not want, but rather we are "capturing" the digits that we do want. Remember, the value matched inside the first set of parentheses is stored in $1. Semantics aside, the net result is that we have the digits we want in a variable that we can use for whatever purpose we need.

Match a number, strip digits, and add a prefix

In this example we need to strip the leading digits as shown, but we also need to place a new prefix before the called number. Assuming that FreeSWITCH receives the number 00123456789 and we need to replace the 00 with 011, we can use the following extension:

```
<extension name="Test4">
  <condition field="destination_number"
    expression="^00(\d+)$">
    <action application="bridge"
      data="sofia/profilename/011$1@x.x.x.x"/>
  </condition>
</extension>
```

Call a registered device

This example shows how to bridge to devices that have registered with your FreeSWITCH system. In this example we assume that you have set up a Sofia profile called local_profile and your phones are registering with the domain example. com. Note the % instead of @ in the dial string:

```
<extension name="internal">
  <condition field="source" expression="mod_sofia"/>
  <condition field="destination_number" expression="^(4\d+)$">
    <action application="bridge"
      data="sofia/local_profile/$0%example.com"/>
  </condition>
</extension>
```

The use of % instead of @ is a FreeSWITCH-specific feature. Using the form user%domain tells FreeSWITCH that a user is registered with domain, and that domain is being serviced by the FreeSWITCH directory.

Try party A, then party B

The following example shows how it is possible to call another action if the first action fails.

If the first action is successful, the call is bridged to `1111@example1.company.com` and will exist until one of the parties hangs up. After this, no other processing will be done because the caller's channel is closed. (In other words, `1111@example2.company.com` is not called.)

If the initial call to `1111@example1.company.com` was not successful, the channel will not be closed and the second action will be called.

```
<extension name="find_me">
  <condition field="destination_number" expression="^1111$">
    <action application="set"
      data="hangup_after_bridge=true"/>
    <action application="set" data="continue_on_fail=true"/>
    <action application="bridge"
        data="sofia/local_profile/1111@example1.company.com"/>
    <action application="bridge"
        data="sofia/local_profile/1111@example2.company.com"/>
  </condition>
</extension>
```

Route DIDs to extensions

To route incoming calls that come in to a certain DID via the context public to a fixed extension in the context `inhouse`, do something like the following:

```
<context name="public">
  <extension name="test_did">
    <condition field="destination_number"
      expression="^\d{6}(\d{4})$">
      <action application="transfer" data="$1 XML inhouse"/>
    </condition>
  </extension>
</context>
```

This will capture only the last four digits of a ten-digit number and transfer the caller to that number via the `inhouse` context. Note the parentheses around `\d{4}` that allow us to capture only the last four digits.

Alternate outbound gateways

In this example we send ten-digit outbound calls from OfficeA to gateway 1 and from OfficeB to gateway 2. This assumes OfficeA and OfficeB are both using the same FreeSWITCH box but need different routing for outbound calls. It assumes both offices have 4-digit extensions, and that OfficeA's extensions start with 2 and OfficeB's extensions start with 3.

```xml
<extension name="officeA_outbound">
  <condition field="caller_id_number"
             expression="^2\d{3}$"/>
  <condition field="destination_number"
             expression="^(\d{10})$">
      <action application="set"
        data="effective_caller_id_number=8001231234"/>
      <action application="set"
        data="effective_caller_id_name=Office A"/>
      <action application="bridge"
             data="sofia/gateway/myswitch.com/$1"/>
  </condition>
</extension>
<extension name="officeB_outbound">
  <condition field="caller_id_number"
             expression="^3\d{3}$"/>
  <condition field="destination_number"
             expression="^(\d{10})$">
      <action application="set"
        data="effective_caller_id_number=8001231235"/>
      <action application="set"
        data="effective_caller_id_name=Office B"/>
      <action application="bridge"
        data="sofia/gateway/otherswitch.com/$1"/>
  </condition>
</extension>
```

Multiple endpoints with enterprise originate

Consider this example: a customer wants to know if they can route a call to two different people. Person number one (Alice) prefers that her desk phone ring first, and then her mobile phone. Person number two (Bob) prefers that his desk phone and his mobile phone ring simultaneously. Whoever answers first—Alice or Bob—will take the call and all the other outbound calls will stop ringing.

This complicated scenario requires the use of FreeSWITCH's enterprise originate. The basic idea of an enterprise originate is that there are individual originates that are connected in a larger "enterprise". In our example, Alice's phones might be dialed like this:

```
<action application="bridge"
data="[leg_timeout=10]user/Alice|
[leg_timeout=20]sofia/gateway/my_gw/${alice_mobile}"/>
```

And for Bob:

```
<action application="bridge"
data="[leg_timeout=10]user/Bob|
[leg_timeout=20]sofia/gateway/my_gw/${bob_mobile}"/>
```

Each of these individual bridge attempts would work for calling either Alice or Bob, but not both at the same time. To accomplish this, put both of these into a single bridge action and separate them with the special :_: sequence. Here is an example:

```
<action application="bridge"
data="<ignore_early_media=true>[leg_timeout=10]user/Alice|
[leg_timeout=20]sofia/gateway/my_gw/${alice_mobile}:_:
[leg_timeout=10]user/Bob|
[leg_timeout=20]sofia/gateway/my_gw/${bob_mobile}"/>
```

In this case, when the inbound leg hits this bridge app, FreeSWITCH will initiate two separate "originates"—one for reaching Alice and the other for reaching Bob. The effect here is that FreeSWITCH tries to reach Alice, by calling her desk phone and then her mobile while at the same time calling Bob at his desk phone and his mobile phone. If anyone answers then the whole "enterprise" stops and the call is connected to the endpoint that answered.

Note that we are forced to use ignore_early_media=true, because we are creating so many call legs. There is no way to pick just one source of early media (ringing) and use it. Be sure to set the ringback or transfer_ringback variables if you need to supply some kind of ringing signal to the calling party.

Summary

In this chapter we delved very deeply into the operation of the FreeSWITCH Dialplan. Building upon the foundation laid in *Chapter 5, Understanding the XML Dialplan*, we discussed many advanced Dialplan concepts:

- How Dialplan parsing works
- Using global variables and channel variables
- Advanced use of regular expressions
- Various advanced routing concepts

The Dialplan system in FreeSWITCH is one of the most important concepts you can learn. The power of FreeSWITCH is truly unleashed within the Dialplan system itself, and understanding the complexities of using various functions within FreeSWITCH is key to ensure that the FreeSWITCH performs exactly the way you want.

In the next chapter, we will lay the foundation for doing very powerful FreeSWITCH configurations that do not rely solely on the static XML files.

9
Moving Beyond the Static XML Configuration

Up to now, we've concentrated on using the static XML example configuration files that get installed with FreeSWITCH by default. In this chapter, we'll move on to show you how you can have a fully configured FreeSWITCH with only the most minimal static XML. FreeSWITCH offers several ways of letting you control it dynamically. Although each method has a different focus, some of their functions overlap. For example, both mod_xml_curl and the language bindings allow you to create dynamic configurations. In this chapter we will cover the following methods:

- **mod_xml_curl**: This module allows you to pull a configuration file from a web server. Configurations include Dialplans, user directory, and general configuration files. It also allows for dynamic configuration with a static fallback in case of a server failure.

- **Language bindings**: In a way similar to mod_xml_curl, you can use the supported scripting languages (Lua, Perl, Java, Python, and so on) to generate dynamic configurations.

- **originate API**: The originate API is unique in a way that it can create new phone calls on the system, hence the name originate. We will briefly demonstrate how to create a new call with the originate API using fs_cli.

- **Event Socket/ESL**: The Event Socket and **ESL (Event Socket Library)** provide a very powerful means of controlling FreeSWITCH. We briefly introduce the Event Socket in this chapter and then go into greater detail in *Chapter 10, Controlling FreeSWITCH Externally*.

The mod_xml_curl basics

The mod_xml_curl module is a module that uses the well-known cURL library (curl.haxx.se) to pull XML configuration files from a web server. FreeSWITCH can parse these files on-the-fly and use them as it would use the static XML configuration files. Since you control the web server, you get the benefit of being able to change the XML that is delivered from one request to the next. This can be useful when configuring more than one FreeSWITCH server from the same web server. One big benefit of a setup like this is the ability to make configuration changes in a single place and have them affect an entire cluster of servers.

All of the mod_xml_curl examples in this chapter require a web server configured to run PHP scripts. The examples have been tested on Apache2 with mod_php since it can run under Linux/UNIX and Windows.

To make mod_xml_curl load on FreeSWITCH startup, follow these steps:

1. Open conf/autoload_configs/modules.conf.xml in your favorite text editor and add the following line near the top of the modules to load mod_xml_curl:

```
<load module="mod_xml_curl"/>
```

2. Save the file.

 mod_xml_curl is built by default in Windows but not in Linux/Unix. Be sure to enable mod_xml_curl in the modules.conf file in the FreeSWITCH source folder, and then execute the command make mod_xml_curl-install.

As you can imagine, we need to give FreeSWITCH a URL to be used for pulling the configuration files it needs. We do that by editing the xml_curl.conf.xml file. Follow these steps:

3. Open conf/autoload_configs/xml_curl.conf.xml in a text editor and enter the following lines:

```
<configuration name="xml_curl.conf" description="curl
conf">
<bindings>
  <binding name="arbitrary_name">
    <param name="gateway-url"
    value="http://localhost/xml_curl/index.php"
    bindings="configuration|dialplan|directory"/>
  </binding>
</bindings>
</configuration>
```

4. Save the file.

5. Restart FreeSWITCH.

The `binding name` attribute can be anything you want, although we recommend something descriptive. The `param` inside `binding` has a value for the URL that gets requested each time a configuration is needed. In our example we use a local PHP script, however you could also use a public web server. As you can see by the `bindings` attribute we have selected `configuration`, `dialplan`, and `directory` to be requested from the web server by FreeSWITCH (we'll see these later when we talk about the `section` value in the `index.php` file discussed next).

It is critical that you handle the scenario where FreeSWITCH requests something from your script that it doesn't know how to handle. Use the following response to tell FreeSWITCH that you don't know how to handle the request and that it should look locally for the configuration file:

```
<?xml version="1.0" encoding="UTF-8" standalone="no"?>
<document type="freeswitch/xml">
  <section name="result">
    <result status="not found"/>
  </section>
</document>
```

This is especially useful if you want to handle only a few extensions or contexts in the Dialplan or if you only want to serve up special options for just a couple of modules. In the following sections, we'll show you some examples of doing exactly this. First we'll cover the `index.php` file which acts as the driver for all requests. Place the following `index.php` file in an appropriate location for your server:

```php
<?php
  function not_found( $msg = '' ) {
    print "<document type=\"freeswitch/xml\">\n";
    print "  <section name=\"result\">\n";
    print "    <result status=\"not found\"/>\n";
    print "  </section>\n";
    print "  <!-- $msg -->\n";
    print "</document>\n";
    exit;
  }
  header( "Content-Type: text/xml" );
  print "<?xml version=\"1.0\" encoding=\"UTF-8\"
standalone=\"no\"?>\n";
  if ( !array_key_exists( 'section', $_REQUEST ) ) {
    not_found( 'no section passed' );
  }
```

```
  if ( !preg_match( '/^(directory|dialplan|configuration)$/',
  $_REQUEST['section'] ) ) {
    not_found( 'section not valid' );
  }
  $gen_file = "${_REQUEST['section']}.php";
  if ( file_exists( $gen_file )  && is_readable($gen_file) ) {
    include $gen_file;
  } else {
    not_found( '$gen_file not found' );
  }
```

The not_found() function will just print out the chunk of not found XML that we mentioned earlier. In the event that we decide that we want the static XML to handle the request or if something is wrong with the request, then we'll respond with the not found XML block.

The next couple of lines (that start with header and print) will make sure that a browser or FreeSWITCH will recognize the response as XML and handle it appropriately.

The next three-line block will make sure that the request contains a section so that we know what to serve back to FreeSWITCH. If there is no section passed, we'll return the not found XML.

The three-line block following that checks to make sure that the section is either dialplan, directory, or configuration. Any other sections that get requested will receive a response to with the not found XML chunk indicating that FreeSWITCH should look locally for the configuration that it's seeking.

The last if block makes sure that we have a file in place to handle the section being requested and that the file is readable.

In the following section we'll go on to see how the Dialplan requests are handled with the dialplan.php file in the same folder as the index.php file.

The mod_xml_curl Dialplan

In this section we'll show you how you can handle the `book_test` dialplan context with `mod_xml_curl` and let all other contexts fall back to the static XML Dialplan. Add the following `dialplan.php` file to the same subfolder as your `index.php` file:

```php
<?php
  if ( !array_key_exists( 'Hunt-Context', $_REQUEST ) ||
  $_REQUEST['Hunt-Context'] != 'book_test' ) {
    not_found('not our context');
  }
  print "<document type=\"freeswitch/xml\">\n";
  print " <section name=\"dialplan\">\n";
  print "   <context name=\"${_REQUEST['Hunt-Context']}\">\n";
  print "     <extension name=\"no_name\">\n";
  print "       <condition>\n";
  print "         <action application=\"info\">\n";
  print "       </condition>\n";
  print "     </extension>\n";
  print "   </context>\n";
  print " </section>\n";
  print "</document>\n";
```

FreeSWITCH will send many POST parameters to our web application on every request. A couple of frequently used parameters are Hunt-Context and Hunt-Destination-Number, which correspond to the Dialplan context and the destination_number that you normally see in the static XML Dialplan). The first three lines of `dialplan.php` make sure that there exists a Hunt-Context in our request, and that the Hunt-Context is book_test, else it will return the now familiar not found XML to tell FreeSWITCH to keep looking elsewhere for the context. The remainder of this script just prints out the XML for our Dialplan context which contains a single extension.

A useful tool for testing your web server is the `curl` command line tool. On a Linux/ UNIX system issue this command from the command prompt:

```
curl -D- http://localhost/xml_curl/index.php -d
'section=dialplan&Hunt-Context=book_test'
```

The resulting output will look something like the following:

```
HTTP/1.1 200 OK
...Content-Type: text/xml
...
<?xml version="1.0" encoding="UTF-8" standalone="no"?>
<document type="freeswitch/xml">
  <section name="dialplan">
    <context name="book_test">
      <extension name="no_name">
        <condition>
          <action application="info"/>
        </condition>
      </extension>
    </context>
  </section>
</document>
```

Many of the examples you see will use cURL from the command line. We'll usually use the -D option to dump the headers of the response. In our usage, -D- tells cURL to dump the headers on the screen instead of a file, so we can see them immediately.

Notice that the <condition> tag has no attributes. The reason is that we can make the routing decisions in our script real-time and only return XML for the decision we've already made. However, you still have the choice of printing out conditions with field and expression attributes to allow FreeSWITCH to evaluate them and make decisions. Most implementations will return the single extension, but others will return an entire context and mod_xml_curl is used simply to keep configurations uniform across multiple machines.

The examples in this chapter show the use of cURL on a Linux/UNIX command line. However, curl.exe is available for both 32-bit and 64-bit versions of Windows. Visit http://curl.haxx.se/dlwiz/?type=bin to download an executable for your platform.

The mod_xml_curl folder

In this section we'll show you how to respond to folder requests from FreeSWITCH. This example will allow any user to register with the password 1234. This is meant only to be a demonstration of returning valid XML to FreeSWITCH and should never be deployed on a production machine because of inherent security implications.

Add the directory.php file to the same folder that contains your index.php file.

The following is the `directory.php` file:

```php
<?php
  if ( !array_key_exists( 'domain', $_REQUEST ) ||
  !array_key_exists( 'user', $_REQUEST ) ) {
    not_found( 'missing domain or user' );
  }
  print "<document type=\"freeswitch/xml\">\n";
  print "  <section name=\"directory\">\n";
  print "    <domain name=\"${_REQUEST['domain']}\">\n";
  print "      <groups>\n";
  print "        <group name=\"default\">\n";
  print "          <users>\n";
  print "            <user id=\"${_REQUEST['user']}\">\n";
  print "              <params>\n";
  print "                <param name=\"password\"
value=\"1234\">\n";
  print "              </params>\n";
  print "              <variables>\n";
  print "                <variable name=\"user_context\"
value=\"default\">\n";
  print "              </variables>\n";
  print "            </user>\n";
  print "          </users>\n";
  print "        </group>\n";
  print "      </groups>\n";
  print "    </domain>\n";
  print "  </section>\n";
  print "</document>\n";
```

As with `dialplan` requests, `directory` requests will send a number of POST parameters that will help you to determine how to respond to the request. The most commonly used are the `domain` and `user` parameters. In the first three lines of this script, we make sure that both of them exist before we proceed. As with earlier examples, we return the `not found` XML if either of our required parameters are not present.

The remainder of the script goes on to print out the XML that FreeSWITCH will need to process. Notice that in the `<domain>` and `<user>` tags we simply echo back what was requested from us. This will return a valid XML response with the password `1234` for any user on any domain. Again, it's a very bad idea to use this example on any production server as it could allow would-be attackers to authenticate against your server and make calls from protected contexts. This example is meant only for demonstrating the steps required to return a valid response to a directory request. In production systems you will most likely store your user information in a database and your script will query the database in order to return the required information.

At the system command prompt issue the following command:

```
curl -D- http://localhost/xml_curl/index.php -d
'section=directory&domain=example.com&user=1000'
```

The results will appear similar to the following:

```
HTTP/1.1 200 OK
...
Content-Type: text/xml
...
<?xml version="1.0" encoding="UTF-8" standalone="no"?>
<document type="freeswitch/xml">
  <section name="directory">
    <domain name="example.com">
      <groups>
        <group name="default">
          <users>
            <user id="1000">
              <params>
                <param name="password" value="1234"/>
              </params>
              <variables>
                <variable name="user_context" value="default"/>
              </variables>
            </user>
          </users>
        </group>
      <groups>
    </domain>
  </section>
</document>
```

Pay close attention to the name attribute of the <domain> tag, and the id attribute of the <user> tag and notice how they change if you post different parameters from the curl request. Keep in mind that all of the groups and users inside a <domain> tag belong to the same domain. Likewise, all of the users inside a <group> tag belong to the same group.

The mod_xml_curl configuration

You can supply FreeSWITCH with a number of configuration files using mod_xml_ curl and the configuration binding. In this section we'll dynamically generate a sofia.conf file and build a bit of a framework for doing other configurations with ease. We will be adding a few new files and subfolders to our web server.

Add the following `configuration.php` file to the same folder that has the `index.php` file:

```php
<?php
  if ( array_key_exists( 'key_value', $_REQUEST ) ) {
    $conf = $_REQUEST['key_value'];
    if ( is_file( "configuration/$conf.php" ) ) {
      include_once( "configuration/$conf.php" );
    } else {
      not_found( "unable to find config script ($conf.php)" );
    }
  }
}
```

Note that the `configuration.php` file will look for specific configurations in a subfolder appropriately named `configuration`. Create this subfolder under the same folder that contains `index.php` and `configuration.php`.

Next, add the following `sofia.conf.php` file in the `configuration` subfolder:

```php
<?php
  print "<document type=\"freeswitch/xml\">\n";
  print "  <section name=\"configuration\">\n";
  print "    <configuration name=\"sofia.conf\">\n";
  print "      <profiles>\n";
  print "        <profile name=\"internal\">\n";
  print "          <settings>\n";
  print "            <param name=\"sip-ip\"
value=\"${_SERVER['REMOTE_ADDR']}\"/>\n";
  print "            <param name=\"rtp-ip\"
value=\"${_SERVER['REMOTE_ADDR']}\"/>\n";
  print "            <param name=\"sip-port\" value=\"5060\"/>\n";
  print "          </settings>\n";
  print "        </profile>\n";
  print "      </profiles>\n";
  print "    </configuration>\n";
  print "  </section>\n";
  print "</document>\n";
```

There's really nothing to the `sofia.conf.php` file except printing out the XML response for FreeSWITCH. We assume that since the `configuration.php` successfully found this file and loaded it, then the only sensible thing to do is print the XML. The one thing that's worth noting is that the `sip-ip` and `rtp-ip` will be set to the IP address that sent the request, so we use 127.0.0.1 in our example.

Let's test our configuration. At the system command prompt issue the following command:

```
curl -D- http://localhost/xml_curl/index.php -d
'section=configuration&key_value=sofia.conf'
```

The output will be similar to the following:

```
HTTP/1.1 200 OK
...
Content-Type: text/xml
...
<?xml version="1.0" encoding="UTF-8" standalone="no"?>
<document type="freeswitch/xml">
  <section name="configuration">
    <configuration name="sofia.conf">
      <profiles>
        <profile name="internal">
          <settings>
            <param name="sip-ip" value="127.0.0.1"/>
            <param name="rtp-ip" value="127.0.0.1"/>
            <param name="sip-port" value="5060"/>
          </settings>
        </profile>
      </profiles>
    </configuration>
  </section>
</document>
```

As previously mentioned, the rtp-ip and sip-ip are both the IP addresses from which the request came. In this scenario we use 127.0.0.1, which isn't terribly useful at all. Imagine if you had a cluster of a dozen FreeSWITCH boxes where all profiles were exactly the same with the exception of the IP addresses that they're bound to. Suddenly this example starts showing signs of usefulness in a real world situation.

Another thing you might notice as you start inspecting some of these requests is that there are a few requests for configuration files with a post_load_ prefix. These files are requested to let you provide settings in files that are required before mod_xml_curl can be loaded (for example, modules.conf.xml and switch.conf.xml). The contents allowed in these post_load_ files are the same as the regular static files. For example, you can have your modules.conf.xml load only mod_xml_curl and then load the remainder of your required modules in post_load_modules.conf via the mod_xml_curl response.

The mod_xml_curl summary

Most of the mod_xml_curl examples we've shown you will print the same XML every time so they're essentially static with a few dynamic bits here and there.

You may have also noticed, and silently mocked, the fact that we're just using print statements to output the XML file. In PHP, as in the case of other languages, there are XML generating libraries/classes that can help you generate valid and compliant XML with different character encodings. For example, PHP has the SimpleXML extension (http://php.net/manual/en/book.simplexml.php) that can also be used. As a general rule, you should use such a library if you plan on doing any serious implementation.

Generating configurations dynamically with language bindings

If you would rather not set up a web server to process scripts, FreeSWITCH gives you the option of handling the same binding requests with the built-in scripting languages. All of the scripting language modules allow you to set the parameters so that you can have a script that handles requests which is the same as the mod_xml_curl script. The most commonly used languages are as follows:

- Lua with mod_lua
- Perl with mod_perl
- Python with mod_python

> FreeSWITCH also supports Microsoft .NET languages by means of mod_managed. However, its usage is different than that of the scripting languages of Lua, Perl, and Python. More information can be found online at http://wiki.freeswitch.org/wiki/Mod_managed.

Looking in conf/autoload_configs/ you will see configuration files for each language:

- lua.conf.xml
- perl.conf.xml
- python.conf.xml

Open any one of these and you'll see some parameters like the following:

```
<param name="xml-handler-bindings"
value="dialplan|directory|configuration"/>
<param name="xml-handler-script"
value="/path/to/script.ext"/>
```

As you might have guessed, the `xml-handler-bindings` are the configuration sections that you wish to be handled by your script. Therefore, `xml-handler-script` is the path to the script that you want to execute to handle the requests.

> While we use `mod_lua` in these examples, the principles also apply to `mod_perl` and `mod_python`.

The major difference between `mod_xml_curl` and `mod_lua` is that since `mod_lua` is embedded into FreeSWITCH there's no need for setting `Content-Type` and printing XML output for FreeSWITCH to read in. Instead, you just set a special variable named `XML_STRING` that contains the XML content to be parsed by FreeSWITCH. You can see this in the following example:

```
local xml_header = [[<?xml version="1.0" encoding="UTF-8"
standalone="no"?>
<document type="freeswitch/xml">
]]
local xml_body
if XML_REQUEST['section'] == 'configuration' and
XML_REQUEST['key_value'] == 'sofia.conf' then
local ip_v4 = params:getHeader( 'FreeSWITCH-IPv4' )
xml_body = string.format([[
  <section name="configuration">
    <configuration name="sofia.conf">
      <profiles>
        <profile name="internal">
          <settings>
            <param name="sip-ip" value="%s"/>
            <param name="rtp-ip" value="%s"/>
            <param name="sip-port" value="5060"/>
          </settings>
        </profile>
      </profiles>
    </configuration>
  </section>]], ip_v4, ip_v4)
else
```

```
    xml_body = [[
      <section name="result">
        <result status="not found"/>
      </section>
    ]]
  end
  local xml_footer = [[</document>]]
  XML_STRING = xml_header .. xml_body .. xml_footer
```

This example should look pretty familiar. This is essentially the same thing that we did in the mod_xml_curl configuration example earlier in this chapter. We generate the XML opening and closing sections which will always be the same. Then, if the section is configuration and the key_value is sofia.conf, we generate a minimal sofia.conf. If there's any other section or any other configuration is requested, then we just return the same not_found XML chunk from the mod_xml_curl examples earlier in this chapter.

At first glance, it might seem like a bit of a hassle trying to keep these scripts in sync across several machines in a cluster. However, if you consider the possibility of using Box, Dropbox, or one of the many other options for keeping files in sync across multiple boxes, then you could have a graceful alternative to using mod_xml_curl that does not require the use of a web server.

Making calls from the command line interface

You can make calls with no users on a system. For this example, we're going to assume that you have an endpoint to which you can make unauthenticated calls. This endpoint could be an IP phone, a soft phone, or even another FreeSWITCH server with a registered user or two. The only requirement is that the URI you call should ring a phone that you can answer. In our examples, we'll use my.open.endpoint.example.com as the target domain. Be sure to use the appropriate user and domain or IP address for your configuration.

Open fs_cli and execute this command:

```
originate sofia/internal/1234@my.open.endpoint.example.com &echo()
```

Obviously, this isn't going to be very useful in the real world. Hearing yourself say, "Hello, testing one, two, three…" can prove to be a good test of bi-directional audio and such, but to make this a productive example we should probably do something bit more interesting with our call.

In the following example, we'll originate a call to our endpoint, and then bridge it to the public FreeSWITCH conference using the example default Dialplan that comes as part of the default FreeSWITCH install.

```
originate sofia/internal/1234@my.open.endpoint.example.com
&transfer(9888 XML default)
```

As with the previous example, this one will dial our endpoint first. When we pick up, we'll be transferred into the `default` XML dialplan context where the 9888 will match the `freeswitch_public_conf_via_sip` extension in the `default` context and `bridge` the call.

The next example will also `bridge` us to the public FreeSWITCH conference via SIP, but without the need for a Dialplan since we're doing the `bridge` from the `originate` command:

```
originate sofia/internal/1234@my.open.endpoint.example.com
&bridge(sofia/internal/888@conference.freeswitch.org)
```

It could be argued that the previous two examples aren't very useful either, unless of course, it's Wednesday at around 1PM EST. In that case, you'll likely find yourself right in the middle of the weekly community FreeSWITCH users conference call.

That said, you can slightly modify these examples to create a click to call script for a website. You could make a form on your site where users enter their phone number and have it post to a form handler that does an `originate` to your main IVR.

```
originate sofia/gateway/my_provider/12125551234 &ivr(main_menu)
```

This originate will call `12125551234` through the provider gateway named `my_provider` and drop the person who answers into the IVR named `main_menu`. You may be wondering how to get that phone number from the web form into the `fs_cli`. One way is to have the form handler launch a system command that contains `fs_cli`, such as the following:

```
fs_cli -x 'originate sofia/gateway/my_provider/12125551234
&ivr(main_menu)'
```

Notice the use of `fs_cli` with the -x (to execute) parameter. Using `fs_cli -x` is simple and clean. However, it may not be the most scalable or efficient method, depending upon your scenario. The following section will introduce you to one of the most powerful aspects of FreeSWITCH, the event socket and ESL.

Using ESL to execute commands

In our previous examples we've originated calls from `fs_cli`. In this section we'll show you a couple of code samples that will do the same things from your favorite scripting language. For our examples, we're going to use Lua, since you've probably become accustomed to it by now. The ESL API is the same whether you use Python, Lua, PHP, Perl, or whatever, so the adventurous minds could follow along in their own favorite language.

ESL scripts versus built-in languages

Keep in mind that ESL-based programs are not the same as using built-in languages. The FreeSWITCH event socket is a TCP-based connection to FreeSWITCH. The ESL is an abstraction library that is available for more languages than just the few that are built-in to FreeSWITCH. You must first install the Lua, Perl, Python, or PHP for your system before using ESL. For Lua see http://www.lua.org for more information.

First, since the ESL modules aren't built as part of the default install, we'll need to build them before we can do anything with it. Linux/UNIX users should follow these steps:

1. Navigate to the FreeSWITCH ESL folder:

   `cd ${FS_SRC}/libs/esl`

2. Execute the following command:

   `make luamod`

Assuming these commands run successfully, you should now have the Lua ESL module built and saved in `${FS_SRC}/libs/esl/lua` as `ESL.so`.

If you have trouble installing the Lua ESL module then try installing the Lua development module for your platform.

You can move the `ESL.so` file to one of the paths that is in the Lua module's path search to make it load no matter what folder you're in when you run the script. The easiest way to find those folders is to run `./lua/single_command.lua` from the `${FS_SRC}/libs/esl` folder. Doing that should give you output resembling the following:

```
no file './ESL.so'
no file '/usr/local/lib/lua/5.1/ESL.so'
no file '/usr/lib/x86_64-linux-gnu/lua/5.1/ESL.so'
no file '/usr/lib/lua/5.1/ESL.so'
```

We notice here that the system looks for `ESL.so` in the present working folder (represented by `.`) and then in a couple of built-in Lua library search paths. Since we don't want to have a copy of `ESL.so` in every single folder from which we ever plan to run a Lua script we'll copy it to the next path in the search list, that is `usr/local/lib/lua/5.1`. In this example however, your system may have a different path. Be sure to run `single_command.lua` as shown previously to find out the correct paths for your case. Run these commands:

```
sudo mkdir -p /usr/local/lib/lua/5.1/
sudo cp lua/ESL.so /usr/local/lib/lua/5.1/
./lua/single_command.lua
```

Note that we create the folder if it doesn't already exist and then copy our `ESL.so` file into the folder. Lastly we run `single_command.lua` again to make sure it found our `ESL.so`.

> Windows users must build `mod_esl` with Microsoft Visual Studio (the pre-compiled binaries will not suffice). Right-click on `mod_esl` and click on **Build**. It will create `esl.dll`. Place this file in your Lua installation's `clib` sub-folder. When running a Lua script in Windows, use the command prompt and execute `lua` followed by the name of the script. For example: `lua single_command.lua`.

If all went as expected, you should now have a new error that looks similar to the following:

```
/usr/bin/lua: Error in api (arg 2), expected 'char const *' got 'nil'
stack traceback:
        [C]: in function 'api'
        ./lua/single_command.lua:9: in main chunk
        [C]: ?
```

If that's the case for you, then all went well. This new error is just telling us that we didn't pass a mandatory command to our `single_command.lua` script. Let's do that now. Run this command:

```
./lua/single_command.lua status
```

Passing the `status` API command to our `single_command.lua` script should give us output that looks similar to the following:

```
UP 0 years, 0 days, 5 hours, 6 minutes, 27 seconds, 223 milliseconds, 190
microseconds
FreeSWITCH (Version 1.2.8) is ready
0 session(s) since startup
0 session(s) - 0 out of max 30 per sec
1000 session(s) max
min idle cpu 0.00/96.00
Current Stack Size/Max 240K/240K
```

If you see what you expect to see here, then you should be able to pass any API command using a script similar to `single_command.lua`. So you could take the `originate` examples from earlier, and use them over ESL from Lua. Try something like this:

```
./lua/single_command.lua 'originate
sofia/gateway/my_provider/12125551234 &ivr(main_menu)'
```

One thing that could make this even more useful than it already is would be the option to run this script on a separate machine than the one your FreeSWITCH process is running on. Thankfully, you have that option. Details for configuring mod_event_socket to allow you to control it externally are covered in greater detail in the next chapter, appropriately named *Controlling FreeSWITCH Externally*.

Summary

Using the strategies covered in this chapter, you could have a cluster of FreeSWITCH boxes that have a bare minimal XML configuration and get the bulk of their configurations from a web server. There's no need for any of these boxes to have a user directory or Dialplan on them, because those can also be pulled from the web server in real-time as needed. Add in the process that involved you to bridge calls over ESL from your favorite scripting language to originate calls, manage voicemails, and so on, you now have a cluster of FreeSWITCH servers that you can manage almost completely remote without ever having to log into the shell.

These are just a small sample of the ways to configure and control FreeSWITCH without relying solely on static XML files. In the next chapter we learn about an even more useful way to control FreeSWITCH as we now delve into the extremely powerful FreeSWITCH event socket.

10
Controlling FreeSWITCH Externally

The FreeSWITCH **event system** is one of the most exciting components of FreeSWITCH. You have already learned how FreeSWITCH operates when it utilizes various static configuration files and scripting languages. The event system allows for tremendous real-time dynamic behavior and control of FreeSWITCH. Utilizing the event system is where FreeSWITCH really comes alive.

The event system allows external software programs to act as listeners regarding activity happening on the system. This allows for real-time interaction with telephony operations on the telephony softswitch in conjunction with externally running software or hardware. Almost everything that happens within the FreeSWITCH system causes some sort of **event message** to be generated. These events can be watched by external entities. This is similar to the publish/subscribe (or "pub-sub") system used by common message queuing software solutions, although it is specifically tailored for FreeSWITCH events.

The event system is bi-directional: In addition to allowing external programs to listen to events, external programs can also send events to FreeSWITCH. You can send and/or receive events in real time from your own programs. This combination allows you to use FreeSWITCH in almost any way you can imagine.

In this chapter, we will discuss the following:

- General overview of the event system
- Event system architecture
- Accessing the event socket
- Event socket library
- Example ESL program in PHP
- Creating a conference manager using the event system

General overview

The event system is the nerve center of FreeSWITCH, allowing both internal and external software to subscribe to a stream of activity happening inside the switching system. In FreeSWITCH, almost everything that happens generates (or "fires") an event. Receiving a new phone call results in an event. Ending a call results in an event. Committing a log entry to disk results in an event. Even speaking or going silent can generate an event. Each event becomes part of an **event stream**, which is tagged with an **event type**, **event category**, and various other details about the event. Other pieces of software can then listen for these events and act on them in any way they wish, such as streaming them to you via a TCP socket connection in plain text.

Events provide yet another way to extend functionality within FreeSWITCH. Events are different from hooks or modules (which can affect the actual processing and handling of calls in real time). Events provide an asynchronous (or non-blocking/queued) method of keeping track of activity on the system. They are generated by one part of the software in one place, and then are consumed by another part of the software. In practice, this is useful in scenarios where you may have more activity happening on the switch than you can actually process in an external program.

As an example, you may suddenly have a large spike in call volume which generates new call events. You may also be attempting to consume these events via a web browser, but the web browser cannot immediately keep up with the number of new calls that happen. By using a queued event system you avoid blocking the core switching engine (and thus, blocking the calls themselves) from being handled while you wait for the web browser to catch up to the volume that is occurring.

In this chapter, we will review all the different aspects of the event system — from receiving and processing events to sending events to FreeSWITCH from external programs. We will cover the modules that enable the event system externally, the types of events that can be generated, and the ways in which you might utilize events. Finally, we will consider a sample scenario and code to help you get started in creating your own programs to control FreeSWITCH.

Event system architecture

The event subsystem in FreeSWITCH was designed to maximize throughput and prioritize events depending on their type and the system load. There are two layers within the event system of FreeSWITCH. The first layer provides internal event handling routines and an interface for absorbing (or "consuming") events within FreeSWITCH itself. The second layer is provided by the modular architecture and provides the client-facing access to those events. By keeping these two units of functionality separate, the availability of a publish/subscribe style event system becomes apparent.

Within the internal event layer, FreeSWITCH provides core functionality that handles events occurring both on a system-level and a channel-level. Events can be published or broadcast by any part of the system, including modules. Two core types of events generally exist—system events and logging events. System events are generated by the core subsystem components or by modules. They include everything from the system's internal timer heartbeat to conference subsystem events, such as a party joining or leaving a conference room. Logger events are generated every time a log entry is attempted to the FreeSWITCH log file. These subsystems actually consist of three event queues, each with its own thread and priority level. If a queue fills up, the system fails over to the next queue until the entire event system is full. As calls or system functions progress, events are produced and stored in memory via these backend threads while they await pickup from internal subscribers. Once a message has been picked up by all subscribed modules and subsystems, the event message is destroyed. This allows the event system to scale better as events that are thrown do not cause a call to block while waiting for event consumers to pick up queued events.

FreeSWITCH uses its modular architecture to make events available to external software. An event handling module can subscribe to internal event messages, format them and send them to an external program. Such modules are called, appropriately, **event handlers**. There are not a lot of event handlers bundled with FreeSWITCH, but the ones that do exist are quite rich in their abilities, mostly because the underlying event system is so rich to start with. We will review these modules and how to utilize them.

Event-based modules

There are a number of modules that can handle events. By far the most commonly used module is `mod_event_socket`. We will focus most of our attention on this module and then briefly touch on a few of the others.

mod_event_socket

`mod_event_socket` is the most common module in FreeSWITCH for sending and receiving events via third-party programs. This module provides a TCP socket which you can connect to from external software programs. Once authenticated, you can send and receive plain-text event information that is easy to understand and parse. It allows for bi-directional communication for both consuming events from and sending events to FreeSWITCH.

Utilizing event sockets is generally easy. First, you connect from an external program to a preconfigured socket which is configured for `mod_event_socket`. You authenticate to the system, then you begin sending event messages to FreeSWITCH. You can also initiate a request to receive events, at which point `mod_event_socket` will attach event listeners to the event system, queue event messages, and send them to you as fast as you can process them.

The `mod_event_socket` module exposes an interface where you can request to receive plain text, serialized copies of events, and generate events of your own. You can optionally request to receive data formatted as XML. The module includes an event filtering mechanism, allowing you to subscribe only to the event types that are of interest to you. For example, your program may be designed only to operate on conferences; therefore, you need only to receive conference-related events. The module itself is ultimately responsible for capturing events from the internal event system, and echoing them to each active TCP connection it has established. It does the work of setting up and maintaining an individual queue for each individual TCP connection, as each of the connections are likely to consume events at a different rate. The queuing itself however, is part of the core operation of FreeSWITCH.

Configuring event socket settings

You enable the event socket system simply by loading `mod_event_socket` in your `modules.conf.xml` configuration file. Once loaded, `mod_event_socket` is configured by editing the `event_socket.conf.xml` configuration file. The following parameters are available:

- `listen-ip`: The IP address to listen on, for event socket connections. External programs would connect to this IP address. The default settings allow socket connections only from the local host. You can specify a specific IP address or use 0.0.0.0 to listen on all local IP addresses.

  ```
  <param name="listen-ip" value="127.0.0.1"/>
  ```

- `listen-port`: The TCP port to listen on for inbound connections.

  ```
  <param name="listen-port" value="8021"/>
  ```

- `password`: The authentication password that is required when connecting to this port.

  ```
  <param name="password" value="ClueCon"/>
  ```

- apply-inbound-acl: **Access Control List (ACL)** is used to control the connections to this port. This allows you to have a fine-grained control over who is actually able to connect to the IP:port combination specified previously. You can either use a known access control list name (as specified in conf/autoload_configs/acl.conf.xml) or you can use an actual IP address range.

  ```
  <param name="apply-inbound-acl" value="<acl_list|cidr>"/>
  ```

  Following is an example for apply-inbound-acl:

  ```
  <param name="apply-inbound-acl" value="known_machines"/>
  <param name="apply-inbound-acl" value="10.20.0.0/16"/>
  ```

  Note that multiple apply-inbound-acl parameters will not work.

Reading events

When reading events from mod_event_socket, the data will be in the format of name/value pairs, separated by a colon. An event message is terminated with two end-of-line (EOL) sequences. FreeSWITCH uses the traditional DOS/Windows EOL sequence of carriage-return linefeed (CRLF) characters. Your external program should connect to the event socket and read as many characters as it can, up until two linefeeds are encountered. Following is an example of a single key/value pair line:

```
Event-Name: CHANNEL_EVENT
```

Some key/value pairs contain multiple line breaks within the value itself. In this scenario, FreeSWITCH still wants to present the value as a single "line" to you. To do this, FreeSWITCH will URL encode the data so it still appears as one line. Following is an example of a multi-line value response:

```
variable_switch_r_sdp: v%3D0%0D%0Ao%3DUAC%206407%206867%20IN%20IP4%20
192.168.27.72%0D%0As%3DSIP%20Media%20Capabilities%0D%0Ac%3DIN%20
IP4%2061.231.8.102%0D%0At%3D0%200%0D%0Am%3Daudio%2012916%20RTP/AVP%20
0%2018%20101%0D%0Aa%3Drtpmap%3A0%20PCMU/8000%0D%0Aa%3Drtpmap%3A18%20
G729/8000%0D%0Aa%3Dfmtp%3A18%20annexb%3Dno%0D%0Aa%3Drtpmap%3A101%20
telephone-event/8000%0D%0Aa%3Dfmtp%3A101%200-15%0D%0Aa%3Dmaxptime%3A2
0%0D%0A
```

The preceding example is a URL Encoded SDP body from a call that FreeSWITCH is processing. It originally looked as follows:

```
variable_switch_r_sdp: v=0
o=UAC 6407 6867 IN IP4 192.168.27.72
s=SIP Media Capabilities
c=IN IP4 61.231.8.102
t=0 0
m=audio 12916 RTP/AVP 0 18 101
a=rtpmap:0 PCMU/8000
a=rtpmap:18 G729/8000
a=fmtp:18 annexb=no
a=rtpmap:101 telephone-event/8000
a=fmtp:101 0-15
a=maxptime:20
```

If one of the name/value pairs is a Content-Length header, you need to read exactly that many bytes from the socket after the initial headers and two CRLFs are encountered. Once you have read all the bytes in the content length, the next packet will start on the subsequent byte. When you have an event containing the Content-Length header, this is an indication that additional content is generated with the event, which is not in the key/value form and may contain its own native formatting.

The following is an example of an event notifying of a change in a channel's state:

```
Content-Length: 646
Content-Type: text/event-plain
Channel-State: CS_EXECUTE
Channel-State-Number: 4
Channel-Name: sofia/default/1006%4010.0.1.250%3A5060
Unique-ID: 74775b0d-b112-46e2-95af-c28258650b1b
Call-Direction: inbound
Answer-State: ringing
Event-Name: CHANNEL_STATE
Core-UUID: 2130a7d1-c1f7-44cd-8fae-8ed5946f3cec
FreeSWITCH-Hostname: localhost.localdomain
FreeSWITCH-IPv4: 10.0.1.250
FreeSWITCH-IPv6: 127.0.0.1
Event-Date-Local: 2012-12-16%2022%3A33%3A18
Event-Date-GMT: Mon,%2017%20Dec%202012%2004%3A33%3A18%20GMT
Event-Date-timestamp: 1197865998931097
Event-Calling-File: switch_channel.c
Event-Calling-Function: switch_channel_perform_set_running_state
Event-Calling-Line-Number: 620
```

Note the highlighted line shows that the Event-Name is CHANNEL_STATE. This event relates to a change in the channel's state.

Minimum event information

Every event you receive from FreeSWITCH via `mod_event_socket` will contain a minimum amount of information, regardless of the event type. The fields provided for any event are made available to help you understand not only what event type to expect, but also to help you understand when the event actually happened and on which server. In a multi-server environment, these fields are particularly useful as the `Core-UUID` header can be used to understand which system generated the event, while the timestamps ensure that events can be reconstructed and handled in the proper order.

The fields you will also receive in any event are illustrated by the following event:

```
Event-Name: CHANNEL_EVENT
Core-UUID: 689fd828-e85b-ca43-a219-39332bc55860
Event-Date-Local: 2012-05-09%2018%3A48%3A59
Event-Date-GMT: Wed,%2009%20May%202012%2016%3A48%3A59%20GMT
Event-Calling-File: switch_channel.c
Event-Calling-Function: switch_channel_set_caller_profile
Event-Calling-Line-Number: 840
```

The preceding information is always included, no matter which event is being received. That means that every event will be tagged with the following:

- `Event-Name`: The event's name, which is a description of the type of event it is

- `Core-UUID`: The UUID of the current instance of the FreeSWITCH core

- `Event-Date-Local`: The date/time of the event according to the system clock

- `Event-Date-GMT`: The date/time of the event in GMT (that is UTC) time

- `Event-Calling-File`: The C source file from which the event was fired

- `Event-Calling-Function`: The name of the function that fired this event

- `Event-Calling-Line-Number`: The exact line number of the C source file where this event was fired

The last three headers are particularly useful for testing and troubleshooting. After the preceding information, event-specific information will be included depending on the type of event being sent. There is no line break or spacing between the mentioned event key/value pairs and the event-specific key/value pairs.

Sending events

You can send events into the FreeSWITCH core via `mod_event_socket` over the same TCP connection you receive events over (the connection is bi-directional). All commands are formatted with a command name and arguments. Some commands require additional fields after the command itself. The formatting for additional fields when you send events is similar to the format you use when you receive events. You send FreeSWITCH a list of key/value pairs specifying the event name and specific flags related to the event, and FreeSWITCH injects the message into the event subsystem for modules or the FreeSWITCH core to handle.

An example of a basic command is as follows:

```
api sleep 5000
```

This would run the API command `sleep` and pass it the argument `5000`, causing the system to sleep for five seconds.

A more complicated example might be injecting messages directly into the FreeSWITCH event queue system. You can inject events into the FreeSWITCH system with the `sendevent` command, followed by associated parameters.

An example of the `sendevent` command is as follows:

```
sendevent NOTIFY
profile: internal
content-type: application/simple-message-summary
event-string: check-sync
user: 1005
host: 192.168.10.4
content-length: 5
hello
```

This would send a `NOTIFY` event with associated information. In this case, we are requesting that a `NOTIFY` message be sent to user `1005@192.168.10.4` on Sofia's `internal` profile. If `mod_sofia` is loaded and listening for these types of messages, it will generate the appropriate SIP packet to user 1005 for the requested `NOTIFY` message and include the `content-type` and `event-string` header in the SIP message, along with the content itself, which in this case is `hello`.

Note that all event messages you send into FreeSWITCH must be terminated by two CRLF character sequences.

The full list of event commands you can send to FreeSWITCH is detailed later in this chapter in the section *FreeSWITCH event system commands*.

Events from the Dialplan

mod_event_socket provides a Dialplan application named socket that allows for outbound TCP connections to be made to an IP and port, where the other end can stream commands for execution back to FreeSWITCH. This is similar to the network-based fast-AGI (FAGI) of Asterisk, but it can operate in full asynchronous mode, allowing commands to be issued and control to be returned immediately in anticipation of additional events or responses.

When you call outbound socket, FreeSWITCH automatically puts the call in park. You can watch calls go into the parked state by watching the event stack for the CHANNEL_PARK event.

The syntax for calling socket from the Dialplan is:

```
<ip>:<port> [<keywords>]
```

The following are examples of how to use it in the Dialplan:

```
<action application="socket" data="127.0.0.1:8084"/>
<action application="socket" data="127.0.0.1:8084 async"/>
<action application="socket" data="127.0.0.1:8084 full"/>
<action application="socket"
        data="127.0.0.1:8084 async full"/>
```

The optional keywords async and full modify the behavior as follows:

- async: The async keyword indicates that all commands will return instantly, making it possible to monitor the socket for events while the stack of commands are executing. If the async keyword is absent, then each event socket command will block until it has finished.

- full: The full keyword indicates that the other end will have the full command set for event socket. This is the same command set an inbound event socket connection has, so you can execute API commands, get global events, and so on. If the full keyword is absent, then the command set and events are limited to that particular call. In other words, if full is not specified, then the commands sent on this socket connection can affect only the channel currently being processed. Likewise, the socket connection will only receive events related to this particular channel.

mod_event_multicast

mod_event_multicast is very similar to mod_event_socket. It allows for sending and receiving events via network multicasts to third-party programs and other FreeSWITCH instances using plain-text event information. Other hosts can be configured to listen for events and parse them, potentially triggering events being fired on those hosts.

Event headers are the same as typical events except that all original headers are prefixed with 'Orig-' and the event is of CUSTOM type with a subtype of multicast::event. A Multicast-Sender header is also added. The following is an example of a packet received outside of FreeSWITCH that was sent by mod_event_multicast:

```
Event-Name: CUSTOM
Core-UUID: 12938281-57ce-11de-9be6-99a22d850f40
FreeSWITCH-Hostname: SYS1
FreeSWITCH-IPv4: 192.168.1.12
FreeSWITCH-IPv6: %3A%3A1
Event-Date-Local: 2010-01-16%2018%3A15%3A10
Event-Date-GMT: Tue,%2016%20Jun%202009%2022%3A15%3A10%20GMT
Event-Date-Timestamp: 1245190510366825
Event-Calling-File: mod_event_multicast.c
Event-Calling-Function: mod_event_multicast_runtime
Event-Calling-Line-Number: 313
Event-Subclass: multicast%3A%3Aevent
Multicast: yes
Multicast-Sender: 5211c5b8-ac42-11e2-8176-d16e41886f24
Orig-Event-Name: CUSTOM
Orig-Core-UUID: 8784372-5ecc-4eaa-9002-9992b7ab7c4d
```

You configure mod_event_multicast by editing the conf/autoload_configs/event_multicast.conf.xml configuration file. This file has four parameters to configure. They are as follows:

- address: IP address of destination where events are to be sent.
- port: TCP port of destination where events are to be sent.
- bindings: Bindings specify what events you want to send to the multicast addresses. This follows the same format as event <arg> <arg>, as specified earlier in this chapter.
- ttl: You can specify the TTL (Time To Live) for packets so that packets get dropped if not delivered in a timely manner. This is dependent on your LAN/WAN switching equipment for following this setting. The value is the number of "hops" to allow.

The following is an example configuration for `mod_event_multicast`:

```
<param name="address" value="225.1.1.1"/>
<param name="port" value="4242"/>
<param name="bindings" value="PRESENCE_IN CUSTOM sofia::register
CUSTOM multicast::event"/>
<param name="ttl" value="1"/>
```

FreeSWITCH event system commands

The following is a list of commands available for use from any event-based utility you use to connect to FreeSWITCH. You can use these commands from ESL (the FreeSWITCH Event Socket Library, discussed later in this chapter), via `mod_event_socket` and via any other standard interface that FreeSWITCH provides for accessing the event system. The syntax is the same for all access methods, although there may be variations in formatting and encoding that are introduced by individual modules.

auth <password>

When you first connect to the FreeSWITCH event system via the `mod_event_socket` module, you must authenticate. The following command allows you to pass your authentication parameters:

```
auth ClueCon
```

api

The `api` command issues an **Application Programming Interface (API)** command. Any API command accessible via the FreeSWITCH command-line interface may be issued. This executes the corresponding command in blocking mode, which means that the control will not return to the open event socket and no other commands will be allowed to execute until this one finishes.

Syntax: `api <command> <arg>`

Examples:

```
api originate sofia/mydomain.com/4158867999@telco.com 1000
```

This will initiate a call to (415) 886-7999 via `telco.com`, and connect it to local extension 1000.

```
api sleep 5000
```

This would execute a `sleep` command for five seconds (5000 milliseconds).

bgapi

The bgapi command will execute a job in the background and return a Job-UUID field with reference to the background job. When the command actually executes and completes, the result will be sent as an event with a UUID to match the one initially given.

The bgapi command accepts the same arguments for commands as the api command explained above. The only difference is that the server returns immediately and is available for processing more commands.

Syntax: bgapi <command> <arg>

Examples:

```
bgapi originate sofia/example/300@foo.com 8600
Content-Type: command/reply
Reply-Text: +OK Job-UUID: c7709e9c-1517-11dc-842a-d3a3942d3d63
```

When the command is done executing, FreeSWITCH will fire an event with the same UUID in the Job-UUID field. The event type of the response message will be BACKGROUND_JOB, so you must be subscribed to receive those types of events in order to see the response. A sample response might look like the following:

```
Content-Length: 625
Content-Type: text/event-plain
Job-UUID: c7709e9c-1517-11dc-842a-d3a3942d3d63
Job-Command: originate
Job-Command-Arg: sofia/default/300%20foo.com
Event-Name: BACKGROUND_JOB
Core-UUID: 42bdf272-16e6-11dd-b7a0-db4edd065621
FreeSWITCH-Hostname: ser
FreeSWITCH-IPv4: 192.168.1.104
FreeSWITCH-IPv6: 127.0.0.1
Event-Date-Local: 2008-05-02%2007%3A37%3A03
Event-Date-GMT: Thu,%2001%20May%202008%2023%3A37%3A03%20GMT
Event-Date-timestamp: 1209685023894968
Event-Calling-File: mod_event_socket.c
Event-Calling-Function: api_exec
Event-Calling-Line-Number: 609
Content-Length: 41
+OK 7f4de4bc-17d7-11dd-b7a0-db4edd065621
```

Note that in the response of the background job, the original job ID is listed in Job-UUID, while the UUID of the call that the `originate` command created (that is, the result of the `originate` command) is in the extra content data, in this case +OK 7f4de4bc-17d7-11dd-b7a0-db4edd065621. If you are building an application that needs to communicate asynchronously with FreeSWITCH, then be sure to use `bgapi` to submit commands and subscribe to BACKGROUND_JOB events. Use the Job-UUID field value to match a `bgapi` command with its corresponding BACKGROUND_JOB event. The BACKGROUND_JOB event will contain the "final" results of the command that was sent via `bgapi`.

event

The `event` command starts or stops the streaming of events. Events are streamed via the module that is executing the event command (that is, `mod_event_socket` TCP connection, `mod_erlang_event`, and so on). You can subscribe to specific event class types, or you can subscribe to all event types.

Subsequent calls to 'event' will override and disable previously requested event sets.

Syntax: `event plain <list of event types | all>`

Examples:

```
event plain ALL
```

This requests a copy of all events.

```
event plain CUSTOM conference::maintenance
```

This requests a copy of CUSTOM events, specifically the conference module's maintenance events.

```
event plain CHANNEL_CREATE CHANNEL_DESTROY CUSTOM
    conference::maintenance sofia::register sofia::expire
```

This requests a copy of events that have to do with the creating or destroying of channels, and all custom events from the `conference` module's maintenance system and Sofia's register and expire system.

noevents

This command disables all events that were previously enabled with the `event` command.

Usage:

```
noevents
```

divert_events

The `divert_events` command allows events which an embedded script would expect to get in the input call back to be diverted to the event socket. This means that a running script in FreeSWITCH that needs input can actually receive it from an outside connecting program which sends the event responses via an event socket connection.

An input callback can be registered in an embedded script using `setInputCallback()`. (We considered an example of using `setInputCallback()` in *Chapter 7, Dialplan Scripting with Lua*.) Setting `divert_events` to `on` can be used for chat messages like a Gtalk channel, automatic speech recognition (ASR) events, and others.

Syntax: `divert_events <on|off>`

Examples:

```
divert_events on
divert_events off
```

filter

Specify event types to listen for. Multiple filters on a socket connection are allowed. Note that this command is a "filter in", not a filter out. (See the section *nixevent*.) Set multiple filters to narrow the types of events you wish to see.

Syntax: filter `<EventHeader>` `<ValueToFilter>`

Examples:

The following example will subscribe to all events:

```
events plain all
Content-Type: command/reply
Reply-Text: +OK event listener enabled plain
```

Subscribes to all events.

```
filter Event-Name CHANNEL_EXECUTE
Content-Type: command/reply
Reply-Text: +OK filter added. [filter]=[Event-Name CHANNEL_EXECUTE]
filter Event-Name HEARTBEAT
Content-Type: command/reply
Reply-Text: +OK filter added. [Event-Name]=[HEARTBEAT]
```

Filters will receive only events of type CHANNEL_EXECUTE and HEARBEAT.

You can filter on any of the event headers. To filter for a specific channel you would filter by uuid using this syntax:

```
filter Unique-ID d29a070f-40ff-43d8-8b9d-d369b2389dfe
```

Use a combination of filters to narrow down the events you wish to receive on the socket.

filter delete

Specify the event filters that you wish to cancel. This can be used if you are accidentally (or intentionally) filtering too much data and wish to receive additional events.

Syntax: `filter delete  <EventHeader> <ValueToFilter>`

Examples:

```
filter delete Event-Name HEARTBEAT
filter delete Unique-ID d29a070f-40ff-43d8-8b9d-d369b2389dfe
```

This deletes the filter which is applied for the given Unique-ID. After this, you will not receive any events for this Unique-ID.

```
filter delete Unique-ID
```

This deletes all the filters which are applied based on the Unique-ID.

nixevents

This command is the opposite of the `filter` command, it prevents a particular type of event from being received.

Usage:

```
nixevents <event types | ALL  | CUSTOM custom event sub-class>
```

sendevent

Send an event into the event system (multiline input for headers).

Syntax: `sendevent  <event-name>`

This generates an event within the internal FreeSWITCH event system. Any of the modules or system processes that have subscribed to this event type will get the event.

If you issue `sendevent` without specifying an event type, and include an `Event-Name` header with the desired event name, you can specify any event type you want. For example:

```
sendevent SOME_NAME
Event-Name: CUSTOM
Event-Subclass: albs::Section-Alarm
Section: 33
Alarm-Type: PIR
State: ACTIVE
```

An example of the `sendevent` command is as follows:

```
sendevent NOTIFY
profile: internal
content-type: application/simple-message-summary
event-string: check-sync
user: 1005
host: 192.168.10.4
content-length: 5
hello
```

sendmsg <uuid>

Send a message to the call of the given UUID (`call-command execute` or `hangup`). Use this command to control the behavior of specific in-progress calls. You need to provide a UUID for the call.

In order to control calls using send message, the calls should be parked. A parked call means the channel is sitting in a sort of limbo state, allowing you to execute applications on the channel without interrupting other applications already executing (Note: A parked call will not receive any media, including music-on-hold.).

You can originate a call directly to park by using the &park() syntax:

```
originate sofia/example/300@foo.com &park()
```

There are two types of core actions that can be performed on a channel: execute and hangup. These two actions are described in detail in the following sections.

execute

The execute command is used to execute Dialplan applications. You can put an application name and application arguments into the execute request, and loop the application multiple times if you wish. A simple example might include playing a .wav file.

The format is as follows:

```
SendMsg <uuid>
call-command: execute
execute-app-name: <one of the applications>
execute-app-arg: <application data>
loops: <number of times to invoke the command, default: 1>
```

As an example, the following SendMsg command would play a file named test.wav to the channel specified in <uuid>.

```
SendMsg <uuid>
call-command: execute
execute-app-name: playback
execute-app-arg: /tmp/test.wav
```

If you have data that exceeds 2048 characters needs to be passed in as an argument via the SendMsg command, you can use a slightly different format when submitting your commands:

```
SendMsg <uuid>
call-command: execute
execute-app-name: <one of the applications>
loops: <number of times to invoke the command, default: 1>
content-type: text/plain
content-length: <content length>
<application data>
```

Note the highlighted lines. You can specify the length of the text used to invoke your application and then send in the application data in full.

hangup

This command hangs up an active call.

Format:

```
SendMsg <uuid>
call-command: hangup
hangup-cause: <recognized hangup cause>
```

nomedia

You can control whether or not FreeSWITCH is in the media path real time with the nomedia command. This command allows you to turn on or off media handling for a specific channel.

Usage:

```
SendMsg <uuid>
call-command: nomedia
nomedia-uuid: <noinfo>
```

log <level>

This command enables log output. You can specify a logging level that you wish to see. This allows you to receive all the log events just as if you were on the FreeSWITCH CLI.

Usage:

```
log <level>
```

nolog

This command disables log output previously enabled by the log command.

Usage:

```
nolog
```

linger

Tells FreeSWITCH not to close the socket connect when a channel hangs up. Instead, it keeps the socket connection open until the last event related to the channel has been received by the socket client.

Usage:

```
linger
```

nolinger

This command disables linger functionality previously enabled by the linger command.

Usage:

```
nolinger
```

FreeSWITCH Console application

Most people do not realize it, but if they have used the FreeSWITCH Console application (fs_cli), then they have already used the FreeSWITCH event socket subsystem. fs_cli is a C application that connects to the FreeSWITCH event socket provided by mod_event_socket. It consumes all system events, colorizes them, and provides an interface for sending commands back in the form of event messages. The entire FreeSWITCH console has been completely recreated by this application. (You can view the source code for fs_cli in libs/esl/fs_cli.c under the FreeSWITCH source directory.)

Event Socket Library

The FreeSWITCH **Event Socket Library** (ESL) is a set of standard APIs made available as loadable modules for various programming languages. Generally speaking, the APIs, when loaded into a programming language of your choice, provide native function calls for accessing FreeSWITCH event functionality — without the need to set up a TCP or network socket or otherwise concern yourself with how FreeSWITCH is reached.

Supported libraries

FreeSWITCH utilizes **SWIG** (www.swig.org) to create a standardized set of APIs. SWIG takes a defined list of variable and function calls and automatically creates libraries that link the core FreeSWITCH code to the programming language's native loadable module interfaces. The following languages are supported by default:

- Perl
- PHP
- LUA
- Python
- Ruby
- C
- TCL
- .NET

The following objects and methods apply to any language that can build ESL extensions. Once you have loaded the corresponding module for your particular programming language, you can utilize any of the standard ESL objects, functions, and variables. The generic function calls are listed in the following section. The FreeSWITCH ESL uses SWIG to take care of most type conversions for you, so try using your language's native type casting or variable structures when using these commands.

ESLObject

ESLObject is the core ESL object. You can set the loglevel information you wish to receive for events that you are receiving from FreeSWITCH.

eslSetLogLevel($loglevel)

eslSetLogLevel($loglevel) sets the log level on the server. $loglevel is an integer between 0 and 7. The values for $loglevel mean the following:

- 0 is EMERG
- 1 is ALERT
- 2 is CRIT
- 3 is ERROR
- 4 is WARNING
- 5 is NOTICE
- 6 is INFO
- 7 is DEBUG

ESLevent object

When an event is received, you will get an `ESLevent` object. This object has various helper functions available to help parse and process the event that was received.

serialize([$format])

`serialize([$format])` turns an event into colon-separated "name: value" pairs similar to a SIP/e-mail packet.

setPriority([$number])

`setPriority([$number])` sets the priority of an event to `$number` in case it is fired.

getHeader($header_name)

`getHeader($header_name)` gets the header with the key of `$header_name` from an event object.

getBody()

`getBody()` gets the body of an event object.

getType()

`getType()` gets the event type of an event object.

addBody($value)

`addBody($value)` adds `$value` to the body of an event object. This can be called multiple times for the same event object.

addHeader($header_name, $value)

`addHeader($header_name, $value)` adds a header where the key is `$header_name` and value is `$value` to an event object. This can be called multiple times for the same event object.

delHeader($header_name)

`delHeader($header_name)` deletes the header with key `$header_name` from an event object.

firstHeader()

firstHeader() sets the pointer to the first header in an event object, and returns its key name. This must be called before nextHeader is called.

nextHeader()

nextHeader() moves the pointer to the next header in an event object, and returns its key name. firstHeader must be called before this method to set the pointer. If you are already on the last header when this method is called, it will return NULL.

ESLconnection object

The ESLconnection object maintains a connection to FreeSWITCH for event handling. This object maintains connectivity to FreeSWITCH and handles sending and receiving of messages.

new($host, $port, $password)

This command initializes a new instance of ESLconnection, and connects to the host $host on the port $port, and supplies $password to the FreeSWITCH server.

This is intended only for an event socket in inbound mode. Use this function when creating a connection to FreeSWITCH that is not initially bound to any particular call or channel.

new($fd)

This command initializes a new instance of ESLconnection, using the existing file number (file descriptor) contained in $fd.

You can use this with Event Socket outbound connections. It will fail on inbound connections, even if passed a valid inbound socket.

socketDescriptor()

This command returns the UNIX file descriptor for the connection object if a connection exists. This is the same file descriptor that was passed to new ($fd), when used in outbound mode.

connected()

This command tests if the connection object is connected. IT returns 1 if connected, 0 otherwise.

getInfo()

When FreeSWITCH connects to an "Event Socket Outbound" handler, it sends a CHANNEL_DATA event as the first event after the initial connection. getInfo() returns an ESLevent that contains this Channel Data.

getInfo() returns NULL when used on an "Event Socket Inbound" connection.

send($command)

This command sends a command to FreeSWITCH, and it does not wait for a reply.

You can call recvEvent or recvEventTimed events in a loop to receive a reply. The reply event will have a header named content-type that has a value of api/response or command/reply.

To automatically wait for the reply event, use sendRecv() instead of send().

sendRecv($command)

Internally, sendRecv($command) calls send($command) and then recvEvent(), and returns an instance of ESLevent.

recvEvent() is called in a loop until it receives an event with a header named content-type that has a value of api/response or command/reply, and then returns it as an instance of ESLevent.

Any events received by recvEvent() that are unrelated to this transaction are queued up, and will be returned on subsequent calls to recvEvent() in your program.

api($command[, $arguments])

Send an API command to the FreeSWITCH server. This method blocks further execution until the command has been executed.

api($command, $args) is identical to sendRecv("api $command $args").

bgapi($command[, $arguments])

Send a background API command to the FreeSWITCH server to be executed in its own thread and is non-blocking.

bgapi($command, $args) is identical to sendRecv("bgapi $command $args").

sendEvent($send_me)

Inject an event into the FreeSWITCH event system. This allows you to send an event into FreeSWITCH where event consumers can process and utilize the event.

recvEvent()

This returns the next event from FreeSWITCH. If no events are waiting, this call will block until an event arrives.

If any events were queued during a call to `sendRecv()`, then the first one will be returned, and removed from the queue. Otherwise, the next event will be read from the connection.

recvEventTimed($milliseconds)

This command is similar to `recvEvent()`, except that it will block for (at most) the time specified in `$milliseconds`.

A call to `recvEventTimed(0)` will return immediately. This is useful for polling of events.

filter($header, $value)

See the event socket `filter` command.

events($event_type,$value)

`$event_type` can have the value `plain`, `json`, or `xml`. Any other value specified for `$event_type` gets replaced with `plain`.

execute($app[, $arg][, $uuid])

Execute a Dialplan application, and wait for a response from the server. On socket connections not anchored to a channel (frequently, the case with inbound event socket connections), all three arguments are required. `$uuid` specifies the channel on which to execute the application.

`execute()` returns an `ESLevent` object containing the response from the server. The `getHeader("Reply-Text")` method of this `ESLevent` object returns the server's response. The server's response will contain `+OK [Success Message]` on success or `-ERR [Error Message]` on failure.

executeAsync($app[, $arg][, $uuid])

This command is identical to execute; however, it does not wait for a response from the server. (In programming parlance, executeAsync is "non-blocking".)

This works by causing the underlying call to execute() to append async: true header in the message sent to the channel.

setAsyncExecute($value)

Force async mode on for a socket connection. This command has no effect on outbound socket connections that are set to async in the Dialplan and inbound socket connections, as these connections are already set to async mode.

$value should be 1 to force async mode, and 0 not to force it.

Specifically, calling setAsyncExecute(1) operates by causing future calls to execute() to include the async: true header in the message sent to the channel. Other event socket library routines are not affected by this call.

setEventLock($value)

Force sync mode on for a socket connection. This command has no effect on outbound socket connections that are not set to async in the Dialplan, as these connections are already set to sync mode.

$value should be 1 to force sync mode, and 0 not to force it.

Specifically, calling setEventLock(1) operates by causing future calls to execute() to include the event-lock: true header in the message sent to the channel. Other event socket library routines are not affected by this call.

disconnect()

Closes the socket connection to the FreeSWITCH server.

Events in practice

Let's look at a few specific examples that demonstrate the use of events.

Event Socket Library example – running a command

The following PHP example shows how you can write a simple script to process one-line commands. Using the FreeSWITCH Event Socket Library you can send those commands to FreeSWITCH and wait for the response.

```php
// Include FreeSWITCH ESL Library. Note that ESL.php comes
// with the FreeSWITCH PHP ESL module.
require_once('ESL.php');
if ($argc <= 1) {
  printf("ERROR: You Need To Pass A Command\nUsage:\n\t%s <command>",
$argv[0]);
  exit();
}
// Strip off the executable's name ($argv[0]) array_shift($argv);
$command = sprintf('%s', implode(' ', $argv));
printf("Command to run is: %s\n", $command);
// Connect to FreeSWITCH
$sock = new ESLconnection('localhost', '8021', 'ClueCon');
// Send the Command
$res = $sock->api($command);
// Print the response
printf("%s\n", $res->getBody());
```

Examples of sending events to FreeSWITCH

The following examples are useful in demonstrating what you can do with the event socket by sending (or "injecting") events right into the FreeSWITCH event system.

Setting phone lights

Many phones support turning line lights on and off via SIP presence messages. You can use the event socket to turn these lights on and off yourself.

Turn lights on

You can turn a phone's lights on by sending a presence event to FreeSWITCH, which will then send a SIP presence message to the phone. Connect to the FreeSWITCH event socket and send the following event:

```
sendevent PRESENCE_IN
proto: sip
from: 1000@example.com
login: 1000@example.com
event_type: presence
alt_event_type: dialog
Presence-Call-Direction: outbound
answer-state: confirmed
```

Anyone who has a line button for `1000@example.com` should see that line's light turn on. Note carefully the `answer-state` header—confirmed key/value pair. This means there is an active call happening (or we are simulating one) and the light should be turned on.

Turn lights off

You can turn a phone's light off by sending a presence event to FreeSWITCH, just like turning the lights on. After connecting to the FreeSWITCH event socket send the following event:

```
sendevent PRESENCE_IN
proto: sip
from: 1000@example.com
login: 1000@example.com
event_type: presence
Presence-Call-Direction: outbound
alt_event_type: dialog
answer-state: terminated
```

Note carefully that the `terminated` state of `answer-state` header means there is no call on this line (turn the light off).

Rebooting a phone

FreeSWITCH has the ability to send a request to SIP phones to ask them to reboot. This is useful if you have changed a configuration entry and wish to make the phone get the new configuration, which most phones will do automatically when booting during their provisioning phase.

You will need to know the `Call-Id` field for the registered phone you are interested in rebooting. You can get this from issuing `sofia status profile <profile_name> reg` command and finding the party in the list. You can then issue `sofia profile <profile_name> check_sync <call_id> reboot`. The phone should reboot.

You can connect to the FreeSWITCH event socket to perform both these actions. The commands would be prefaced by `api`, as follows:

```
# Search for the Call-Id of interest from within your program
api sofia status profile <profile_name> reg
# Reboot the phone
api sofia profile <profile_name> check-sync <call_id> reboot
```

Requesting phone reconfiguration

Some phones support the feature of being reconfigured. To have Snom phones reread their settings from the settings server you can use the following:

```
sendevent NOTIFY
profile: internal
event-string: check-sync;reboot=false
user: 1000
host: 192.168.10.4
content-type: application/simple-message-summary
```

Custom notify messages

You can send custom notify messages with arbitrary content via event firing. As an example, if you have sent the following:

```
sendevent NOTIFY
profile: internal
content-type: application/simple-message-summary
event-string: check-sync
user: 1005
host: 99.157.44.194
content-length: 2
OK
```

A packet similar to the following one would be generated:

```
NOTIFY sip:1005@99.157.44.203  SIP/2.0
Via: SIP/2.0/UDP 99.157.44.194;rport;branch=z9hG4bKpH2DtBDcDtg0N
Max-Forwards: 70
From: <sip:1005@99.157.44.194>;tag=Dy3c6Q1y15v5S
To: <sip:1005@99.157.44.194>
Call-ID: 129d1446-0063-122c-15aa-001a923f6a0f
CSeq: 104766492 NOTIFY
Contact: <sip:mod_sofia@99.157.44.194:5060>
User-Agent: FreeSWITCH-mod_sofia/1.0.trunk-9578:9586
Allow: INVITE, ACK, BYE, CANCEL, OPTIONS, PRACK, MESSAGE, SUBSCRIBE,
   NOTIFY, REFER, UPDATE, REGISTER, INFO, PUBLISH
Supported: 100rel, timer, precondition, path, replaces
Event: check-sync
Allow-Events: talk, presence, dialog, call-info, sla, include-
   session-description, presence.winfo, message-summary
Subscription-State: terminated;timeout
Content-Type: application/simple-message-summary
Content-Length: 2
OK
```

Note that aside from the SIP notify message itself being generated because of our request, the specific fields we included in the request were passed directly into the SIP message.

Summary

Once you understand how rich the event system in FreeSWITCH is and have tried it out yourself, you begin to realize that there are literally thousands of things you can do with the FreeSWITCH application. Unlike previous topics on making phone calls or configuring modules, this is one piece of FreeSWITCH that truly lets you and your users interact with FreeSWITCH in real time, in any way you can possibly imagine. The event engine is powerful and robust, and its applications are limitless.

In the following chapter, we will look at a more lightweight means of controlling FreeSWITCH. Read on to learn about controlling FreeSWITCH with `mod_httapi`.

11
Web-based Call Control with mod_httapi

The relatively new mod_httapi module was built to allow you to make your IVRs and other call control applications more dynamic. With it you can generate custom IVRs based on user input. FreeSWITCH's mod_httapi employs a simple HTTP POST operation to send various bits of information to a web application for a RESTful way to control FreeSWITCH call flows. In this chapter we will discuss:

- The syntax of HTTAPI markup
- HTTAPI configuration
- Basic HTTAPI operation, including the httapi Dialplan application
- A sample PHP library that makes HTTAPI applications easier to develop

As you read this chapter, keep in mind that mod_httapi employs an iterative call handling process; that is, there are repeated HTTP POST requests to the web server for a single phone call. This gives the application developer a great amount of flexibility and power in designing an application. It is not necessary to generate all the possible call flow logic in a single response. A phone call controlled by the httapi application will perform the actions specified in the HTTP response (that is, the HTTAPI "document") and then send another HTTP POST request to the server. In effect, the httapi application gets instructions from the web server, processes them, and then contacts the web server to say, "I'm done with those instructions. What's next?". This iteration happens until the call ends or has been transferred outside the control of the httapi Dialplan application.

HTTAPI syntax

HTTAPI markup is really nothing more than specifically crafted XML. In its most basic form an HTTAPI document looks like this:

```
<document type="text/freeswitch-httapi">
 <variables/>
 <params/>
 <work/>
</document>
```

This document is returned from the web server in response to the HTTP POST operation that requested it.

An HTTAPI response must have a content type of `text/xml`. All HTTAPI responses must include the document tag with the type attribute of `text/freeswitch-httapi`. Aside from that, you may use any one, or all, of the child tags in a given response. The child tags available are:

- `params`: These are the POST `params` (that is, "parameters") that FreeSWITCH passes to the web server on each request. You can use the `<params>` tag to tell FreeSWITCH to pass custom POST `params`.

- `variables`: These are channel variables from the channel that is calling the `httapi` Dialplan application. The `<variables>` tag allows you to set channel variables that can be used by the FreeSWITCH Dialplan or read back into `httapi` on subsequent requests. (This is described in more detail later in this chapter.)

- `work`: This is where most of the interesting stuff happens. There are many different `action` tags that can be used as children of the `<work>` tag to make FreeSWITCH do just about anything with the phone call being controlled: logging a message at the console, playing a sound file, doing Automatic Speech Recognition, collecting DTMF keypresses, and so on. The available `action` tags and the attributes that correspond to each action are covered in great detail in the next section.

Many of the following actions have the ability to add **bindings** to them that allow you to have FreeSWITCH collect and pass information back to you. This is handled much like an HTML form on a web page. Each element will have a "name" and any data collected for that element will be passed to your web application as a POST `param` of the same name. The bindings will have a regular expression (or `regex`) against which to match, and an optional digit value to strip from the end of the input value.

Work actions

The HTTAPI work actions are described in this section. In the following definitions, *DATA* is the content of the tag (that is, `<tag>*DATA*</tag>`).

All work actions have two tags that are always available:

- `action`: Changes the new default target URL.
- `temp-action`: Changes target URL to submit the next request. Subsequent requests will use the default URL or whatever is specified in the `action` tag.

The following is a list of `work` actions and their descriptions:

playback

`playback` plays a file and optionally collects input. It has the following attributes:

- `file`: The path to the file to play
- `name`: Param name to save result
- `error-file`: Error file to play on invalid input
- `digit-timeout`: Timeout waiting for digits after file plays (when input bindings are present)
- `input-timeout`: Timeout waiting for more digits in a multi-digit input
- `loops`: Maximum number of times to play the file (when input bindings are present)
- `asr-engine`: Automated Speech Recognition (ASR) engine to use
- `asr-grammar`: Automated Speech Recognition (ASR) grammar to use
- `terminators`: The keys that you want to use to immediately stop and process the digits collected

Example:

```
<document type="text/freeswitch-httapi">
  <work>
    <playback action="http://newurl/index.php"
      temp-action="http://newtempurl/index.php"
      name="playback_user_input"
      error-file="ivr/ivr-error.wav"
      file="ivr/ivr-welcome_to_freeswitch.wav"
      asr-engine="pocketsphinx"
      asr-grammar="my_default_asr_grammar"
      digit-timeout="5"
```

```
        input-timeout="10"
        loops="3"
        terminators="#">
        <bind strip="#">~\\d{3}</bind>
      </playback>
    </work>
  </document>
```

The `playback` action is analogous to the `playback` Dialplan application.

vmname

`vmname` plays a voicemail name and optionally collects input. It has the following attributes:

- `id`: User's name to play passed as `user@domain`
- `name`: `Param` name to save result
- `error-file`: Error file to play on invalid input
- `digit-timeout`: Timeout waiting for digits after file plays (when input bindings are present)
- `input-timeout`: Timeout waiting for more digits in a multi-digit input (when input bindings are present)
- `loops`: Maximum number of times to play the file (when input bindings are present)
- `terminators`: The keys that you want to use to immediately stop and process the digits collected

Example:

```
<document type="text/freeswitch-httapi">
  <work>
    <vmname action="http://newurl/index.php"
      temp-action="http://newtempurl/index.php"
      name="vmname_user_input"
      error-file="ivr/ivrerror.wav"
      id="1007@192.168.1.101"
      digit-timeout="5"
      input-timeout="10"
      loops="3"
      terminators="#">
      <bind strip="#">~\\d{3}</bind>
    </vmname>
  </work>
</document>
```

record

record records a file, optionally collects input, and posts the file back to the target URL. It has the following attributes:

- `file`: The file path to record
- `name`: Param name to save result (will be a multipart form file upload)
- `error-file`: Error file to play on invalid input
- `beep-file`: File to play as an indicator to start recording message (that is, a voicemail beep)
- `digit-timeout`: Timeout waiting for digits after file plays (when input bindings are present)
- `limit`: Upper limit of number of seconds to record
- `terminators`: The keys that you want to use to immediately stop and process the digits collected

Example:

```
<document type="text/freeswitch-httapi">
  <work>
    <record action="http://localhost/newurl.php"
      temp-action="http://localhost/newtempurl.php"
      name="playback_user_input"
      error-file="ivr/ivr-error.wav"
      beep-file="tone_stream://$${beep}"
      file="12345.wav"
      digit-timeout="5"
      limit="60"
      terminators="#">
      <bind strip="#">~\\d{3}</bind>
    </record>
  </work>
</document>
```

The record action is analogous to the record Dialplan application.

pause

pause waits for input for a specific amount of time. It has the following attributes:

- `milliseconds`: Number of milliseconds to pause
- `name`: Param name to save result
- `error-file`: Error file to play on invalid input

- digit-timeout: Timeout waiting for digits after file plays (when input bindings are present)

- input-timeout: Timeout waiting for more digits in a multi-digit input

- loops: Maximum number of times to play the file when input bindings are present.

- terminators: The keys that you want to use to immediately stop and process the digits collected

Example:

```
<document type="text/freeswitch-httapi">
  <work>
    <pause action="http://localhost/newurl.php"
      temp-action="http://localhost/newtempurl.php"
      name="pause_user_input"
      error-file="ivr/it_was_that_bug.wav"
      digit-timeout="5"
      milliseconds="15000"
      terminators="#">
      <bind strip="#">~\\d{3}</bind>
    </pause>
  </work>
</document>
```

speak

speak reads text to the caller using the TTS (Text-to-Speech) engine, optionally collecting input. It has the following attributes:

- text: The text to be spoken to the caller

- name: Param name to save result

- error-file: Error file to play on invalid input

- digit-timeout: Timeout waiting for digits after file plays (when input bindings are present)

- input-timeout: Timeout waiting for more digits in a multi-digit input

- loops: Maximum number of times to play the file when input bindings are present

- engine: Text-to-Speech (TTS) engine to use

- voice: Text-to-Speech (TTS) voice to use

- terminators: The keys that you want to use to immediately stop and process the digits collected

Example:

```
<document type="text/freeswitch-httapi">
  <work>
    <speak action="http://localhost/newurl.php"
      temp-action="http://localhost/newtempurl.php"
      name="speak_user_input"
      error-file="ivr/ivr-error.wav"
      digit-timeout="5"
      engine="flite"
      voice="slt"
      text="Hello from flite text to speech engine"
      terminators="#">
      <bind strip="#">~\\d{3}</bind>
    </speak>
  </work>
</document>
```

The speak action is analogous to the speak Dialplan application.

say

Use the FreeSWITCH say engine to iterate sounds to simulate a human speaker. It has the following attributes:

- text: The text to speak, spell, pronounce, and so on
- name: Param name in which the result will be saved
- error-file: Error file to play on invalid input
- digit-timeout: Timeout waiting for digits after file plays (when input bindings are present)
- input-timeout: Timeout waiting for more digits in a multi-digit input
- loops: Maximum number of times to play the file when input bindings are present
- language: Language of speech
- type: Type (say interface parameter)
- method: Method (say interface parameter)
- gender: Gender (say parameter)
- terminators: The keys that you want to use to immediately stop and process the digits collected

Example:

```
<document type="text/freeswitch-httapi">
  <work>
    <say action="http://localhost/newurl.php"
      temp-action="http://localhost/newtempurl.php"
      name="say_user_input"
      error-file="ivr/ivr-error.wav"
      digit-timeout="5"
      language="en"
      type="name_spelled"
      method="pronounced"
      text="This is what the caller will hear"
      terminators="#">
      <bind strip="#">~\\d{3}</bind>
    </say>
  </work>
</document>
```

The say action is analogous to the say Dialplan application. See the say entry under
Important Dialplan applications in *Chapter 5, Understanding the XML Dialplan.*

execute

execute executes a FreeSWITCH Dialplan application. It has the following
attributes:

- application: The Dialplan application to run
- data: Alternate source for application data
- *DATA*: The application data

Example:

```
<document type="text/freeswitch-httapi">
  <work>
    <execute action="http://localhost/newurl.php"
      temp-action="http://localhost/newtempurl.php"
      application="log"
      data="INFO this is an info log message"/>
  </work>
</document>
```

sms

sms sends an SMS message. It has the following attributes:

- to: The destination number
- *DATA*: The message data

Example:

```
<document type="text/freeswitch-httapi">
  <work>
    <sms action="http://localhost/newurl.php"
      temp-action="http://localhost/newtempurl.php"
      to="sip:1007@192.168.1.101">Message text here</sms>
  </work>
</document>
```

Note: this requires mod_sms to be compiled and loaded. See
http://wiki.freeswitch.org/wiki/Mod_sms for more information.

dial

dial places an outbound call or transfer. It has the following attributes:

- context: Dialplan context
- Dialplan: Dialplan type (usually XML)
- caller-id-name: Caller ID Name
- caller-id-number: Caller ID Number
- *DATA*: Number to dial or originate string

Example:

```
<document type="text/freeswitch-httapi">
  <work>
    <dial action="http://localhost/newurl.php"
      temp-action="http://localhost/newtempurl.php"
      caller-id-name="HTTAPI Test"
      caller-id-number="19193869900"
      context="default"
      Dialplan="XML">
        sip:2019@10.1.1.12
      </dial>
  </work>
</document>
```

The `dial` action will place a call through the Dialplan, and if a new call leg is created, the call being controlled by HTTAPI will be connected to it.

recordCall

`recordCall` initiates recording of the call. The file will be posted when the call ends. It has the following attributes:

- `limit`: Timeout in seconds.
- `name`: If this starts with `http://` then it must specify the URL where FreeSWITCH will PUT the file. Your web server must be set up to handle a PUT request in order to use it this way. If omitted, FreeSWITCH will record to a temporary directory.

Example:

```
<document type="text/freeswitch-httapi">
  <work>
    <recordCall action="http://localhost/newurl.php"
      temp-action="http://localhost/newtempurl.php"
      name="http://localhost/newfile.wav"
      limit="60"/>
  </work>
</document>
```

The `recordCall` action is analogous to the `record` Dialplan application.

conference

`conference` starts a conference call. It has the following attributes:

- `profile`: Conference profile to use
- `*DATA*`: The conference name in which the call will be placed

Example:

```
<document type="text/freeswitch-httapi">
  <work>
    <conference action="http://localhost/newurl.php"
      temp-action="http://localhost/newtempurl.php"
      profile="my_new_profile">
        My_Conference
      </conference>
  </work>
</document>
```

The `conference` action is analogous to the `conference` Dialplan application.

hangup

`hangup` hangs up the call. It has the following attributes:

- `cause`: The hangup cause to send

Example:

```
<document type="text/freeswitch-httapi">
  <work>
    <hangup action="http://localhost/newurl.php"
      temp-action="http://localhost/newtempurl.php"
      cause="NORMAL_CLEARING"/>
  </work>
</document>
```

The `hangup` action is analogous to the `hangup` Dialplan application.

break

`break` exits the `httapi` application and continues in the Dialplan.

```
<document type="text/freeswitch-httapi">
  <work>
    <break/>
  </work>
</document>
```

log

`log` writes a log line to `fs_cli`, console, and log file.

- `level`: The log level to use
- `clean`: If set to a true value, then the log line will not print the log prefix

Example:

```
<document type="text/freeswitch-httapi">
  <work>
    <log action="http://localhost/newurl.php"
      temp-action="http://localhost/newtempurl.php"
      level="info">this is a log message with a prefix</log>
    <log level="warning"
      clean="1">and this is one without</log>
  </work>
</document>
```

The `log` action is analogous to the `log` Dialplan application. Note that the `log` Dialplan application does not have a `clean` option whereas the `httapi log` action does.

continue

`continue` performs no specific work actions and continues (that is, a `no-op` action). This is useful if you want to request a different `action` URL based on the results of a `getVar` or similar.

```
<document type="text/freeswitch-httapi">
  <work>
    <continue action="http://localhost/newurl.php"
      temp-action="http://localhost/newtempurl.php"/>
  </work>
</document>
```

getVar

`getVar` gets a channel variable's contents (depends on permissions). It has the following attributes:

- permanent: When set to a true value this variable gets sent on all subsequent HTTAPI requests for this call, otherwise it is sent only on the next request

- name: The variable name to read from the channel (for example, `caller_id_name`)

Example:

```
<document type="text/freeswitch-httapi">
  <work>
    <getVariable name="caller_id_name"
      action="http://localhost/newurl.php"
      temp-action="http://localhost/newtempurl.php"
      permanent="1"/>
  </work>
</document>
```

voicemail

voicemail calls the voicemail Dialplan application without requiring "execute" permissions. It has the following attributes:

- check: When set to a true value this allows the caller to check messages; that is, the mailbox user. If omitted then the caller will be prompted to leave a voice message in the mailbox.
- auth-only: Authenticate only and move on. In the event this mode is chosen, two new variables will be set on the channel upon successful authentication:
  - ○ variable_user_pin_authenticated is set to true
  - ○ variable_user_pin_authenticated_user is the username of the successfully authenticated user
- profile: Voicemail profile name to use (omit for "default").
- domain: Domain to use (omit for global domain variable).
- id: ID to use (omit to prompt for id).

Example:

```
<document type="text/freeswitch-httapi">
  <work>
    <voicemail action="http://localhost/newurl.php"
      temp-action="http://localhost/newtempurl.php"
      auth-only="1"
      check="1"
      domain="192.168.1.101"
      id="1010"
      profile="default"/>
  </work>
</document>
```

The voicemail action is analogous to the voicemail Dialplan application.

mod_httapi configuration file

The mod_httapi configuration file is found in conf/autoload_configs and is named httapi.conf.xml. It contains several settings parameters as well as a profiles section. The example configuration contains a default HTTAPI profile or you may create your own profiles.

Inside the profile tag you will notice a number of `param` entries. These control things such as default settings for various work actions, permissions control (see the following sections), and the default URL to use for HTTP requests.

You might recall the `gateway-url` parameter from the `mod_xml_curl` configuration in *Chapter 9, Moving Beyond the Static XML Configuration*, and how `mod_xml_curl` would use it to get its configuration from the web server. In `mod_httapi`, there's an identical `gateway-url` parameter that FreeSWITCH can use as a base URL to which information can be pushed and from which information can be pulled, namely a web server. As `httapi` is a Dialplan application, we also have the ability to specify a different URL if we choose. As we look at the following two examples, notice that we don't pass any application data in the first example. This will cause it to use the preconfigured `gateway-url` parameter from the configuration file. In the second example, we give `httapi` a URL that's different than the one in the configuration file.

Example one:

```
<action application="httapi "/>
```

Example two:

```
<action application="httapi"
        data="http://localhost/httapi/index2.php"/>
```

In the next few examples, we'll demonstrate how you can pass extra POST parameters to your web app. Both of the following examples are functionally identical to example two.

The following example passes the URL as a named parameter inside curly brackets (or "braces" – the { and } characters) that FreeSWITCH interprets before sending the request to the web server. The `url` parameter is special and literally means "use this URL for the request".

```
<action application="httapi"
        data="{url=http://localhost/httapi/index2.php}">
```

In our next example, we pass the `url` parameter as before, as well as passing a new parameter to set the HTTP method (for instance, GET, PUT, or POST).

```
<action application="httapi"
 data="{method=POST,url=http://localhost/httapi/index2.php}">
```

Permissions

With all the control that you have in `httapi`, sometimes it becomes necessary to throttle that power a little bit with `permissions` on things such as variables that shouldn't be changed, or applications and APIs that you don't want to execute inadvertently. In the example `httapi.conf.xml` configuration file, you will see the `<permissions>` tag under the `default` profile. Within the `permissions` tag you'll find many different permissions that you can enable, with even more fine-grained control over certain aspects of some of them.

`set-params` is a permission to allow you to set or restrict the setting of the same parameters that can be set from within the {}'s when calling `httapi` from the Dialplan and have them persist throughout the lifetime of the call.

`set-vars` allows you to set or restrict the setting of channel variables. This permission goes a step further than the `set-params` does and allows you to specify which variables you want to allow the setting of, similar to the way access control is handled in `acl.conf.xml`. Notice the default policy and the ability to allow access in the following snippet from the example configuration file:

```
<permission name="set-vars" value="true">
  <variable-list default="deny">
    <!-- Variables here may be changed -->
    <variable name="caller_id_name"/>
  </variable-list>
</permission>
```

The preceding code listed says, in effect, that the ability to set variables is disabled unless they are specifically named within the `variable-list`.

You may have noticed that there's no attribute on the `<variable>` tag that tells it that it should allow setting of the given variable. There is a valid `type` attribute that works the same as the `type` attribute you've seen in ACLs, but the default is to be the opposite of the policy if the type attribute is omitted. That is to say, if your list default is `deny`, then leaving the `type` attribute off of an entry will make it allow the given entity. The opposite is also true:

```
<permission name="set-vars" value="true">
  <variable-list default="allow">
    <!-- Variables here may *not* be changed -->
    <variable name="caller_id_name"/>
  </variable-list>
</permission>
```

Pay close attention to your allow and deny entries, otherwise you may inadvertently allow a program to have access to sensitive data.

As you might expect, the `get-vars` permission allows you the ability to read channel variables from the call. This permission has the same fine-grained controls that the `set-vars` option gives. There is a separate ACL-like control list for getting variables as opposed to setting variables. This exists because there is the possibility that you will want to allow some variables to be set from your application, while others remain read-only, and some are totally inaccessible altogether.

The `extended-data` permission will pass much more information to your web application than without it. The default behavior is to post a succinct overview of the channel and allow you to get the information you need via HTTAPI commands and subsequent callbacks. If you would rather have every set channel variable posted to your application upon the initial request, you only need to enable this option.

If you set the `execute-apps` permission then you'll have the ability to call Dialplan applications from within your `httapi` web application. This will allow you to use applications with an `<execute>` tag as described earlier. This permission has the same sort of ACL-like control that we have seen in a couple of the other permissions already. You have the ability to allow access to all applications, or enable or disable them one by one. In the following code from the example configuration, you will see that we allow access to use applications with a default deny policy, and allow access to the `info` and `hangup` applications:

```
<permission name="execute-apps" value="true">
  <application-list default="deny">
    <application name="info"/>
    <application name="hangup"/>
  </application-list>
</permission>
```

The `expand-vars` permission allows you to use variables in your applications like you normally could from the XML Dialplan. Variables like `${caller_id_number}` would be expanded inline. The expression `${caller_id_number}` would give you the number of the calling party. This also gives you a way to use API commands from within your web applications. Consider this example:

```
${sofia_contact(1010@192.168.1.100)}
```

This line will execute the `sofia_contact` API command with the given argument and have the result inserted in place. As you read this, you might be considering the security implications of allowing access to every possible API command from within your application. No worries! ACL-like control lists are available. You can allow or disallow as many API commands or variables as you need to. Consider the following XML snippet:

```xml
<permission name="expand-vars" value="true">
  <variable-list default="deny">
    <variable name="caller_id_name"/>
    <variable name="caller_id_number"/>
  </variable-list>
  <api-list default="deny">
    <api name="expr"/>
    <api name="lua"/>
    <api name="sofia_contact"/>
  </api-list>
</permission>
```

The preceding code would allow the setting of the `caller_id_name` and `caller_id_number` channel variables and no others. It would allow the execution of the `expr`, `lua`, and `sofia_contact` API commands but no others. This example shows the fine-grained control that you as the application developer and FreeSWITCH system administrator have over HTTAPI applications running on your system.

The `dial` permission allows you to dial a number from your web application that will hit the Dialplan and be routed accordingly.

The `dial-set-Dialplan` and `dial-set-context` permissions allow you to change the Dialplan and, if applicable, the Dialplan context that is used to dial the number.

The `dial-set-cid-name` and `dial-set-cid-number` permissions will let you set the caller ID name and caller ID number when you make the call.

The `dial-full-originate` permission will allow you to dial using the full endpoint/profile/number syntax. (for example: `sofia/internal/1010@192.168.1.100`)

Enabling any one of `dial-set-context`, `dial-set-Dialplan`, `dial-set-cid-name`, `dial-set-cid-number`, or `dial-full-originate` will enable the `dial` permission even if it is set to false elsewhere in the configuration file.

The `conference` permission will allow you to call into conferences, while the `conference-set-profile` permission will allow you to change the conference profile used on each request. If `conference-set-profile` is enabled then conference will be enabled even if it is set to false elsewhere in the configuration file.

One thing to note is that any of the ACL-like control lists can be skipped by simply closing the `<permission>` tag without including the list. This will default to allow all as if you had created the list with `default="allow"`. The following two examples will work exactly the same way.

Example one:

```
<permission name="set-vars" value="true"/>
```

Example two:

```
<permission name="set-vars" value="true">
  <variable-list default="allow">
  </variable-list>
</permission>
```

Exiting

In the event that the user hangs up, FreeSWITCH will pass the "exiting" `param` to let you know that the call is over, and you can tear down any sessions that you might have opened and complete any reporting that you might have been keeping track of. While you can completely ignore this request and FreeSWITCH will recover just fine, it's expecting a plain text response of "OK".

Storing data across successive requests

As you begin thinking about applications that you can write with this newly acquired knowledge, you might be wondering about the best way to store pieces of information from one request to the next. Obviously, you could set and get channel variables, but that could be expensive with having to do multiple requests per set/get operation. If you were writing a web application that a person logged into and used (for example, online banking systems), you could just store those bits of information in a session for easy access later. Thankfully, `httapi` allows you to do this. Each request will include a `session_id` POST or GET parameter. With this `session_id` parameter value you should be able to initialize a session using its value as the session identifier. This level of control is available in just about every web programming language. An example of doing this in PHP would look similar to the following:

```
if ( array_key_exists( 'session_id', $_REQUEST ) ) {
  session_id( $_REQUEST['session_id'] );


}
session_start();
```

After you've started the session, you will have access to a session variable or object that can be used to store information that you can access on subsequent requests.

Some parameters are missing from some requests

If you use the example configuration, you should get all the information from every HTTP request. When you start editing the example configuration, you might notice that if you turn on `extended-data` then you start missing out on some of the data that should be passed to your application. The reason for this is that the default method is a GET request. All the information that is passed with `extended-data` can often exceed the maximum allowed length of CGI parameters, which results in cutting off some of the data from the end of the request. There are a couple of ways to fix this. The most permanent way is to set the `method` parameter in the `httapi.conf.xml` file as shown here:

```
<param name="method" value="POST"/>
```

However, there is a way to set the method per-request if you decide that you only want to set the method to POST on the requests that are causing issues. You can set the method in the URL string as shown here:

```
<action application="httapi"
  data="{url=http://localhost/httapi/index.php,method=POST}"/>
```

Making it easier

As you looked at the examples earlier in the chapter, you may have thought that while there might be a lot of power in this `httapi` thing, you really don't want to learn another XML format to control FreeSWITCH. Also, manually printing all of that XML could be a huge hassle. We couldn't agree more. That's why the `httapi` XML was written to be easy to implement with a helper library in the language of your choice. A couple of such libraries exist in the `freeswitch-contrib` repository for PHP and Python, already.

 The FreeSWITCH Git server (`git.freeswitch.org`) contains several repositories, one of which is `freeswitch-contrib`. This repository (or "repo") contains user-contributed code samples.

Moving forward, we'll show you a couple of examples of using the PHP version to create some basic, but useful IVRs. With all the IDEs that exist nowadays that offer code completion on things such as function and method names, as well as variable names, you should find it much easier to create your custom call flows using a library like this than you would with manually typing out the `httapi` XML.

The demo IVR – in HTTAPI

Before you start, you need to already have a web server set up to serve up PHP files, with the PHP XML extensions installed. Setting up web servers is outside the scope of this book, so if you don't have that set up already, that will be your first step. Once that is ready you may proceed with this section.

Once your web server is set up and ready to serve the PHP files, the next thing you'll need to do is download the PHTTAPI library from the `freeswitch-contrib` repo. All the classes are written into one PHP file to make it easier to install and get going. Obtain the file here: `http://git.freeswitch.org/git/freeswitch-contrib/plain/intralanman/PHP/phttapi/phttapi.php`. Save it as a known path that can be referenced later. You might also prefer to put this in the web directory where you'll be writing or downloading the demo IVR. In the next section, we'll cover the highlights of the `demo-ivr.php` script that are included with the code samples for this chapter.

 Visit the Packt Publishing website (`www.packtpub.com`) to obtain code samples for this publication.

Save the file `1004_11_01.php` as `demo-ivr.php` in the web documents directory on your web server. Open it in a text editor and follow along as we discuss each line of code and what it does.

```
if ( array_key_exists( 'session_id', $_REQUEST ) ) {
    session_id( $_REQUEST['session_id'] );
}
session_start();
```

This block will start the session using the `session_id` like we described earlier in this chapter.

```
if ( array_key_exists( 'exiting', $_REQUEST ) ) {
    session_destroy();
    header( 'Content-Type: text/plain' );
    print "OK";
    exit();
}
```

If we see the `exiting` parameter, we destroy the PHP session and tell FreeSWITCH we understand and then we exit the script.

```
$demo = new phttapi();
```

Here, we create the `httapi` object. This object (`$demo`) allows us to perform operations such as work actions.

```
$opt = array_key_exists( 'main_menu_option', $_REQUEST ) ?
       $_REQUEST['main_menu_option'] : '';
```

This is a simple if/then/else condition that will make sure `$opt` is always set, even if the `main_menu_option` is empty. The `main_menu_option`, which we later bind to the options, is going to be populated with the keys that were pressed by the caller.

```
if ( preg_match( '/^10[01][0-9]$/', $opt ) ) {
    $xfer = new phttapi_dial( $opt );
    $xfer->context( 'default' );
    $xfer->Dialplan( 'XML' );
    $demo->add_action( $xfer );
} else {
```

This block will test if the option matches the extension regex. If it is then we build a new `phttapi_dial` object (`$xfer`), set the destination, and then add the action to the `$demo` object. If it's not an extension, we drop into a `switch` statement that tests for each of the single keypress options.

```
case '1':
    $conf = new phttapi_dial( '9888' );
    $conf->caller_id_name( 'another book reader' );
    $conf->context( 'default' );
    $conf->Dialplan( 'XML' );
    $demo->add_action( $conf );
    break;
```

If option 1 was pressed, then we create a `dial` option that corresponds to the `dial` tag that we described earlier in this chapter. Each of the attributes on the tag have a corresponding method in the `phttapi_dial` class. For example, the `context` method sets the `context` attribute, the `Dialplan` method sets the Dialplan `attribute`, and so on. (Option 1 will send the caller to the public FreeSWITCH conference server.)

Cases 2 through 5 are all `dial` objects and have the same basic logic with the attributes assigned differently to achieve the desired results for each option.

```
case '6':
    if ( array_key_exists( 'sub_menu_option', $_REQUEST ) && $_
REQUEST['sub_menu_option'] == '*' ) {
```

```
                unset( $_SESSION['first_sub_play_done'] );
                $demo->add_action( $c = new phttapi_continue() );
                break;
        }
        $demo->start_variables();
        $demo->add_variable( 'main_menu_option', 6 );
        $demo->end_variables();

        $sub = new phttapi_playback();
        $sub->error_file( 'ivr/ivr-that_was_an_invalid_entry.wav' );
        $sub->loops( 3 );
        $sub->digit_timeout( '15000' );

        if ( !array_key_exists( 'first_sub_play_done', $_SESSION ) ) {
                $_SESSION['first_sub_play_done'] = TRUE;
                $sub->file( 'phrase:demo_ivr_sub_menu' );
        } else {
                $sub->file( 'phrase:demo_ivr_sub_menu_short' );
        }

        $star = new phttapi_action_binding( '*' );
        $sub->add_binding( $star );
        $sub->name( 'sub_menu_option' );

        $demo->add_action( $sub );
        break;
```

Option 6 is a little tricky and should probably be broken out into its own file, as it is technically a separate IVR. We included it in a single file for you here to make it easier to install and test. (Option 6 demonstrates an IVR submenu.)

```
    case '9':
        $continue = new phttapi_continue();
        $demo->add_action( $continue );
        break;
```

With this chunk of code, we simply do a `continue`, which has the effect of "repeating these options" as there are no bindings and no way to pass the `main_menu_option` parameter.

```
    default:
        $intro = new phttapi_playback();
        $intro->error_file( 'ivr/ivr-that_was_an_invalid_entry.wav' );
        $intro->loops( 3 );
        $intro->digit_timeout( '2000' );
```

```
$intro->input_timeout( '10000' );
$intro->name( 'main_menu_option' );
$intro->terminators( '#' );

if ( !array_key_exists( 'first_play_done', $_SESSION ) ) {
    $_SESSION['first_play_done'] = TRUE;
    $intro->file( 'phrase:demo_ivr_main_menu' );
} else {
    $intro->file( 'phrase:demo_ivr_main_menu_short' );
}
```

The `default` case action is to play the intro file. To simulate the way the `ivr` Dialplan application does it, we'll just store something in the session to let us know whether or not we've already played the long intro or not. (The short and long greetings are explained in *IVR menu definitions* in *Chapter 6, Using XML IVRs and Phrase Macros*.)

```
$b1   = new phttapi_action_binding( 1 );
...
$bext = new phttapi_action_binding( '~10[01][0-9]' );

$intro->add_binding( $b1 );
...
$intro->add_binding( $bext );
...
$demo->add_action( $intro );
```

In this section the ellipses indicate that the other options were left out for brevity. You can see here that we create a binding object for each of the digit choices and then add each binding to the `playback` action. Then, just as with our previous examples, we add the action to the `$demo` object. Obviously, we could have built out a single binding with a more complete regex that would have worked for all the digits. However, we did it this way to show that you can have multiple bindings with single digits and/or regexes and things will still work as designed.

```
header( 'Content-Type: text/xml' );
print $demo->output();
```

Here, we set the content type of the response to `text/xml` and print the output of the object we've been building. FreeSWITCH won't understand your responses if you use any other `content-type` than `text/xml`, so be sure to set that however it's done in your language of choice.

Summary

In this chapter we learned about the new functionality unleashed with `mod_httapi`. By combining a web browser with FreeSWITCH it is now possible to do call control using the simple HTTAPI markup. Further, we also discussed a PHP library (`phttapi.php`) that provides an abstraction layer to make it even easier to build telephony applications on a web server. By using `mod_httapi`, enterprises can leverage the knowledge of their web developers to assist with creating telephony applications. Furthermore, web developers need not learn all that a FreeSWITCH administrator needs to know. Rather, they can learn just HTTAPI and still have everything they need to build feature-rich, web-controlled telephony applications.

In the next chapter, we will focus on a very important subject for the VoIP administrator: how to handle NAT.

12
Handling NAT

In the beginning of the book we talked about legacy. The more things change, the more everybody wants it to stay the same. It's just a part of how technology evolution works. Our cars still pretend to have speedometer needles; the graphics on your favorite website look like an old-fashioned set of buttons and switches. We as a society also try to live by the motto: "If it ain't broke, don't fix it!" The same principle applies even to things that seem relatively modern, like "how we get on the Internet". Most of us would prefer to remain blissfully unaware of the details when it comes to how all of our fancy gizmos make it onto the Internet. Those of us who take the plunge into the exciting world of IP Telephony will not make it very far before coming face to face with a fearsome beast known as **NAT (Network Address Translation)**.

In this chapter we will discuss:

- A brief introduction to NAT, including a little history
- The four pitfalls of NAT
- The settings in FreeSWITCH that help overcome NAT
- Troubleshooting tips

A brief introduction to NAT

A good way to explain NAT to someone who could absolutely care less about techno-babble would be with an analogy. Think of a giant office building and its mailroom. An employee on the 10th floor sends a package to you by dropping it off at the mailroom on the ground floor. The package is passed on to the Postal service and it arrives at your house. The return address on the package is actually the address of the entire office building and not the tiny office on the 10th floor. Now say you need to return the package. You put it back through the Postal system and it arrives at the building and the employees in the mailroom must figure out where to deliver the package by mapping your name or office number to the location in the building, and then they take it back up to the employee on the 10th floor. The mailroom is like a NAT router because it proxies the mail between the actual Postal system and the one inside the building. The offices are like the LAN addresses because they do not have any direct access to the mail. What if the name of the office sending the message is messed up or not present on the package and the mailroom employees have no idea which office to send the package to when you return it? This would be a NAT problem and the package may end up getting lost just like your calls. Perhaps you get the package and notice it's missing the office name or number but you know which office sent it because you were expecting this package and then when you return it you write the office number on the label? This would be an ANTI-NAT feature created by you.

NAT versus PAT

There are technical differences between Network Address Translation (NAT) and **Port Address Translation (PAT)**. However, in the VoIP industry (and elsewhere) the term NAT is used quite liberally. In this chapter we follow this liberal use and make no explicit distinction between NAT and PAT.

When it comes to networking, NAT is basically a technique where an entire LAN or Local Area Network (meaning a network that is not directly connected to the Internet) is connected to a device that does have access to the Internet and uses a single public IP address (meaning an IP that is directly connected to the Internet) to provide Internet connectivity to the entire LAN. It's used primarily to reduce the number of public IP addresses that are necessary since we are running out of them fast. We started out with four billion of them and they are all basically used up at the time of writing this.

Putting your local network behind NAT has a side effect of constantly protecting your computers and other devices from attack since they are not visible on the Internet. Experts do not feel this is the ultimate solution for security because there are still ways to compromise devices behind NAT but consider it a bonus protection when used together with other good security practices. By the way, you'll learn more about security when it comes to VoIP in *Chapter 13, VoIP Security*.

Understanding the evolution of NAT

The demand for IPv4 addresses has grown over the years since the Internet has evolved. As the demand increased, the pool of available addresses has been depleted and there is a shortage of available IPv4 addresses. Two major attempts to deal with this situation have become popular over time – NAT and IPv6.

NAT has become a fairly popular way to take a small subset of public IP addresses and utilize them across a larger number of devices on a network. NAT took off in the 1990s as a way to mitigate the IP starvation problem until IPv6 took off, but now it's so popular that many people don't want to let go of it. Meanwhile, system administrators are forced to embrace the looming legacy of NAT and make sure that we can tolerate it across our software and equipment due to popularity.

A new standard for IP addresses called IPv6 can solve the IP starvation problem by adding so many public IP addresses that we can have trillions of IP addresses for every square inch of the surface area of the Earth. We could give a block of IPs, the size of the entire Internet as we know it today, to every creature on the planet and not even put a dent in the total available pool of IPv6 addresses. The IPv6 specification was published in 1998 and has been slowly gaining momentum. IPv6 still takes a back seat to the more widely used IPv4 that was adopted in the 1970s. Most likely, even if we fully adopt IPv6, NAT still won't go away for some time.

 In case you're wondering, FreeSWITCH does support SIP and RTP over IPv6. More information on the subject can be found online at `http://wiki.freeswitch.org`.

For most of us in the IP Telephony world, NAT is a proverbial four-letter word (or is at least used often in sentences with several other four-letter words). I will try to spare you the intimate details of IP networking since you either already know about it or you can easily find endless documentation on it. What you do need to know is that a healthy understanding of the pitfalls of NAT can save you tons of time otherwise spent banging your head against a wall or pulling your hair out. The goal of this chapter will be to explain how you can successfully navigate the treacherous waters of NAT by leveraging the ANTI-NAT features of FreeSWITCH. Good luck, we're all rooting for you!

The key problem we are trying to solve with NAT and VoIP is that since a device (phone) behind NAT is not visible to the Internet, it becomes difficult to contact that device when you want to call it. The next big problem is that some protocols, such as SIP, may break when used over NAT. If you find this whole thing to be completely confusing, take solace in the fact that we have actually simplified it for you. So while it may seem to be crazy right now, the fact is that it was much worse before.

To be honest, the original stance of the FreeSWITCH developers on the NAT issue was, "Not our problem!" In an ideal world, every device behind a NAT firewall is well aware of its circumstances and can successfully solve its own problems. Unfortunately, we do not live in an ideal world (of course if we were in an ideal world, none of us would have a job because there would be no problems to solve). So we decided, "OK fine, we'll give it a shot!" We soon learned that our users had a myriad of devices that they wanted to use with FreeSWITCH, but these devices had absolutely no idea how to deal with NAT. Soon, we began the monumental task of developing techniques to allow these devices to work despite their shortcomings. NAT is a vicious opponent and the faint-hearted do not stand a chance to survive.

The four pitfalls of NAT

There are four basic pitfalls of NAT that everyone should learn. Understand these pitfalls and you will be well-equipped to handle the NAT scenarios that you'll no doubt face:

- NAT can be there even when you don't know about it. The Internet does not have to be involved.

- Any two techniques to defeat NAT used together will cancel each other out.

- Some devices use a SIP **ALG** (**Application Layer Gateway**) to defeat NAT.

- NAT correction techniques can falsely identify a situation and actually make things even worse.

Become familiar with these pitfalls. They are referenced frequently throughout this chapter.

Let's discuss each of these in more detail:

- NAT can be there even when you don't know it. The Internet does not have to be involved.

  If you are using home Internet service from your cable or telephone company, or even in some cases a business-class service, they may on occasion use NAT to put all of their customers in a separate network and then translate that network to other segments in their infrastructure. This could happen not just once but multiple times between your device and its destination and you have no control over it. This can cause some real problems for people trying to use VoIP. Most VoIP protocols only have basic provisions for dealing with NAT and often fall short. This is probably the first problem that most home-users will encounter when trying to use VoIP from their homes. NAT can also be used in this fashion inside a LAN connecting multiple LANs without actually reaching the Internet. Getting on the Internet is just the most popular use for NAT but it can be used just as well to isolate one LAN from another. If you're asking your friendly neighborhood VoIP guru for help and he suggests a NAT problem, don't count it out just because you are not using the Internet or because you don't know NAT is there.

- Any two techniques to defeat NAT used together will cancel each other out.

  This one is tricky and a very popular issue among VoIP users. The best way to visualize it is to picture a game of Othello. Whenever you make a move to block the NAT it flips everything around. If you make a counter move, it flips it all back. This might even be happening more than you think (see the first pitfall). As long as it's an odd number of flips and you started out with a non-working situation you should end up okay, but you should make it a point to do only the most minimal modifications possible to avoid confusion and pain. If your phone supports NAT features and you enable them and also enable them on FreeSWITCH, you may end up with one-way or no audio. What's even more confusing is that there are so many ways to cancel out NAT. Some require only changes on your phone behind the NAT, while some require changes only on FreeSWITCH and some require a change on both ends. Do you get now as to why I was wishing you luck earlier?

- Some devices use a SIP ALG to defeat NAT.

  "Arrrghh, curse you SIP ALG!". We've heard that being exclaimed countless times over IRC or on a community conference call. ALGs mean well but they usually mess things up real bad. They are like a combination of the first two pitfalls because they are usually implemented inside your provider or in your network router and enabled by default without your knowledge. They do the worst and last resort of all the ANTI-NAT techniques that is modifying the SIP packets as they pass through your router. This can lead to misbehaviors and misrouted traffic that will present itself to you as a complete mystery. Heed my words. If you find yourself uttering the phrase, "This makes absolutely no sense", the first thing you should check is to see if you are under the evil spell of a SIP ALG. In many cases, simply turning off a SIP ALG resolves NAT-related issues.

- NAT correction techniques can falsely identify a situation and actually make things even worse.

  It helps to understand your surroundings at least enough to know if you actually need to enable ANTI-NAT features. Some SIP agents make use of the more arcane aspects of SIP and do really fancy things with the network addresses in the packet. For those of you familiar with SIP, yes I know it's all arcane but we need to keep things in perspective. So the problem is, completely legitimate packets that are just doing things in a way that resemble NAT can trigger some of the features we use to detect NAT. So you need to be careful, especially with Cisco phones that are notorious for being bad behind NAT and subject to false detection at the same time.

Demystifying NAT settings in FreeSWITCH

Now that we have reviewed the common pitfalls of NAT, we can go over the various types of NAT situations that you may encounter. There are several technical differences between the various implementations of NAT as well, but we won't focus on that because you'll probably fall asleep and miss the point of the chapter which is learning how to use FreeSWITCH in a NATed environment. Basically you will probably be in a situation where either your phone or PBX is behind NAT talking to a SIP endpoint that is not behind NAT (or vice versa). Even worse, you might end up in the dreaded double-NAT situation where both sides of a connection are independently behind their own individual NAT routers at the same time. A double-NAT scenario looks like the following diagram:

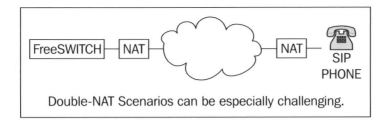

Double-NAT Scenarios can be especially challenging.

Let's start with a sane, yet challenging situation where you have a phone at your house that can't understand NAT and you want to register to your FreeSWITCH server that is on the public Internet. The good news is that this situation is already covered for you by the example FreeSWITCH configuration. The core of FreeSWITCH has a feature called **ACL** (**Access Control Lists**). An ACL lets you create lists of network addresses and control access to things depending on whether or not a particular device is originating from an address defined by the ACL. There is equal value in determining if an address matches or does not match a list and from there deciding if being (or not being) on the list is a good or bad thing.

This feature makes it possible to allow certain devices to authenticate based on their IP address or you can make a list of enemy devices so you can completely block anyone who is on the list. In this case we will use the ACL to determine if a device is behind NAT or not and decide what to do from there.

A device behind NAT is likely to have an IP address within a special range called RFC-1918. The easiest explanation for this is that there is a special set of IP addresses that never lead to the Internet because they are reserved for private use on LANs. This is basically any IP address that starts with 192.168.x.x, 172.16.x.x through 172.31.x.x, or 10.x.x.x. We'll just call them LAN addresses from now on.

 More information about RFC-1918 IP addresses can be found at
`http://en.wikipedia.org/wiki/Private_network`.

Because these addresses are private, there can be endless networks using the same exact IP addresses but they can never connect to each other. Now when you connect these networks to a NAT router, all the phones on these private networks will be able to reach your FreeSWITCH server. The routers work by keeping track of all the traffic coming from the LAN addresses and sending it to the Internet as if it was coming from the public Internet IP on the router. Then, when the destination on the Internet sends a response to the NAT router, it uses the mapping to deliver the packet back to the sender. The source address that FreeSWITCH sees the traffic originating from may never be the same and this makes it very difficult to send an incoming call to the phone. This is where the ACL comes in handy.

FreeSWITCH has a configuration parameter for `mod_sofia` profiles called `apply-nat-acl`. This parameter can be used more than once in the same profile and expects the name of an ACL list. When `mod_sofia` gets SIP REGISTER or INVITE packets, it looks at the contact address and checks the IP referenced in the Contact header against the specified ACL. If there is a match, it concludes that the device must be behind NAT. It's difficult to tell which IPs represent devices behind NAT but we have a bit of a clue. Remember RFC-1918 or LAN addresses as we affectionately call them? Since it's a defined range of IP addresses, we can conclude that if you are coming from one of these addresses then you are calling from behind NAT.

Be careful! Don't forget the fourth pitfall, it's not 100 percent safe to assume every device coming from a LAN address is behind NAT. This may not always be the case but more times than not it is. It's just good to be wary. One case where it may not be true is when FreeSWITCH also has a LAN address because it's behind NAT too. Well, we have a special ACL that is created for you when FreeSWITCH starts, called `nat.auto`. This special ACL already contains the entire RFC-1918 address space but it also checks the machine's local network address and excludes that address space so you won't get any false positives when it gets calls from phones on the same LAN as FreeSWITCH. At the same time this ACL can detect a phone that is actually in a remote location behind NAT. FreeSWITCH comes pre-configured with `apply-nat-acl` set to `nat.auto` and can correct most typical device behind NAT versus FreeSWITCH on the public Internet situations.

How do we solve the problem? Basically, when the phone registers from behind NAT and it's detected, we save the IP and port that we saw the register originate from and store it in the internal database alongside the unreachable LAN address that the unsuspecting phone has provided us. When we need to contact this phone, we consult our database and determine the external IP:port to which the message should be sent. The SIP headers will still have the internal IP:port values that the remote phone is expecting to see. We also tell the phone to register more frequently so that the mapping stays open, since most NAT routers only hold a translation path open for a short period of time. This technique is especially effective in avoiding the other part of the fourth pitfall because we never modified the intended address at all like the evil ALG. This means the phone will happily see everything it expects and never be the wiser.

Here is an example of output from the FreeSWITCH **CLI (Command Line Interface)**. The client is a softphone behind NAT registering to an instance of FreeSWITCH running on a public IP. Notice the Contact field is using the IP 10.0.1.85 that is a LAN address. The status shows that UDP-NAT was detected thanks to the `nat.auto` ACL list. The trick comes in at the end of the Contact. The extra parameters `fs_nat` and `fs_path` are appended to the Contact address of the phone registration so we can figure out how to circumnavigate the NAT. Consider the following:

```
fs_nat=yes
fs_path=sip%3A1006%40206.22.109.244%3A43425%3Brinstance%3Db67dbafc
9baa9465%3Btransport%3Dudp.
```

The `fs_path` field is a SIP **URI (Uniform Resource Identifier)** that actually will lead back to the phone through NAT. It's URL-encoded, so special characters in the URI do not conflict with the real contact. The decoded version of this field is:

```
sip:1006@206.22.109.244:43425;rinstance=b67dbafc9baa9465;transport=udp
```

So even though when we call the phone we will send the INVITE packet to `206.22.109.244:43425`, we will keep it addressed to 10.0.1.85:5060 and that is exactly where it will end up once the NAT translation takes place and the local router delivers it to the phone. You can see the complete set of registration information using the `sofia status profile internal reg` command. The following is an example:

```
freeswitch@myhost> sofia status profile internal reg

Registrations:

================================================================
Call-ID:        ZWU1MjdiZTI2MTg2MmVhNTc5NTk3MDY5YjFmOTVkMTU.

User:           1006@myhost.freeswitch.org

Contact:        "TEST" <sip:1006@10.0.1.85:10118;rinstance=b67dbafc9baa94
65;transport=udp;fs_nat=yes;fs_path=sip%3A1006%40184.58.189.244%3A43425%3
Brinstance%3Db67dbafc9baa9465%3Btransport%3Dudp>

Agent:          eyeBeam release 1104g stamp 54685

Status:         Registered(UDP-NAT)(unknown) EXP(2012-12-09 10:18:07)
EXPSECS(88)

Host:           myhost

IP:             206.22.109.244

Port:           43425

Auth-User:      1006

Auth-Realm:     myhost.freeswitch.org

MWI-Account:    1006@myhost.freeswitch.org

Total items returned: 1

================================================================
```

Notice that the `Contact:` header contains both the `fs_nat` and `fs_path` parameters. Any SIP traffic that FreeSWITCH needs to send to user 1006 will use the URI specified in the `fs_path` parameter.

Making media flow

Now that the SIP messages are flowing properly from FreeSWITCH to the phone, what about the media? A phone call is not very eventful if you can't even hear each other, right? We had many problems where the calls would set up properly until the point where NAT would strike the RTP packets that provide the actual audio of the call, rendering the call with one-way-audio or even no-way-audio in some cases. In light of this injustice, we created a separate feature that is always enabled and only needs to be manually disabled in a very few set of cases inspired by the fourth pitfall. This feature is called RTP auto-adjust. The reason we need it is because when the phone tries to call us from behind NAT, it will naively advertise its unreachable LAN address to FreeSWITCH as the intended destination for the audio.

We could guess that since the device is behind NAT, we should really send the audio to the same address that we saved from the SIP message. But that is not always the case since various types of NAT have restrictions and the port mappings sometimes don't exist until the device behind NAT has actually sent a packet. So, in reality we may have no idea whatsoever as to how to successfully get audio flowing to the phone. Thanks to the auto-adjust feature, we still have a fighting chance. As long as we give the phone a valid address where it can send us audio, we can wait until it sends us some packets and use the originating address to determine where to send the audio back. This is not 100 percent guaranteed, as we know, but it's very effective in an otherwise hopeless situation. Just to be safe we only allow this magical adjustment to happen right at the beginning of the call otherwise evildoers may try to steal people's audio streams.

As previously mentioned, this RTP auto-adjust is pretty much enabled by default and will turn on automatically. The way in which you can tell that it is working is by looking for a log message like the one that follows. The message shows you the original media destination and the new one that was detected. This log line prints at the beginning of any call where auto-adjust has triggered.

```
2012-05-09 10:37:48.183742 [INFO] switch_rtp.c:3607 Auto Changing port
from 10.0.1.85:23010 to 206.22.109.244:34029
```

The following diagram shows this more clearly:

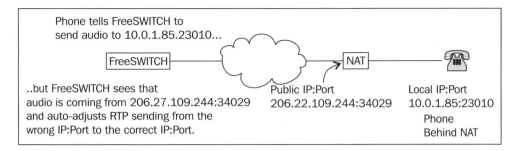

Phone tells FreeSWITCH to
send audio to 10.0.1.85.23010...

FreeSWITCH — NAT — ☎

..but FreeSWITCH sees that
audio is coming from 206.27.109.244:34029
and auto-adjusts RTP sending from the
wrong IP:Port to the correct IP:Port.

Public IP:Port
206.22.109.244:34029

Local IP:Port
10.0.1.85:23010
Phone
Behind NAT

If you do have one of the two percent of cases where this feature triggers the fourth pitfall and actually breaks things for you, then all you need to do is add this parameter to your SIP profile:

```
<param name="disable-rtp-auto-adjust" value="true"/>
```

Otherwise you can also disable it on a per-call basis by setting the channel variable `rtp_auto_adjust=false` at some point before the media stream has started.

Advanced options and settings

Now that we kind of understand how it works, we can look at other ways to trigger the NAT detection. In some cases, the ACL is not enough because maybe a sneaky ALG has messed up the packet or maybe the traffic is passing over a proxy or the phone may think it's handling the NAT case itself but it's not doing it quite right.

We have another option that is not enabled by default because it laughs in the face of the fourth pitfall and basically thinks almost anything slightly out of the ordinary is NAT. This parameter is dangerous but effective in cases where you have no other choice. The name of the parameter is `aggressive-nat-detection` and setting it to `true` in your SIP profile will enable it for all traffic. Basically it looks at the SIP packets and if it sees a variety of IP addresses in various headers, it uses logical deduction to figure out which one is the source address. From there it does the same thing that the ACL based one does, only it may not always be the source address that it writes into the database.

```
<param name="aggressive-nat-detection" value="true"/>
```

The following diagram illustrates such a case:

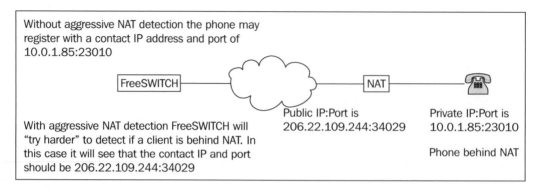

FreeSWITCH has a family of parameters we refer to as "No Device Left Behind" or NDLB. These parameters denote situations where we completely mimic or accept a flaw in a device and pretend everything is peachy or make provisions for the device so it can still work despite the fact that we are utterly offended that we actually had to make it work by modifying the code. One such parameter that is particularly effective in the battle against NAT is called `force-rport`. The purpose of the `rport` attribute in SIP is a minimal attempt to conquer NAT by appending `;rport` to the request.

When FreeSWITCH sees this attribute, it will respond in kind with a `rport=host:ip` attribute so the phone will realize it's behind NAT. The funny thing is, some phones can react properly when they see the `rport` in the response but never request it. The `force-rport` parameter causes FreeSWITCH to pretend that every device we talk to has supplied an `rport` parameter so we respond as if they did and hence unlock the functionality that would otherwise be unobtainable.

This parameter is also not enabled by default, as is the case for most NDLB options. It also opens up vulnerability to the fourth pitfall, since it can break many devices. You can either set it to `true` to always assume `rport` or set it to `safe` to only enable it for devices where we know it's required to make things work. You can also set it to `client-only` or `server-only` to only do it depending on the direction of the call but with any luck you will never need those options.

 Polycom phones provide a classic use case for setting `ndlb-force-rport` to `true` or `safe` because these phones do not support `rport`. In most cases you will want to use `safe` since most phone models do support `rport`. If for some reason you need to use `ndlb-force-rport=true` then create a new SIP profile with this parameter. Make sure that only the Polycom phones use this SIP profile.

FreeSWITCH on the client side

We have covered some of the common cases where your phone is behind NAT talking to FreeSWITCH who isn't. Now we can move on to cases where your local copy of FreeSWITCH is behind NAT and talking to a SIP provider or another FreeSWITCH server on the public Internet. Luckily, we have also dressed up the example configuration to have the best chance to work under these NAT circumstances.

I recommend you try the unaltered example configuration on a test instance of FreeSWITCH every so often just to see if there are any more new default behaviors you may be missing out on. FreeSWITCH supports two client-side NAT-busting protocols by default called NAT-PMP and UPnP. Both of these protocols use slightly different methods but the basic gist is the same.

Both methods use a network protocol to discover your NAT router and communicate with it, so rather than making the NAT mappings on-the-fly, it asks the router to open a port and actually learns the details of the port mapping, so when FreeSWITCH talks to another server it's putting the correct information in the packets for both the SIP and the media. That is cool! Beware though, now we're opening the door to the second, third, and fourth pitfalls.

 More information about NAT-PMP and UPnP can be found online at http://en.wikipedia.org/wiki/NAT_Port_Mapping_ Protocol and http://en.wikipedia.org/wiki/Universal_ Plug_and_Play, respectively.

We have now disguised the fact that we are behind NAT so the other side cannot detect it. An ALG might be hiding in our midst and mess with the packet thinking that it still needs to when it doesn't. The other side might be using something similar to aggressive NAT detection and spring a double anti-NAT trap. The great thing is, if you have some very strict NAT routers or firewalls, this feature will not only solve the address mapping dilemma, but also unlock otherwise blocked ports held tight by the firewall. Wait, there's more! You can also use the FSAPI interface to map and unmap ports in the event your application has some need for such a mapping.

There are a set of parameters in the SIP profile called ext-sip-ip and ext-rtp-ip. These parameters are used to supply information about how to behave in regards to external IP addresses. The default configuration defines both of these parameters with auto-nat. This is used together with the NAT router control feature we were just talking about to just do the right thing. Some of us will not have a router that supports NAT-PMP or UPnP, or worse, it will claim to support one or the other and then not work at all because either it's inherently broken or due to some other deadly combination of the pitfalls.

We can disable this functionality when we start FreeSWITCH by supplying the `-nonat` command-line option. With this option disabled, we still have some tricks up our sleeve. You can put an IP address in either field when you already know what it is, for example when you have a static external IP address. Better yet, you can set it to `autonat:x.x.x.x` (where x.x.x.x should be replaced with your public IP) so it uses your known external IP and still does a bit of dynamic magic.

Additionally, you can make use of dynamic DNS or STUN by setting it to `host:my.domain.com` or `stun:stun.myhost.com` (where `my.domain.com` or `stun.myhost.com` are your own dynamic domain or STUN server, respectively) to do lookups as needed. This has disadvantages because it can slow things down or stop working. As usual we have already shipped the best options by default but you still deserve to know about the other options. If you do control your own routers, you can also create permanent NAT mappings that route specific traffic right to your FreeSWITCH server or phones, and the `ext-sip-ip` and `ext-rtp-ip` can come in very handy in that case. Also, if you have the means, you could use a VPN to route two independent networks to each other when both are behind NAT, assuming you can actually control the router at both ends.

Other creative uses of FreeSWITCH in a NAT situation

FreeSWITCH can be used to conquer NAT by simply wedging it between devices. You can configure a local FreeSWITCH and register all of your phones to it, then register that instance of FreeSWITCH to the SIP provider on behalf of all of your phones, carving a hole right through the NAT and keeping everyone happy. Also, you can set up FreeSWITCH on a public IP somewhere on the Internet, then register all of your phones or local FreeSWITCH instances from multiple locations to that common server, so even if both locations are behind NAT, they can still make calls between sites without a problem.

Conclusion

We wish you well on your journey into the world of NAT! Hopefully, this chapter will prove useful when you are stuck or prepare you in advance for a battle with an ALG .That would really be awful! If you memorize everything in this chapter and somehow still have problems, you can always come online and ask other FreeSWITCH community members for help. See *Appendix B, The FreeSWITCH Online Community*. One final word of wisdom that can make you look smart is that if next time you notice someone complaining that their calls fail 30 seconds after they start, then yes, it's a NAT problem. This has been shown in the following diagram:

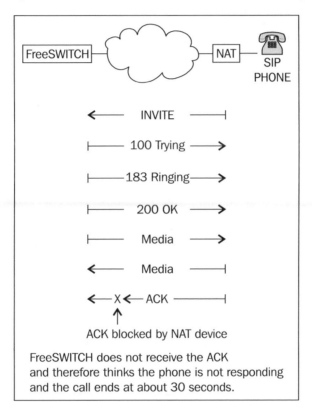

In some cases FreeSWITCH can't fix the problem and you will need to fix or replace the NAT device.

Summary

That's a lot of information to swallow in one sitting, so I'll understand if you're still confused. Can you believe this is actually the watered-down high-level explanation? Luckily, the FreeSWITCH developers have already been down this road and have done their best to tailor the defaults so that it just works. So, in this chapter, we've identified the pitfalls of NAT and if even one reader is spared the searing pain caused by a first encounter with an ALG or NAT router then our journey into madness was not in vain.

We've also covered all of the options you have in FreeSWITCH to mitigate NAT-related problems and now you can venture into the wilderness and make phone calls where nobody thought phone calls were possible. Before we move on to VoIP security, I'll leave you with a few more tips so hopefully you will get things working perfectly even when plagued by NAT. The following are the tips you should remember:

- Learn the four pitfalls of NAT and keep your eyes open for them

  It's very easy to get distracted and fall prey to one of the pitfalls. If you notice it's taking too long, start over and make sure that you haven't made a mistake somewhere that is leading you astray.

- Try to make the least changes necessary to get NAT working

  The more you mess with NAT settings, the easier it is to do something wrong or make things incompatible. It's very easy to get one end working and break the other and go back and forth for hours at the mercy of the second pitfall.

- If you have access to your own router, configure it to make conditions as favorable as possible for NAT

  The best way to make things simple is to tune your surroundings so you have the ideal environment. Choose basic NAT settings and stick with defaults that are usually tuned to working the best for the majority of cases.

In our next chapter we will change our focus from overcoming NAT issue and look at ways to improve VoIP security.

13
VoIP Security

VoIP Security is an increasingly important topic for protecting your FreeSWITCH system. Protection strategies include both proactive and defensive technologies. Proactive technologies in FreeSWITCH include multiple types of encryption for both SIP and RTP communication which discourages tampering or eavesdropping with phone calls. Defensive technologies in FreeSWITCH, when combined with other open source tools, can block suspicious or malicious transmissions from unknown sources and prevent abuse or fraud. The importance of combining FreeSWITCH capabilities with generally available open source VoIP tools is essential when running in a production environment.

This chapter is divided into the following four sub-sections:

- Network level protection
- Protecting signaling
- Protecting audio
- Protecting passwords

Network level protection

Most malicious individuals utilize open network ports to break into VoIP systems. They look for anything from weak passwords to known software bugs and attempt to exploit those setups to control the configuration and routing of a phone system. The general goal is to commit fraud, eavesdrop on calls, or steal information (such as voicemail messages).

Since the network is the entry point to your system, it's important to pay close attention to how your network is setup and take advantage of some of the functionality within FreeSWITCH to secure your system further.

Separating interfaces and restricting traffic

SIP is a technology that is commonly targeted for abuse on the open Internet. In most cases, malicious hackers will attempt to scan a range of IP addresses by sending UDP packets on port 5060 and look for servers that respond. Once they find a server which responds, they will attempt to brute-force common passwords or simply try to dial out. In some cases they will also simply flood the server with fake registration or other packets, crippling the system's ability to operate properly.

One of the most basic ways by which you can protect your FreeSWITCH system is by separating your SIP interfaces and enforcing firewall or IPTables rules that are different on each interface.

As you've learned in previous chapters, FreeSWITCH allows you to set up different Sofia SIP interfaces so that you can send and receive SIP traffic via different IP addresses and ports on the same system. What may not be obvious is that this setup is useful for providing an extra layer of security and stability.

In terms of security, Sofia SIP profiles have default contexts for which they will route inbound calls to. Those contexts can default to fairly restrictive Dialplans. If you combine restrictive contexts and Dialplans with the relevant SIP profile, you are less likely to allow someone to send fraudulent SIP traffic through your system, even if you accidentally create a misconfiguration.

In addition, each Sofia SIP profile can have a different **Access Control List (ACL)**. In this way, you can put more stringent restrictions on public facing IP addresses and looser restrictions on private IP addresses.

In terms of stability and performance, a little known fact about FreeSWITCH's design is that each Sofia SIP interface is a separate thread. It means that by having separate threads for each port and IP, you somewhat help in minimizing any disruptions someone can cause to the system. While this is by no means a foolproof way of protecting your system, any additional time you get to resolve an issue when being attacked maliciously is helpful.

Sample setup – simple

In its most simple form, having an interface where your carriers or **Internet Telephone Service Providers (ITSPs)** reach you versus an interface that your phones use is inherently beneficial. Most malicious activity starts with someone discovering that you are accepting and responding to SIP traffic on port 5060 via a port scan. At this point they will try various combinations of authentication methods until they find one that works, or otherwise abuse that port. If you restrict access on this IP and change the port to a random number and solely allow inbound calls from carriers using ACLs, you immediately prevent anyone from gaining access to your system, even if they have the right username and password.

The following diagram shows how people set up their FreeSWITCH system by default:

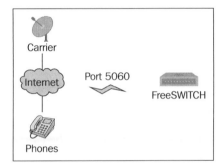

In an alternate setup, you can utilize unique and unusual ports that make it harder for hackers to find. In addition, you can use a firewall to restrict carriers to one port while keeping the other port open for phones. This has been demonstrated in the following diagram:

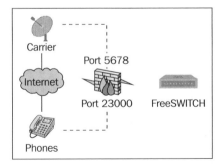

To achieve the previous example where carriers communicate via port 5678 and phones communicate on port 23000, you could set up a configuration like the following:

```
<profile name="incoming_from_pstn">
  <settings>
    <param name="auth-calls" value="true"/>
    <param name="apply-inbound-acl" value="my_carriers"/>
    <param name="context" value="inbound_call"/>
    <param name="sip-port" value="5678"/>
    ... other settings here ...
  </settings>
</profile>
```

In the previous Sofia profile, inbound calls from your carriers must come in on port 5678. When they hit this port, the my_carriers ACL will be applied, making sure only carriers get through. If you make an error in your my_carriers ACL, no big deal – the context the caller reaches is inbound_call and only allows for inbound calls, not outbound. These are a fairly solid set of restrictions.

In addition, since you know only your carriers should be contacting you on port 5678, you could modify your firewall or IPTables software firewall rules to allow traffic on this port only from your carrier's IP addresses. This is a fairly fool proof methodology for inbound access.

You would then create the following profile for your users to utilize:

```
<profile name="customer_access">
  <settings>
    <param name="auth-calls" value="true"/>
    <param name="apply-inbound-acl" value="default_deny_list"/>
   <param name="context" value="customer_call"/>
    <param name="sip-port" value="23000"/>
    ... other settings here ...
  </settings>
</profile>
```

In this Sofia SIP profile, calls that your customers make would need to hit SIP port 23000. This port requires authentication and uses an ACL called default_deny_list which denies all traffic by default. This will force traffic to be authenticated, meaning the user must provide a valid username and password to be able to utilize the system. Once the user provides that information they will be sent to the customer_call context where the calls will be processed.

Sample setup – complex

A more complex example indicates isolation of networks and assumes you have network routing gear that allows you to split network access either physically (separate network cables and routers) or via subnets or VLANs (see next section).

In the more complex setup, you would additionally use different IP addresses which, via your operating system, are bound to different network cards. In addition to mapping the SIP ports to different interfaces, you would also map the event socket and other FreeSWITCH ports to a management interface.

To do this, you might set up two Sofia SIP profiles like the following:

```
<profile name="incoming_from_pstn">
  <settings>
    <param name="auth-calls" value="true"/>
    <param name="apply-inbound-acl" value="my_carriers"/>
    <param name="context" value="inbound_call"/>
    <param name="sip-port" value="5678"/>
    <param name="sip-ip" value="2.3.4.5"/>
    ... other settings here ...
  </settings>
</profile>
<profile name="customer_access">
  <settings>
    <param name="auth-calls" value="true"/>
    <param name="apply-inbound-acl" value="default_deny_list"/>
    <param name="context" value="customer_call"/>
    <param name="sip-port" value="23000"/>
    <param name="sip-ip" value="212.222.33.111"/>
    ... other settings here ...
  </settings>
</profile>
```

In the previous scenario, note carefully the sip-ip setting which differs for each interface. One interface is 2.3.4.5 and the other is 212.222.33.111. FreeSWITCH will attempt to utilize the network interface on the physical server which represents the IP address that you have specified in the Sofia SIP profile. This allows you to use different firewalls and network links for each interface powering your FreeSWITCH system.

In this scenario, 2.3.4.5 could be an internal IP address that is not routable on the public Internet and 212.222.33.111 could be a public IP address that is routable. The IP address 212.222.33.111 would only have to be open to carriers unless you have users with phones outside your local network. As an alternative for allowing softphones, you could allow your staff to VPN into your network. This would be the most secure strategy possible.

The previous scenario can also be illustrated with the following diagram:

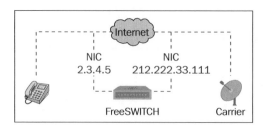

In the previous diagram, the phone talks on the **Network Interface Card** (**NIC**) on the FreeSWITCH box assigned to 2.3.4.5, while the carrier talks to FreeSWITCH via the NIC on 212.222.33.111.

VLANs

VLANs are a fantastic way to isolate phones from data communications on your local network and if done correctly, they can improve call quality while preventing malicious activity.

VLANs are often overlooked as optional but in fact, a lot of damage can be done by having phones on the same network as computers. It is simple to identify the IP address of a device and log in to it when they are on the same network. From there, it is trivial to lift the SIP username and passwords of many phones. For example, if you log in to a Polycom phone, you can export the configuration which contains the phone's credentials and view them in plain text. It is more challenging to do this when a phone is on a private segment of the network.

In addition to manipulating a phone directly, VLANs prevent tools running on computers from sending bogus information into the voice network. This includes scenarios as simple as unauthorized softphones that are used to hijack an extension to send bogus BYE messages causing calls to hang up intentionally when they should have continued.

It's worth noting that VLANs are available on most networks as either port-based tagging, where a specific physical port on a switch is part of a virtual LAN or software-based tagging, where the network interface card or operating system tags each packet with a specific virtual LAN number in the IP header.

Setting up VLANs is beyond the scope of this book. However it should be noted that nearly all popular desk phone models and recent network gear support VLANs, including both software and port-based VLAN tagging.

Intrusion detection

Detecting intruders attempting to gain access to the system or who are intentionally creating a denial-of-service or similar type of disturbance can be a challenge. While it may seem obvious what type of traffic would be considered unusual, there are edge cases that must be considered when setting up rules for automatic detection and blocking of hacking attempts.

Registration monitoring

Some tools overwhelm VoIP systems by sending fake authorization attempts to them without ever responding to the challenge request that is used in SIP. One popular tool is often referred to as friendly scanner or SIPvicious. These types of tools keep a system busy by handling bogus requests, overloading the system, making it difficult to handle real requests, and so on. In addition, some suspicious behavior can be detected from someone simply trying to make long distance or international calls repeatedly within a short time period.

FreeSWITCH provides the ability to log a warning when an attempt is made to utilize credentials in the system (recognized or not). Programs such as Fail2Ban may then be used to monitor the frequency in which this logline is produced. If the frequency hits a threshold where the traffic is suspicious, the IP address causing the traffic can be blocked for a period of time (or permanently). It is generally considered suspicious if a large number of authorization attempts occurs from the same IP address within a relatively short period of time.

To ensure that a warning is generated when FreeSWITCH receives an invalid authentication attempt, you can modify your SIP profiles and include the following setting:

```
<param name="log-auth-failures" value="true"/>
```

A log line will be generated for authentication attempts that looks as follows:

[WARNING] SIP auth challenge (REGISTER) on sofia profile 'customer_access' for [user_rdkj7h@2600hz.com] from ip 184.106.157.100

These warnings can be counted automatically and are used to ban the IP address `184.106.157.100` in the previous example.

Fail2Ban

Fail2Ban is a third-party program that runs in the background and monitors logs. When specific loglines such as the authentication challenge line shown previously, are seen a certain number of times, Fail2Ban takes an action. It can be programmed to e-mail you with an alert or automatically use IPTables to block an offending IP address after too many invalid attempts occur within a certain period of time.

This book is not intended to be a complete guide for using Fail2Ban. However some sample scripts are given later in the chapter.

To configure Fail2Ban you will need to create several files which instruct Fail2Ban what to look for in your logs and what to do when it finds a match.

For filters, Fail2Ban has by default, a folder where you can place filters. These filters contain strings which can be used to match against your logs. You can have as many filters as you want to look for different types of traffic in your logs. When combined with FreeSWITCH's error log which shows invalid login attempts, this can become a useful filter mechanism.

The second file, known as the `jail` configuration file applies the filters to rules such as how often an error is allowed to occur and what action to take after that threshold has been exceeded. The `jail` configuration file effectively specifies how to react (when filters match).

Filter configurations

Let's first review a `filter` configuration file. This file would typically be placed in `/etc/Fail2Ban/filter.d/` and named according to the particular filter you are looking for. In this case we might call the file `freeswitch-auth.conf`. The file would contain a filter to look for failed authentication attempts. The format is a standard regular expression. In this case we consider a failure in FreeSWITCH anytime someone tries to register or make a call using invalid credentials. The file would look like the following:

```
# freeswitch-auth.conf Fail2Ban filter configuration file
[Definition]
failregex = SIP auth failure \((?:[REGISTER|INVITE])\) on sofia
profile \'[^']+\' for \[.*\] from ip <HOST>
```

This will watch the FreeSWITCH logs for failed REGISTER or INVITE messages.

Jail configurations

Now, combine this filter with a `jail` entry which blocks an IP address if too many failed INVITEs or REGISTERs are received within a certain period of time. To do this edit `/etc/Fail2Ban/jail.conf` and add the following entry:

```
[freeswitch-auth]
enabled  = true
# place your custom port entries in here if needed (per the Sofia
settings above)
port     = 5060
filter   = freeswitch-auth
logpath  = /var/log/freeswitch/freeswitch.log
maxretry = 50
findtime = 30
bantime  = 6000
action   = iptables-allports[name=freeswitch, protocol=all]
```

The earlier settings indicate the use of `freeswitch-auth` filter and after 50 failed INVITE or REGISTER authorization attempts (`maxretry`) within a 30 second period, blocks the IP address of the offender. If the filter is met (meaning 50 failed INVITE or REGISTER authorization attempts occur) within a 30 second period, the IP address will be banned in full for 6000 seconds.

Other considerations

The Fail2Ban script must be tuned so that a large site is not accidentally kicked offline just because they are busy. For example, if you have a rate limit Fail2Ban entry, you would not want to set up Fail2Ban to block IP addresses if they happen to send 50 authentication requests in a 5 second period, because if the site has 50 phones and their power goes out, when their power comes back on all phones will attempt to register at once, resulting in them being banned. This is not the intent.

Care must be taken when setting up Fail2Ban to test for edge case scenarios like the power outage scenario just described.

Encryption

Keeping voice communication secure is essential to any communications platform. This is especially critical for PSTN communication routed over the Internet because end-users often assume secure lines when speaking about confidential matters or conducting financial transactions.

VoIP encryption is based on two concepts – encrypting signaling and encrypting media (audio/video) communication. Like any standard encryption mechanism, VoIP encryption utilizes standard cryptography libraries and involves key exchanges and password negotiation to securely transmit and receive information. The two main encryption algorithms used in VoIP (which are detailed later) are very similar to SSL over the web and key exchange is used when connecting to remote servers via SSH. In either exchange, the main goal is to end up with an encryption algorithm and a common encryption secret between the two parties that only they know, which can be used to encrypt and decrypt the actual content – the phone call.

Many people toss around the terms TLS, SSL, and SRTP without fully understanding them. It should be understood that in order to fully protect communications it is recommended to choose both an encryption strategy for signaling and an encryption strategy for audio encryption.

In the following sections, we'll review each cryptography strategy in more detail.

Protecting SIP signalling

SIP signaling is important to encrypt. It contains both authentication information your phone utilizes to make and receive calls and it includes the Caller ID Name and Number of the caller and callee, by default in plain text. This is easy to sniff and to spoof. Encryption makes that harder. In addition, if you are using SRTP (Secure RTP), the SIP signaling contains the cryptography key used to keep your audio secure. Someone who observed this key in plain-text would easily be able to defeat the media encryption utilized.

Choosing between encryption options

There are a variety of encryption options available for FreeSWITCH. You can encrypt the signaling (that is, the SIP messages), the media (that is, the audio in the RTP stream), or both. **Transport Layer Security (TLS)** V1 encrypts everything over the TCP connection; this has the downside that jitter or delays due to TCP can occur. UDP is generally preferred for RTP and using TLSV1 has some additional traffic overhead. ZRTP has the advantage that it allows for end-to-end encryption without pre-exchanging keys or certificates but is a bit more complex to set up, especially for some clients. Finally there is **Secure Sockets Layer (SSL)** v2/3; this encrypts the SIP control channel over an encrypted TCP connection using SSL certificates, but by default doesn't provide anything for the RTP data. The login information and call metadata is transmitted over the control channel, so if this is what you care about, protecting this is enough and adds no overhead to the RTP data. If you want to encrypt the voice data itself (so the voice data cannot be understood) it can be combined with SRTP. SRTP enables encryption of the RTP data with minor overhead to each of the RTP UDP packets. This has the benefit that the call data are encrypted but is still over UDP, so there should be virtually no difference with SRTP on or off it. The encryption key used for SRTP is exchanged over the control channel (which SSLv2/3 encrypts), which gives you best results of both the worlds. Generally SSLv2/3 + SRTP is the most firewall friendly(has the fewest changes for existing installations). SSLv2/3 + SRTP is also fairly easy to configure on the FreeSWITCH server and most likely the most supported encryption method for most clients and SIP phones, so generally they should be where someone wants to start encrypting call data.

> ZRTP is a protocol that was co-designed by the same individual who created PGP encryption. More information can be found at `http://zfone.com`.

Encryption with SSL

SSL encryption works in the same way as negotiation via a website or any other SSL-based service. A third-party is used to validate (sign) certificates used between a sender and a receiver to exchange messages. These certificates are based on a public and private hash that should in theory, be loaded on the phone itself and the server respectively.

FreeSWITCH supports SSL v2/3 encryption of SIP packets. By default, enabling SSL only encrypts SIP, it doesn't provide anything for the media or RTP data. Information on how to encrypt the media is provided via this encrypted SSL control channel to allow for RTP data to be encrypted, but only if SRTP is also enabled. The call information and call metadata is transmitted over the protected connection so if this is what you care about protecting, you can use SSL encryption alone with no RTP encryption or overhead. For example, if you don't want packet sniffing of phone numbers to work, SSLv2/3 will be sufficient for encrypting your SIP packets. If you want to encrypt the voice data itself (so the voice data cannot be understood) it can be combined with SRTP (refer to the earlier part of this chapter).

Setting Up SSLv2/3

In order to utilize SSL encryption you must compile FreeSWITCH with the OpenSSL enabled library. In addition, you'll need to generate and self-sign or professionally sign an SSL certificate. These certificates work in the exact same way as web server SSL certificate signing works.

To compile FreeSWITCH with the OpenSSL enabled library, ensure that the OpenSSL development libraries are installed. Then run the configure command with the `--with-openssl` flag set. Note that this flag is set by default so, most likely, you already have this library compiled in, but this provides a fail-safe way to be sure.

FreeSWITCH includes a simple script to help you generate self-signed certificates quickly to use on the Internal SIP Profile that ships by default. If your server internal hostname is `pbx.freeswitch.org`, you can run:

```
bin/gentls_cert setup -cn pbx.freeswitch.org -alt
DNS:pbx.freeswitch.org -org freeswitch.org
bin/gentls_cert create_server -cn pbx.freeswitch.org -alt
DNS:pbx.freeswitch.org -org freeswitch.org
```

Some phones check the hostname for matches, so in the previous commands, modify the hostname to match your server. You can generate multiple certificates for each domain name you host, if necessary. These scripts generate and self-sign certificates which are automatically placed into your `conf/ssl/` folder for your FreeSWITCH installation.

Once you've generated your certificates, you will need to tell FreeSWITCH which SIP profiles use these certificates and enable SSL encryption support on those profiles. To do this, set these variables in your Sofia SIP profile:

```
<param name="tls" value="true"/>
<param name="tls-version" value="sslv23"/>
<param name="tls-cert-dir" value="/opt/freeswitch/conf/ssl"/>
```

If you generated your certificates with a passphrase protecting the files themselves, you can enter that password here:

```
<param name="tls-passphrase" value=""/>
```

You can generate different certificates for different SIP profiles if you wish, for added security.

Once you've installed the certificates and started FreeSWITCH you should be able to enable SSL on your endpoint device and all SIP packets should be encrypted.

Encryption with TLS

TLS is an alternative encryption mechanism for establishing secure signaling. It is generally seen as a more mature strategy. TLS encrypts everything over a TCP connection and maintains that connection for the duration of a dialog.

Like SSL, TLS requires the OpenSSL libraries. To compile FreeSWITCH with the library enabled OpenSSL, ensure that the OpenSSL development libraries are installed. Then, run the configure command with the `--with-openssl` flag set. Note that this flag is set by default, so most likely you already have this library compiled in, but this provides a fail-safe way to be sure.

To enable TLS encryption for signaling simply add the following to your Dialplan:

```
<param name="tls-version" value="tlsv1"/>
```

There are a number of gotchas and snafus possible with TLS. TLS (and its forerunner, SSL) runs on TCP, rather than UDP. This has the downside that when FreeSWITCH needs to make a connection toward the phone (such as delivering an inbound call to the phone) and if the phone is sitting behind a firewall or NAT traversal mechanism, the phone may be unreachable. You must make sure that all firewalls are configured to work with TCP inbound traffic. Also, ensure that the time is configured properly on your endpoint as you will get cryptic `bad certificate` error messages if the time is too far off, and it will fail to handshake properly.

As in the previous example with SSL, you must also specify the folder where your certificates reside:

```
<param name="tls-cert-dir" value="/opt/freeswitch/conf/ssl"/>
```

If you generated your certificates with a `passphrase` protecting the files themselves, you can enter that password here:

```
<param name="tls-passphrase" value=""/>
```

Once you've installed the certificates and started FreeSWITCH, you should be able to enable TLS on your endpoint device and all SIP packets should be encrypted.

Protecting audio

Audio content (also known as the RTP stream) is perhaps the most valuable part of a VoIP conversation. This makes it one of the most important parts for VoIP security. Encryption of the RTP stream ensures that the actual content of phone calls cannot be listened in on, recorded, or otherwise illegally obtained. There are multiple ways to achieve this security.

At its core, the theme for encryption algorithms requires that both sides involved in the encryption agree on a method and an encryption algorithm for encrypting and decrypting the data being transmitted and received. In other words, you can't use an encryption method that isn't supported by both sides. In addition, encryption algorithms are based on key exchanges, generally at the beginning of a call. These key exchanges are similar to exchanging passwords by both parties, but in an electronic and often automated way.

There are two popular forms of encryption generally used when encrypting audio and media streams. These forms of encryption are SRTP and ZRTP.

SRTP was developed in 2004 by a small team of IP protocol and cryptographic experts from Cisco and Ericsson. SRTP defines a method of transmitting and receiving RTP with message authentication and integrity and replay protection to the RTP data. It is designed to work in both unicast and multicast applications. Because it is older and was developed by key IP telephony hardware players, it has seen adoption in most standard equipment. SRTP is available on numerous devices available in the world today.

ZRTP was developed in 2006 by Phil Zimmermann (creator of PGP). It is a newer entrant that makes key negotiation automatic, significantly simplifying the setup and operation of ensuring secure and encrypted RTP calls. It also has the added advantage of not being dependent on server-side encryption. Encryption can occur between servers that are otherwise unaware of the contents of the RTP stream. This should allow the speed of adoption to increase significantly as dependencies are greatly reduced. However, most hardware manufacturers will need to implement ZRTP for this protocol to be fully successful.

Both SRTP and ZRTP technologies are supported by FreeSWITCH and are described in this chapter.

Encryption with SRTP

SRTP is an encryption mechanism that is negotiated during call setup via SIP. Both sides of the SIP conversation must agree to support RTP encryption and exchange keys for encryption in the SIP packets. The encryption key used for SRTP is exchanged over the control channel. This information is then used to encrypt the audio stream.

SRTP enables encryption of the RTP data with minor overhead to each of the RTP UDP packets. This has the benefit that the call data are encrypted but still transmit via UDP, minimizing latency or network traversal mechanisms that would normally be used in an unencrypted stream.

Generally SSLv2/3 and SRTP are the most firewall friendly strategies for existing installations since the actual work has already been done to get RTP to transmit properly over the network. SSL and SRTP are also fairly easy to configure within FreeSWITCH.

Note that unless you enable encryption of the SIP packets as well (discussed later) the key for the SRTP goes in the clear. For a fully secure connection between your phone and FreeSWITCH you should combine SIP encryption with SRTP encryption. This prevents any snooping or man-in-the-middle attacks. If only SRTP is enabled, only payload packets of type RTP packets will be secured.

Enabling SRTP

You can enable SRTP from your Dialplan on a per-call basis by setting the following flag:

```
<action application="set" data="sip_secure_media=true"/>
```

This needs to be done on both legs and on both inbound and outbound calls to be fully effective. Of course, your provider may not support SRTP so you may only be able to enable this on legs from FreeSWITCH to the endpoint.

You can check if media is secured properly within the Dialplan by checking for the variable ${sip_secure_media_confirmed} to be set. As an example, the following block will play a bong tone when SIP media is secured:

```
<extension name="is_secure">
  <condition field="${sip_secure_media_confirmed}"
  expression="^true$">
    <action application="sleep" data="1000"/>
    <action application="gentones" data="${bong-ring}"/>
  </condition>
</extension>
```

When debugging encryption, a helpful hint is in the SIP packet as to whether the phone is properly requesting encryption. You will see SIP packets that include the a=crypto line if you have offered encrypted RTP in your SIP setup.

Encryption with ZRTP

ZRTP is an SRTP-based encryption algorithm that differs from SRTP by exchanging encryption keys within the media stream, making the encryption more secure and also transparent to servers that don't understand the protocol. This allows ZRTP to be more flexible than SRTP and gives complete control to the endpoints to handle all levels and requirements of encryption without the risk of a man-in-the-middle attack. ZRTP also does not require a key exchange prior to media setup. The key exchange occurs during the initial portion of the RTP conversation.

ZRTP establishes keys over RTP when it is in an initially insecure state using the Diffie-Hellman key exchange protocol. The ZRTP protocol is fully laid out in RFC 6189.

Learning about cryptography

When first learning about cryptography, it is easy to get lost in a sea of unfamiliar expressions such as Diffie-Hellman and key exchange. These are part of a larger field of cryptography known as **PKI (Public Key Infrastructure)**. We recommend that you consult some of the many excellent resources available for learning more about this field.

One of the major strong points of ZRTP is its ability to work via proxies. Typically with SRTP, every point communicating via the encrypted stream needs to be aware of the encryption protocol, and also able to encrypt and decrypt the audio stream. This allows for snooping the encryption mid-stream if you have access to a server where the stream traverses. With ZRTP, the opposite is true; the servers in the middle do not need to be aware of the encryption protocol at all. They believe they are simply passing standard RTP packets. Since the servers are unaware of what the content of the RTP stream contains, only the two endpoints need to support ZRTP in order for the conversation to be completely secure. The proxies don't need to understand, or pass encryption information.

Another major advantage of ZRTP in FreeSWITCH is that it's enabled by default. The ZRTP protocol itself inserts negotiation packets into every initial RTP conversation and waits for a reply. If a reply is received, ZRTP encryption is automatically enabled when the other endpoint requests it.

Because ZRTP is a less popular protocol, there has been work to not only build ZRTP-enabled phones and soft clients but also work on a ZRTP software proxy. This proxy allows you to simply install a ZRTP plug-in software program, known as Zfone, and RTP traffic will be automatically encrypted, even with a software that doesn't natively support ZRTP. Zfone runs in the background unobtrusively and pops up to notify you when a key exchange has occurred. There is additionally an SDK available to help developers build ZRTP-enabled software and hardware as well.

You can enable or disable ZRTP support from within your Dialplan using the following command:

```
<action application="set" data="zrtp_secure_media=[true|false]"/>
```

When ZRTP is being negotiated, you will see the following line on the FreeSWITCH console indicating ZRTP is being offered:

[DEBUG] switch_rtp.c:928 [zrtp main]: START SESSION INITIALIZATION.

The ZRTP protocol will then begin injecting ZRTP negotiation packets into the RTP stream. If ZRTP is successfully started for a session, you will see a series of ZRTP log messages followed by a confirmation message that the channel is now secure, such as the following:

[zrtp protoco]:   Enter state SECURE (DH).

You will also see that a cache of the selected shared secret was auto-stored, which will be used for comparison purposes on the next call:

[zrtp cache] Storing ZRTP cache to </usr/local/freeswitch/db/zrtp.dat>...

You must ensure that ZRTP was compiled when FreeSWITCH was built. If you are unsure, you can use the flag `--enable-zrtp` to force ZRTP to be enabled during compiling, via the `configure` program.

Protecting passwords

Passwords are used in FreeSWITCH when phones register. When FreeSWITCH registers to external gateways and when administrators authenticate into the FreeSWITCH system itself. Most of these areas utilize weak plaintext passwords.

In addition, many users set their passwords to simple easy-to-guess combinations. Worse yet, some don't ever change or set up their voicemail boxes, leaving the defaults in place.

These passwords are very often targeted and once gained, they are exploited to commit fraud.

There are a few mechanisms available to mitigate this.

Registration passwords

Registration credentials do not need to be passed or kept on disk in plain-text. When defining SIP credentials in your folder, instead of including the following line:

```
<param name="password" value="samiam"/>
```

replace it with a pre-calculated `a1-hash` of the password, like the following:

```
<param name="a1-hash" value="c6440e5de50b403206989679159de89a"/>
```

To generate `a1-hash`, get the `md5` of the string `username:domain:password`, which is your username, domain name, and password all tied together with a colon. As an example:

```
echo -n "darren:2600hz.com:pass1234" | md5sum
  b62d1e3e27773ffd173c87e342a6aace
```

You would utilize the returned hash in your folder entry. This means you did not have to store the actual SIP registration on disk and someone who finds a way to compromise the folder file can't see the password either.

 In Mac OSX, use md5 instead of md5sum.

A full example would look something like the following:

```
<user id="darren">
  <params>
    <param name="a1-hash"
       value="c6440e5de50b403206989679159de89a"/>
  </params>
</user>
```

Voicemail passwords

Voicemail boxes have a history of being compromised for a variety of reasons. Besides simply listening to someone else's messages, voice mailboxes are often exploited because they have call-back or forward features which can be turned on remotely. One of the most popular strategies is to hack a voicemail box and forward that person's calls to an expensive international destination, racking up thousands of dollars of calls in a short amount of time. This makes voicemail password hacking popular even today.

Protection against weak voicemail passwords is fairly simple. FreeSWITCH stores voicemail passwords in plain-text in the database, allowing you to scan for passwords which are weak, such as 1111 or 1234. You can also scan for people who are using their extension number as their voicemail password which is another popular (and insecure) password strategy.

To scan for weak passwords you'll need to write a script that looks for passwords in the voicemail configuration database. Assuming you are using the defaults in FreeSWITCH, the voicemail database is stored in a SQLite file in your FreeSWITCH DB folder. This folder will be in one of various locations depending on how you installed FreeSWITCH, but most commonly it is in /opt/freeswitch/db, /usr/local/freeswitch/db, or /var/lib/freeswitch/db.

A sample way to check your database could be using the following simple SQLite query:

```
sqlite3 db/voicemail_default.db "select * from voicemail_prefs
where password=1234 or password=1111"
```

This command would use the SQLite3 linux client to look in the `voicemail_prefs` table for any passwords that are `1111` or `1234`. It will print all information about that mailbox on the screen, including the username and domain name of the user who has this password. You can then take corrective action by either resetting the password forcefully or contacting the user to advise them to change their password.

Summary

This chapter is only a brief guide to the most common VoIP security technologies prevalent today. There are a plethora of additional resources including sites such as `www.hackingvoip.com`, books on Hacking VoIP, and RTP encryption.

Taking the basic steps outlined in this chapter will provide you sufficient amount of security against today's most common hacks, DoS attacks, and abuses. This should allow most small to medium sized PBXes or hosted VoIP systems to operate securely and reliably.

We now move on to the last chapter in this book where we consider a variety of subjects that don't fit into any particular category. We will also present the reader with other resources for learning more about SIP, VoIP, and FreeSWITCH.

14

Advanced Features and Further Reading

There are two general categories of applications that can utilize FreeSWITCH—ones that are built in C as modules that live inside FreeSWITCH, and the others that control or manage FreeSWITCH externally. Both topics will be covered briefly in this chapter.

FreeSWITCH contains a variety of application modules that provide functionality and features that direct calls and make switching decisions while calls are in progress. These modules range from Caller ID lookup modules to real-time billing modules to multi-party conferencing modules. Modules can be used with each other to enrich the general Dialplan application set, to supervise calls, or to provide other functionality.

In addition, an entire community of open source FreeSWITCH applications has grown to provide various software programs that can fully (or partially) manage FreeSWITCH.

In this chapter, we'll presume you already have some basic understanding of how FreeSWITCH operates. We'll review various applications or modules which enable various features within FreeSWITCH, scratching only the surface of what they do. We'll also briefly cover some third-party tools that you can use to expand your utilization of FreeSWITCH further.

We will discuss the following topics in this chapter:

- Multi-user conferencing (`mod_conference`)
- Real-time billing (`mod_nibblebill`)
- Other endpoint types: Skype, GSM, and TDM
- Web GUIs and other projects

Multi-user conferencing

FreeSWITCH includes a powerful built-in multi-user conferencing module `mod_conference`, which allows the mixing of audio channels between callers in a multi-user audio conferencing system. This system also allows for full control of all audio mixing and caller interaction features, such as detection of touch-tones, management of send and receive audio paths per channel, volume controls, gain controls, and more. You can create as many conferences as you like, as long as free system resources (that is, memory, CPU cycles, and so forth) are still left there.

Configuration

The `mod_conference` configuration is configured in the `conference` section of the XML files. This is generally located in the `autoload_configs/conference.conf.xml` file. The configuration defines how conferences behave, through a series of profiles. These profiles can be applied to conferences when they are created via the Dialplan. The `conference` configuration file is divided into several sections, each with its own set of parameters. These sections are detailed in this chapter.

Conference profiles

Conference profiles are templates of the settings that can be applied to a particular conference. In combination with caller-controls (discussed in this section), conference profiles allow for the complete customization of the behavior of individual conferences. You can create template types and apply them across many conferences, create a profile for each conference you intend to utilize, or you can simply utilize the defaults.

Conference profiles are named profiles that contain lists of parameters within each named profile element. The general structure is as follows:

```
<profiles>
  <profile name="default">
    <param name="paramName" value="paramValue"/>
  </profile>
</profiles>
```

You can have any number of `<profile>` tags, and each `<profile>` tag can have any number of `<param>` tags. The following is a list of parameters that are available:

- `rate`: The `rate` parameter specifies the default (and highest) sampling rate that the conference bridge will utilize. All callers who call into this channel will have their audio transcoded into this sampling rate if they are not already transcoded at that rate. For the purposes of audio mixing, this defines the lowest sampling rate in relation to the system—if two callers have HD phones but call into a conference where the rate is 8000, those callers will have their audio sampled down to the lower rate.

    ○ Parameter syntax: `<param name="rate" value="8000"/>`

    ○ Default: `8000`

    ○ Available options: `8000`, `12000`, `16000`, `24000`, `32000`, and `48000` (possibly others in the future)

- `caller-controls`: This parameter specifies the `caller-controls` profile to use with this conference bridge.

    ○ Parameter syntax: `<param name="caller-controls" value="default"/>`

- `auto-record`: This parameter specifies whether to automatically record conferences or not. Recording will begin once two or more parties are on the line. This option, if set, must consist of a path that can be written to for the purposes of recording the conference.

    ○ Parameter syntax: `<param name="auto-record" value="filename"/>`

    ○ Default: off

    ○ Sample filename: `/usr/local/freeswitch/sounds/ conferences/${conference_name}.wav`

The sample filename listed would record conferences into a file based on the conference bridge's name.

- `interval`: This parameter specifies the number of milliseconds per frame that are mixed. This setting is similar to how `ptime` works, but does not need to match the actual `ptime` of a caller. Higher numbers require less CPU usage, but can cause conversation quality issues, so experiment with your setup. The default is usually OK.

    ○ Parameter syntax: `<param name="interval" value="20"/>`

    ○ Default: `20`

- energy-level: This parameter specifies the energy level (or strength/volume of audio) required for audio to be sent to the other users. The energy level is a threshold that dictates the level at which a person is determined to be speaking versus the background noise received. This feature helps remove background or ambient noise from being mixed into the conference. If this option is too high, it can result in clipping at the beginning and end of people's sentences. The value 0 disables the detection and will bridge all packets even if they are only background noise.
  - Parameter syntax: <param name="energy-level" value="20"/>
  - Default: 20
  - Set 0 to disable completely

- member-flags: This parameter allows for setting member-specific flags or parameters on individual conference members. These options include whether to be *wasteful* with packet mixing (that is, send audio to individuals even when no speaking is happening in the conference), whether or not a specific member is the leader of a conference (and thus, the conference should terminate when they leave), and so on. Options should be separated by a pipe | character.
  - Parameter syntax: <param name="member-flags" value="waste|endconf"/>
  - The options for the member-flags parameter are as follows:
    - deaf: Prevents the members from listening to other members in the conference by default (this can be changed after the conference has begun via events).
    - waste: Sends audio to channels even when no conversation is occurring.
    - dist-dtmf: Distributes DTMF signals to each channel. When someone pushes a DTMF tone, it is normally absorbed and processed by FreeSWITCH. This option prevents that from happening and instead echoes the DTMF tone to all other members.
    - endconf: Specifies that the conference should end when this party exits.

- conference-flags: This parameter sets the conference-wide flags that dictate how the conference behaves. The only currently available option is to force users to wait for the moderator before the conference begins. Moderators are determined via the Dialplan, when bridged to the conference, by passing an extra flag. While waiting for the moderator to join, callers hear music on hold.
  - Parameter syntax: <param name="conference-flags" value="wait-mod"/>

- `tts-engine`: This parameter specifies the Text-To-Speech engine to utilize within this conference bridge.
  - Parameter syntax: `<param name="tts-engine" value="cepstral"/>`

- `tts-voice`: This parameter specifies which Text-To-Speech engine voice to utilize within this conference bridge.
  - Parameter syntax: `<param name="tts-voice" value="david"/>`

- `pin`: This parameter specifies the PIN code (that is pass code or password) that must be entered before user is allowed to enter the conference.
  - Parameter syntax: `<param name="pin" value="12345"/>`

- `max-members`: The maximum number of members allowed in the conference. If this number is reached and an additional member tries to join, the `max-members-sound` will be played and the caller will not be allowed to enter the conference bridge.
  - Parameter syntax: `<param name="max-members" value="20"/>`

- `caller-id-name`: This parameter instructs the caller ID name to set when making an outbound call from within this conference bridge.
  - Parameter syntax: `<param name="caller-id-name" value="John Doe"/>`

- `caller-id-number`: This parameter instructs the caller ID number to set when making an outbound call from within this conference bridge.
  - Parameter syntax: `<param name="caller-id-number" value="4158867900"/>`

- `comfort-noise`: This parameter instructs the volume level of background white noise to get added to the conference. Sometimes callers think they have been dropped from a conference if the audio level remains too quiet. This comfort noise setting provides white noise on the line so the caller knows the line is still connected. Note that at higher audio sampling rates, this noise can become bothersome, so you may wish to tweak this setting if you go above 8000 Hz sampling rates.
  - Parameter syntax: `<param name="comfort-noise" value="1000"/>`

- **announce-count**: The parameter will speak the total number of callers in the conference when a new person joins, but only when the threshold specified in this parameter is reached. It requires a valid text-to-speech engine.
  - Parameter syntax: `<param name="announce-count" value="5"/>`

- **suppress-events**: This parameter is for use with the FreeSWITCH event system. This special configuration option denotes that certain types of events should NOT be fired to other parties who may be listening for conference events.
  - Parameter syntax: `<param name="suppress-events" value="true"/>`

- **sound-prefix**: This parameter sets a default path from which to retrieve conference audio files.
  - Parameter syntax: `<param name="sound-prefix" value="/usr/local/freeswitch/sounds/"/>`

The following parameters are available for setting custom sounds to play from within the conference bridge when certain activities occur. All sounds are played to individual caller channels and not to all parties in the conference, with the exception of `enter-sound` and `exit-sound`, which are played to all members.

All sound files are specified with the format: `<param name="sound-name" value="file.wav"/>`

The custom sounds available are as follows:

- **muted-sound**: This sound is played when a caller has been muted.
- **unmuted-sound**: This sound is played when a caller is no longer muted.
- **alone-sound**: This sound is played to a caller when they are the only remaining party.
- **enter-sound**: This sound is played to all members when a new caller joins the conference.
- **exit-sound**: This sound is played to all members when a caller leaves the conference.
- **kicked-sound**: This sound is played when a caller is kicked out from the conference.
- **locked-sound**: This sound is played to callers who try to join a locked conference.
- **is-locked-sound**: This sound is played to conference participants when a conference is locked.

- `is-unlocked-sound`: This sound is played to conference participants when a conference is unlocked.

- `pin-sound`: This prompt is used while asking for a conference pin.

- `bad-pin-sound`: This sound is played when an invalid PIN number is entered.

- `perpetual-sound`: A special setting — this plays a sound in a continuous loop forever, when parties are in the conference.

- `moh-sound`: A file or resource handle that plays a particular music-on-hold stream to the conference, when there is only one member in the conference. When a second member joins, the audio will stop, unless the `mod-wait` settings have been specified (as mentioned earlier).

- `max-members-sound`: If someone tries to join a conference that already has the maximum amount of members, this file is played.

Caller controls

Conferences allow caller controls which specify what commands are available to callers via touch-tones from within an active conference. Commands can include modifying the volume of the conference, mute/un-mute, or more advanced options such as playing menus to individuals or moving people from one conference to another.

Caller controls are based on pre-configured templates that are applied when a conference is first started. For example, you can specify a list of controls that are available (such as the *0* key for mute, *1* to lower the volume, and *3* to increase the volume) and then apply those controls to three different conferences. The settings are applied when the conference begins and remain the same for the duration of the conference.

Keep in mind that you cannot have one party entering the conference with one set of controls and another party with another set of controls.

 Warning: Do not name your `caller-controls` as default or none. Those words are reserved for the default key mappings or no key mappings, respectively.

The following is an example of the `caller-controls` configuration:

```
<caller-controls>
  <group name="standard-keys" >
    <control action="vol talk dn" digits="1"/>
    <control action="vol talk zero" digits="2"/>
    <control action="vol talk up" digits="3"/>
```

```
        <control action="transfer" digits="5"
          data="100 XML default"/>
        <control action="execute_application" digits="0"
          data="playback conf_help.wav"/>
        <control action="execute_application" digits="#"
          data="execute_dialplan conference-menu"/>
    </group>
  </caller-controls>
```

The preceding example shows how to create a `caller-controls` profile named `standard-keys`. The keys *1, 2,* and *3* lower, normalize, and raise the volume respectively, the key *5* transfers the caller who pressed the key to an extension `100`, and the keys *0* and *#* each execute a specific Dialplan application.

Advertise

The `advertise` section of the conference configuration file allows you to generate presence events (advertisements) to services and subscribed parties via the FreeSWITCH event system. The idea is to set up permanent room names that generate presence events just like a phone or other device would. An outside program can then monitor whether a conference room is in use or not.

Advertise settings contains a room name in each element within `advertise` tags, as shown in this example:

```
<advertise>
  <room name="888@$${domain}" status="FreeSWITCH"/>
</advertise>
```

Sending and receiving XMPP events

The conference module allows for XMPP servers such as Gtalk to accept commands via Jabber/XMPP. These commands can include things such as kicking users, transferring calls, and likewise. The configurations are simple to use and the examples are as follows:

```
<chat-permissions>
  <profile name="default">
    <user name="bob@somewhere.com" commands="all"/>
    <user name="harry@somewhere.com"
      commands="|deaf|dial|energy|kick
               |list|lock|mute|norecord
               |play|record|relate|say|saymember
               |stop|transfer|undeaf|unlock
               |unmute|volume_in|volume_out|"/>
  </profile>
</chat-permissions>
```

Connecting callers to the conference

Callers reach conferences via the `conference` application, which is usually invoked from the XML Dialplan or from the event socket via API calls. The general syntax for connecting a caller to a conference is as follows:

```
<action application="conference" data="confname@profilename"/>
```

`confname` is the conference room's name, and `profilename` is the profile to use from the conference configuration file (as specified earlier in this chapter).

You can optionally pass specific parameters in to the conference by appending `+flags` at the end of a conference profile name, as shown in the following code:

```
<action application="conference"
  data="confname@profilename+ConfPIN+flags{
  mute|deaf|waste|moderator}
  "/>
```

Conferences are created on-demand when the first participant arrives in the bridge. Upon creation, the settings from the active profile, along with the specified conference PIN number, are recorded in memory with the conference. This is important to note because changes you load into memory won't take effect on in-progress conferences. For example, once a conference has been started with a PIN number, any future participants who join the conference must specify the same PIN number.

The profile name you specify should match a named profile from your `conf/ autoload_configs/conference.conf.xml` file.

Dynamically created conferences stay alive until the number of members drops to zero.

The following are some examples of values to specify in the data section when bridging a call to a conference:

Action data	Description
confname	Profile is "default", no flags or PIN
confname+1234	Profile is "default", PIN is 1234
confname@profilename+1234	Profile is "default", PIN is 1234, no flags
confname@profilename++flags{mute|waste}	Profile is "default", multiple flags, no PIN
confname+1234+flags{mute|waste}	Profile is "default", multiple flags with PIN

Note that while some parameters are optional, their order is very important.

Controlling active conferences

A number of CLI and API commands exist for controlling an active conference. The most commonly used commands involve kicking members, adjusting volumes, and originating calls (to add people to a conference). While these items are outside the scope of this tutorial, you should consult the FreeSWITCH wiki for more examples of how to use CLI commands to control a conference bridge.

 Further detailed information about conferencing can be found online at `http://wiki.freeswitch.org/wiki/Mod_conference`.

Nibblebill

`mod_nibblebill` is a credit/debit module for FreeSWITCH. The module was initially written by Darren Schreiber to fill the gaps of a professional grade trunking system that lacked the ability to detect fraud in real-time. Its purpose is to allow real-time debiting of credit or cash from a database while calls are in progress.

Darren had the following goals:

- Debiting credit/cash from accounts real-time
- Allowing for billing at different rates during a single call
- Allowing for warning callers when their balance is low (via audio, in-channel)
- Allowing for disconnecting or re-routing calls when balance is depleted
- Allowing billing functions listed previously to operate with multiple concurrent calls

Use cases

`mod_nibblebill` can be used in a variety of use cases, some of which are listed in the following topics.

Billing (pre-pay)

You can allow people to put cash into an account and "nibble" away at it. In addition, when callers have almost depleted their account, a tone or other message can play (or another action can occur) warning the caller about this.

Upon full depletion of their account, the call can either be transferred to an extension that allows them to recharge their balance via touch-tones or otherwise, or the call can simply be disconnected.

Billing (post-pay)

If your database column allows it, you can make the warning and out-of-cash thresholds a negative number. Callers can "dip into" negative numbers in the database, and then you can bill them after their usage. In this way, you are also able to protect yourself from abuse, since callers will still be terminated if they go below some (negative) threshold you set (that is, they spend too much money in a month).

This is a more typical approach to billing for landlines and it allows for an account to be automatically cut off, if excessive usage occurs without someone paying their bill.

Pay-per-call service billing

You could bill for providing a special service, either via fixed fee or via per-minute after a certain event (for example, entering a credit card number and being approved).

Maximum credit and/or fraud prevention

You can set up a credit field that gets depleted by your users, similar to pre-pay as we had seen earlier, but just not tell them about it. When they deplete all their credit for a day, week, month, and so on they can't make any more calls. You can use an external script to deposit more credit into their account at a pre-set interval. This would allow something such as "100 minutes a day free" or other such promotions to work.

Design goals

If you plan to use `mod_nibblebill` please keep in mind the design goals of the module:

- **Concurrent design**: This allows for supervision of multiple in-progress channels that belong to the same account/account code.

- **Scalability**: This allows for different heartbeat intervals (or turning off supervision during calls altogether). This allows the administrator to tweak checks depending on system load.

- **Flexibility**: This allows warning levels and "out-of-funds" levels to be flexible on a global and/or per-user basis, and allows customization as to what happens when the caller is out of funds.

- **Customizable**: These settings should be customizable, including when people are terminated or warned and what happens when they are terminated or warned.

Installation and configuration

mod_nibblebill is part of the main FreeSWITCH source tree. It requires database/ODBC support to function properly. The ODBC designated name must be known to configure mod_nibblebill, just like other ODBC modules within FreeSWITCH. Linux/Unix users must compile mod_nibblebill as it is disabled by default.

Enabling mod_nibblebill is very similar to the process we used in *Chapter 2, Building and Installation* where we enabled mod_flite:

1. Open modules.conf in the FreeSWITCH source directory and locate the following line:

    ```
    #applications/mod_nibblebill
    ```

    Remove the # and save the file.

2. Compile the module with the following command:

    ```
    make mod_nibblebill-install
    ```

3. Open the conf/autoload_configs/modules.conf.xml file and locate the following line:

    ```
    <!-- <load module="mod_nibblebill"/> -->
    ```

    Remove the <!-- and --> tags and save the file.

4. Modify the database connection settings in conf/autoload_configs/nibblebill.conf.xml:

    ```
    <param name="odbc-dsn" value="database:user:password"/>
    ```

5. Save the file and exit.

Now mod_nibblebill will load automatically when FreeSWITCH starts. Note that you may also load or unload mod_nibblebill without restarting FreeSWITCH. This allows you to make changes to your nibblebill configuration without bringing down your entire system.

> More information about **Data Source Names (DSN)** in FreeSWITCH can be found at http://wiki.freeswitch.org/wiki/Data_source_name.

Database tables

For your configuration file (from `nibblebill.conf.xml` which we had seen before), make sure you have an ODBC database driver and database that is accessible and contains the correct database, table, and column names. While a discussion of ODBC configurations is beyond the scope of this book, a basic `odbc.ini` file might look something like the following:

```
[NIBBLEBILL]
Description = Nibblebill
Driver    = MySQL
SERVER    = localhost
PORT      = 3306
DATABASE = nibblebill
OPTION    = 67108864
Socket    = /var/lib/mysql/mysql.sock
User     = db_user
Password = db_pass
```

A sample table is shown in this example:

```
mysql> use nibblebill;

mysql> select * from accounts;

+--------+--------------+---------+
| id     | name         |    cash |
+--------+--------------+---------+
|      1 | Darren       | 41.4161 |
|      2 | Joe          |      50 |
|      9 | tester9      |      50 |
|     10 | tester10     | 44.8213 |
| 837269 | My Company   |      50 |
+--------+--------------+---------+
    5 rows in set (0.00 sec)
```

In the previous example, a table named `accounts` exists in the database `nibblebill`. That table contains `id` and `cash` columns for use by the billing script. The `id` column represents the account code for the user and `cash` represents the amount of money the user currently has in his or her account. The corresponding settings in your `nibblebill.conf.xml` file for the previous setup would be as follows:

```
<param name="db_dsn" value="nibblebill:user:password"/>
<param name="db_table" value="accounts"/>
<param name="db_column_cash" value="cash"/>
<param name="db_column_account" value="id"/>
```

Creating the database table for PostgreSQL

Use the following SQL command to create a table in Postgres:

```
create table accounts (
 id bigserial not null,
 name varchar( 256 ),
 cash double precision not null
);
```

Creating the database table for MySQL

Use this SQL command to create a table in MySQL:

```
CREATE TABLE accounts
(
 id int NOT NULL PRIMARY KEY,
 name VARCHAR(255),
 cash double precision NOT NULL
);
```

Note that your business logic may require more columns in the `accounts` table. The `nibblebill` database will only use `id`, `name`, and `cash`; it will ignore all other columns.

Billing a call

There are several methods available to employ billing calls. This section discusses the relevant methods and related options.

The nibble method (default)

The default method of billing is based on the concept of a FreeSWITCH heartbeat. For every x seconds, we deduct y amount from an account.

To bill a call, you must set a minimum of two variables on an in-progress channel. The variables are `nibble_rate` and `nibble_account`. As a neat feature, `mod_nibblebill` doesn't really care where you set up the billing variables from, as long as they exist before a `hangup` occurs. That means that you can set them in the Dialplan inside the directory in Lua script anywhere that you can manipulate channel variables.

In its simplest form, you can add this to a user's directory entry:

```
<variable name="nibble_rate" value="0.03"/>
<variable name="nibble_account" value="18238"/>
```

Now that user will be billed $0.03/minute for every call made or received. The billing will go against account 18238.

By default, a heartbeat is set at 60 seconds. This means that every 60 seconds, $0.03 is deducted from their account. Note that all mathematical calculations are done using FreeSWITCH's internal microseconds counters. This means a few things:

1. If a heartbeat does not fire exactly on time, you will get a fraction of a cent billed. You should make sure your underlying database can support that.

2. Counters count the time in-between ticks exactly. There is no "lost" billing.

3. Billing of minimums does not exist (yet).

You can modify the heartbeat interval globally with this parameter:

```
<param name="global_heartbeat" value="300">
```

That would make the heartbeat fire every 300 seconds, or every five minutes. Heartbeats can go as low as every second (though this is really not wise, as you're making a database call every second, per channel).

An alternative to nibble billings

It is possible to use this module without heartbeats enabled. That means you just bill a call at the end of the call. You set the same variables as listed previously, but you also set one additional variable in your mod_nibblebill.conf.xml file:

```
<param name="global_heartbeat" value="off">
```

By doing this, billing will only occur at the end of a call (on hang up). The time calculation will be from when the call was answered until the end of the call. If a call is never answered, billing is skipped.

The formula used to bill calls when this parameter is set as follows:

```
([time call ended] - [time call answered]) x [rate per minute] = total
charge
```

 NOTE: This method does not allow for any supervision of a call in progress, meaning fraud can occur and people can go over their allotted limits.

Examples

The following examples demonstrate how to implement various billing scenarios.

Different rates per user

It is possible to have different rates per minute, per user. This can work in addition to the Dialplan examples listed later, as long as you take care not to delete the variables. Consider the following example.

Let's say you have two users—one is billed at $0.05/minute and the other at $0.10/minute. Neither is billed when calling a toll-free 800 number. You would set up their directory entries as follows:

```xml
<user id="dschreiber">
  <params>
    <param name="password" value="1234"/>
  </params>
  <variables>
    <variable name="nibble_rate" value="0.05"/>
    <variable name="nibble_account" value="8182"/>
    <variable name="default_areacode" value="415"/>
    <variable name="toll_allow"
      value="domestic,international,local"/>
    <variable name="user_context" value="default"/>
  </variables>
</user>
<user id="expensive_guy">
  <params>
    <param name="password" value="1234"/>
  </params>
  <variables>
    <variable name="nibble_rate" value="0.10"/>
    <variable name="nibble_account" value="2932"/>
    <variable name="default_areacode" value="212"/>
    <variable name="toll_allow"
      value="domestic,international,local"/>
    <variable name="user_context" value="default"/>
  </variables>
</user>
```

Then in your Dialplan, override the bill rates for toll-free calls only:

```
<extension name="tollfree800">
  <condition field="destination_number"
    expression="^1"(800\d{7})$">
    <action application="set" data="nibble_rate=0"/>
    <action application="bridge"
      data="sofia/gateway/flowroute/$1"/>
  </condition>
</extension>
```

All non-800 number calls will be billed at the rates set on the user's account, while toll-free calls will be billed 0 (equivalent to no billing).

Single rate for all users

On your user accounts type the following code:

```
<user id="mercutioviz">
  <params>
    <param name="password" value="1234"/>
  </params>
  <variables>
    <variable name="toll_allow"
      value="domestic,international,local"/>
    <variable name="user_context" value="default"/>
    <variable name="nibble_account" value="1"/>
  </variables>
</user>
```

Append the following code as well:

```
<user id="dschreiber">
  <params>
    <param name="password" value="1234"/>
  </params>
  <variables>
    <variable name="toll_allow"
      value="domestic,international,local"/>
    <variable name="user_context" value=" default"/>
    <variable name="nibble_account" value="2"/>
  </variables>
</user>
```

In the Dialplan add an entry on the extension you want to bill as follows:

```
<extension name="outbound">
  <condition field="destination_number"
    expression="^91"(\d{10,})$">
    <action application="set" data="nibble_rate=0.05"/>
    <action application="set"
      data="nibble_account=${nibble_account}"/>
    <action application="bridge"
      data="sofia/gateway/flowroute/1$1"/>
  </condition>
</extension>
```

Different rates per area code

This example bills all calls at $0.05/minute, except calls to area code 919 which are $0.07/minute and calls to 800 numbers, which are free. Calls are billed to whatever account code is set for the user in their directory profile.

In the following example, we set the rate from the Dialplan. Be careful! This overrides any variable set on the user/directory level:

```
<extension name="tollfree800">
  <condition field=" destination_number"
    expression="^1?(800\d{7})$">
    <action application="set"
      data="nibble_account=${accountcode}"/>
    <action application="set" data="nibble_rate=0"/>
    <action application="bridge"
      data="sofia/gateway/flowroute/1$1"/>
  </condition>
</extension>
<extension name="special919rate">
  <condition field="destination_number"
    expression="^1?(919\d{7})$">
    <action application="set"
      data="nibble_account=${accountcode}"/>
    <action application="set" data="nibble_rate=0.07"/>
    <action application="bridge"
            data="sofia/gateway/flowroute/1$1"/>
  </condition>
</extension>
<extension name="domestic">
  <condition field="destination_number"
```

```
          expression="^1?(\d{10})$">
      <action application="set"
        data="nibble_account=${accountcode}"/>
      <action application="set" data="nibble_rate=0.05"/>
      <action application="bridge"
        data="sofia/gateway/flowroute/1$1"/>
    </condition>
  </extension>
```

Different rates per service delivery

This idea encompasses the concept of changing the `nibble_rate` entity while the call is in progress.

Here is an idea: a caller could call in and for the first part of their call, they might be getting billed at $1.00/minute, maybe to talk to `tier1` support. If they need `tier2` support, the rate goes to $5.00/minute. The rate changes when the call is transferred, simply by changing the variable. You can even set the amount to 0 while the caller is on hold or in a FIFO queue. In the following example, extension 2000 routes to the first tier agent at extension 1000. Extension 2001 routes to the second tier agent at extension 1001:

```
<extension name="tier1">
  <condition field="destination_number" expression="^2000$">
    <!-- Save anything billed at a previous rate -->
    <action application="nibblebill" data="flush"/>
    <!-- Change the rate -->
    <action application="set" data="nibble_rate=1.00"/>
    <!-- Transfer to Tier1 rep -->
    <action application="transfer" data="1000 XML default"/>
  </condition>
</extension>
<extension name="tier2">
  <condition field="destination_number" expression="^2001">
    <!-- Save anything billed at a previous rate -->
    <action application="nibblebill" data="flush"/>
    <!-- Change the rate -->
    <action application="set" data="nibble_rate=5.00"/>
    <!-- Transfer to Tier2 rep -->
    <action application="transfer" data="1001 XML default"/>
  </condition>
</extension>
```

Another possible use of this is to bill a caller while they're talking to support, but to stop billing after the call when you give them a survey. Its the same concept as the previous instant, except done as follows, where extension 2002 routes to the survey:

```
<extension name="survey-after-call">
  <condition field="destination_number" expression="^2002">
    <!-- Handle support request here at $1.00/minute via
      extension 1001 -->
    <action application="set" data="nibble_rate=1.00"/>
    <action application="set"
      data="hangup_after_bridge=false"/>
    <action application="bridge"
      data="sofia/internal/1001@$${domain}"/>
    <action application="nibblebill" data="flush"/>
      <!-- Set rate to 0, then xfer caller to survey IVR -->
    <action application="set" data="nibble_rate=0.00"/>
    <action application="bridge"
      data="sofia/internal/1002@$${domain}"/>
  </condition>
</extension>
```

WARNING: There is a "catch" to this method. You should flush the current call's billings to the database before the call's rate changes. This is to write out any billed seconds since the last query to DB with the old rate. See flush in the section *Application/CLI/API commands* later in this chapter.

Hang up the call when the balance is depleted

When the balance of an account drops below the setting you have specified in the configuration for nobal_amt, the call gets transferred to an extension of your choice. This allows you to play a message such as, "Your call has been terminated due to insufficient funds." Since we're really just transferring the call to an extension and suspending the billing process, you could get fancy and potentially make the user key in their credit card number to replenish their funds.

In your conf/autoload_configs/nibblebill.conf.xml file add something like the following:

```
<param name="nobal_amt" value="0"/>
<param name="nobal_action" value="hangup XML default"/>
```

In this example, note the `nobal_action` parameter of `"hangup XML default"`. This tells `mod_nibblebill` to transfer the call to the extension named `hangup` in the `default` context of your XML Dialplan when the balance reaches the `nobal_amt` threshold. You can then add this to your Dialplan:

```
<extension name="hangup">
  <condition field="destination_number"
    expression="^(hangup)$">
    <action application="playback" data="no_more_funds.wav"/>
    <action application="hangup"/>
  </condition>
</extension>
```

In this example, when a caller's balance reaches zero their call will be transferred to the `hangup` extension. That extension will play a message stating that they are out of funds (assuming you record a sound file named `no_more_funds.wav`) and the call will disconnect.

Note carefully that the B leg currently also gets transferred to the same extension. In other words, the other party will also hear the announcement about no more funds.

Application/CLI/API commands

The following commands can be used from the Dialplan, CLI, or API. The syntax is basically the same for each, with somewhat obvious difference being that applications are in the following format:

```
<action application="nibblebill" data="action [params]"/>
```

Whereas CLI and API commands are just as follows:

```
nibblebill <channel-uuid> <action> [params]
```

Check

Inserting the `check` command in your application or using it on the CLI with a UUID returns the balance that has been billed so far. This does not include any increments that are not written to the database yet.

```
<action application="nibblebill" data="check"/>
```

Flush

Insert the following code in your Dialplan:

```
<action application="nibblebill" data="flush"/>
```

The preceding code will immediately write any pending billings to the database. Billing will continue, but everything that needed to be billed up to this point in time will be calculated and recorded. This has no effect when billing is paused.

Pause

Insert the following code in your Dialplan:

```
<action application="nibblebill" data="pause"/>
```

This will set a flag to pause billing. If the call is terminated while billing is paused, no billing since the time the call was paused will be calculated, but billing prior to the pause will still get recorded. You can also manually resume billing later on during the call with the resume command (see the following section).

Note that if you call the pause command when a call is already paused, then the pause command will be ignored.

Resume

Insert the following code in your Dialplan:

```
<action application="nibblebill" data="resume"/>
```

This will resume billing during a call that was previously paused. The time in between pause and resume is not billed. Note that you can pause and resume a call multiple times. The time between each pause and resume will not be billed.

Reset

Insert the following code in your Dialplan:

```
<action application="nibblebill" data="reset"/>
```

This will reset the billing timer to the current time. But note that all you are doing here is resetting all the internal counters that track the call's progress to the current time, so any time that would have been billed prior to now (but has not yet been committed to disk) will be "lost" and considered "free."

Any amounts already deducted in the database for a particular account are considered committed—a done deal. This command has no impact on commits already made to disk/database.

Adding and deducting funds

Insert an `adjust` command in your Dialplan:

```
<action application="nibblebill" data="adjust 5.00"/>
```

It adds or deducts a certain amount of funds from an account (in this case, we are adding $5.00). Note that this occurs immediately and currently circumvents any protections that exist for when the database is down. It is your responsibility to deal with having a functioning database when you use this command.

Use negative numbers to deduct from an account.

Enabling session heartbeat

Enabling the session `heartbeat` is done during a call as follows:

```
<action application="nibblebill" data="heartbeat 60"/>
```

This sets the heartbeat for the current call (only) to 60 seconds. You can set this differently per call.

Bill based on B Leg only

If you want to bill only the B Leg, `enable_heartbeat_events` variable must be enabled on the B Leg channel. You can enable these heartbeats by setting the heartbeat events in the `bridge` command. As we discussed earlier in the book, variables in brackets on the `bridge` command are passed to the B Leg. Here is an example:

```
<action application="bridge"
data="{enable_heartbeat_events=5,nibble_rate=1,nibble_
account=0838833133}sofia/external/$1@tel.co."/>
```

Alternative endpoints

While most users of FreeSWITCH will use SIP (and thus `mod_sofia`), there are other ways for FreeSWITCH to communicate with the world. Here are brief descriptions of three methods that you may wish to investigate further.

Skype and GSM endpoints

Not everyone has the budget to buy hardware or services to connect to the Skype and GSM (Global System for Mobile Communications) networks, especially when first learning a new technology. FreeSWITCH has an alternative to offer to those willing to do a little work: a pair of endpoints (that is, channel drivers) that allow inbound and outbound voice calls and messaging (chatting and SMSs) in the cheapest possible way.

Both mod_skypopen and mod_gsmopen support full integration with all the FreeSWITCH features, have CLI commands for diagnostic and control, full events interaction, and can be used in the same way as the Sofia SIP workhorse endpoint module.

Both the mod_skypopen and mod_gsmopen modules have the same general structure: they control an external entity (an "interface") via its own signalling protocol, and redirect the audio stream from/to FreeSWITCH via the interface to/from the destination network.

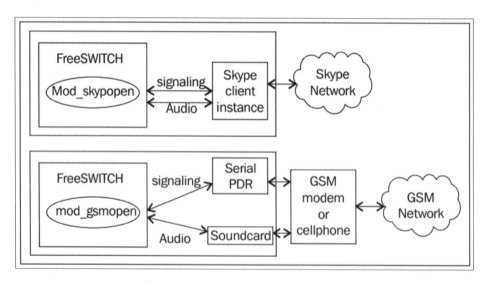

For mod_skypopen, the "interface" is an instance of the regular Skype client software that interacts natively with the Skype network, redirecting the audio flow to FreeSWITCH. The Skype client instance is controlled by mod_skypopen through the Skype API native commands (signalling).

For mod_gsmopen, the "interface" is a GSM modem (or perhaps a second-hand cell phone) that interacts natively with the GSM network. The GSM interface is controlled by mod_gsmopen via serial port commands, often regular AT commands (signalling), while the audio flows through a soundcard.

Both mod_skypopen and mod_gsmopen fully support voice calls and chatting, using the regular FreeSWITCH APIs, Dialplans, and events. So, if your application works with SIP or Jabber, both for voice and/or messaging, it will work unmodified on GSM and Skype networks as well, including inbound/outbound chatting and SMS messages.

Skype with mod_skypopen

The mod_skypopen module effectively connects a running Skype instance on the server with FreeSWITCH using the public Skype APIs. Skype was not reverse engineered and requires no external hardware for this feature to work. mod_skypopen is simply a legal usage of the Skype API. While mod_skypopen uses the Skype API in full accordance with the Skype license agreement, it is not endorsed, certified, or otherwise approved in any way by Skype.

Because of these properties, mod_skypopen requires a running copy of Skype, which is what provides access to the Skype APIs. Running Skype usually requires X Windows, which can eat some resources. The process is fairly simple, mod_skypopen operates by creating a dummy audio driver which Skype sends and receives audio to/from. This dummy driver actually just retransmits the data to/from FreeSWITCH instead of going to a real set of speakers and a microphone on your soundcard.

In order to use mod_skypopen, you will need to compile and load the mod_skypopen module, and start at least one instance of the regular native Skype client on the same machine on which FreeSWITCH is running on.

Linux and Windows are fully supported and you can have dozens of concurrent Skypopen calls on a machine that has enough RAM and CPU power to run dozens of Skype client instances. On Mac, only one instance is possible as of this writing.

On Linux and Windows, you can have multiple instances answering inbound Skype calls/chat for the same Skype username (that is, dozens of concurrent inbound calls for "mycompany_tech_support").

Multiple outbound calls/chat can be originated from the same Skype username on Linux (that is, dozens of concurrent calls placed by "mycompany_sales" Skype username), while on Windows, each outbound call has to be placed by a different Skype username ("mycompany_sales01", "mycompany_sales02", and so on).

Both on Linux and Windows Skypopen, the Skype client instances can run "headless", without the need (and the overhead) of a desktop installation (for example, on a regular "server" installation, on Linux using Xvfb).

Skypopen allows for placing and receiving outbound/inbound calls to/from other Skype usernames (the classic regular "Skype-to-Skype" calls), for placing "SkypeOut" calls to PSTN or cell phone numbers around the world (you must buy credit from Skype for the Skype username used by the "interface" Skype client instance), for receiving "SkypeIn" calls originally destined for a PSTN number somewhere in the world (you must buy the service from Skype), and for chatting (inbound/outbound) with other Skype usernames. The Skype SMS service is not yet supported as of this writing.

Extremely detailed information on setting up and using mod_skypopen can be found online at http://wiki.freeswitch.org/wiki/Mod_skypopen.

GSM with mod_gsmopen

You will need to compile and load the mod_gsmopen module, and the following:

- One or more GSM modems or second-hand cell phones (the "interface")
- One or more serial ports (most often just a USB port)
- One or more soundcards (most often a cheap USB "dongle")
- Cables for the serial and audio connection between the "interface" and serial port/soundcard

Each "interface" is the combination made by all of the listed items.

Most cell phones out there can be directly connected to a serial port (USB) via their own data cable, while for audio you will need to make an audio cable from the hands-free jack to the in/out jacks of the soundcard.

There are very nice cheap embedded compound devices in the market (fully supported by GSMOpen) that comprise the GSM modem, the soundcard, and an internal USB hub (a complete "interface"). With those devices, you'll have only one standard USB cable running from the FreeSWITCH machine to the "black box" complete interface.

Each GSM modem supports one concurrent call. To add more lines (numbers), just connect USB hubs and additional devices. See the Wiki at the next link for more details, including supported cell phones and devices. For usage as a SMS gateway only (no voice calls needed) you only want the serial part of the "interface" (no soundcard and no audio cable). You can connect as many second-hand cell phones as you wish with USB hubs (multi-serial support is very good in Linux), and the CPU load at full SMS throughput is negligible.

Each "interface" has its own SIM card, with its own mobile number. Ideally, you will have a good mobile plan from your GSM carrier. Note that most carriers offer free intra-carrier calls, "SME plans", "family plans", free minutes, or special offers on special hours.

You can mix and match interfaces with different carriers and plans, and have outbound calls and SMSs made from the less costly "interface" via Dialplan and least cost routing.

At the time of writing, GSMOpen runs only on Linux, however Windows support will be available soon.

 More detailed information about mod_gsmopen and supported GSM dongles can be found online at http://wiki.freeswitch.org/wiki/GSMopen.

TDM with FreeTDM

FreeSWITCH is fully compatible with many types of telephony interface cards. Various types of interface cards are manufactured by Sangoma, Digium, OpenVox, Rhino Technologies, RedFone, and others. The FreeSWITCH developers originally created a BSD-licensed abstraction library named OpenZAP. This abstraction layer allowed FreeSWITCH to communicate with both Sangoma and Digium-based cards and their requisite drivers. FreeTDM, sponsored by Sangoma Technologies Corporation, is a new abstraction layer that has completely replaced OpenZAP.

 Detailed information on configuring various analog and digital (T1/E1 and PRI) cards can be found online at http://wiki.freeswitch.org/wiki/FreeTDM.

Configuration tools and related projects

The FreeSWITCH community has grown tremendously over the past few years with many different people using the software for a variety of purposes. These purposes range from running small home PBXs to large telephone companies. Along the way a variety of people have created different bits of code that allow you to save time or allow FreeSWITCH to operate in unique ways. Contributions range from complete open source GUIs and frameworks to small single-purposes libraries. We briefly discuss some of these items next.

Web GUIs

There are a number of **Web Graphical User Interfaces (Web GUIs)** available for FreeSWITCH today. Some are graphical tools that generate XML configuration files while others take the approach of abstracting the switch configuration completely and providing simplified but flexible user interfaces to end-users. We cover some of the more popular ones below.

Note that choosing the right GUI is really a personal decision based on your preferences. Some people prefer one language over another. Some people are concerned strictly about features. Some people focus on scalability. Since most distributions come with easy to install ISOs, you should try out all the interfaces you can find before making a decision on which one you like the most.

FusionPBX

FusionPBX is an open source graphical interface written in PHP. The project started as the FreeSWITCH package on the pfSense firewall. Later it was renamed to FusionPBX and released with multi-platform support including Linux, BSD, Windows, Mac OS X, and others. It supports multiple databases including PostgreSQL, MySQL, and SQLite.

Features include unlimited extensions, IVR menu, voicemail-to-e-mail, hunt groups, fax server, interactive conference controls, viewing active calls and extensions, queues, call forward, click-to-call, DISA, provisioning, multi-tenant, and more.

FusionPBX is highly customizable. For example, a user assigned to the "superadmin" group can log in to the web interface and perform many administrative functions including customizing the menu, content, themes, user groups, multi-tenant configuration, and feature permissions.

Additional information, such as documentation and screenshots, are available on the website (`http://www.fusionpbx.com`). See also the IRC channel `#fusionpbx` on `irc.freenode.net`.

FreePyBX

FreePyBX is a Python-based FreeSWITCH GUI written by Noel Morgan. It allows for configuration and web-based administration of FreeSWITCH. It has a multitude of features including multi-tenant, call center, a built-in ticketing system, and more. You can learn more at `http://www.freepybx.org`.

blue.box

`blue.box` is an open source PHP/MySQL based project by the 2600hz team which provides a graphical user interface for configuring the XML files that FreeSWITCH utilizes. It is designed to power small and medium sized FreeSWITCH installations using solely the built-in features of FreeSWITCH and XML configurations managed by the GUI. It is highly customizable and has modular functionality allowing various features to be implemented over time, but users can install only what they need. It also supports multi-tenancy.

Additional information is available at `http://www.2600hz.org/`. See also the IRC channel #2600hz on `irc.freenode.net`.

Kazoo

Kazoo is an open source platform from the 2600hz team that aims to bring distributed cloud communications to the masses. The project was a natural next step in development for open source telephony platforms. It is designed to help service providers scale to medium and large installation sizes and allows for network and site redundancy across the internet or a large private WAN. The entire stack was designed to expose all functionality as APIs so all functions can be fully automated by external software. The GUI, call-handling APIs, database storage engine, and messaging engines have all been abstracted into independent modules, allowing you to choose which pieces to utilize for your own application.

If you are interested in the hosted or distributed communications market, you should check out Kazoo. You can learn more about the Kazoo platform at `http://2600hz.com/platform.html`.

Supporting libraries

In addition to the **Event Socket Library** (**ESL**) abstraction library supplied with FreeSWITCH, there are third-party libraries that expand upon (or eschew entirely) ESL while adding specific functionality to certain programming languages.

Liverpie (Ruby)

Liverpie (language independent IVR proxy) is a free piece of software, written in Ruby, that talks to FreeSWITCH on one side, and to any web application on the other, regardless of language, platform, and so on. It translates FreeSWITCH `mod_event_socket` dialogue into HTTP markup (embedding various parameters in HTTP headers), so you can write your own HTTP-speaking finite state machine and hook it to FreeSWITCH via Liverpie. Note also that Liverpie expects the response in YAML so you can save yourself the pain of providing XML if you are comfortable with Liverpie doing the translation.

You can learn more about Liverpie at `http://www.liverpie.com`.

FreeSWITCHeR (Ruby)

FreeSWITCHeR is an `EventMachine`-based Ruby library for interacting with FreeSWITCH. The FreeSWITCHeR library interacts through `mod_event_socket`. It can create both inbound and outbound event listeners and can power an entire call from a Ruby library. Significant amounts of documentation and sample code to get you started are available.

You can learn more about FreeSWITCHeR at `https://github.com/bougyman/freeswitcher`.

Librevox (Ruby)

Librevox eventually came to life during a major rewrite of FreeSWITCHeR. Harry Vangberg, who participated in the original FreeSWITCHeR code, decided to rewrite FreeSWITCHeR and this is the result. From the website: "Librevox and Freeswitcher look much alike on the outside, but Librevox tries to take a simpler approach on the inside." As with FreeSWITCHeR, there is a good amount of documentation and sample code to get you started.

You can learn more about Librevox at `https://github.com/vangberg/librevox`.

EventSocket (Python/Twisted)

EventSocket is a Twisted protocol for the FreeSWITCH event socket. This protocol provides support for both inbound and outbound methods of the event socket in a single-file class. It may be used for a wide variety of purposes. It aims to be simple and extensible, and to export all the functionality of FreeSWITCH to Twisted-based applications. Moreover, it is totally event-driven and allows easy implementation of complex applications aiming at controlling FreeSWITCH through the event socket.

This code is part of the core of the Nuswit Telephony API (http://nuswit.com), a full-featured web-based dialer currently operating in Brazil and Colombia.

Source code, examples, and documentation are available at http://github.com/fiorix/eventsocket.

FSSocket (Perl)

The FSSocket Perl library, based on the **Perl Object Environment (POE)** framework, allows for easy integration with the FreeSWITCH event socket system from Perl. It parses FreeSWITCH events into hashes. You can ask for as many event types as you like or all for everything.

Source code, examples, and documentation are available at: http://search.cpan.org/~ptinsley/POE-Filter-FSSocket-0.07/.

Vestec Automatic Speech Recognition

While FreeSWITCH works with the PocketSphinx project, those who want professional-grade speech recognition should consider Vestec. Vestec has an ASR platform that works well with FreeSWITCH and that is suitable for real-world applications. Vestec is a commercial offering, however the company will offer a free, unlimited, full-featured developer license to anyone who uses FreeSWITCH. Contact Vestec via email at info@vestec.com for more information. Supported languages are listed at http://www.vestec.com/acoustic_models.

Summary

FreeSWITCH provides a powerful toolset for creating rich applications. The modules bundled with FreeSWITCH today are an early example of what you can do with the powerful internal APIs that are available. In addition, a thriving community of FreeSWITCH enthusiasts is taking the software development available to the next level. Expect many hosted, cloud, and premise-based solutions to thrive in the coming years for various purposes in the VoIP and communications space, based on the FreeSWITCH core.

A
The FreeSWITCH Online Community

One of the good things about many open source software projects is that people from around the world connect on a regular basis to form a community of interested, and in many cases passionate users. FreeSWITCH is certainly one of these.

In this appendix we will introduce several aspects of the online community. They are as follows:

- FreeSWITCH mailing lists
- Real-time interaction via IRC
- Main FreeSWITCH website and wiki
- The annual ClueCon telephony conference in Chicago

This appendix will help you to become a part of this vibrant, worldwide community.

The FreeSWITCH mailing lists

The FreeSWITCH project maintains several mailing lists at `http://lists.freeswitch.org`. The primary list for most users is appropriately named **freeswitch-users**. Like many projects, the lists are powered by the GNU mailing list manager, MailMan.

To join one of the lists, simply browse to `lists.freeswitch.org` and click on the name of the list as shown in the following screenshot:

New users should join only the **FreeSWITCH-users** list until they are comfortable with the project. The other lists are very technical in nature, except for the **Freeswitch-biz** list, which is used for discussing commercial endeavors with FreeSWITCH.

You will need to input a username and password when subscribing to a list. Keep this information handy so that you can make adjustments to your e-mail subscriptions. One important setting that you can change is whether or not to receive "digest" e-mails. A digest is an amalgamation of several e-mails into a single transmission. The digest method is handy for those who may be casual readers of the e-mail traffic flowing through the mailing lists. However, if you wish to interact with others then you should not use the digest because it will be difficult to participate in a particular discussion thread.

Some points to keep in mind when using the mailing list are as follows:

- Use an e-mail client that handles threads so that you can more easily follow specific discussions.

- Do not "hijack" threads! A hijack occurs when someone replies to an existing thread and changes the subject line of the e-mail. Always start with a new message to the list if you need to discuss a new subject.

- Try not to become overwhelmed when you first join. There are lots of messages coming through each day. You can only absorb so much, so pace yourself and give yourself time to get acclimated.

- Use the site archives to search for discussions on a particular subject. An example is to use Google. Search Google for `site:lists.freeswitch.org` `"early media"` to see all list threads that discuss the topic of "early media".

The mailing lists are a great resource for interacting with people all over the world. However, sometimes you need to have a dialog. In cases like this you will appreciate chatting with others in real time.

Talking in real time via IRC

IRC or Internet Relay Chat is a venerable means for chatting with other users.

The FreeSWITCH team have several chat rooms on `irc.freenode.net`. They are as follows:

- `#freeswitch`
- `#freeswitch-dev`
- `#freeswitch-social`
- `#freetdm`

Various community members around the world also have chat rooms in other languages. Some of them are as follows:

- `#freeswitch-de`
- `#freeswitch-es`
- `#freeswitch-fr`

Using IRC is simple once you know what to do. You will need an IRC client for your computer. There are many to choose from, including the following:

- **Chatzilla**: A Firefox add-on
- **IRSSI**: A text-based IRC client
- **Colloquy**: An IRC client for Mac OS X
- **mIRC**: An IRC client for Windows

You can also join the `#freeswitch` channel using the Java applet on the main FreeSWITCH website.

To use IRC you will need to choose a nickname, known as a "nick" for short. Choose something unique, and if possible register your nick with Freenode. Visit `http://freenode.net/faq.shtml#userregistration` to learn more about setting up your nick and getting it registered.

A few nicks that you will probably see online are as follows:

- `anthm`: Anthony Minessale
- `bkw_`: Brian K West
- `MikeJ`: Michael Jerris
- `mercutioviz`: Michael S Collins
- `pyite`: Darren Schreiber
- `intralanman`: Raymond Chandler
- `SwK`: Ken Rice

These are all active members of the FreeSWITCH community. There are many others who stay online throughout the day (and night, depending on your time zone).

Following are a few things to keep in mind when using IRC:

- It is a public place with people from varying backgrounds and standards of decency.

- Be polite, even when others are not.

- Do not "flood" the channel with long pastes of information. If you have more than two or three lines of information to share, then use the pastebin found at `http://pastebin.freeswitch.org`.

- When joining the room there is no need to ask if you may pose a question. Simply ask your question. For example, "I'm a new user trying to set up a gateway. Why does FreeSWITCH say that username and password are REQUIRED parameters when my provider uses IP authentication?".

- Be patient! Usually someone will answer within a few minutes, but keep in mind that usually there are more people in the channel during North American business hours.

- People from all backgrounds are welcome. The main `#freeswitch` channel is in English, but there are many who speak other languages, including Spanish, French, Italian, German, Portuguese, and Chinese. (See also the previously mentioned IRC channels dedicated to specific languages.)

- Always respect user c888!

Feel free to join the FreeSWITCH IRC channel and see what topics are being discussed.

The FreeSWITCH main website and wiki

There are two primary websites for the FreeSWITCH project:

- `www.freeswitch.org`: The main project page
- `wiki.freeswitch.org`: The public wiki page

The main FreeSWITCH page – www.freeswitch.org

The FreeSWITCH main web page is the starting point for all things related to the project. From the main page you can do many things as follows:

- Read up on FreeSWITCH and VoIP news
- Download or browse the source code
- Report bugs or feature requests
- View documentation
- Join the `#freeswitch` IRC channel with the Freenode Java applet

New content is added to the main page every week, so check back frequently.

The FreeSWITCH wiki page – wiki.freeswitch.org

The FreeSWITCH wiki is the primary source for FreeSWITCH documentation. A wiki is a website that allows users to add, edit, or delete content and link to other content. A classic example of a wiki page is Wikipedia. The FreeSWITCH wiki page uses MediaWiki (`http://www.mediawiki.org`), the same wiki engine used by Wikipedia.

The FreeSWITCH wiki is a community resource. While Michael S. Collins is the primary wiki administrator, all FreeSWITCH users are welcome to add or update content on the site. Like most wiki sites there is a lot of content. Sometimes searching for information can be challenging. We recommend that you use Google site search (`site:wiki.freeswitch.org <search topic>`) if you are having trouble locating a particular subject. After using the wiki for a while you will begin to get a feel for where certain pieces of information are located.

Prospective wiki contributors should keep the following things in mind:

- Do a search before adding content—it may be that the information you want to add is already on the wiki and simply needs to be updated or better indexed
- Make sure that any content you add is properly linked to
- Make sure that any content you add is part of a site category
- Feel free to make mistakes! Others will be happy to help you make corrections

Documentation of open source software is almost always a challenge, so if you are in a position to assist, please contact Michael at `msc@freeswitch.org`. There is always a need for skills such as proofreading, verifying facts, testing configurations and examples, and translating text into other languages.

The annual ClueCon open source developer conference

Each year in Chicago, we have a three-day conference where open source telephony professionals and enthusiasts gather to discuss many topics. The conference is held in the first week of August and is a great way to interact with a wide range of personalities in the telephony world. Visit `http://www.cluecon.com` to see details about the upcoming conference and to get links to presentations and videos from previous conferences.

Although ClueCon is "by developers, for developers", it has been growing each year and many non-developers have been attending. Most presentations are still relatively technical in nature; however, there are many talks that focus on non-technical aspects of telephony, such as demonstrations of new products. The conference is designed for users, developers, and vendors to connect with one another. Users appreciate being able meet developers and vendors in person, and vendors appreciate the focus being on interacting with developers and vendors rather than on spending many hours in a sales booth.

ClueCon invites people from all open source telephony projects to come and give presentations. Over the years there have been presentations on Asterisk, FreeSWITCH, Kamailio, and OpenSIPS, as well as from vendors such as Sangoma and Vestec, who have been supportive of open source telephony projects.

We encourage all FreeSWITCH users to become acquainted with one another by means of these resources.

B

Migrating from Asterisk to FreeSWITCH

Special thanks to Stefan Wintermeyer for his contribution to this appendix.

This appendix is for administrators and programmers who use Asterisk but want to learn how to switch their existing system to FreeSWITCH. Because this is a book about FreeSWITCH and not Asterisk, we will not describe the Asterisk examples in detail. It is assumed that the reader is familiar with the Asterisk concepts of extensions, priorities, and applications.

The information in this appendix is not meant to be an exhaustive reference on how to convert every configuration item on your Asterisk system over to a FreeSWITCH installation. Rather, it is meant to get you started on such a conversion by comparing some of the basic things you do in Asterisk and how those would be done in FreeSWITCH. The topics presented here are:

- Stopping and starting Asterisk and FreeSWITCH
- Setting the debug verbosity levels
- Reviewing the basic configuration file directory structures for each software
- Setting up two SIP users in Asterisk and then in FreeSWITCH
- Simple voicemail configuration in each software

You can find additional information on leveraging your existing Asterisk knowledge by consulting the "Rosetta Stone" found on the FreeSWITCH wiki: `http://wiki.freeswitch.org/wiki/Rosetta_stone`.

> Use migration to FreeSWITCH not only to get a better software platform but also to tidy up your dialplan and setup. We all know the results of coding projects that are "improved" over time by a few new functions without taking the time to optimize the total system. A new conversion is an opportunity to start with a clean slate.

Getting started

For this documentation we run an Asterisk and a FreeSWITCH on a Debian Linux system that has the IP address 10.0.0.10. We could run both services simultaneously, but for the sake of easier configuration examples we manually stop Asterisk or FreeSWITCH before starting the other. We use the latest versions of both software but actually the version number of either is not that important to understand the difference in architecture. The SIP phones use the IP addresses 10.0.0.20 and 10.0.0.21. See *Chapter 4, SIP and the User Directory* for tips on configuring different SIP phones.

> You can have Asterisk and FreeSWITCH installed on the same server. However, you cannot run them simultaneously unless they each bind to a different IP and/or port number. For example, in `/etc/asterisk/sip.conf` you can change the SIP port for Asterisk. As long as they both don't try to use port 5060 on the same interface then you will be able to run them simultaneously if you so choose.

Starting and stopping Asterisk or FreeSWITCH

On a default installation of Asterisk you can start Asterisk with the command `asterisk`. That will start Asterisk and backgrounds the process. To stop Asterisk you can use the command-line interface with `asterisk -r` and type `core stop now`. A typical session might look like this:

```
debian*CLI> core stop now
debian*CLI>
Disconnected from Asterisk server
```

```
Executing last minute cleanups
Asterisk cleanly ending (0).
root@debian:#
```

On a typical FreeSWITCH installation you can start FreeSWITCH in the background with the following command:

```
/usr/local/freeswitch/bin/freeswitch -nc
```

To stop FreeSWITCH execute the same command but with the -stop argument:

```
/usr/local/freeswitch/bin/freeswitch -stop
```

Basic debugging

During the following examples you might want to see what is going on. Preferences vary but in general you will want to see more verbose debugging. We recommend that you try different verbosity levels to find one that suits your needs.

Asterisk

If you have an already running Asterisk you can use asterisk -r to open a command-line interface to it. With the command core set verbose 3 you set the log level to 3. Do not use core set debug 3 because that will overwhelm you with debugging information for Asterisk programmers (those guys who program Asterisk itself). Type core set debug 0 to reset the level to 0. A typical session might look like this:

```
debian*CLI> core set verbose 3
Set remote console verbosity to 3
debian*CLI>
```

FreeSWITCH

If you have an already running FreeSWITCH, you can use the aforementioned fs_cli command to open the command-line interface. With the command /log info you can set the log level to 6. You can do the same with /log info as seen in this example session:

```
freeswitch@internal> /log info
+OK log level info [6]
```

Now that we have debugging available let's take a brief look at the example configurations that come with Asterisk and FreeSWITCH.

Configuration files

Both Asterisk and FreeSWITCH have large directory structures for their example configuration sets. To view the Asterisk configuration tree, execute this command:

```
tree /etc/asterisk
```

For FreeSWITCH, execute this command:

```
tree /usr/local/freeswitch/conf
```

As you can see, both projects have what appear to be intimidating file and directory structures for their respective configurations. Like all complex software, it's important to figure out where to focus your attention since most of the files won't need to be edited.

The biggest difference is that each configuration file for Asterisk has a specific meaning. For example, Asterisk will look up the dialplan in the file extensions. conf. FreeSWITCH doesn't expect configuration in specifically named files. It reads one big XML file that is split into smaller ones. How these are named is totally up to you. The default files are just an example. You are free to name and order your configuration FreeSWITCH configuration files in any way it makes sense for you. In fact, the only configuration file that is absolutely required is freeswitch.xml. (Be sure to review *Chapter 3, Test Driving the Example Configuration* if you have any questions about the FreeSWITCH example configuration files.)

In the following sections we will look more closely at some of these configuration files.

Whenever we use the word "replace" we do mean replace. Do not try to open the existing file to add the given example. Just delete the file and create a new one with the editor of your choice. Once you understand the basic logic of the software you can have a look into these default files. They burst with examples and are a good source to code by cut and paste. But they are not a good start to understand the basics.

Two SIP phones

The smallest PBX example is a two SIP phone setup. We create one with the extension 2000 and the other one with the extension 2001. Each phone should be able to call the other one by dialing the other's extension.

The first SIP account is 2000 with the password 1234. The second SIP account is 2001 with the password 1234. Please set up your SIP phones with these accounts.

Asterisk configuration

Asterisk stores its SIP account information in the configuration file /etc/asterisk/
sip.conf. Please replace the default sip.conf with a new one that contains the
following code:

```
[general]
port=5060
bindaddr=0.0.0.0

[2000]
type=friend
secret=1234
context=default
host=dynamic

[2001]
type=friend
secret=1234
context=default
host=dynamic
```

The dialplan is stored in /etc/asterisk/extensions.conf. Please replace it with
this code:

```
[default]
exten => _200[1-2],1,Dial(SIP/${EXTEN})
```

As we bring up Asterisk (asterisk -c) and set the verbose level to 3 (core set
verbose 3) we can see how the phones register:

```
*CLI>      -- Registered SIP '2000' at 10.0.0.21:2048
    -- Registered SIP '2001' at 10.0.0.20:3072
    -- Unregistered SIP '2001'
    -- Registered SIP '2001' at 10.0.0.20:3072
```

Now we can make a phone call from one phone to the other. During such a call
the command sip show channels will display some basic information about the
current call:

```
*CLI> sip show channels
Peer              User/ANR           Call ID           Format        Hold
Last Message      Expiry      Peer
10.0.0.21         2000               150b1e3879a2bff   (ulaw)        No
Tx: ACK                       2000
10.0.0.20         2001               ea88263cebdd-1a   (ulaw)        No
Tx: ACK                       2001
2 active SIP dialogs
```

Now that we've established a call on Asterisk, let's do the equivalent on a FreeSWITCH. If necessary shut down Asterisk with the `core stop now` command.

FreeSWITCH configuration

FreeSWITCH doesn't have a fixed file and directory structure. The structure you see in `/usr/local/freeswitch/conf` is just an example. You could put everything into one XML file or separate it into numerous XML files all named as you like. The sample configuration already contains a couple of example SIP accounts and demo extensions. However, we want to recreate the preceding Asterisk example.

Create the file `/usr/local/freeswitch/conf/directory/default/2000.xml` with the following content for your first SIP account:

```
<include>
  <user id="2000">
    <params>
      <param name="password" value="1234"/>
    </params>
    <variables>
      <variable name="user_context" value="default"/>
    </variables>
  </user>
</include>
```

Then create a second file, `/usr/local/freeswitch/conf/directory/default/2001.xml`, with the configuration for the second SIP account:

```
<include>
  <user id="2001">
    <params>
      <param name="password" value="1234"/>
    </params>
    <variables>
      <variable name="user_context" value="default"/>
    </variables>
  </user>
</include>
```

Finally, let's create a new Dialplan file for our two new SIP accounts. Create the new file, `/usr/local/freeswitch/conf/dialplan/default/01_New.xml`, with this Dialplan content:

```xml
<?xml version="1.0" encoding="utf-8"?>
<include>
  <context name="default">
    <extension name="Local_Extension">
      <condition field="destination_number"
        expression="^(200[1-2])$">
        <action application="export"
          data="dialed_extension=$1"/>
        <action application="bridge"
          data="user/${dialed_extension}@${domain_name}"/>
      </condition>
    </extension>
  </context>
</include>
```

After you have saved these three files, start FreeSWITCH:

```
/usr/local/freeswitch/bin/freeswitch -nc
```

Wait a few moments for the FreeSWITCH process to start, then connect to it with `fs_cli`:

```
/usr/local/freeswitch/bin/fs_cli
```

Make sure that your two SIP phones are on and have attempted to register. (You will need to restart them or perform a re-registration if they were recently connected to your Asterisk server.) To see the status of your registrations, issue this command:

```
sofia status profile internal reg
```

The output will be like this:

```
freeswitch@internal> sofia status profile internal reg


Registrations:
Call-ID:        a270263caa23-uocan9j61z5y
User:           2000@127.0.0.1
Contact:        "2000" <sip:2000@10.0.0.20:3072;line=0tqusdnm>
Agent:          snom821/8.4.35
Status:         Registered(UDP)(unknown) EXP(2013-01-13 06:46:31)
EXPSECS(3529)
Host:           debian
IP:             10.0.0.20
Port:           3072
Auth-User:      2000
Auth-Realm:     10.0.0.10
MWI-Account:    2000@127.0.0.1


Call-ID:        3c26708e4d57-yzfzr61f7x4l
User:           2001@127.0.0.1
Contact:        "2001" <sip:2001@10.0.0.21:2048;line=9r6kyu0i>
Agent:          snom360/8.4.35
Status:         Registered(UDP)(unknown) EXP(2013-01-13 06:46:45)
EXPSECS(3543)
Host:           debian
IP:             10.0.0.21
Port:           2048
Auth-User:      2001
Auth-Realm:     10.0.0.10
MWI-Account:    2001@127.0.0.1


Total items returned: 2
freeswitch@internal>
```

Now you can make a call from 2000 to 2001 and vice versa.

You can analyze the used channels during the call with `show channels`. Make a call between the two phones, and then issue the command `show channels`. You will see output like this:

```
freeswitch@internal> show channels

uuid,direction,created,created_epoch,name,state,cid_name,cid_num,ip_
addr,dest,application,application_data,dialplan,context,read_
codec,read_rate,read_bit_rate,write_codec,write_rate,write_bit_
rate,secure,hostname,presence_id,presence_data,callstate,callee_
name,callee_num,callee_direction,call_uuid,sent_callee_name,sent_callee_
num

af6dc664-5cb3-11e2-ae64-41a8c0d6e735,inbound,2013-01-12
13:29:18,1357993758,sofia/internal/2000@10.0.0.10,CS_EXECUTE,2000
,2000,10.0.0.20,2001,bridge,user/2001@127.0.0.1,XML,default,PCMU,8
000,64000,PCMU,8000,64000,,debian,2000@10.0.0.10,,ACTIVE,Outbound
Call,2001,SEND,af6dc664-5cb3-11e2-ae64-41a8c0d6e735,Outbound Call,2001

af861bd8-5cb3-11e2-ae6d-41a8c0d6e735,outbound,2013-01-12
13:29:18,1357993758,sofia/internal/sip:2001@10.0.0.21:2048,CS_EXCHANGE_ME
DIA,2000,2000,10.0.0.20,2001,,,XML,default,PCMU,8000,64000,PCMU,8000,640
00,,debian,2001@127.0.0.1,,ACTIVE,Outbound Call,2001,SEND,af6dc664-5cb3-
11e2-ae64-41a8c0d6e735,2000,2000

2 total.

freeswitch@internal>
```

You have set up SIP users on both Asterisk and FreeSWITCH.

 If you edit a FreeSWITCH XML configuration file while FreeSWITCH is running, be sure to execute the command `reloadxml`. Alternatively, you can press the *F6* key.

Analysis

FreeSWITCH uses XML and Asterisk uses traditional "ini" files. XML has the big advantage that it can easily be checked for syntax errors. Asterisk is somewhat loose in this area and in some cases does not give enough feedback to the system administrator. On several occasions we had an Asterisk Dialplan that looked fine and which worked most times but in some edge cases it didn't. Many times this was because of syntax errors in the Dialplan that weren't found by Asterisk itself. So having a strict XML configuration is a good thing, but it does take some time to get used to it. A good XML editor might be helpful in this transition phase.

> A text editor with syntax highlighting is invaluable when reviewing or editing FreeSWITCH configuration files.

The syntax of the SIP account definitions is quite different between these two pieces of software. The Dialplan is also very different. We defined the SIP accounts with a default context (literally "default") for Asterisk and FreeSWITCH. Each software searches for a `default` context in its configurations. Asterisk uses the configuration file `extensions.conf` for that and a customized syntax. Within the `[default]` context it searches for a matching extension. The regular expression `_200[1-2]` matches the dialed number and starts the Dial application, which initiates a call with the SIP protocol to `${EXTEN}`, which is a variable that was set automatically by Asterisk and contains the dialed number.

FreeSWITCH searches for the `default` context too (because the SIP accounts were defined within this context). It runs through all defined extensions within this context until it finds one that has a matching `condition` field. Conditions can be many things such as a time or as in this example a `destination_number` that is matched with the regular expression `^(200[1-2])$`. A `condition` itself contains code that is fired up when the condition is true. In our example it is this code:

```
<action application="export" data="dialed_extension=$1"/>
<action application="bridge"
  data="user/${dialed_extension}@${domain_name}"/>
```

We could write it in one line like this:

```
<action application="bridge" data="user/$1@${domain_name}"/>
```

But setting a `dialed_extension` variable is often very handy. It might remind the Asterisk veteran of `${EXTEN}`. Also, we can see that FreeSWITCH's `bridge` is the equivalent of Asterisk's `Dial` application. In FreeSWITCH we see a reference to `@${domain_name}` in the `bridge` argument. The channel variable `${domain_name}` is set elsewhere in the example configuration.

More information is presented in *Chapter 5, Understanding the XML Dialplan*, and in *Chapter 8, Advanced Dialplan Concepts*.

Voicemail

We now shift our attention to a feature that is available in both systems: voicemail.

Asterisk

The Asterisk dialplan application, `Dial`, offers the ability to add the number of seconds the phone can ring. It will wait for that amount of seconds (for example, 10) for the called party to answer and then move to the next priority. In this example we have the `VoiceMail` application. Please replace the `/etc/asterisk/extensions.conf` with this content:

```
[default]
exten => _200[1-2],1,Dial(SIP/${EXTEN}, 10)
exten => _200[1-2],n,VoiceMail(${EXTEN},u)
```

Asterisk needs some additional configuration for the voicemail boxes. Please replace the file `/etc/asterisk/voicemail.conf` with:

```
[general]
format = wav
attach = yes
[default]
2000 => 1234,Mr. X
2001 => 1234,Mr. Y
```

Now you can make a call and after approximately 10 seconds the `Dial` application stops calling. Asterisk increases the priority by 1 and starts the `VoiceMail` application for the voicemail box `${EXTEN}`, and the calling party can leave a message.

FreeSWITCH

Voicemail configuration in FreeSWITCH is very different. Please replace the file /usr/local/freeswitch/conf/dialplan/default/01_New.xml with this content:

```xml
<?xml version="1.0" encoding="utf-8"?>
<include>
  <context name="default">
    <extension name="Local_Extension">
      <condition field="destination_number"
       expression="^(200[1-2])$">
        <action application="export"
          data="dialed_extension=$1"/>
        <action application="set" data="call_timeout=10"/>
        <action application="set"
          data="hangup_after_bridge=true"/>
        <action application="set"
          data="continue_on_fail=true"/>
        <action application="bridge"
          data="user/${dialed_extension}@${domain_name}"/>
        <action application="answer"/>
        <action application="sleep" data="1000"/>
        <action application="bridge"
data="loopback/app=voicemail:default ${domain_name} ${dialed_
extension}"/>
      </condition>
    </extension>
  </context>
</include>
```

The FreeSWITCH dialplan is a bit more complex but also gives more control. With call_timeout=10 you can set the maximum time in seconds the bridge application tries to call the other party. The setting hangup_after_bridge=true tells FreeSWITCH to hang up after a bridged call has occurred. (This is also important for when the caller goes to voicemail and hangs up.) The setting continue_on_fail=true handles the scenario when the called party is busy. After the bridge application we have the answer, which means that FreeSWITCH kind of "picks up the phone" itself. After a one second sleep (which just feels a bit more human than without it) it bridges the call to a loopback destination for the voicemail application. You can also use the voicemail application without the loopback channel; however, by using this specific syntax we allow for attended transfers into a user's voicemail box.

Accessing voicemail

Now that we've configured the system to record voicemail messages for our users, let's discuss how to access those messages. In each case, be sure to call and leave a voicemail message for a user and then follow the instructions for retrieving.

We'll create dialplans that allow us to check voicemail boxes by dialing 4000.

Asterisk

Please replace the /etc/asterisk/extensions.conf file with this content:

```
[default]
exten => _200[1-2],1,Dial(SIP/${EXTEN}, 10)
exten => _200[1-2],n,VoiceMail(${EXTEN},u)
exten => 4000,1,VoiceMailMain(${CALLERID(num)})
```

The Asterisk application VoiceMailMain offers a gateway to a caller's personal voicemail box. The function ${CALLERID(num)} returns the number of the caller. Don't mix it up with ${EXTEN}, which is the number you are dialing and would be 4000 in this example.

FreeSWITCH

First we need to define a password for accessing the voicemail box by the owner. For simplicity we use 1234 as a password again.

Open /usr/local/freeswitch/conf/directory/default/2000.xml and locate this line:

```
<param name="password" value="1234"/>
```

Add a new param line:

```
<param name="password" value="1234"/>
```

Save the file. Repeat for /usr/local/freeswitch/conf/directory/default/2000.xml.

At this point you can dial 4000 to retrieve a message because the example FreeSWITCH dialplan already defines 4000 as the message retrieval extension. You can alternatively dial *98 to access voicemail.

Notice that the system asks you to key in both your "ID number" (that is, 2000 or 2001) as well as your password. Some people prefer to have the system assume that if you dial voicemail from a particular extension then it should attempt to log in to that extension's voicemail box. This is easily achieved. Open the file /usr/local/freeswitch/conf/dialplan/default.xml and locate this extension:

```
<extension name="vmain">
  <condition field="destination_number" expression="^vma
  in$|^4000$|^\*98$">
    <action application="answer"/>
    <action application="sleep" data="1000"/>
    <action application="voicemail" data="check default ${domain_
    name}"/>
  </condition>
</extension>
```

Notice the highlighted line with the voicemail application. Let's modify the arguments to the voicemail application so that it assumes the caller ID number is the voicemail box to which the caller wants access. Change the argument to this:

```
data="check default ${domain_name} ${caller_id_number}"
```

Notice that we added ${caller_id_number} to the arguments. This tells the voicemail application to assume that the caller ID number (that is, 2000 or 2001) is the voicemail box to which the caller wants access.

Save the file and then issue the reloadxml command (or press *F6*) from fs_cli. Dial 4000 and now the system only asks for the password.

 FreeSWITCH global voicemail settings are found in /usr/local/freeswitch/conf/autoload_configs/voicemail.conf.xml.

Summary

Moving from Asterisk to FreeSWITCH can be a daunting task; however, it can be done. Think back to those days when you were first learning Asterisk, and compare what you know now versus then. It took some time but you learned many things. Learning FreeSWITCH requires a similar amount of time and effort. Fortunately, by leveraging the knowledge and experience you have from your months and years of using Asterisk you will be able to get up to speed very quickly.

C

The History of FreeSWITCH

In order to properly explain the origin of FreeSWITCH, we have to go back to the time before we even had the idea to write it. The VoIP revolution really began to take shape at the turn of the century with the creation of both the Asterisk PBX and OpenH323. Both of these pioneering software packages enabled many developers to have access to VoIP resources without paying for a costly commercial solution. This led to many new innovations in both projects, and the rapid spread of the evidence that true usability of IP telephony did indeed exist.

I first got involved in the industry in 2002, when my company at the time was selling outsourced technical support and we needed a way to manage the calls and send the traffic to an off-site location. We were using a commercial solution but it was costly to deploy and had very over-priced per-seat charges on top of that. I had done a lot of work with open source applications such as Apache and MySQL in my past duties as a web hosting platform architect, so I decided to do some research on the existence of any open source telephony applications. Enter Asterisk.

When I first downloaded Asterisk, I was amazed. I got some analog telephone cards to use with it and here I was at my house, with a dial tone on a phone that was plugged into the back of my Linux PC. Wow! That's crazy! It wasn't long before I started immersing myself in the code, trying to figure out how it worked. I learned quickly that it was possible to extend this software to do other things based on loadable dynamic modules just like Apache. I started digging around and worked up a few test modules. This was better than ever. Now I was not only making my phone talk with PC, I was making it execute my own code when I dialed a certain number.

I played around with a few ideas and then the thought dawned on me. Hey! I really like Perl, and this telephone stuff is pretty cool too. What if I try to combine them? I looked into the documentation on embedding Perl into a C application and before I knew it I had `app_perl.so`, a loadable module for Asterisk that would allow me to execute Perl code of my choice when a call was routed to my module. It wasn't perfect, and I started to learn quickly about the challenge of embedding Perl in a multi-threaded application, but it was at least an awesome proof of concept and quite the accomplishment for a few days of tinkering.

As time progressed, I was drawn deeper into the Asterisk online community. After playing with the code for a few weeks, I began working on some call-center solutions using Asterisk as the telephony engine and some home-grown web applications as a frontend. Along the way, I encountered some bugs in Asterisk, so I submitted them to the issue tracker for inclusion to the development branch. The more this process repeated, the deeper my involvement in the project grew, and I began creating improvements to the software as well as just sporadic fixes to bugs. By 2004, I was actually fixing bugs that other people reported as well as my own. It was the least I felt I could do for having a free solution to all of my problems. If my problems would actually be solved still remained to be seen.

Taking things to the next level

When I was testing my application, I would make many calls to the system and watch for the web page to update, control the queues, and watch the stats build up. However, one thing I was not paying attention to was the number of simultaneous calls and the call volume itself. I was really only making a call or two at a time, and I was not really fully testing my application. When I put it into production for the first time, it was also the first time I ever saw what happened when multi-threaded software had an irresolvable conflict in the locking contention, better known as a dead lock. I was quite familiar with the segmentation fault, as I had encountered many of those along the way when I was working on my own modules, but I was surprised to also see a rise in the number of inexplicable random ones happening only some of the time.

A segmentation fault is a violation that an application commits where it makes inappropriate access to memory by destroying the same memory more than once or accessing memory addresses that are out of bounds or do not exist. You will run into them a lot in C programming, since you have lower-level access to the operating system and there is nothing to protect you from making errors besides your own discipline. I don't give up easily, which you could consider a curse or a blessing, so when I started to encounter some problems, I was prepared to get to the bottom of it. I spent countless hours studying the output from the GNU debugger and trying to simulate the traffic that caused my problems. After a little trial-and-error, we found success! I managed to duplicate the crash in my test lab using a load generator. I even managed to figure out where the problem was and fixed it! That was a great feeling that lasted right up until later that afternoon, when I learned there was another new problem with similar symptoms somewhere else in the code.

I managed to slowly back out the features in my application that increased the likelihood of a deadlock or segmentation fault, but I could not completely eliminate all the problems. I eventually discovered that the app_queue module was causing most of my grief, which was not the best news considering that was the module I was using the most in my call-center application. Some of the changes I wanted to make were too intrusive for inclusion in the main code distribution, so I ended up using my own copy of the code so I could continue to update the rest of Asterisk. This kept things stable, but only stable enough to seek another solution.

By this time I had written a fairly large amount of features into Asterisk and was really starting to have some big ideas for new functionality. I created a new concept called "function variables" allowing modules to expose an interface that could be expanded from the Dialplan (if you read the rest of this book, that idea may sound familiar). I was still wrestling with the queue problems, so I got together with another Asterisk community member and started brainstorming on a new ACD queue module for Asterisk called mod_icd.

ICD stood for Intelligent Call Distribution, a play on the acronym ACD meaning Automatic Call Distribution. We had identified all the shortcomings of the app_queue module with regards to functionality, and we had a common interest in making a more stable module that would not cause countless crashes and deadlocks. We had a working prototype and a lot of work to do. We used state machines and higher-level memory management abstractions with data pools and several other inspiring concepts that we felt were lacking in the standard Asterisk. The problem was, I think we over-engineered the module too much, almost as if we were trying to edge out the entire Asterisk core, which was of course not completely possible being only a loadable module within that core.

We never quite finished `mod_icd`. It was late 2004 and my opportunities with call-center solutions lay smashed on the rocks, washed away by the unforgiving seas of segmentation faults and deadlocks. We started focusing more on other telephony services that did not involve queuing. I developed a new offering of toll-free termination and fax-to-e-mail services. Using several new features I added to the mainline Asterisk and some of my less-popular modules that were not approved, I built a cluster of seven Asterisk boxes and connected them to a large telecom circuit. This deployment of Asterisk was not problem-free but, on the bright side, if some of the machines crashed, there were more to take its place while we restarted them.

New ideas and a new project

At this point I had accumulated several new ideas: some tested, some not, some that were going to require some major changes to Asterisk. My team—Brian West, Michael Jerris, and I—were donating a lot of time to the Asterisk project. We helped maintain the issue tracker. We fixed bugs and helped out every week by hosting a developer's conference call. We even hosted a mirror of the code on our site. We were very involved yet some of our new ideas were causing some political turmoil in the Asterisk community, as there was an unnecessary competition among the various developers. Every contributor to Asterisk must sign a form stating that all the code you write that may be included in the Asterisk code base will automatically have a royalty-free license for Digium, the owner of Asterisk, to do what it pleases with your code. This was so they could sell the unrestricted licensing to would-be buyers for a high price. Not exactly the spirit of open source but that's another story. I think this alienation caused some strife between the volunteer developers like myself and the developers who were hired outright by Digium to work on Asterisk.

Even with the tension, we were dedicated to the project and really wanted to see it succeed. We were having those regular weekly conference calls, and they were really starting to help get the developers motivated. We decided that we should have a live in-person meeting so we could all share our knowledge of telephony and hang out for a few days. We had no idea what we were doing, but we decided to do it anyway and call it ClueCon. Having a clue meant you knew what you were doing, so ClueCon was a conference to help everyone to "get a clue". I do acknowledge, I just said we did not know what we were doing either, so there was a bit of irony that people with no clue would start a clue con. However, that turned out to be more of a blessing than a problem, and the clue we were referring to was in regards to telephony, not to running conferences.

Therefore, with several months until the first ClueCon, in the spring of 2005, we had one of our usual weekly conference calls and began talking particularly in detail about several shortcomings of Asterisk. This is not uncommon, because our primary goal was to identify the problems and convert them into solutions. There was, at the time, a fairly large unruly crowd who was tired of the endless problems they were experiencing with Asterisk. Many of them joined this weekly call, hoping to persuade us to look at one of their issues. The more I thought about it, the bigger the task seemed to unravel some of the big architectural problems that were plaguing us. Many concepts were monolithic in nature and would not scale. Many features had several users dependent on them, and changing them with a goal of improvement could lead to regressions in functionality. It just seemed like some of the problems could only be solved with a sledgehammer, yanking out some older code and doing some serious rewrites to some of the deeper recesses of the core code. This did not seem very viable since it would render Asterisk unusable for months if not a year or more. That's when I had the idea: let's make a 2.0!

It was not the worst idea; I knew it would be challenging but, hey, I thought we could start a new code base alongside the old one, so we could tear out the parts of the code that caused the most problems and replace them while still maintaining the original code for the users who depended on something that worked. I was pretty excited about the idea and equally shocked when the project leader reacted to my suggestion of the idea, and he appeared equally shocked that I would even suggest such a thing, so, in short, we did not make an Asterisk 2.0. Here I was, with a ton of ideas and a clear mind on exactly what I did and did not like about Asterisk with nowhere to write them down.

I gazed at that empty text-editor buffer open in an empty directory for an hour. I knew what I wanted to do, but it was hard to bring it to words. I never could find the words until I added in several oddly arranged punctuation around them. Those were not your everyday words; they were symbol names and variable declarations. I was writing C code. In a few days, I drafted up a basic application in C, tying together some of my favorite tools from my past experience in programming. I had the Apache Portable Runtime or APR library, the Perl language, and a few other packages. I built a core and a loadable module structure, a few helper functions to use memory pools, and I had a simple command-line prompt that would allow you to type help if you wanted to see a sarcastic comment about there being no help for you, and exit to shut the application down. I made a sample module that would let you telnet to a specific TCP port and have it echo back everything you typed and a very basic state machine. I called it Choir. I thought of my idea as a series of parts working together to make one unified voice like a choir. After that initial coding session, I put it down for a while. ClueCon was coming and I did not want to rush things as I still thought that there was much to consider.

The first ClueCon

August of 2005 was the first annual ClueCon conference. We had several open source VoIP project leaders including Craig Southeren, one of the authors of OpenH323, and Mark Spencer, creator of Asterisk and the same person who did not like my Asterisk 2.0 idea. However, it was awesome to get these guys in the same room. We filled the day with presentations, with discussions going back and forth, and we really got everyone thinking. It was a huge success, and I left the conference energized and ready to work on my Choir code again. However, I didn't. Instead I talked it through on our conference call for months while trying to keep my struggling Asterisk based platform afloat. It was Fall now and the turmoil in the Asterisk community finally erupted into a rebellion. A sizable percentage of the community forked Asterisk into a new application called OpenPBX.

I totally understood why they did it, and I supported them the best I could. I donated all the code I had written for Asterisk, for them to do what they pleased. I helped when I had a chance, but could never fully get involved with the effort because I still had the same problem—I saw a need to really tear everything down to the basic level and the founders of the new project were mostly interested in fixing specific pressing issues that were not being addressed in a timely manner by the Asterisk core team. We still had the conference calls, but mostly nobody would show up from the Asterisk project because they were not happy with the idea of cavorting with the rebels. I apologized one day because I could not try to solve any problem in OpenPBX that would not boil down to totally gutting everything and writing a new core. That's when someone asked me, "How long do you think it would take to get your new code to make a call?" Like Mr. Owl from the Tootsie Pop commercials, I had no idea so I decided to find out. A-one, a-two, a-three weeks (give or take).

The first module that actually produced sound was called `mod_woomera`; it was an endpoint module using the Woomera protocol written by Craig Southeren, the same person I had just met at ClueCon. I made a similar module for Asterisk and it was a simple protocol and required no codecs or anything fancy. The idea was that it would take the complexity out of H323 and allow applications to use it via this simple protocol that could be easily integrated into VoIP applications, so it seemed like a great place to start. As I started to work, I realized that I needed more elements in my basic core and slowly started to bring the code together to a point where I could make a call to the Woomera-powered H323 listener process and get activity in my Pandora code. Yes, I renamed it to "Pandora" because nobody liked the name Choir. I joyously listened to the Alan Parsons Project hit *Sirius* stream into my speakers from my application for the first time. This was even more exciting than the first time I made Asterisk work because I actually wrote this code myself from scratch and it was doing something.

Now I was getting somewhere; I figured out how to make two channels bridge to each other, then how to support some other protocols and do a few basic things beyond a sarcastic help message and an exit routine. The idea came and went to dub this code OpenPBX 2, and finally when I had enough with naming arguments, I decided once and for all what I wanted to call the application: FreeSWITCH. I finally had a name I knew I was going to stick with and some working code, and a lot of ambition. I put my head down and just began coding. There was work to be done everywhere. It was too overwhelming to think about it really. I just kept plowing through the code and by the time I reached January of 2006, I had enough to share with the public. We opened up our code repository to developers asking them to register for a developer account to gain access to the code as a way to make sure only those who were serious would bother to complete the registration process. We had some people checking it out and providing feedback, and we really started to feel like we had a real project.

We had a module to bridge calls, one to play sounds, a few codecs, some examples of Dialplan modules, and a few other things. Oh, and did I mention it worked on Windows too?

Our original site is still preserved, though none of the links are active:
`http://www.freeswitch.org/old_index.html`

Introducing FreeSWITCH

Somewhere along the way from all that planning, we actually produced code that could run on Windows as well as Linux and Mac OSX. My original teammates, Michael and Brian, were there from the beginning, and Mike, having a lot of experience in Windows, made sure we could compile and run the code in MSVC. It was a struggle at first, but after having to correct tons of compiler errors on many occasions, I began to learn how to code in a way that would be friendly on most platforms on the first try. Time started to fly and before I knew it, it was ClueCon time again. That year I gave my first presentation on FreeSWITCH, demonstrating the core design and fundamentals that are outlined in the opening chapter of this book. We saw very exciting modules, such as an endpoint module that can communicate with Google Talk. My presentation featured a live demonstration of several thousand calls being set up and torn down by our `mod_exosip` SIP module. It was a nice demo, but we still weren't happy.

Exosip was a SIP library that was really nothing more than a helper library to Osip, an open source SIP library that provided most of the functionality. The Exosip made it a bit easier to get an endpoint moving, and we decided to use it, but we encountered several mishaps with it, and I started to feel that same sinking feeling I had when I was trying to get Asterisk working, so we started looking for a replacement. It didn't help that there was potential licensing conflicts because Exosip claimed to be GPL despite the fact that its parent library was LGPL (which, in my opinion, is a much more reasonable license). As we chose MPL for our project, it was forbidden by the GPL to allow GPL'd code to be included in an MPL app. License debates are fun and a good way to get people excited, but that was not the time for one.

We searched the land of open source far and wide, for both a new SIP stack and an RTP stack to use in FreeSWITCH since there was quite the high demand for SIP functionality. We auditioned several libraries for both roles and we ended up trying at least five different stacks for both protocols. I never found an RTP stack that satisfied me, so I wrote my own. I was not foolish enough to try the same thing with SIP. Having a front row seat to the mess caused by Asterisk trying to write a SIP stack from scratch and the failure with Exosip in my rear-view window, I continued to search for a SIP stack until I found Sofia-SIP, a SIP stack written by Nokia. We built a functional `mod_sofia` to test things out, and we were highly impressed. We continued to polish the module until we reached the point where we could drop `mod_exosip` and use `mod_sofia` as our primary SIP endpoint module. This was only the beginning really, as I still find myself adding code to `mod_sofia` on a regular basis to this day. SIP is a complicated and frightening protocol that brings many unpleasant thoughts to mind even saying its name, but now is not the time for that conversation.

We gave another presentation on FreeSWITCH at ClueCon 2007, this time with a new SIP module and a lot more code. Now we also had OpenZAP, a TDM library to connect FreeSWITCH to telephone hardware. OpenZAP was later replaced to FreeTDM and is now maintained by Sangoma Corporation. I experienced the joy of making the very same cards I got working on Asterisk so long ago to work with FreeSWITCH as well. We had announced that soon we would be releasing the 1.0 edition of FreeSWITCH. Anyone who read our original home page that I posted earlier might notice we announced that an official release was "coming soon" way back then. This was announced in January of 2006, and we were trying desperately to make things the way we wanted them ever since. We really wanted to focus on making a stable core before all else, and we were making real progress, but we still were not ready to release 1.0.

By spring of 2008 we had stable SIP, we had the event socket to remotely control FreeSWITCH, we had a module to interface with our API commands over HTTP, we had XML curl and a nice big list of features. We finally decided it was the right time for a release, so we bit the bullet and released FreeSWITCH 1.0 Phoenix. I chose Phoenix as the release name because I felt that all of our hard work was born from the ashes of our previous failures, and though it had been used by a lot of others, including NASA who was launching the Phoenix to Mars at the same exact time, I think it was the appropriate title.

ClueCon 2008 featured the announcement that 1.0 had been finally released earlier that year in late May. Several presentations also related to FreeSWITCH as well as the other open source projects such as Asterisk, who had produced a 1.6 release that year. We spent the next entire year focusing on wideband audio support and other advanced features such as on-the-fly re-sampling of unlike audio streams. We added many new SIP features such as presence indications and other fancy things beyond simple call setup and a follow-up 1.0.1 release.

In 2009, we released 1.0.2 to 1.0.4 versions and presented FreeSWITCH again at the fifth annual ClueCon. Some of our early innovations matched up with reality by that time, as we were able to demonstrate Polycom phones using high-definition audio on their new Siren codec as well as support for the Skype protocol as an endpoint module. The FreeSWITCH presentation was an overview of the things you probably didn't realize you could do unless you learn to think fourth-dimensionally, as Dr. Emmett Brown (from *Back To The Future*) and I both like to put it. We have some similarities to Asterisk in behavior, but we also have an entirely new paradigm that opens the door to some incredible things you can do with just a PC and a telephone.

In 2010 we had ClueCon MMX at the Trump Tower! It was one of the most memorable ClueCons ever, and the first edition of this book was released. We even gave a few away as prizes! We gave a detailed presentation on FreeSWITCH and performance. We released 1.0.5 and 1.0.6. The theme that year seemed to be Erlang. Everyone was getting on the bandwagon for doing event-driven architecture, so we were definitely in the right place at the right time!

2011 was a big transition year for the project. Inspired by our own presentation on performance the year before we made some drastic changes to the Sofia SIP module to try to de-serialize it at the point where the messages met the application so we could push the message processing for each call into its own thread. This change yielded a lot more parallelization of operations and reduced the likelihood of the entire SIP stack getting stuck behind an issue happening on a single channel. For ClueCon that year, we went Euro at the fabulous Sofitel. We demonstrated a bunch of new features added to help developers, such as the concept of array variables and scoped variables so you can set a channel variable that is only set during the execution of a particular app.

In early 2012 we announced a new initiative to create a stable branch to the FreeSWITCH code repository. This is a daunting task because you must separate your mature code from your newer code and do additional checks on changes to respective branches to make sure everything is running smoothly. We've been working hard on this, and the refresh of this book will mark the beginning of the FreeSWITCH 1.2 stable branch. We had a great ClueCon at the Hyatt and showcased several new features such as faxmodem emulation designed to work with Hylafax and also `mod_htttapi` that is covered in an earlier chapter in this book.

At the time of the writing of this book we have most of 2013 ahead of us. Having survived the Mayan apocalypse, we look on to bridging the gap between telephony and HTML5 with support for WebRTC and the first alpha releases of FreeSWITCH 1.4. ClueCon will be held at the Hyatt again, and they have remodeled the entire building for our enjoyment. We hope to see you all there, and I hope you have managed to learn a little bit more about FreeSWITCH and why I decided to start typing those first few characters in that empty text-editor that has blossomed into nearly half a million lines of code just inside the core components of FreeSWITCH.

Index

P

PARAMETERS parameter 192
params 264
parsing
about 98
phrase 190
passwords
about 320
registration 320
voicemail passwords 321
PAT
versus NAT 288
pause
digit-timeout 268
error-file 267
input-timeout 268
loops 268
milliseconds 267
name 267
terminators 268
pause command 344
PCRE 32, 95, 163
Perl Compatible Regular Expressions. *See*
PCRE
Perl Object Environment (POE) 353
perpetual-sound 329
Phrase Macro 17, 118
phrases
Phrase Macros, calling 126
using, with IVRs 126
voicemail system 127-131
pin parameter 327
pin-sound 329
PKI (Public Key Infrastructure) 318
Plain Old Telephone Service.
See POTS lines
play_and_get_digits application 108
playback
about 265
asr-engine 265
asr-grammar 265
digit-timeout 265
error-file 265
file 265
input-timeout 265
loops 265

name 265
terminators 265
playback application 106
polycom phones 59, 60, 298
Port Address Translation. *See* PAT
POTS lines 8
pre_answer application 110
pre-processor 21
presence 185
proxied 170
ptime 325
public context 172

R

rate parameter 325
record
beep-file 267
digit-timeout 267
error-file 267
file 267
limit 267
name 267
terminators 267
recordCall
limit 272
name 272
recvEvent() 256
recvEventTimed($milliseconds) 256
regex command 97
regex operator
all value 186
any value 186
values 186
xor value 186
regular expression pattern-matching 12
regular expressions 46, 96, 97
reloadxml command 74, 79
reset command 344
RESPOND_ON parameter 192
resume command 344
RFC-1918 IP addresses
URL 293
RFC (request for comment) 11
ROUTING 48
RTP stream. *See* audio content encryption

S

sample sub-menu 62
say
  application 106
  digit-timeout 269
  error-file 269
  gender 269
  input-timeout 269
  language 269
  loops 269
  method 269
  name 269
  terminators 269
  text 269
  type 269
say module 9
scripting tips 164, 165
Secure Sockets Layer. *See* SSL
send($command) 255
send_display command 194
sendevent 248
sendEvent($send_me) 256
sendevent command 240
sendmsg <uuid> 249
sendRecv($command) 255
serialize([$format]) 253
service 42
session_id parameter 280
Session Initiation Protocol. *See* SIP
session:ready() method 145
set 185
  versus export 205
set application 110
setAsyncExecute($value) 257
setEventLock($value) 257
set_global 185
setInputCallback method 151
set-params permission 277
setPriority([$number]) 253
set_profile_var 185
set_user 185
set-vars permission 277
show calls command 53
show channels command 53
SIP
  about 11, 67

contact parameters 203, 204
digest authentication 54
modifying 310
settings 53
SIP Endpoint module 48
SIP phone
  analysis 372
  Asterisk configuration 367
  configuring 53
  FreeSWITCH configuration 368-371
SIP profiles 84
SIP registrar 54
SIP signalling
  about 313
  encryption options, selecting 313
  SSL, encryption with 314
  SSLV2/3, setting up 314
  TLS, encryption with 315
SIP telephone 23
Skype
  with mod_gsmopen module 347, 348
Skype endpoint 346, 347
slash command 51
sleep application 109, 185
sms
  DATA 271
  to 271
Snom phones 60, 61
socketDescriptor() 254
sofia_contact API command 279
Sofia-SIP
  URL 11
Sofia SIP module 69
soft phone
  about 53
  X-Lite soft phone 54-56
software-based SIP softphone 23
sound-prefix parameter 328
source
  downloading 29
speak
  about 268
  digit-timeout 268
  engine 268
  error-file 268
  input-timeout 268
  loops 268

name 268
terminators 268
text 268
voice 268
SRTP
about 316
enabling 318
encryption with 317
SSL
encryption with 314
SSLV2/3 encryption
about 314
setting up 314, 315
stable source project 29
status command 20, 53
string conditioning 202
string.gsub function 162
subclass 19
suppress-events parameter 328
SWIG 252

T

TDM
with FreeTDM 349
telephony revolution 7, 8
temp-action 265
terminators 265
Tetris extension 61
text-only editors
about 29
Emacs 28
Notepad++ 28
Vi/Vim 28
Text-to-Speech (TTS) 13
TGML 152
three-way call 46
timeout attribute 13, 120
timers module 9
TLS
encryption with 315
toll_allow variable 71
Tone Generation Markup Language.
See **TGML**
tone stream 49
transfer application 110
Transport Layer Security. *See* **TLS**

TTS 31
tts-engine attribute 121
tts-engine parameter 327
tts-voice attribute 121
tts-voice parameter 327

U

Unix-like 25
unloop 99
unmuted-sound 328
unset 185
unstable branch 29
UPnP
URL 299
URI (Uniform Resource Identifier) 295
url parameter 276
user
adding 72-75
user agents 84
user_context variable 71
user features 70, 71
user groups 77, 78

V

var 202
variables
about **264**
caller profile fields 197
channel variables 197
global variables 199, 200
passing, via call headers 206
testing, with regular expressions 197
utilizing 197
verbose_events 185
version command 53
Vestec Automatic Speech Recognition
about 353
URL 353
Visual C++ Express Edition. *See* **MSVCEE**
VLANs 308
vmname
digit-timeout 266
error-file 266
id 266
input-timeout 266
loops 266

Thank you for buying
FreeSWITCH 1.2

About Packt Publishing

Packt, pronounced 'packed', published its first book "*Mastering phpMyAdmin for Effective MySQL Management*" in April 2004 and subsequently continued to specialize in publishing highly focused books on specific technologies and solutions.

Our books and publications share the experiences of your fellow IT professionals in adapting and customizing today's systems, applications, and frameworks. Our solution based books give you the knowledge and power to customize the software and technologies you're using to get the job done. Packt books are more specific and less general than the IT books you have seen in the past. Our unique business model allows us to bring you more focused information, giving you more of what you need to know, and less of what you don't.

Packt is a modern, yet unique publishing company, which focuses on producing quality, cutting-edge books for communities of developers, administrators, and newbies alike. For more information, please visit our website: www.packtpub.com.

About Packt Open Source

In 2010, Packt launched two new brands, Packt Open Source and Packt Enterprise, in order to continue its focus on specialization. This book is part of the Packt Open Source brand, home to books published on software built around Open Source licences, and offering information to anybody from advanced developers to budding web designers. The Open Source brand also runs Packt's Open Source Royalty Scheme, by which Packt gives a royalty to each Open Source project about whose software a book is sold.

Writing for Packt

We welcome all inquiries from people who are interested in authoring. Book proposals should be sent to author@packtpub.com. If your book idea is still at an early stage and you would like to discuss it first before writing a formal book proposal, contact us; one of our commissioning editors will get in touch with you.

We're not just looking for published authors; if you have strong technical skills but no writing experience, our experienced editors can help you develop a writing career, or simply get some additional reward for your expertise.

FreeSWITCH 1.0.6

ISBN: 978-1-847199-96-6   Paperback: 320 pages

Build robust high performance telephony systems using FreeSwitch

1. Install and configure a complete telephony system of your own even if you are using FreeSWITCH for the first time

2. In-depth discussions of important concepts like the dialplan, user directory, and the powerful FreeSWITCH Event Socket

3. The first ever book on FreeSWITCH, packed with real-world examples for Linux/Unix systems, Mac OSX, and Windows, along with useful screenshots and diagrams

FreeSWITCH Cookbook

ISBN: 978-1-849515-40-5   Paperback: 150 pages

Over 40 recipies to help you get the most of your FreeSwitch server

1. Get powerful FreeSWITCH features to work for you

2. Route calls and handle call detailing records

3. Written by members of the FreeSWITCH development team

Please check **www.PacktPub.com** for information on our titles

Building Telephony Systems With Asterisk

ISBN: 978-1-904811-15-2   Paperback: 176 pages

An easy introduction to using and configuring Asterisk to build feature-rich systems for small and medium businesses

1. Install, configure, deploy, secure, and maintain Asterisk

2. Build a fully-featured telephony system and create a dial plan that suits your needs

3. Learn from example configurations for different requirements

Building Telephony System with OpenSIPS 1.6

ISBN: 978-1-849510-74-5   Paperback: 284 pages

Build scalable and robust telephony systems using SIP

1. Build a VoIP Provider based on the SIP Protocol

2. Cater to scores of subscribers efficiently with a robust telephony system based in pure SIP

3. Gain a competitive edge using the most scalable VoIP technology

Please check **www.PacktPub.com** for information on our titles

5682578R00236

Printed in Great Britain
by Amazon.co.uk, Ltd.,
Marston Gate.